THE
MORTGAGE ENCYCLOPEDIA

SECOND  EDITION

THE AUTHORITATIVE GUIDE TO MORTGAGE PROGRAMS, PRACTICES, PRICES, AND PITFALLS

JACK GUTTENTAG
"THE MORTGAGE PROFESSOR"

New York   Chicago   San Francisco   Lisbon
London   Madrid   Mexico City   Milan   New Delhi
San Juan   Seoul   Singapore   Sydney   Toronto

1 2 3 4 5 6 7 8 9 0 DOC/DOC 1 5 4 3 2 1 0

ISBN 978-0-07-173958-0
MHID 0-07-173958-0

McGraw-Hill books are available at special quantity discounts to use as premiums and sales promotions or for use in corporate training programs. To contact a representative, please e-mail us at bulksales@mcgraw-hill.com.

Topics

Topics

Topics

Topics

Topics

Topics

Preface to the Second Edition

Since the first edition of this book in 2004, the home mortgage market has run through an incredible cycle: from bubble to crisis to a crisis aftermath for which there is not yet an adequate descriptive noun.

A bubble is a marked rise in prices that becomes self-reinforcing: buyers attracted by prior price increases enter the market in order to resell at the still higher prices expected in the future. The housing bubble began slowly in 2000, generated momentum as it proceeded, and then collapsed in 2007.

The housing bubble corrupted the mortgage credit system. Rising house prices convert "bad" loans—those that in a stable market would have defaulted and caused loss to investors—into good loans. Borrowers who couldn't pay could sell their houses at a profit, and if they did default, the equity in the houses from rising prices protected investors against loss. As a result, loans became available at terms that were unthinkable before the bubble to categories of borrowers who earlier would have been rejected outright. The flood of mortgage credit, in turn, reinforced the bubble by further stimulating housing demand.

The corruption of the mortgage credit system was across the board. The cash required to qualify gradually declined, and, by 2006, a large proportion of all mortgages had no down payment. The credit status required to qualify was downgraded through the creation of new underwriting categories labeled "Alt-A" and "subprime." And the initial mortgage payment that borrowers had to prove they could manage declined through adoption of potentially toxic types of mortgages that offered low initial payments in exchange for higher payments in later years.

Preface to the Second Edition

When house prices stopped rising in late 2006 and then began falling, the bubble collapsed. Mortgage defaults and foreclosures rose first in the weakest areas and then metastasized in all directions: from loans written in 2006, which were hit the hardest, to those from earlier vintages; from subprime loans, which tanked first to Alt-A and finally to those classified as prime; and from mortgages to securities issued against mortgages. Markets for mortgage securities that were not guaranteed by the federal government largely ceased functioning.

Losses to mortgage lenders and investors were horrendous. Smaller subprime lenders were quick to fold, followed by many with familiar names: Countrywide, Wachovia, Bear Stearns, Lehman Brothers, Merrill Lynch, Fannie Mae, and Freddie Mac. Of these, all but Lehman Brothers were merged into stronger firms or, in the case of Fannie and Freddie, were placed in a government conservatorship. Lehman Brothers was allowed to fail, causing losses to creditors all over the world and badly shaking confidence in institutions and markets.

To prevent the deterioration of confidence in financial institutions from causing a worldwide meltdown with potentially catastrophic consequences, the Federal Reserve and Treasury provided massive amounts of assistance to shaky firms that were viewed as "too big to fail." Assistance included loans, stock purchases, and guarantees of liabilities, and recipients were in multiple industries. The largest single assistance package was provided to AIG, an insurance conglomerate with extensive global operations.

By 2009, when I wrote this book, confidence in financial institutions had been largely restored, but the mortgage market was a long way from any semblance of normality. House prices were about 30 percent below their 2006 peak, and many millions of homeowners were "underwater," owing more on their mortgages than their houses were worth. Partly for this reason, foreclosure rates remained abnormally high. A federal program to reduce foreclosures by incenting servicing firms to modify mortgage contracts was not working well. This was partly because servicers did not have the systems needed to handle the crushing workload and partly because the modification program did not target the negative equity that was driving many foreclosures. The high unemployment rates did not help either.

A bright spot was that interest rates were very low for borrowers who could take advantage of them, but many could not. Either they didn't have enough equity because of the decline in market values, or they did not meet current underwriting standards, which had flipped 180 degrees from what they had been. As one example, the seven or so modes of documentation that existed prior to the crisis, designed to meet the needs of different categories of borrowers, had been reduced to one: "full doc." Few self-employed borrowers in 2009 could meet the full-doc requirement, regardless of how good their credit was and how much equity they had.

The market in 2009 was functioning only because of federal guarantees. About 90 percent of all new loans were either being sold to Fannie Mae and Freddie Mac, or insured by the FHA, VA, and the U.S. Department of Agriculture. The private secondary market remained shut, and it was not clear when, if ever, it would reopen. Lurking in the background was a fear that inflation was not far down the road because of all the money that the Federal Reserve had pumped into the system, and that rising interest rates would come with it.

I am looking forward to a third edition in 2014, maybe even sooner.

Acknowledgments

Much of what I have learned about the home mortgage market has been stimulated by the many thousands of borrowers who, ever since I hung up my Web-based shingle in 1998, have e-mailed me questions and related their experiences. Numerous mortgage brokers and loan officers have also contributed to my education about what goes on in the mortgage trenches, often by being combative, sometimes with good reason. Among the most helpful have been Catherine Coy, Chris Cruise, Jeffrey Jaye, Kevin Iverson, and Jack Pritchard. This book could not have been written without the steadfast support of my wife, Doris, who made our home a productive as well as a loving place.

A-Credit *A borrower with the best credit rating, deserving of the lowest prices that lenders offer.*

Also referred to as a "prime" borrower. Most lenders require a FICO score above 720. There is seldom any payoff for being above the A-credit threshold, but you pay a penalty for being below it. *See* **Credit Score/*Use of FICO Scores by Lenders***.

A-Minus *A general mortgage risk categorization that falls below A because the borrower's credit rating, debt-to-income ratio, and other factors do not, in combination, meet A standards.*

Acceleration Clause *A contractual provision that gives the lender the right to demand repayment of the entire loan balance in the event that the borrower violates one or more clauses in the note.*

Such clauses may include sale of the property, failure to make timely payments, or provision of false information.

I have never seen a note that did not have such a clause. Borrowers need not concern themselves with it except where the lender has discretion to exercise it without conditions. This would be referred to as a "demand feature," and it would be flagged on the Truth in Lending Disclosure Statement. If that statement shows "This loan has a Demand Feature . . . ," the note should be read with care. *See* **Demand Clause**.

Accrued Interest *Interest that is earned but not paid, adding to the amount owed.*

For example, if the monthly interest due on a loan is $600 and the borrower pays only $500, $100 is added to the amount owed by the borrower. The $100 is the accrued interest. On a mortgage, accrued interest is usually referred to as **Negative Amortization**.

Adjustable-Rate Mortgage (ARM) *A mortgage on which the interest rate can be changed by the lender.*

Adjustable-Rate Mortgage (ARM)

While ARM contracts in many countries abroad allow rate changes at the lender's discretion (**Discretionary ARMs**), in the United States the rate changes on ARMs are mechanical. They are based on changes in an interest rate index over which the lender has no control. Henceforth, all references are to such **Indexed ARMs**.

Reasons for Selecting an ARM: Borrowers may select an ARM in preference to a fixed-rate mortgage (FRM) for three reasons, which are not mutually exclusive:

- They need the low initial payment on an ARM to qualify for the loan they want.

- They want the low initial rates and payments on ARMs because they expect to be out of their house before the initial rate period ends.

- They expect that they will pay less on the ARM over the life of the loan and are prepared to take the risk that rising interest rates will cause them to pay more.

I will return to these reasons later.

How the Interest Rate on an ARM Is Determined: There are two phases in the life of an ARM. During the first phase, the interest rate is fixed, just as it is on an FRM. The difference is that on an FRM the rate is fixed for the term of the loan, whereas on an ARM it is fixed for a shorter period. The period ranges from a month to 10 years.

At the end of the initial rate period, the ARM rate is adjusted. The adjustment rule is that the new rate will equal the most recent value of a specified interest rate index plus a margin. For example, if the index is 5% when the initial rate period ends, and the margin is 2.75%, the new rate will be 7.75%. The rule, however, is subject to two conditions.

The first condition is that the increase from the previous rate cannot exceed any rate adjustment cap specified in the ARM contract. An adjustment cap, usually 1 or 2% but ranging in some cases up to 5%, limits the size of any interest rate change.

The second condition is that the new rate cannot exceed the contractual maximum rate. Maximum rates are usually five or six percentage points above the initial rate.

During the second phase of an ARM's life, the interest rate is adjusted periodically. This period may be but usually is not the same as the initial rate period. For example, an ARM with an initial rate period of 5 years might adjust annually or monthly after the 5-year period ends.

Adjustable-Rate Mortgage (ARM)

The Quoted Interest Rate: The rate that is quoted on an ARM, by the media and by loan providers, is the initial rate—regardless of how long that rate lasts. When the initial rate period is short, the quoted rate is a poor indication of interest cost to the borrower. The only significance of the initial rate on a monthly ARM, for example, is that this rate may be used to calculate the initial payment. *See* **How the Monthly Payment on an ARM Is Determined**.

The Fully Indexed Rate: The index plus margin is called the "fully indexed rate," or FIR. The FIR based on the most recent value of the index at the time the loan is taken out indicates where the ARM rate may go when the initial rate period ends. If the index rate does not change, the FIR will become the ARM rate.

For example, assume the initial rate is 4% for one year, the fully indexed rate is 7%, and the rate adjusts every year subject to a 1% rate increase cap. If the index value remains the same, the 7% FIR will be reached at the end of the third year.

The FIR is thus an important piece of information, the more so the shorter the initial rate period. Nevertheless, it is not a mandated disclosure, and loan officers may not have it. They will know the margin and the specific index, however, and the most recent value of the index can be found on the Internet, as explained below.

ARM Rate Indexes: Every ARM is tied to an interest rate index. An index has three relevant features:

- Availability
- Level
- Volatility

All the common ARM indexes are readily available from a published source, with the exception of one called the **Cost of Savings Index**, or **COSI**, which is no longer offered on new loans.

In principle, a lower index is better for a borrower than a higher one. However, lenders take account of different index levels in setting the margin. A 3% index with a 2% margin provides the same FIR as a 2% index with a 3% margin. Assuming volatility is the same, there is nothing to choose between them.

An index that is relatively stable is better for the borrower than one that is volatile. The stable index will increase less in a rising rate environment. While it will also decline less in a declining-rate environment, borrowers can take advantage of declining rates by refinancing.

Adjustable-Rate Mortgage (ARM)

The most stable of the more widely used rate indexes is the 11th District Cost of Funds Index, referred to as COFI (pronounced like "coffee"). Most of the others are significantly more volatile. These include the Treasury series of constant (1-, 2-, or 3-year) maturity, 1-month, 6-month, and 12-month LIBOR, 6-month CDs, and the prime rate.

Another series known as MTA is a 12-month moving average of the 1-year Treasury constant maturity series. MTA is a little more volatile than COFI but less volatile than the other series.

An ARM should never be selected based on the index alone. That would be like buying a car based on the tires. But if an overall evaluation (see below) indicates that two ARMs are very close, preference could be given to the one with the more attractive index.

The most complete source of current and historical values of major ARM indexes can be found on the Web site www.mortgage-x.com.

How the Monthly Payment on an ARM Is Determined: ARMs fall into two major groups that differ in the way in which the monthly payment of principal and interest is determined: fully amortizing ARMs and negative amortization ARMs.

Fully amortizing ARMs adjust the monthly payment to be fully amortizing whenever the interest rate changes. The new payment will pay off the loan over the period remaining to term if the interest rate stays the same.

For example, a $100,000 30-year ARM has an initial rate of 5%, which holds for 5 years, after which the rate is adjusted every year. (This is referred to as a "5/1 ARM.") The payment of $536.83 for the first 5 years would pay off the loan if the rate stayed at 5%. In month 61, the rate might increase to, say, 7%. A new payment of $649.03 is then calculated, at 7% and 25 years, which would pay off the loan if the rate stayed at 7%. As the rate changes each year thereafter, a new payment is calculated that would pay off the loan over the remaining period if that rate continued.

Negative amortization ARMs allow payments that don't fully cover the interest. They have one or more of the following features:

- **Payment Rate Below the Interest Rate:** The payment rate, which is the interest rate used to calculate the payment, may be below the actual interest rate. If the payment rate is so low that the initial payment does not cover the interest, the result will be negative amortization.

- **More Frequent Rate Adjustments Than Payment Adjustments:** If, e.g., the rate adjusts every month but the payment adjusts every year, a large rate increase within the year will lead to negative amortization.

- **Payment Adjustment Caps:** If a rate change is large and a payment adjustment cap limits the size of a change in payment, the result will be negative amortization.

Virtually all ARMs are designed to fully amortize over their term. This means that negative amortization can only be temporary and that at some point or points in the ARM's life history the monthly payment must become fully amortizing.

Two contract provisions are used to assure that negative amortization ARMs pay off at term.

- A recast clause requires that periodically, usually every 5 years, the payment must be adjusted to the fully amortizing level.

- A negative amortization cap is a maximum ratio of loan balance to original loan amount, for example, 110%. If that maximum is reached, the payment is immediately adjusted to the fully amortizing level, overriding any payment adjustment cap. In a worst-case scenario, the required payment increase may be very large.

Identifying ARMs: There are no industry standards for identifying ARMs, and practices vary across lenders. Some identify their ARMs by the index used, e.g., "COFI ARM" or "6-month LIBOR ARM." Some identify their ARMs by the rate adjustment periods, e.g., "5/1" or "3/3."

None of these shorthand descriptions are of much use to borrowers because there are so many differences within each. Indeed, even if the features of each were standardized, to compare one type of ARM with another, one needs to know exactly what those features are.

Selecting an ARM to Qualify: It is easier to qualify with an ARM than with an FRM. In deciding whether an applicant has enough income to meet the monthly payment obligation, lenders usually use the initial interest rate on an ARM to calculate the payment, even though the rate may rise at the end of the initial rate period.

That's why, when market interest rates increase, ARMs become more common and FRMs less common. Some borrowers who could have qualified with an FRM at the lower rates would now require an ARM to qualify.

However, many borrowers who appear to require an ARM to qualify in fact could qualify with an FRM. It just takes a little more work. *See* **Qualification/*Meeting Income Requirements/Is an ARM Needed to Qualify?***

Adjustable-Rate Mortgage (ARM)

After the financial crisis erupted in 2007, it became common to qualify borrowers using the FIR rather than the initial rate. If this practice continues, it will reduce cyclical sensitivity in the market share of ARMs relative to FRMs.

Taking Advantage of Low Initial Rates: Borrowers with short time horizons can take advantage of the relatively low initial interest rates on ARMs. For example, at a time when a borrower is quoted 6.5% on a 30-year FRM, the quoted initial rates on 3/1, 5/1, 7/1, and 10/1 ARMs might be 6%, 6.125%, 6.25%, and 6.375%, respectively.

The correct choice depends on how long the borrower expects to have the loan and on what the borrower's attitude is toward risk. For example, a borrower who expects to hold the mortgage for 6 years might play it safe by selecting a 7/1. Or he might take the 5/1 on the grounds that the savings over 5 years justifies taking the risk of having to pay a higher rate in year 6.

Borrowers who take this risk, whether deliberately as in the example above or inadvertently because they aren't sure how long they will hold the loan, should consider what can happen at the end of the initial rate period. Suppose the borrower deciding between the 5/1 and 7/1, for example, finds that the indexes, margins, and maximum rates are the same, but the rate adjustment caps are 2% on the 5/1 and 5% on the 7/1. This could tilt the decision toward the 5/1.

If the ARMs being compared differ in a number of ways, however, comparing one with another (or with an FRM) can be very confusing. In this situation, borrowers with short time horizons seeking to take advantage of low initial rates on ARMs are no different from borrowers with longer horizons who seek to pay less on the ARM over the life of the loan and are prepared to take the risk that they will pay more. Both should analyze the potential benefits and risks with calculators, as explained below.

Gambling on Future Interest Rates: Taking an ARM (when an FRM is an option) is a gamble, and the question is whether it is a good gamble in any particular case. A good gamble is one where the borrower can reasonably expect that the **Interest Cost (IC)** or **Total Horizon Cost (THC)** will be lower on the ARM than on a comparable FRM over the period the mortgage is held, and where the borrower won't face extreme hardship if interest rates explode.

On my Web site, there are six calculators in the Comparing Two Mortgages (9) series that compare IC or THC, and there are six in the

Adjustable-Rate Mortgage (ARM)

Mortgage Payment (7) series that show mortgage payments month by month. All of them allow the user to specify the time period and the interest rate scenario. The calculators cover FRMs and ARMs with and without negative amortization

Information Needed: All the calculators require the following information about each ARM:

Basic Loan Information

- New loan amount or existing loan balance
- Points
- Other settlement costs
- Initial interest rate on new loan or current rate on existing loan
- New loan term or remaining term on existing loan, in months

Interest Rate Index

- Most recent value of the index
- Margin that is added to interest rate index

First Rate Adjustment

- Period over which initial rate holds
- Maximum interest rate change on first rate adjustment

Subsequent Rate Adjustments

- Duration between subsequent rate adjustments
- Maximum interest rate change on subsequent rate adjustments

Maximum and Minimum Rates

- Maximum interest rate over life of mortgage
- Minimum interest rate over life of mortgage

On negative amortization ARMs, the following are also needed:

Payment Information

- Initial monthly payment of principal and interest
- Payment adjustment period, in months
- Payment adjustment cap, in percent
- Payment recast period, in years
- Negative amortization cap, in percent

Adjustable-Rate Mortgage (ARM)

Assumptions About Future Interest Rates

- Stable index: interest rate index stays unchanged for the life of the mortgage
- Worst case: ARM rate rises immediately to the maximum extent permitted by the loan contract

• Rising trend: index rises:	Number of Years	Percent/Year
	5	1

• Declining trend: index falls:	Number of Years	Percent/Year
	3	0.5

• Volatile: index rises/falls:	2	1
• Volatile: index falls/rises:	2	1

The stable index or "no-change" scenario provides the closest approximation to an "expected" result and is an excellent benchmark. The worst case is exactly that—the ARM rate rises as far and as fast as the loan contract permits. The worst case is so improbable that borrowers may want to design something less extreme, such as the rising trend scenario used below.

An Illustration: On September 4, 2009, I compared the 5/1 no-negative amortization ARM and 30-year FRM shown below.

	FRM	ARM
Loan amount	$300,000	$300,000
Points	$3193	$1785
Other settlement costs	$2442	$2442
Initial interest rate	4.75%	3.625%
Term	30 Years	30 Years
Rate index value		1.291%
Margin		2.25%
Initial rate period	30 Years	5 Years
Maximum initial rate change		5%
Rate adjustment period		1 Year
Maximum rate adjustment		2%
Maximum lifetime rate		8.625%
Minimum lifetime rate		1%

Adjustable-Rate Mortgage (ARM)

I used my calculator 9ai to calculate the total horizon costs on these mortgages over varying periods, using three rate scenarios for the ARM. The upward trend assumes an increase of 1% during each of the first 3 years. I assumed the borrower had an interest opportunity cost of 2% and was in the 27% tax bracket.

Total Horizon Cost on ARM and FRM, September 4, 2009				
	FRM	5/1 ARM		
Period		Stable Rates	Upward Trend	Worst Case
5 years	$57,829	$44,307	$44,307	$44,307
7 years	79,372	60,506	72,347	80,652
12 years	133,675	101,622	143,022	172,830
30 years	319,607	251,124	373,914	469,568

It is clear that the 5/1 ARM is a winner for any borrower who expects to be out of the house within 5 years, and is very confident that he or she will be out within 7 years. In the worst case, the borrower who stays 7 years fares a little worse with the ARM than with the FRM, but not much; and with anything less than the worst case, the ARM does better. Any borrower who expects to stay more than 7 years, however, should avoid the ARM.

For many consumers, the bottom line is what might happen to the payment. On the FRM, the payment is $1,547 for the life of the loan. On the ARM, the payment calculator 7b covering no-negative amortization ARMs shows the following payments under the three scenarios:

The payment on the ARM is $1,368 for the first 5 years. Under the stable rate scenario, it drops a little to $1,356 in month 61. On the upward trend scenario, the payment jumps to $1,827 in month 61, a 34% increase. And on a worst case, the payment would jump to $2,194 in month 61, which is a 60% increase. The upshot is that borrowers who are sure they will be out within 7 years, and are therefore very likely to profit from the ARM over the full period they have it, must nonetheless be prepared to deal with a sizable payment increase in month 61.

Mandatory Disclosures: The theory underlying the Federal Reserve's disclosure rules for ARMs is that consumers should first receive a general education on ARMs and then should receive specific information about any ARM program in which they might be interested. This is a reasonable approach.

The general education is provided by a *Consumer Handbook on Adjustable Rate Mortgages*, sometimes referred to as the "CHARM Booklet." The booklet is a passable effort, but it is too long and so few people read it.

The second part of ARM disclosure is a list of ARM features that must be disclosed and an explanation of "each variable-rate program in which the consumer expresses an interest." This is where the process breaks down. The list of ARM features is too long and includes all kinds of pap.

Overwhelming borrowers with more information than they can handle is counterproductive. Disclosing everything is much the same as disclosing nothing—it just takes longer.

Lenders don't make this mistake. They know they can't sell an ARM (or anything else) by overwhelming the customer. They tend to focus on a single theme or hook—an easy-to-understand ARM feature that is appealing. For example, in 2003 they sold COFI ARMs based on the stability of the COFI, and in 2005–2006 they sold option ARMs based on the low initial payment.

ARM disclosures would be a useful counterweight to lender sales pitches if they were limited to critically important information and presented clearly. Instead, borrowers are presented with a list of ARM features, including those needed to derive useful tables, provided that the borrower knows (a) which items are relevant and (b) how to derive the tables from them. But such borrowers don't need mandatory disclosure; they can get the information they want by asking for it. Mandatory disclosure is for borrowers who don't know what they need and, therefore, don't know what to look for in voluminous disclosures.

In addition to the list of ARM features, lenders are required to describe each program, but there is no requirement for clarity. So long as the mandated items are included, it seemingly doesn't matter whether the descriptions are comprehensible. I have seen a few that are pretty good, but most are unreadable.

In the fall of 2009, the Fed released a major set of proposals to revise Truth in Lending, which included substantial changes in ARM disclosures. The CHARM Booklet would be replaced by a one-page explanation of the basic differences between ARMs and FRMs, and loan program descriptions would be streamlined and simplified. These were pending when this book went to press. *See* **Mandatory Disclosure**.

Convertible ARMs: Some ARMs have an option to convert to an FRM after some period, at a market rate. The advantage, relative to a refinance, is that the conversion avoids settlement costs. The disadvantage is that the borrower loses the flexibility to shop the market.

The conversion interest rate on the FRM is usually defined in terms of the value of a rate index at the time of conversion plus a margin. To determine whether the conversion option has value, assume you can convert immediately. Find the current index value, add the margin, and compare it with the best FRM rate you can obtain in the market. If the second rate is lower, which is likely to be the case, the conversion option has little value.

Market conditions do change, and it is possible that the option could have value in the years ahead. But don't give up anything important for it.

Also see **Points, Partial Prepayments (or Paying Off Early)/***Effect of Early Payment on Monthly Payments***/ARMs, Qualification/***Meeting Income Requirements***/Is an ARM Needed to Qualify?, Interest-Only Mortgage/ Interest-Only ARMs, Second Mortgage, Option ARM.**

Adjustment Interval *On an ARM, the time between changes in the interest rate or monthly payment.*

These are the same on a fully amortizing ARM, but may not be on a negative amortization ARM. *See* **Adjustable-Rate Mortgage.**

Affordability *A consumer's capacity to afford a specified house price.*

Affordability can be viewed in two ways. One way is through an analysis of the household's income-generating capacity and pattern of expenditures. This approach requires detailed budgetary data over a considerable period showing how the household tends to allocate its income. Using this approach, two households with the same income might have very different affordability levels because one spends more of its income on discretionary items than the other.

Prospective homebuyers should use this approach in assessing their own capacity to afford a house, but this is *not* how lenders do it. The budgetary approach is too messy and excessively dependent on data

11

Affordability

provided by the borrower which can't be verified except at great expense. The lender approach described below looks at only one category of non-housing expenses, namely debt service, which can be verified. All other categories of spending are disregarded.

Calculating the Maximum Affordable Sale Price: When done properly, affordability as viewed by a lender is calculated three times using an "income rule," a "debt rule," and a "cash rule." The final figure is the lowest of the three. When affordability is measured on the back of an envelope, usually it is based on the income rule alone, ignoring the other two. This can result in error.

The Income Rule: The borrower's monthly housing expense (MHE), which is the sum of the mortgage payment including mortgage insurance if any, property taxes, and homeowner insurance premium, cannot exceed a percentage of the borrower's income specified by the lender. If this maximum is 28%, for example, and John Smith's income is $4,000, MHE cannot exceed $1,120. If taxes and insurance are $200, the maximum mortgage payment is $920. At 7% and 30 years, this payment will support a loan of $138,282. Assuming a minimum 5% down payment, this implies a sale price of $145,561. This is the maximum sale price for Smith using the income rule.

The Debt Rule: The borrower's total housing expense (THE), which is the sum of the MHE plus monthly payments on existing debt, cannot exceed a percentage of the borrower's income specified by the lender. If this maximum is 36%, for example, the THE for Smith cannot exceed $1,440. If taxes and insurance are $200 while existing debt service is $240, the maximum mortgage payment is $1,000. At 7% and 30 years, this payment will support a loan of $150,308. Assuming a 5% down payment, this implies a sale price of $158,218. This is the maximum sale price for Smith using the debt rule.

The Required Cash Rule: The borrower must have cash sufficient to meet the down payment requirement plus other settlement costs. If Smith has $12,000 and the sum of the down payment requirement and other settlement costs is 10% of the sale price, then the maximum sale price using the cash rule is $120,000. Since this is the lowest of the three maximums, it is the affordability estimate for Smith.

When the cash rule sets the limit on the maximum sale price, as in the case above, the borrower is said to be cash constrained. Affordability of

Affordability

a cash-constrained borrower can be raised by a reduction in the down payment requirement, a reduction in settlement costs, the willingness of a home seller to pay the settlement costs, or access to an additional source of down payment—a parent, for example.

When the income rule sets the limit on the maximum sale price, the borrower is said to be income constrained. Affordability of an income-constrained borrower can be raised by a reduction in the maximum MHE ratio or by access to additional income—sending a spouse out to work, for example.

When the debt rule sets the limit on the maximum sale price, the borrower is said to be debt constrained. The affordability of a debt-constrained borrower (but not that of a cash-constrained or income-constrained borrower) can be increased by repaying debt.

Affordability will be affected by changes in the assumed maximum MHE and THE ratios, which vary from loan program to program and can also vary with other characteristics of the loan such as the down payment or credit score. Affordability may also be affected by changes in the assumptions made regarding settlement costs, taxes and insurance, interest rate, and term.

Some Estimates: The table below provides some ballpark estimates of how much house a borrower can afford with a 7.5% two-point mortgage for 30 years. For each of seven sale prices, the table shows the total cash required to meet down payment requirements and settlement costs, the total monthly housing expense, the minimum income required to cover housing expenses, and the maximum amount of debt service allowable on the minimum income.

These numbers were calculated from the Housing Affordability calculator (5a) on my Web site. The assumptions used are not likely to apply exactly to any individual situation. However, readers can use the calculator to change any of the assumptions as they please.

The table assumes that the borrower pushes buying power to the limit. In particular, the table assumes that the down payment is the lowest that lenders are willing to accept, which requires mortgage insurance that increases borrowing cost. This may not be prudent. *See* **Housing Investment**.

How Much House Can You Afford with a 7% 2-Point 30-Year Mortgage?						
To Spend This Amount on a House ...	You Need At Least This Gross Monthly Income ...	To Cover This Monthly Housing Expense ...	Other Monthly Debt Payments Should Not Exceed ...	And You Need at Least This Much Cash ...	For the Down Payment Lenders Are Most Likely to Require ...	And the Closing Closts
$400,000	$11,290	$3,160	$903	$59,200	$40,000	$19,200
350,000	10,260	2,871	820	51,800	35,000	16,800
300,000	8,790	2,461	703	44,400	30,000	14,400
250,000	7,330	2,051	586	37,000	25,000	12,000
200,000	6,280	1756	502	19,800	10,000	9,800
150,000	4,710	1317	376	14,859	7,500	7,359
100,000	3,230	903	258	7,940	3,000	4,940

Notes: Minimum monthly income is based on a ratio of monthly housing expense to income of 28%. Closing costs excluding points are assumed to total 3% of the sale price. The maximum monthly debt service payment is assumed to be 8% of minimum monthly income. Monthly housing expense includes principal and interest, mortgage insurance, taxes, and hazard insurance. Taxes and hazard insurance are assumed to be 1.825% of sale price. The down payment requirement is assumed to be 10% on prices of $250,000–400,000, 5% on $150,000–200,000, and 3% on $100,000. Mortgage insurance premium rates are assumed to be 0.9% with 3% down, 0.78% with 5% down, and 0.52% with 10% down.

Agreement of Sale *A contract signed by buyer and seller stating the terms and conditions under which a property will be sold.*

Alt-A *A general mortgage risk categorization that falls below A, usually because the borrower's income and assets are not fully documented.*

This categorization developed alongside "subprime"; both disappeared with the financial crisis in 2007–2008. *See* **Documentation Requirements**.

Alternative Documentation *Expedited and simpler documentation requirements designed to speed up the loan approval process.*

Instead of verifying employment with the applicant's employer and bank deposits with the applicant's bank, the lender will accept paycheck stubs, W-2s, and the borrower's original bank statements. Alternative documentation remains "full documentation," as opposed to the other documentation options. *See* **Documentation Requirements**.

Amortization *The repayment of principal from scheduled mortgage payments that exceed the interest due.*

The **Scheduled Mortgage Payment** is the payment the borrower is obliged to make under the note. The scheduled payment less the interest equals amortization. The loan balance declines by the amount of the amortization plus the amount of any extra payment. If such payment is less than the interest due, the balance rises, which is negative amortization.

The Fully Amortizing Payment: The monthly mortgage payment that will pay off the loan at term is called the fully amortizing payment. On an FRM, the fully amortizing payment is calculated at the outset and does not change over the life of the loan. For example, on an FRM for $100,000 at 6% for 30 years, the fully amortizing payment is $599.56. If the borrower makes that payment every month, the balance will be extinguished with the 360th payment.

On an ARM, the fully amortizing payment is constant only so long as the interest rate remains unchanged. When the rate changes, the fully amortizing payment also changes. For example, an ARM for $100,000 at 6% for 30 years would have a fully amortizing payment of $599.55 at the outset. But if the rate rose to 7% after 5 years, the fully amortizing payment would jump to $657.69.

Amortization on Standard Loans: Except for simple interest loans, which are discussed below, the accounting for amortized home loans assumes that there are only 12 days in a year, consisting of the first day of each month. The account begins on the first day of the month following the day the loan closes. The borrower pays "per diem interest" for the period between the closing day and the day the record begins. The first monthly payment is due on the first day of the month after that.

Amortization

For example, if a 6% 30-year $100,000 loan closes on March 15, the borrower pays interest at closing for the period March 15–April 1, and the first payment of $599.56 is due May 1.

The payment is allocated between interest and principal, which is a reduction in the loan balance. The interest payment is calculated by multiplying 1/12 of the interest rate times the loan balance in the previous month. Going back to our example, 1/12 of 0.06 is 0.005. The interest due May 1, therefore, is 0.005 times $100,000, or $500. The remaining $99.56 is principal that reduces the balance to $99,900.44.

The process repeats each month, but the portion of the payment allocated to interest gradually declines while the portion allocated to principal gradually rises. On June 1, the interest due is 0.005 times $99,900.44, or $499.51, while principal rises to $100.06

While the payment is due on the first day of each month, lenders allow borrowers a "grace period," which is usually 15 days. A payment received on the 15th is treated exactly in the same way as a payment received on the 1st. A payment received after the 15th, however, is assessed a late charge equal to 4 or 5% of the payment.

Interest and Principal Payments on a Fixed-Rate Mortgage of $100,000 at 6% for 30 Years

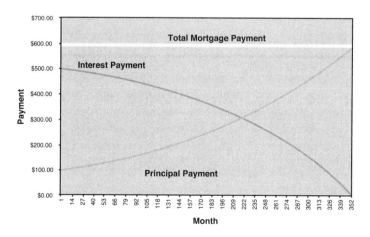

Amortization Schedule: This is a table that shows the mortgage payment, broken down by interest, principal, and the loan balance. Schedules prepared by lenders will also show the tax and insurance payments if made by the lender, as well as the balance of the tax and insurance escrow account.

Amortization

Readers are encouraged to develop an actual amortization schedule, which will allow them to see exactly how they work. They can do that using one of my calculators. For straight amortization without extra payments, use calculator 8a. To see how amortization is impacted by extra payments, use calculator 2a.

Readers who want to maintain a continuing record of their mortgage under their own control can do this by downloading one of two spreadsheets from my Web site. These are "Extra Payments on Monthly Payment Fixed-Rate Mortgages" and "Extra Payments on ARMs." As the titles indicate, the spreadsheets will allow you to take account of extra payments in addition to regular payments.

Payment Rigidity: The payment requirement of the standard mortgage is absolutely rigid. Skip a single payment and you accumulate late charges until you make it up. If you skip May, for example, you make it up with two payments in June plus one late charge, and you record a 30-day delinquency in your credit file. If you can't make it up until July, the price is three payments plus two late charges plus a 60-day delinquency report in your credit file. Falling behind can be a slippery slope.

Amortization on a Simple Interest Mortgage: On a simple interest mortgage, interest is calculated daily based on the balance on the day of payment, rather than monthly, as on the standard mortgage.

For example, using a rate of 7.25% and a balance of $100,000 on both, the standard mortgage would have an interest payment in month one of 0.0725 times $100,000 divided by 12, or $604.17. On a simple interest mortgage, the interest payment per day would be 0.0725 times $100,000 divided by 365, or $19.86. Over 30 days this would amount to $589.89, while over 31 days it would amount to $615.75.

A borrower who pays on the first day of every month in both cases would come out the same over the course of a year. But borrowers who pay late while staying within the usual 15-day grace period provided on the standard mortgage will do better with that mortgage. If they pay on the 10th day of the month, for example, they get 10 days free of interest on the standard mortgage; whereas on the simple interest mortgage, interest accumulates over the 10 days.

Similarly, borrowers who make extra payments of principal do better with the standard mortgage. For example, if they make an extra payment of $1,000 on the 15th of the month, they pay 15 days of interest on the $1,000 on the simple interest mortgage, which they would save on a standard mortgage.

The only borrowers who will do better with the simple interest mortgage are those in the habit of making their monthly payments early. If you make your payment 10 days before it is due, you will receive immediate credit with the simple interest mortgage, saving the interest on the portion of the payment that goes to principal reduction for the 10 days. With the standard mortgage, a payment received 10 days early is credited on the due date, just like a payment received 10 days late.

Amount Financed *On the Truth in Lending form, the loan amount less "prepaid finance charges," which are lender fees paid at closing.*

For example, if the loan is for $100,000 and the borrower pays the lender $4,000 in upfront fees, the amount financed is $96,000. This is a useless number, perhaps less than useless. It allows loan officers to say, with a straight face, "The finance charges are deducted from the amount financed." And you are supposed to say to yourself, "Oh, that's all right then," as if that meant that you won't have to pay the charges. Don't fall for it; you will have to pay them.

Annual Percentage Rate (APR) *A measure of the cost of credit that must be reported by lenders under Truth in Lending regulations.*

The APR was designed to be a comprehensive measure of all costs, which borrowers could use to compare one type of loan with another, as well as to compare offers for the same type of loan from different loan providers. Under the regulations, whenever lenders disclose an interest rate, they must disclose the APR alongside it. For reasons indicated below, it has never served this purpose adequately and is much inferior to **Time Horizon Cost**.

The Comprehension Problem: Very few borrowers understand the APR, which is expressed as a percent, the same as the interest rate, except that the APR is somehow a composite of the percentage rate and dollar costs. The algebraic expression, shown at **Mortgage Equations/*Annual Percentage Rate***, is mysterious to many. The mystery is even deeper on ARMs because the ARM rate is subject to unknown change in the future.

Annual Percentage Rate (APR)

Few loan officers or mortgage brokers understand it either. Indeed, within most lender firms, the only ones who understand how the APR is calculated are the technologists responsible for having it programmed, and sometimes they get it wrong.

The Comprehensiveness Problem: Despite the intent, the APR has never been the comprehensive measure of cost it was supposed to be. To serve its purpose, the APR should include all charges that would not arise in an all-cash transaction. In fact, charges paid to third parties, such as title insurance premiums and appraisal fees, are not included. In principle, this is an easy problem to fix; and in its 2009 proposal to amend Truth in Lending regulations, the Federal Reserve promised to fix it. It has only taken the Fed 30 years.

Meanwhile, incomplete fee coverage means that the APR understates the true credit cost. If the understatement was consistent, this would not be a major problem, but it is not consistent. Fees that are not included in the APR are sometimes paid by the lender, in exchange for a higher interest rate. The APR in such cases indirectly includes fees that are excluded when paid by the borrower. Mortgage shoppers should not use the APR to compare loans where they pay settlement costs with loans where the lender pays them.

Assumption That Loans Run to Term: The APR assumes that all loans run to term, when in fact more than 90% are paid off before term. Because the APR calculation spreads upfront fees over the life of the loan, the longer the assumed life, the lower the APR. The point is illustrated in the chart, which shows what the APR would be if the loan were terminated in any month over a 30-year period. It applies to a 7% loan with fees equal to 5% of the loan amount.

Suppose a borrower was deciding between this 7% loan with 5% fees and a 7.75% loan and zero fees. The APR on the 7% loan is 7.52%, whereas the 7.75% loan has an APR of 7.75%. But if the borrower expects to be out of her house in 10 years, the 7% loan would have a 10-year APR of 7.76%, and over 5 years it would be 8.26%. Mortgage shoppers with short time horizons should not use the APR to compare loans. They should use **Time Horizon Cost** or **Interest Cost** calculated over their own time horizon, which they can do using calculators 9a, 9ai, 9b, 9bi, 9c, and 9ci on my Web site. *See* **Time Horizon Cost** *and* **Interest Cost**.

Annual Percentage Rate (APR)

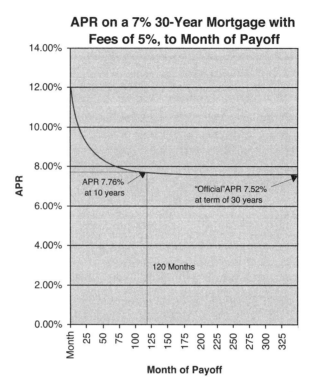

APR on a 7% 30-Year Mortgage with Fees of 5%, to Month of Payoff

Ignoring Borrower-Specific Characteristics That Affect Costs: A major difference between borrowers that affects their mortgage costs is their time horizon, which was discussed above. A second difference is their income tax bracket, which is important because mortgage interest and points are deductible. A third difference is their investment opportunity costs. APR ignores all these differences, in contrast to **Time Horizon Cost**, which takes account of them.

Ignoring the Paid-Off Loan on a Cash-Out Refinance: The APR is also deceptive for borrowers raising cash who are choosing between a cash-out refinance and a second mortgage. The APR on a cash-out refi ignores the interest rate on the existing mortgage that is being paid off.

For example, you have a $200,000 first mortgage at 7% and you need to raise $20,000 in cash. Assume a second mortgage for $20,000 has an APR of 8.5%, while a cash-out refi for $220,000 has an APR of 7.5%. The APR comparisons make it appear as if the cash-out refi is less costly, but that is not the case. The APR on the cash-out refi ignores the loss to the

20

borrower from increasing the APR on the $200,000 from 7% to 7.5%. An APR that took account of this loss would be well above the 8.5% on the second mortgage.

Borrowers and loan consultants comparing the cost of a second mortgage with that of a cash-out refi should ignore the APRs. They can use calculator 3d on my Web site, "Refinance to Raise Cash or Take Out a Second Mortgage."

APR on an ARM: On an ARM, the quoted interest rate holds only for a specified period. In calculating an APR, therefore, some assumption must be made about what happens to the rate at the end of the initial rate period.

The rule is that the initial rate is used for as long as it lasts, and the new rate or rates are those that would occur if the interest rate index used by the ARM stays the same for the life of the loan. This is a "no-change" or "stable-rate" scenario.

Under a stable-rate scenario, at the end of the initial rate period, the interest rate used in calculating the APR adjusts to equal the "fully indexed rate," or FIR, subject to the adjustment cap. The FIR is the value of the interest rate index at the time the ARM was written plus a margin that is specified in the note.

For example, if the start rate on a 3/1 ARM is 4%, the current index 2%, and the margin 2.25%, the APR calculation will use 4% for 3 years and 4.25% for 27 years. But if the current index is 4% and the rate adjustment cap is 2%, the APR calculation will use 4% for 3 years, 6% for 1 year, and 6.25% for 26 years.

When the FIR is above the initial rate, as it was during most of the 1990s, the rate increases on a no-change scenario. The APR is above the initial rate even if there are no lender fees. When the FIR is below the initial rate, as it was during most of the first 10 years of the new century, the rate decreases on a no-change scenario. If not offset by high upfront fees, this will produce an APR below the initial rate.

There is nothing wrong with the procedure used to calculate the APR on ARMs, but borrowers don't understand it. Further, the APR does not tell borrowers anything about the potential riskiness of an ARM, which is their major concern.

APR on a HELOC: The APR on a HELOC is the initial interest rate. It thus does not reflect points, other upfront costs, or expected future rates. The most important price feature of a HELOC, the margin, is not a required disclosure. *See* **Home Equity Line of Credit (HELOC)/*Truth in Lending (TIL) on a HELOC*.** *Also see* **Interest Cost (IC)/*IC Versus APR* and Time Horizon Cost.**

Application *A request for a loan that includes the information about the potential borrower, the property, and the requested loan that the solicited lender needs to make a decision.*

In a narrower sense, the application refers to a standardized application form called the "1003" which the borrower is obliged to fill out.

Application Fee *A fee that some lenders charge to accept an application.*

It may or may not cover other costs such as a property appraisal or credit report, and it may or may not be refundable if the lender declines the loan.

Appraisal *A written estimate of a property's current market value prepared by an appraiser.*

Appraisal Fee *A fee charged by an appraiser for the appraisal of a particular property.*

Appraisal Management Company (AMC) *A firm that hires appraisers as employees, intermediating between the appraiser and the lender ordering an appraisal.*

AMCs began to thrive in 2009 following adoption of a rule by Fannie Mae and Freddie Mac designed to guarantee that appraisals were free of influence by lenders and others interested in the outcome of an appraisal *See* **Home Valuation Code of Conduct (HVCC)/*Emergence of Appraisal Management Companies*.**

Appraiser *A professional with knowledge of real estate markets and skilled in the practice of appraisal.*

When a property is appraised in connection with a loan, the appraisal is ordered by the lender, but the appraisal fee is usually paid by the borrower.

Approval *Acceptance of the borrower's loan application.*

Approval means that the borrower meets the lender's **Qualification Requirements** and also its **Underwriting Requirements**. In some cases, especially where approval is provided quickly as with **Automated Underwriting** systems, the approval may be conditional on further verification of information provided by the borrower.

APR

See **Annual Percentage Rate**.

ARM

See **Adjustable-Rate Mortgage**.

Assignment *The transfer of ownership rights, or interests in property, by one person, the assignor, to another, the assignee.*

Assumable Mortgage *A mortgage contract that allows, or does not prohibit, a homebuyer from assuming the mortgage contract of the seller.*

When a homebuyer assumes responsibility for a home seller's existing mortgage, the buyer assumes all the obligations under the mortgage, just as if the loan had been made to her.

Assumable Mortgage

Value of Assumptions to Buyers and Sellers: The major driving force behind assumptions is the lower interest rate on the assumed mortgage relative to current market rates. If the home seller has a 5.5% mortgage, for example, and the best the buyer can get in the current market is 7%, both parties can be better off if the buyer assumes the 5.5% loan. An assumption also avoids the settlement costs on a new mortgage.

During periods when market rates are low, there is little interest in assumptions. But when rates increase after a long period of low rates, so does the interest in assumptions.

The value of an assumption depends on the difference in rate between the old assumed mortgage and a new one, the balance and period remaining on the old loan, the term of the new loan, the length of time the buyer expects to have the mortgage, and the "investment rate"—the rate the buyer could earn on the savings from the lower rate. Assuming that the 5.5% loan has a $100,000 balance with 200 months remaining while the 7% loan would be for 30 years, and assuming that the buyer expects to be in the house for 5 years and can earn 4% on investments, the value is about $7,000. A spreadsheet that makes this calculation is available on my Web site.

The $7,000 of savings does not include the settlement costs on a new loan. On the other hand, the savings would be reduced if the buyer has to supplement the existing loan balance with a new second mortgage at a higher rate. This could well be the case if the existing loan balance has been paid down appreciably or the house has appreciated since that mortgage was taken out. The buyers who do best on assumptions are those who have the cash to pay the difference between the sale price and the balance of the old loan.

However, buyers should not expect to receive the full value of an assumption. The seller must benefit as well; typically, the parties share the savings. The seller's share will be in the form of a higher price for the house. Indeed, some economists believe that the full value of the assumption should be reflected in the price of the house, but this is as implausible as the opposite view, that only the buyer benefits.

Assumptions a Cost to Lenders: The benefit to buyer and seller from assuming an old loan comes at the expense of the lender. Instead of having the 5.5% loan repaid, which would allow the lender to convert it into a new 7% loan, the 5.5% loan stays on the books. Back in the 1970s and 1980s, lenders couldn't do anything about this. Mortgage notes at that time did not prohibit assumptions, and the courts ruled that lenders could not prevent them.

Following that experience, however, lenders began to insert **Due-on-Sale Clauses** in their notes. (An exception is FHA and VA mortgages; see below.) These stipulate that if the property is sold, the loan must be repaid. Even with a due-on-sale clause, the lender may allow an assumption—keeping the loan on the books avoids the cost of making a new loan—but the interest rate will be raised to the current market rate.

Illegal Assumptions—Wraparounds: Raising the interest rate to the current market rate removes most of the benefit of the assumption to the buyer and seller. In some cases, they attempt to retain the benefit by agreeing to a sale using a wraparound mortgage without the knowledge of the lender. The seller takes a mortgage from the buyer, which may be for a larger amount than the balance of the old loan, and continues to pay the old mortgage out of the proceeds of the new one. The new mortgage "wraps" the old one.

This is a dangerous business, particularly to the seller, who gives up ownership of the house but retains liability for the mortgage. The seller is in deep trouble if the buyer fails to pay or if the lender discovers the sale and demands immediate repayment of the original loan. I wouldn't do it even if I were selling the house to my mother.

Legal Assumptions Under Garn–St. Germain: Whether a mortgage includes a due-on-sale clause or not, assumptions are explicitly allowable on certain types of transactions under the Garn–St. Germain Act of 1982. For example, if the title is transferred after a death or a divorce, or if the transfer is to an inter vivos living trust where the borrower is the beneficiary and remains the occupant, a due-on-sale clause cannot be enforced. Borrowers with low-rate mortgages who are involved in a transfer of ownership that is something other than the standard arm's-length purchase and sale should consult an attorney on whether the transaction falls under the Garn–St. Germain exemptions.

Offering Assumability at a Price, as an Option: When borrowers are concerned that interest rates could go much higher, they may be willing to pay for an assumable mortgage. For example, a borrower taking a 6.5% 30-year FRM might be willing to pay 6.875% for the right to allow a homebuyer to take it over when he sells his house. The higher rate is akin to an insurance premium. If market rates are above 16% when he sells, as they were in 1981, being able to offer a 6.875% loan to prospective buyers would have substantial value.

An assumable mortgage has some similarities to, and some differences from, a **Portable Mortgage**. If your mortgage is assumable when you sell your home, it can be transferred to the buyer; if the mortgage is portable, it can be transferred to a new property that you buy. Portability is of no value if you decide to rent, go to a nursing home, or die, whereas an assumable mortgage retains its value in these situations. On the other hand, some portion of the value of an assumable mortgage must be shared with the purchaser. A mortgage that is both assumable and portable would have the greatest value to the borrower.

Lenders who offer assumable mortgages will require that any new borrower meet the lender's qualification requirements. Borrowers purchasing the option will need to be confident that the lender won't tighten its requirements when market rates increase. The best assurance would be a commitment to accept approval under one of the automated underwriting systems developed by Fannie Mae or Freddie Mac.

FHA and VA Loans Are Assumable: Loans insured by FHA or guaranteed by VA have always been assumable. During periods when borrowers are concerned about future rate increases, this gives them an edge.

Old Loans: FHA loans closed before December 14, 1989, and VA loans closed before March 1, 1988, are assumable by anyone. Buyers who assume these mortgages don't have to meet any requirements at all, but the seller remains responsible for the mortgage if the buyer doesn't pay.

Any seller who allows assumption by a buyer without a release of liability is looking for trouble. Even if the buyer pays, and that is a crapshoot, the seller's ability to obtain another mortgage will be prejudiced by her continued liability on the old one.

If an old FHA or VA loan is attractive to a buyer, the seller can request that the agency underwrite the buyer. If the buyer is approved, the seller will be released from liability. At this point, there can't be many of these loans left with balances large enough to be attractive to buyers.

New Loans: Assumption of FHA and VA loans closed after the dates shown above requires approval of the buyer by the agencies. The process is much the same as it would be for a new borrower. Upon approval of the buyer and sale of the property, the seller is relieved of liability. FHA allows lenders to charge a $500 assumption fee and a fee for the credit report. VA allows a $255 processing fee and a $45 closing fee, and VA itself receives a funding fee of ½ of 1% of the loan balance.

FHA and VA loans that were closed during the low-rate years 1996–2009 will become attractive targets for assumption if interest rates rise in future years. Potential sellers who have one of these loans can use the spreadsheet on my Web site to estimate how much the assumption would be worth to a potential buyer.

Assumption *A method of selling real estate where the buyer of the property agrees to become responsible for the repayment of an existing loan on the property.*

Unless the lender also agrees, however, the seller remains liable for the mortgage. *See* **Assumable Mortgage**.

Auction Sites

See **Lead-Generation Sites**.

Authorized User *Someone authorized by the original credit card holder to use the holder's card.*

While authorized users are not responsible for paying any charges, including their own, they are sometimes dunned for the unpaid bills of the card holder. *See* **Credit Score/*Some Misperceptions About Credit/*Authorized Credit Card Users Are Safe**.

Automated Underwriting *A computer-driven process for informing the loan applicant very quickly, sometimes within a few minutes, whether the application will be approved, denied, or forwarded to an underwriter.*

The quick decision is based on information provided by the applicant that is subject to later verification and other information obtained electronically, including information about the borrower's credit history and the subject property.

Automated Underwriting System *A particular computerized system for doing automated underwriting.*

Mortgage insurers and some large lenders have developed such systems, but the most widely used are Fannie Mae's "Desktop Underwriter," Freddie Mac's "Loan Prospector," and FHA's "Scorecard."

"Bad Faith" Estimate *Deliberately underestimating closing costs as a way of enticing borrowers.*

Unscrupulous lenders may lowball their figures for settlement costs because they know that many borrowers look at total settlement cost figures in shopping lenders. They lowball their own charges as well as third-party charges, since under RESPA, all are viewed as "estimates." They can almost always get away with it because it is very difficult to prove that an estimate was given in bad faith. Under revisions to RESPA effective January 1, 2010, this problem may largely go away.

Bailout *Government support to a firm in trouble, which is usually limited to protecting creditors and employees.*

Whenever government is involved in a program to assist a private firm in trouble, much of the press reports it as a "bailout." Back in the 1980s when the savings and loan industry was in trouble, the operations of the Resolution Trust Corporation (RTC), which the federal government chartered to manage and liquidate the assets of failed associations, were frequently, yet erroneously, described in this way, and they still are.

For readers who don't bother absorbing the details, the term "bailout" suggests that everybody connected to the troubled enterprise is being rescued, including those who were responsible for its plight. For this reason, it often generates a hostile public response—"one more example of how government protects the big guys."

In fact, a core if unstated principle of federal government intervention since the 1980s has been that the shareholders of the firms involved lose all or most of their investment and that some or all of the top executives lose their jobs. This was the case in the savings and loan episode, as well as in the more recent interventions involving the investment bank Bear Stearns, the government-sponsored enterprises Fannie Mae and Freddie Mac, and the insurance conglomerate AIG. Those protected by the intervention were the creditors of the firm, and the employees if the firm continued as a going concern.

The erroneous inferences hasty readers draw when they see the term "bailout" used in connection with a government intervention derives from the other common uses of the term. The most familiar one is bailing out a leaking boat, which protects everybody in the boat. It is not possible to bail for one but not for another. Similarly, only one pilot bails out of a damaged airplane, and only one accused felon is bailed out of jail. In describing government interventions in connection with individual firms in trouble, we need another term that does not carry this baggage.

Balance *The amount of the original loan remaining to be paid.*

It is equal to the original loan amount less the sum of all subsequent payments of principal, plus any lender charges that have been added to the balance rather than paid directly by the borrower.

Balloon *The loan balance remaining at the time the loan contract calls for full repayment.*

Balloon Mortgage *A mortgage that is payable in full after a period that is shorter than the term.*

In the 1920s most balloon loans were interest-only—the borrower paid interest but no principal. At maturity, usually 5 or 10 years, the balloon that had to be repaid was equal to the original loan amount. The balloon loans offered today, in contrast, calculate payments on a 30-year amortization schedule, so there is some principal reduction. Assuming a rate of 6.5%, for example, a $100,000 loan would have a balance remaining at the end of the fifth year of $93,611.

Comparing a Balloon Mortgage and an ARM: It is useful to compare 5- and 7-year balloons with ARMs that have the same initial rate periods. Both offer a rate in the early years below that available on a fixed-rate mortgage, and both carry a risk of higher rates later on. But there are some important differences.

Favoring the Balloon:

- Balloon loans are much simpler, easier to understand, and therefore easier to shop for.

- The interest rate on a 5-year or 7-year balloon is typically lower than that on a 5/1 or 7/1 ARM.

Favoring the ARM:

- The risk of a substantial rate increase after 5 or 7 years is greater on the balloon. The balloon must be refinanced at the prevailing market rate, whereas a rate increase on most 5- and 7-year ARMs is limited by rate caps.

- Borrowers with 5- or 7-year balloons incur refinancing costs at term, whereas borrowers with 5/1 or 7/1 ARMs don't unless they elect to refinance.

- Borrowers who are having payment problems may find it difficult to refinance balloons. The balloon contract allows lenders to decline to refinance if the borrower has missed a single payment in the prior year. This is not a problem with ARMs, which need not be refinanced.

- Borrowers may find it difficult to refinance balloons if interest rates have spiked. The balloon contract allows lenders to decline to refinance if current market rates are more than 5% higher than the rate on the balloon.

Bimonthly Mortgage *A mortgage on which half the monthly payment is paid twice a month.*

It should be called a "semimonthly mortgage," but market practice often trumps logic. In contrast to a biweekly, a bimonthly mortgage involves no extra payments. The 24 half payments a year add to the same total as 12 full payments. Advancing the payment by half a month saves a little interest, but the effect is negligible. A 7% 30-year loan pays off in 29 years, 11 months. Check it out with the bimonthly spreadsheet on my Web site.

Biweekly Mortgage *A mortgage on which half the monthly payment is paid every two weeks.*

This results in 26 payments per year, which is the equivalent of 13 monthly payments rather than 12. Because of the extra payment, the biweekly mortgage amortizes before term. For example, a 7% 30-year loan that is converted into a biweekly pays off in 286 months (23 years, 11 months).

Biweekly Mortgage

Benefit of a Biweekly: Borrowers do not need a biweekly to make extra payments. They can do it themselves in a variety of ways described below, but all require self-discipline. Having a third party set up the procedure and legally obligating borrowers to make the additional payments forces the discipline on them.

New Biweeklies: Borrowers taking out a new loan who need the discipline provided by a biweekly can usually do better with a straight monthly payment loan carrying a shorter term. A 30-year loan converted into a biweekly carries the 30-year rate, whereas shorter-term loans often carry lower rates. In particular, 15-year loans generally carry rates 3/8 to 5/8% below those on 30s.

Rolling Your Own Biweekly: For borrowers who already have a 30-year mortgage and are attracted by the prospect of paying it off early, there are a number of options. One is to open a new account with a bank that has an automatic payment privilege and arrange for it to make their monthly mortgage payment every month. If they pay half the monthly payment into this account every two weeks, after a year the account will have enough money for a double payment.

This procedure exactly mimics that of a third-party biweekly provider. The only difference is that the borrower rather than the third party earns interest on the account.

Making a Double Payment Once a Year: A borrower who makes a double payment once a year will pay off on the same schedule as one using a biweekly. This can be a convenient method for borrowers who regularly receive bonuses or similar compensation at the end of the year.

Increasing the Monthly Payment by 1/12: Another simple method is to divide the monthly payment by 12 and add that amount to the payment every month. Paying an extra 1/12 of the payment every month for 12 months is the equivalent of one full extra payment. This method pays off a loan a little sooner than a biweekly or a double payment at year-end because balance reductions begin with the first extra payment rather than after a year. A 30-year 7% loan will pay off in 285 months rather than 286.

Simple Interest Biweeklies: On a simple interest biweekly, the biweekly payment is applied to the principal every two weeks, which results in a faster payoff. Again, however, the difference is small. The simple interest version pays off the 7% 30-year loan in 284 months.

Readers can check the numbers cited here and test other possibilities with the biweekly spreadsheet on my Web site. *Also see* **Partial Pre-payments (or Paying Off Early)/***Monitoring the Lender*.

Blemished Borrowers *Mortgage borrowers with one or more important risk factors adversely affecting their ability to qualify for a loan.*

Blemished borrowers have one or more of the following risk factors: they can make only a small or no down payment; they cannot fully document their income and assets; their property is something other than a single-family home; their loan is intended to raise cash or to purchase an investment property; they have low credit scores; their income is low relative to their expected total obligations.

During the go-go years 2000–2006, the mortgage market was extraordinarily tolerant of risk factors. It was not unusual to see five of them present in an accepted mortgage, a phenomenon termed "risk layering." Lending to a borrower who had no money for a down payment, who could not document adequate income, and who had a poor credit history was a kind of market insanity associated with the rapid run-up in house prices. Inflation of house prices converts even the worst loans into good loans.

When the housing bubble burst in 2006, the chickens came home to roost in the form of mortgage defaults. During 2007–2009, defaults rose to levels not seen since the depression of the 1930s.

Markets tend to overreact. Just as the housing bubble was accommodated by insanely liberal lending terms, in the crisis that followed, the pendulum swung toward Scroogelike stringency. "Cream-puff borrowers"—those with no blemishes—could borrow at the unusually low rates that emerged after the crisis. But borrowers with blemishes on their applications paid much higher prices, and faced a much higher risk of being turned down altogether. Roughly speaking, a borrower with two risk factors paid a substantially higher price, and borrowers with three were rejected.

Bridge Financing *The financing used by a home purchaser who needs the equity in her current house to buy a new house but has to close on the new house before the old house can be sold.*

Homeowners who need to finance a home purchase before they can cash out the equity in their current house, and who have exhausted all possibilities of borrowing from family, friends, or retirement accounts, have several other options.

Unsecured Bridge Loans: A bridge loan provides funds needed for a short period until another source of funds becomes available. In the home loan market, a bridge loan, sometimes called a "swing" loan, allows a homebuyer to close on a new home purchase before closing on the old home sale.

A bridge loan lender accepts two types of protection. One type is a binding contract of sale on the old house. The lender who knows that on a certain date you will be receiving enough money to repay the loan can avoid the trouble and expense of placing a lien on that property.

I used an unsecured bridge loan on my last home purchase, and it was relatively simple and hassle-free. While the rate may be high, the interest payment won't amount to much because the period is short.

Banks aren't crazy about bridge loans because they realize they are one-shot affairs and they are unlikely to see the borrower again. For this reason, you should go to the institution where you currently hold your deposit, whether it is a commercial bank, savings and loan association, or credit union. If the officers there give you any flak, let them know (in a polite way) that as a customer, you expect this service, and if you don't get it, you have lots of other choices of where you hold your account.

Secured Bridge Loans and HELOCs: If you don't have a binding contract of sale on your old house, you can't get an unsecured bridge loan, but you can get a secured bridge loan or a home equity line of credit (HELOC). Both are secured by the house you are trying to sell, and can be for an amount up to some portion of the equity, perhaps 85 or 90%.

A secured bridge loan is offered by the lender providing the new loan, as an accommodation or a marketing inducement. "Take your purchase loan from us, and you won't have to worry about whether your old home sells before the new one is purchased." The downside of this is that it eliminates your ability to shop for the best possible terms on the purchase loan.

The advantage of a HELOC is that the HELOC lender is not looking to get your purchase loan. HELOCs are a profitable stand-alone business. On the other hand, HELOC lenders are not much interested in a deal that will last only a few months. If they know the house is up for sale, they probably will not give you a HELOC on it. If they do go ahead, there likely will be a cancellation charge, and you may have to pay the closing costs that they otherwise would waive to get your business.

In sum, assuming you need cash out of your old house to do the best deal on the new one:

- If your old house is under contract, take an unsecured bridge loan.
- If the old house is not yet on the market, take a HELOC.
- If the old house is on the market but unsold, take a secured bridge loan.

Builder-Financed Construction *Having the builder borrow the money needed for construction.*

See **Construction Financing/*Should the Builder Finance Construction?***

Buy-Down *A way to reduce the mortgage payment by paying more up front.*

A permanent buy-down is the payment of points in exchange for a lower interest rate. *See* **Points**. A temporary buy-down requires funding a special account from which monies are withdrawn to supplement the borrower's reduced payments in the early years of the loan. *See* **Temporary Buy-Down**.

Buy-Up *Reducing upfront costs by increasing the interest rate.*

See **Negative Points**.

Cash-Out Refinance *Refinancing for an amount in excess of the balance on the old loan plus settlement costs.*

While not all lenders define "cash-out refinance" in the same way, the most widely used definition is that of the two federal secondary market purchasers, Fannie Mae and Freddie Mac. Their rules define a cash-out refinance by exclusion; i.e., they define an ordinary or no-cash-out refinance, and any refinance that does not meet that definition is considered a cash-out.

A no-cash-out refinance is one that (a) is used to pay off a first mortgage or junior mortgages that were used in their entirety to buy the subject property and (b) is for an amount not in excess of the loan balance, plus settlement costs, plus 2% of the new loan amount or $2,000, whichever is less. If the borrower has a mortgage balance of $150,000 and settlement costs are $5,000, for example, the loan can be no larger than $157,000.

Any refinance that does not meet these specs is a cash-out refinance and will carry a higher interest rate.

Why Cash-Out Refinancing Carries a Higher Rate: The major reason for the higher rate is that studies of delinquency and default indicate that borrowers who do a cash-out subsequently have poorer payment records than borrowers who don't. The presumed reason for this is that borrowers who need cash are financially weaker than borrowers who don't, and in some cases they may be in financial distress.

Refinancing a Second Mortgage Is Cash-Out: The agencies assume that refinancing borrowers who want to repay second mortgages that they acquired after they purchased their house are cut from the same cloth as refinancing borrowers who want a large amount of cash. While those refinancing a second don't need cash now, they did need cash when they took a second mortgage. If they were in financial distress then, perhaps they still are. The presumption of distress does not apply, however, if the second mortgage was taken out when the house was purchased.

Loan on a Property with No Mortgage Is Cash-Out: If a homeowner who paid all cash for a property or who has paid off all mortgages elects to take a new mortgage, the agencies consider it cash-out. This is also based on the presumption that the need for cash may signal financial distress.

Portfolio Lenders May Be More Flexible: Lenders who originate loans to hold rather than to sell in the secondary market may be more flexible in their definitions of what constitutes a cash-out. They may not view a loan for the purpose of repaying a second mortgage as cash-out if the borrower has had the loan for some time or if the loan had been used to improve the property. Property improvement might also exempt a loan on a property with no mortgage. Borrowers should be prepared to document the improvements, however.

Cash-Out Versus Second Mortgage: Borrowers who want to raise cash should compare the cost of a cash-out refinance against the cost of a second mortgage. This will depend on the interest rates, the points and terms of both loans, the amount of cash required relative to the loan balance, the borrower's tax rate, and other factors. *See* **Refinance/ Refinancing to Raise Cash**.

Cash-Out Refinance by Predators: Cash-out refinance is a tool used by some predators to exploit unwary borrowers who are dazzled by the prospect of putting a sizable amount of money in their pocket. This applies to many of those who have become homeowners with assistance from Habitat for Humanity, who have refinanced the zero interest rate loans provided them by the program into high-rate loans in order to get cash. *See* **Predatory Lending/*Targets of Predators*/Cash Dazzled**.

Closing *On a home purchase, the process of transferring ownership from the seller to the buyer, the disbursement of funds from the buyer and the lender to the seller, and the execution of all the documents associated with the sale and the loan.*

On a refinance, there is no transfer of ownership, but the closing includes repayment of the old lender.

Closing Costs *Costs that the borrower must pay at the time of closing in addition to the down payment.*

See **Settlement Costs**.

Closing Date *The date on which the closing occurs.*

On a purchase transaction, there is no financial advantage to the buyer-borrower in closing on any day of the month, as compared with any other day. Buyers should select the closing date as close as possible to the moving date, regardless of the day of the month that is.

The interest clock on the loan starts ticking on the closing date, because the lender expects to be paid beginning the day the funds are disbursed. There is no point in paying interest before you are prepared to move.

While borrowers pay interest beginning the closing date, they may pay it in different ways, depending on when during the month they close. The first payment on a home loan is due on the first day of a month and includes interest for a full month. Since loans may close anytime within the month, there is always an interest adjustment at closing based on the exact closing date. This is **Per Diem Interest** or "prepaid interest."

If you close on July 29, for example, you pay 3 days of interest at closing, covering July 30 and 31 and August 1. Your first monthly payment is due

September 1. So at closing you pay interest for the last 3 days of July, and the first monthly payment on September 1 pays the interest for the full month of August.

Closing on different days during the month will shift the amount of interest you pay at closing, but it will not affect the total interest you pay beginning at closing.

In principle, refinancing should work in the same way as a purchase. If you close a refinance on July 29, you should pay the new lender per diem interest for 3 days and the old lender for 29 days. Unfortunately, because of glitches in the system, it doesn't work out that way. Borrowers often are charged interest by both lenders for 1 day and sometimes 2 or 3 or more.

The major reason is that the funds don't move directly from the new lender to the old lender. The funds are held by an intermediary until the new documents have been recorded, and that process takes time. Because recording offices are usually closed on the weekend, borrowers who close on a Friday are especially likely to pay double interest for several days. So don't close a refinance on a Friday if you can avoid it.

Furthermore, FHA requires that interest be paid for a full month, regardless of when a loan is closed during the month. Those refinancing out of an FHA, therefore, should try to close as near to the end of the month as possible.

Coborrowers *One or more persons who have signed the note and are equally responsible for repaying the loan.*

When One Coborrower Has Much Better Credit Than the Other: A problem that arises frequently with coborrowers is that one has much better credit than the other. If they buy the house together as co-owners and coborrowers, the deadbeat's bad credit will result in a bad credit rating for the transaction and a corresponding high interest rate.

One option is for "good-credit" to buy the house alone, leaving "bad -credit" out of the deal. But then the mortgage would be limited to the amount that the income of "good-credit" can support. Whether this option works depends on whether the mortgage that "good-credit" can carry, plus the down payment the partners can make, permits them to purchase the house that they want. *See* **Affordability/*Calculating the Maximum Affordable Sale Price*.**

Coborrowers

Before the financial crisis, if the first option didn't work, the partners could have "good-credit" buy the house using a program that did not require verification of income. A number of such programs were available with different twists. (*See* **Documentation Requirements**.) Then the mortgage amount would not be limited by the income of "good-credit." However, these programs were scrapped during the crisis, and full documentation became the rule. In early 2010 there were no signs of their coming back.

Still another possibility is to have a third party with good credit and income replace "bad-credit" as the coborrower. Usually only a parent would be willing to play this role.

When Coborrowers Split: Problems can arise when coborrowers split, whether they are married or not. However, difficulties seem to arise more frequently with unmarried couples, perhaps because unmarried couples purchasing a house together more often do it blindly. When they split, issues that should have been foreseen, but weren't, may prevent a clean and amicable separation.

Here are the major issues to resolve with your partner *before* you buy.

Split with Sale: There is much to be said for an agreement that the house must be sold if either partner aborts the relationship. This avoids the thorny issues, discussed below, that can arise when one partner stays with the house.

If a split leads to a sale, the only issue is how the proceeds are to be divided. Equal shares may or may not be equitable. A partner who pays the down payment, or a larger share of current expenses, deserves a larger share of the proceeds.

One approach is to divide the net proceeds by each partner's contribution to the equity in the house when it is sold. Suppose, for example, that the partners pay $100,000 for a house, take a mortgage of $80,000, pay $20,000 down plus $3,000 in settlement costs, and sell it after five years when the loan balance is $74,000. Total contributions of the partners to equity in the house at the time of sale consist of $23,000 in cash at purchase, plus $6,000 in reducing the loan balance. If one partner contributed 60% of the cash and paid 40% of the expenses, that partner's share of net proceeds would be [0.6($23,000) + 0.4($6,000)]/$29,000, or 56%.

In some cases, this rule would not be fair. For example, one of the partners might unilaterally work on improving the house, which would call for a higher share.

Coborrowers

The point is that the partners ought to agree at the outset on the terms of the split. If they can't agree, they should reconsider whether they really want to cohabit.

Split with One Partner Staying: The terms of settlement are more complex when one of the partners remains in the house. There is no sale price, so the partners must agree on an appraisal procedure and on who will pay for it. They should also agree on whether a real estate sales commission should be deducted from the valuation used in the settlement. If they wait until the event, this is invariably contentious.

Another problem arises if the partner remaining in the house doesn't have the money to pay off the partner who is leaving. The more equity they have in the house, the more cash the resident partner needs to raise. A home equity loan is not possible unless both partners become responsible, which is the last thing the departing partner wants.

The largest problem, however, is the departing partner's continuing responsibility for the mortgage. Many departing partners believe that they are off the hook because the partner remaining in the house has agreed to assume full responsibility for the mortgage. They (and often their lawyers) overlook the fact that the lender was not a partner to their agreement.

As far as the lender is concerned, the departing partner remains liable. If the departing partner seeks to purchase another house, the old mortgage will show up on his credit report, reducing the size of the loan for which he can qualify.

Lenders have no incentive to remove one partner from the note. Some can be induced to do it if the partner remaining with the house has a perfect payment record and can document that she has been solely responsible for the payments. But in the best situation this takes time, perhaps a year.

If the lender refuses, the only way to get the departing partner off the note is for the remaining partner to refinance in her own name. But if this was not part of the original agreement, it is unlikely that the remaining partner will agree later—unless refinancing becomes financially advantageous at the time.

If both the original lender and the remaining partner refuse to help, a new lender may be willing to ignore the old mortgage obligation if presented with evidence that the remaining partner has been meeting the payment obligations. Unlike the old lender, a new lender has something to gain by wiping the departing partner's slate clean.

Of course, if the remaining partner has not been making payments on time, neither lender will be willing to help the departing partner.

If I were drafting an agreement for a loved one, not knowing whether she was more likely to be the remaining or the departing partner, it would grant the remaining partner 14 months to make the settlement payment and to remove the departing partner from the note. Otherwise, the house must be sold and the mortgage paid off.

COFI *Cost of Funds Index, one of many interest rate indexes used to determine interest rate adjustments on an adjustable-rate mortgage.*

See **Adjustable-Rate Mortgage (ARM)/*ARM Rate Indexes***.

Collateralized Debt Obligation (CDO) *A security issued against the collateral of a pool of assets, which may include mortgages or mortgage securities.*

CDOs were one of the mechanisms through which the United States exported its mortgage crisis abroad. *See* **Subprime Market/*Exporting the Crisis***.

Conforming Mortgage *A loan eligible for purchase by the two major federal agencies that buy mortgages, Fannie Mae and Freddie Mac.*

Conforming mortgages cannot exceed a legal maximum amount, which was $417,000 during 2006–2009. The practice before 2006 was to raise it each year to keep pace with rising home prices, but it was not reduced when prices started to decline in 2006. Instead, as a crisis measure, the limit was raised.

The financial crisis disabled the private secondary market in which most jumbos were sold, enlarging the conforming-jumbo yield spread substantially. Prior to the crisis, a mortgage in excess of the conforming maximum, which was identical in other respects, might have an interest rate about 3/8% higher. After the crisis, because of the breakdown in the secondary market for nonconforming loans, the spread was three times or more larger.

To compensate, Congress increased the conforming loan limit of $417,000 to a maximum of $729,500 on a county-by-county basis—low-cost counties remained at $417,000. Loans larger than $417,000 eligible for purchase by the agencies became "conforming jumbos." Because the agencies paid less for conforming jumbos, there were two **Pricing Notch Points** for every county that had a jumbo maximum above $417,000. One was $417,000, and the other was the county jumbo maximum. Authorization for conforming jumbos was scheduled to expire at the end of 2010.

Conforming loans must also meet the agencies' underwriting requirements regarding credit, documentation, property features, and other factors. Prior to 2007, these tended to become more liberal over time, but the process reversed itself after the crisis hit. Documentation requirements in particularly were severely tightened. *See* **Documentation Requirements**.

Construction Financing *The method of financing used when a borrower contracts to have a house built, as opposed to purchasing a completed house.*

Construction can be financed in two ways. One way is to use two loans, a construction loan for the period of construction, followed by a permanent loan from another lender, which pays off the construction loan. Borrowers who use two loans must decide whether they will take out the construction loan or have the builder do it. The second approach is to use a single combination loan, where the construction loan becomes permanent at the end of the construction period.

Some lenders (primarily commercial banks) will only make construction loans. Others will only make combination loans. And some will do it either way.

Two Loans Versus One Loan: Two loans mean that you shop twice and incur two sets of closing costs. One loan means that you shop only once and incur only one set of closing costs. But to do it effectively, you must shop for construction loans and permanent loans at the same time.

Construction loans usually run for six months to a year and carry an adjustable interest rate that resets monthly or quarterly. In addition to points and closing costs, lenders charge a construction fee to cover their costs in administering the loan. (Construction lenders pay out the loan in stages and must monitor the progress of construction.) In shopping for construction loans, one must take account of all these dimensions of the "price."

Lenders offering combination loans typically will credit some of the fees paid for the construction loan toward the permanent loan. The lender might charge four points for the construction loan, for example, but apply three of the points toward the permanent loan. If the borrower takes the permanent loan from another lender, however, the construction lender retains the three points. This credit and the one set of closing costs are major talking points of loan officers pushing combination loans.

The rebate offered on combination loans makes it difficult to compare these loans with the two-loan alternative. For example, lender A offers a construction loan at four points with three points applicable to a permanent loan, while B offers an untied construction loan at two points. Going with A means saving one point on the construction loan, but this is no bargain if A's terms on permanent loans are not competitive.

Suppose A offers a permanent loan at 6% and three points, while lender C offers the same 6% loan at one point. Then if you selected A, you would pay a total of four points on both loans; but if you had selected B for the construction loan and C for the permanent loan, you would have paid only three points in total. A is above the best price available in the permanent loan market by more than it is below the best price available in the construction loan market.

Further, once you accept a combination-loan deal that involves a significant rebate from the construction loan, shopping other lenders for a permanent mortgage after construction ends is likely to prove fruitless. So long as the combination lender is not above the market for permanent loans by more than the rebate plus closing costs, you cannot do better by finishing the deal with another lender. You're hooked!

This means that you cannot properly assess a lender's combination loan without comparing that lender's terms on permanent loans with those of other permanent lenders. You should shop for construction loans and permanent loans at the same time. If the combination lender is above the market on permanent loans by an amount that is less than the saving on the construction loan plus closing costs, you go with the combination loan. Otherwise, you go with two loans.

If you go the two-loan route, you have the option of having the builder take the construction loan. Then you have only the permanent loan to worry about.

Should the Builder Finance Construction? The advantage of having the builder finance construction is that you need to take out only one mortgage, and you have assurance that the builder has sufficient financial capacity to do the job. Further, a builder paying interest on a construction loan has an incentive to get the job done as quickly as possible.

The downside is that you don't know what you are paying for the financing because it is embedded in the price of the house. Since the builder must include the financing cost in the price before the construction period is known, his inclination may be to assume a longer period (and therefore a higher financing cost) than is actually the case.

In addition, the builder must have title to the land in order to obtain construction financing, and switching title is costly in some states. Finally, a builder who owns the property and is on the hook for the loan may be reluctant to make any modifications in the design that would negatively affect the house's marketability in the event that the deal falls through.

Contract Chicanery *Inserting provisions into a loan contract that severely disadvantage the borrower, without the borrower's knowledge and sometimes despite oral assurances to the contrary.*

Prepayment penalties are perhaps the most frequently cited subject of such abuse. *See* **Prepayment Penalty/*Surreptitious Penalties***.

Conventional Mortgage *A home mortgage that is not insured or guaranteed by FHA, VA, or USDA.*

Conversion Option *The option to convert an ARM to an FRM at some point during its life.*

See **Adjustable-Rate Mortgage (ARM)/*Convertible ARMs***.

Correspondent Lender *A lender who delivers loans to another (usually larger) lender against prior price commitments the larger lender has made to the correspondent.*

Mortgage brokers sometimes evolve into correspondent lenders when they accumulate enough capital to acquire the credit lines needed to close loans in their own names. Correspondents like brokers depend on price commitments from larger lenders to protect them against the risk that market prices will decline while they are holding loans. *See* **Mortgage Lender/*Retail, Wholesale, and Correspondent Lenders***.

Cosigning *Assuming responsibility for someone else's debt obligation in the event that the party defaults.*

The economic distress of 2008–2009 battered the credit scores of many potential borrowers, while causing lenders to increase the scores they were willing to accept. The result was a growing number of cosigning requests.

Cosigning Provides Limited Help on a Mortgage: Cosigning is used less often on home mortgages than on other types of loans. A cosigner with good credit cannot overcome the bad credit of a mortgage borrower. Lenders use the credit of the borrower whose income is used to qualify. They will not use the credit of a cosigner.

While a cosigner cannot improve the credit score used to price the loan, the cosigner's income may be added to the borrower's income in determining the size of loan for which the borrower qualifies. On FHA loans, 100% of the cosigner's income can be used to raise the qualifying loan amount up to the FHA loan limit. However, the cosigner's debt is added to the borrower's debt in determining the qualifying loan amount. This means that if the cosigner's debt is large, her inclusion could add little or nothing to the qualifying loan amount.

On conventional (non-FHA and non-VA) loans, the picture is very different. Most conventional loan programs don't allow nonoccupant cosigners at all. Those that do typically limit the incremental income to 50% of the cosigner's income, but they include 100% of the cosigner's debt. As a result, there aren't many cosigners on conventional loans.

Cosigning Means Assuming a Major Risk: Some cosigners have had their lives severely disrupted when the borrower for whom they cosigned stopped paying, leaving it up to the cosigner to make the loan good. Most of the mail I get on the subject is from cosigners in this situation. They now regret they did it, and they invariably ask me how they can get out of it. I discuss this question below.

Most Cosignings Have a Happy Ending: On the other hand, probably the great majority of cases of cosigning have a happy ending. Stories with happy endings seldom get into my mailbox, but I had one in my own family that illustrates the potential benefits of cosigning. When my younger son left the military, he had no credit but needed an automobile, so I cosigned his note. Within 18 months, he had paid off the loan and his credit was well established. I never had to cosign for him again.

I cosigned his note because he was my son, but that was only part of the reason. The other part was that I had information about him that the lender did not have. Specifically, I knew he was a straight arrow who always met his commitments.

Cosigning fails when the borrower defaults and the cosigner has to make good on her pledge. Sometimes a responsible borrower draws a bad card from the deck of life, such as illness or job loss. A cosigner can't avoid that risk. The risk a cosigner can and should avoid is cosigning for someone who is not responsible.

The Big Mistake: Cosigning for Someone Who Is Not Responsible: I recently read through some of the letters I have received where cosigning ended in default by the borrower and in severe distress for the cosigner. What struck me was that in most of these cases the cosigners had no better information about the capacity and willingness of the borrower to repay than the lender. Indeed, in many cases, the cosigners had persuasive evidence that the borrower was not reliable, which evidence they chose to ignore.

Why? Usually the reason was strong feelings of obligation to help a relative, friend, or lover. The guilt they would have felt in refusing, along with the fear that refusal would destroy the relationship, overwhelmed their better judgment. When it is someone near and dear, it is hard to say no.

But if you are not fully confident that, absent unusual circumstances, the borrower will meet her obligation, no is what you need to say. It can destroy the relationship, that's the borrower's call, but the relationship will also be destroyed if the borrower defaults. And if that happens, your financial security could be destroyed with it.

How Can You Get Out of a Cosigning Obligation? The letters below are typical of many I receive from people who cosign without giving it much thought or who are asked to cosign with false assurances.

I cosigned a loan for my brother-in-law who has since left my sister and has stopped paying the note . . . The lender is now after me to pay. How can I get out of this?

You can't. Once you cosign a note, there are only two ways to get out of it. Either the loan must be repaid in full by the borrower or you, or the lender must agree to take you off.

The lender is not going to let you off the hook because the borrower stopped paying. The risk of nonpayment is why the lender required a cosigner in the first place! The lender doesn't care that the borrower left your sister; he just wants to be repaid.

My nephew has asked me to cosign his mortgage. He says that after the loan is closed, I will be taken off the deed and my obligation will terminate. Is this right?

No, removal of your name from the deed does not eliminate your obligation.

My brother-in-law has asked me to cosign for a home, and the real estate agent tells me that after 6 months of good payment by the borrower, I can be removed from the title and loan. Is this true?

Probably not. It is strictly up to the lender, who might let you off the hook in 6 months, or perhaps after 12 months, or perhaps never.

Cosigning Can Affect Your Qualifications for a Loan: Lenders impose limits on the amount of existing debt a borrower can carry, and a cosigning obligation is considered debt for qualification purposes.

In a weak moment I agreed to help a friend get a mortgage by cosigning her note. My friend has always made the payments, but I discovered that her mortgage shows up as debt on my credit report, and it prevents me from getting a mortgage of my own. How do I deal with this?

The loan qualification problem that may arise from a cosigning can usually be remedied by documenting that the borrower has been making the payments on time for a reasonable period. The lender in such case will probably remove the debt from your loan application. You remain a cosigner, but the lender is ignoring your obligation to the other lender in assessing your ability to repay a new loan.

Cosigning a Lease: The only difference between cosigning for a lease and cosigning for a loan is that the lease—and with it, the cosigner's obligation—is likely to be for a shorter period.

Cost of Savings Index (COSI) *One of many interest rate indexes used to determine interest rate adjustments on an adjustable-rate mortgage.*

COSI was an index developed for use by a single lender, World Savings, which was subsequently acquired by Wachovia, which stopped employing it in 2008.

Credit Report *A report from a credit bureau containing detailed information bearing on creditworthiness, including the individual's credit history.*

A typical credit report shows some personal information including social security number; current and past addresses; employment history; public record information such as liens, foreclosures, bankruptcies, and garnishments; collection accounts; and credit information. The last covers individual credit relationships and shows the creditor, the current status of each account including the amount outstanding and the maximum line if any, prior payment history, and recent activity. A credit report also shows a list of companies that have requested the individual's file and the date the request was made.

There are three major repositories of credit information: Equifax, Experian, and TransUnion. The information provided by the three is not exactly the same because not all credit grantors report information to all three.

At one time, underwriters with responsibility for determining whether or not a mortgage applicant was "creditworthy" spent much of their time studying and interpreting credit reports. Starting in the 1990s, these judgments increasingly came to be based on credit scores. However, the financial crisis slowed down that process.

Credit Score *A single numerical score, based on information in an individual's credit report, that measures an individual's creditworthiness.*

Credit scores are based on statistical studies of the relationship between the different items in a credit report and the likelihood of default. The most widely used credit score is called FICO for Fair Isaac Co., which developed it. FICO scores range from 350 to 850, the higher the better.

Major Determinants of FICO Scores:

Payment History: This is the most important determinant of credit scores. It includes information on the extent to which the subject has made timely payments on mortgage loans, auto loans, credit cards, personal loans, and charge accounts. Delinquencies reduce the score, while timely payments raise it.

Payment history also includes information on bankruptcies, foreclosures, legal judgments, liens, and wage garnishments. These will have a major adverse impact, although the impact declines with the passage of time.

Amount and Distribution of Current Debts: This is the next most important determinant of credit scores. Unlike payment history, however, it is not always intuitively obvious whether more or less debt, or whether more or fewer creditors, will improve a score. Past some point, more debt will lower the score by raising questions about the ability of the borrower to pay it all off. But not having debt will not generate a good score, because without debt the subject cannot demonstrate a good payment history.

The FICO genie who generates a score does not have information on a subject's income or financial assets. The genie must make judgments about how much debt is too much from information on the debt alone. On debts with debt limits, it focuses on the relationship between the two. It reduces the score when it sees debts that are at or close to the maximum. On installment loans, the genie likes to see the balances going down. A large number of accounts does not disturb the genie, so long as most of them have no balances.

Age of Accounts: The FICO genie likes old accounts much better than new ones. Old ones indicate stability in credit relationships, whereas new ones might indicate financial distress—if there are many of them.

The genie understands, however, that shopping multiple credit sources can generate many inquiries without indicating financial distress. All inquiries regarding either mortgage loans or auto loans in any 14-day period are treated as one inquiry, and inquiries within 30 days of a score date are disregarded. The genie also disregards inquiries of your own and inquiries from lenders who are considering you for a loan "preapproval."

Mix of Credit: This is not an important factor in the equation, which is good because Fair Isaac doesn't reveal exactly what it means. Reading between the lines, however, one can surmise that the genie is allergic to finance company loans.

Reason Codes: Every FICO score is returned with up to four "score factors," ranked by importance, that indicate why the score was not higher. Examples are "too many delinquencies," "ratio of balances to credit limits is too high," and "too many finance company accounts."

The reason codes mean little to someone with a high score. Those with low scores looking to improve, however, will do well to focus their efforts on the major problem areas indicated by the codes.

Credit Score

Correcting Errors: Credit reports often contain mistakes that lower the subject's credit score. Perhaps the most common is the inclusion of someone else's accounts. Borrowers who find mistakes must take the initiative to get them fixed, which means writing to the repository reporting the erroneous information and detailing the particulars of the error.

Under the Fair Credit Reporting Act (FCRA), a repository has 5 days from receipt of such a letter to contact the credit grantor that reported the erroneous information and another 35 days to complete its investigation and report back to the borrower. The report must indicate that the error was corrected, or there was no error, or the credit grantor did not respond, in which case the disputed item is dropped from the report.

To exercise your rights under FCRA, you must follow the correct procedures. These are spelled out on my Web site in an article on how to correct your credit file.

Because fixing errors takes time, it is a good idea for borrowers to check their credit well in advance of entering the market. Your FICO score is available for $14.95 from www.myfico.com.

Some Misperceptions About Credit: Many borrowers have misperceptions about how their behavior will affect their FICO score.

A Skipped Payment Results in One Delinquency: One misperception is that a skipped payment results in one delinquency record. In fact, however, a skipped payment generates a stream of delinquencies until it is paid.

Under the accounting rules used for amortized mortgages, lenders always credit a payment against the earliest unpaid obligation. If you skip the payment for May, the payment intended for June will be credited to May, leaving the June payment delinquent. Similarly, the payment intended for July will be credited to June, leaving the July payment delinquent.

It would be nice if the mortgage contract allowed a skipped payment now and then. Such contracts exist in the United Kingdom and some other countries, but they have appeared in the United States only very recently and are not yet widely available. Unless you have one, if you skip a payment but pay regularly thereafter, you remain delinquent (and accumulate late fees) until the skipped payment is made good.

Paying Off Delinquent Loans Improves the Score: Another misperception is that a credit score will improve if loans that have been delinquent are made current or paid off. This isn't so. Delinquencies lower credit scores because they show a weak commitment toward meeting obligations. This evidence is not wiped away when the loan is repaid. Only the passage of time, along with a better payment record, will wipe it away. The same is true of bankruptcies, tax liens, and judgments. They remain on the record for a period, even after they have been discharged or released.

Consolidating Balances Improves the Score: Still another misperception is that the consolidation of credit card balances into a smaller number of cards will increase a credit score. It is true that the FICO genie is much more favorably disposed to 4 credit cards than to 15. However, the genie is even more concerned with the relationship between the balances on the cards and the maximums. It sees cards that are "maxed out" as an indication of financial distress. So if the consolidation resulted in a smaller number of cards with balances close to their maximums, the score might drop rather than rise.

Authorized Credit Card Users Are Safe: Some borrowers have been surprised to find that their credit score has been reduced by delinquencies on credit cards for which they are not responsible. They are authorized users of cards on which the original credit card holder stopped paying. Even though they are not responsible for making the payment, credit grantors sometimes report authorized users to the credit-reporting agencies as delinquent. Unable to collect from the responsible parties, the original card holders, the credit grantors hope that maybe the authorized users will pay in order to keep their credit records clean.

To fix this, write the credit-reporting agency, as follows:

I'm an authorized user only and am not financially responsible for this debt. By reporting me delinquent, you are impugning my credit reputation in full violation of the Fair Credit Reporting Act (FCRA). I am aware of my rights under the Act. I intend to enforce them if you don't immediately remove all derogatory information from my credit profile that you placed there as a result of nonpayment by the financially responsible party.

If this doesn't work, go to my Web site and read the article "Are Authorized Users at Risk?"

Credit and Income Can Be Separated in a Loan Application: Some couples want to use the credit score of one spouse (the one with the good score) while qualifying with the income of the other. This doesn't work. Lenders are concerned with the credit score of the borrower whose income they are depending on to service the loan.

Use of FICO Scores by Lenders: Most lenders now incorporate FICO scores in their pricing and qualification requirements, but they do it in all sorts of ways. One lender might have 10 different interest rates corresponding to 10 FICO score categories. Another might only use three categories. Still another might set a single FICO score minimum for all loans, but require higher scores for borrowers who want no-down-payment loans or less than full documentation. Some lenders use FICO scores but supplement them with other information from the credit report that they believe is not adequately weighted in the score.

Because the different credit repositories may have different information, lenders may get two FICO scores and use the lower of the two. Sometimes they get three and use the middle score.

Lenders dealing with applicants who have low scores because of a foreclosure or bankruptcy will often request a letter of explanation. The purpose is to determine whether the event was caused by recklessness and, therefore, likely to recur or by unusual and unforeseeable misfortunes that were beyond the applicant's control.

Applicants in this situation should realize that the burden of proof is on them. They must persuade the lender that the misfortune was a one-time event that is very unlikely to recur.

Cumulative Interest *The sum of all interest payments to date or over the life of the loan.*

This is not a good measure of the cost of credit to the borrower because it does not include upfront cash payments and it is not adjusted for the time value of money. *See* **Interest Cost**.

Current Index Value *The most recently published value of the index used to adjust the interest rate on an indexed ARM.*

See **Indexed ARMs**.

Danish Mortgage System *A simple and efficient housing finance system based on specialized mortgage banks that place every new loan in a bond that is actively traded.*

The strength of the system is its low origination cost, the absence of sharp practices by loan originators, and complete transparency. It does not serve as large a segment of the population as the U.S. system, and partial prepayments are too costly to be practical.

Mortgage Banks: The core of the Danish system is eight mortgage banks that specialize in making mortgage loans. They fund their loans by selling bonds in the capital markets. The bonds are in all major respects identical to the mortgage loans they fund.

For example, if I borrow $200,000 for 30 years at a fixed rate, the loan would be placed in a large pool of 30-year fixed-rate loans that serve as collateral for an equal amount of mortgage bonds held by investors. The mortgage bank on my behalf would sell an additional $200,000 of these bonds in the capital market and credit the proceeds to me. As I repay the loan, the mortgage bank passes along the payments to the bondholders in proportion to the amount of the total pool that they own.

Mortgage banks are not exposed to interest rate risk from funding long-term assets with short-term liabilities. The Danish system is built on the principle of "match funding," meaning that mortgages are funded with bond issues that have the same characteristics as the mortgages. Five-year ARMs, for example, are funded by bonds on which the rate is reset every 5 years.

Although referred as "mortgage bonds" because they are liabilities of the mortgage banks, the bonds could as well be termed "mortgage-backed securities," because the cash flows on the mortgages are passed through to the bondholders. See **Mortgage-Backed Security.**

Shopping by Consumers: Shopping for a loan in Denmark is easy. The interest rate is the bond yield on the day the terms are locked plus the mortgage bank's markup. Bonds are traded on the Copenhagen stock market. The yields are readily available to everyone through the media, including the Internet. Price shopping thus focuses entirely on the banks' markups, which are very low and subject to competition between the banks.

On a given day, all borrowers pay the same rate on the same type of loan. (This is not true of commercial mortgages, on which rates are negotiated individually.) Loans are either fixed rate for 20 or 30 years or adjustable for periods ranging from 1 to 10 years. Each loan type has its corresponding bond, which determines the rate for that type.

No Points in Denmark: Danish mortgage banks do not adjust the interest rate for points, as lenders do in the United States. Nor do banks tack on a series of fixed-dollar charges to cover their expenses, as they do in the

Danish Mortgage System

United States. All borrowers in Denmark pay the same upfront fees: 1/10 of 1 percent of the loan amount plus a modest fixed charge.

Refinancing: Borrowers with fixed-rate mortgages can refinance, when market interest rates go down, as easily in Denmark as in the United States. They refinance by buying bonds in an amount equal to their mortgage balance. When interest rates go up, borrowers in Denmark can stay put as they do in the United States, or they can refinance by buying back bonds at the depressed market price. They realize a capital gain in exchange for accepting a new higher rate on their loan.

Weaknesses: The most important weakness of the Danish system, relative to the U.S. system, is its limited reach. Loans are not priced for risk, so borrowers with poor credit are not served. Borrowers must also put 20% down. Second mortgages are available for 15%, but not through the bond system. The mortgage bank acts as agent for nonbank investors in placing second mortgages at rates well above the first mortgage rate.

A second weakness is that partial prepayments on fixed-rate mortgages are not practical. Many borrowers in the United States pay a little more each month to pay their loans off sooner, but this doesn't work in Denmark. It would require a small bond purchase every month, which costs about $100 regardless of the amount of the purchase. On ARMs, borrowers can prepay at a small cost, but only when the rate is adjusted.

Impact of the Financial Crisis: The Danish system fared much better during the worldwide financial crisis that erupted in 2007 than the U.S. system. A major reason was that the Danish system was much less caught up in the housing bubble during the years preceding the crisis than the U.S. system. There were no toxic ARMs in Denmark to entice gullible borrowers to erode their equity in order get a temporary reduction in payment. There was no Danish equivalent of subprime loans to attract tenants into ownership who were not qualified to be owners. Denmark did not have alternative documentation rules that allowed borrowers to claim higher incomes than they actually had. And zero-down loans, which resulted in homebuyers having negative equity in their homes the day they moved in, were unknown in Denmark.

One of the reasons the liberalization of lending terms was less pronounced in Denmark than in the United States is that Denmark did not have mixed private-public institutions attempting to increase the homeownership rate among the disadvantaged by liberalizing mortgage terms. *See* **Secondary Mortgage Markets/*Fannie Mae and Freddie Mac*/Role in the Housing Bubble**.

While house prices declined in Denmark during the crisis, negative equity did not become a problem because the great majority of borrowers had substantial equity in their homes when the crisis struck. This was a major reason why the rise in defaults in Denmark was small and manageable.

The Danish financial system was impacted by the worldwide loss of confidence in financial institutions and the associated liquidity squeeze. In 2008 the Danish government guaranteed the unsecured creditors of all banks including the mortgage banks. However, the guarantee did not include mortgage bonds, because it was not considered necessary.

The Danish mortgage bond market continued to function normally during the crisis, which meant that new loans could continue to be written as before. This is in marked contrast to the U.S. experience, where markets in mortgage-backed securities that were not guaranteed by a U.S. government entity (Fannie Mae, Freddie Mac, or GNMA) ceased functioning.

Deadbeat *A borrower who doesn't pay.*

Debtaholic *A borrower who has not been able to handle debt without getting in over his head.*

For some, "debtaholicism" is an incurable disease, like alcoholism, where complete abstinence is the only satisfactory way to cope. Others can learn to use credit responsibly, but lenders will put the burden of proof on them to demonstrate it.

To do that, the debtaholic must establish new relationships with credit grantors who are prepared to deal with people who have bad credit histories. They are a tough lot: they make borrowers pay a high rate, keep them on a short leash, and when they fall behind in their payments, badger them in every legal way and sometimes beyond. This is the only way for them to make money lending to a population that includes a sizable number of incurables.

While these firms catch a lot of flak from community organizations that object to the way they treat borrowers, the firms perform an important public service: they give debtaholics a second chance when no one else will. If debtaholics pay on time every month, their credit scores will gradually rise. If they stick to it, they make the transition from deadbeat to solid citizen.

Debt Consolidation *Rolling short-term debt into a home mortgage loan, either at the time of home purchase or later.*

The Case for Consolidation: Borrowers consolidate in order to reduce their finance costs. Usually, the interest rate on the mortgage is below that on short-term debt, and mortgage interest is also tax deductible. Borrowers also like the convenience of making fewer payments.

The Case Against Consolidation: When borrowers consolidate, they convert unsecured debt into secured debt. That is the major reason the mortgage interest rate is usually lower. Borrowers who encounter financial distress and fail to pay their unsecured debts lose their good credit, but they don't lose their home. By increasing the size of the claim against their home, they increase the risk of losing it.

If consolidation causes the mortgage amount to exceed the property value, borrowers may also lose their mobility. Sale of the property requires that all mortgages be repaid, which means that the seller must come up with enough cash to cover the deficiency. Borrowers in this situation may also have to pass on opportunities for profitable refinance, since it is impossible to refinance when debt exceeds value.

Consolidation that reduces the borrowers' total monthly payments while eliminating their short-term debt may encourage them to build up that debt all over again. This could result in so much debt that they never get out from under.

Consolidating Intelligently: To consolidate intelligently, borrowers need to compare their options. Three debt consolidation calculators on my Web site can help you do this. These calculators are designed for three categories of borrowers with nonmortgage debt:

- **Those About to Purchase a House.** Their options are to either consolidate in the new purchase mortgage or not.

- **Those with an Existing First Mortgage.** Their options are to consolidate by refinancing the first mortgage to include the nonmortgage debt, or by taking out a new second, or neither.

- **Those with Existing First and Second Mortgages.** Their options are to (a) consolidate existing nonmortgage debt in a new (cash-out refinance) first mortgage, leaving the second mortgage as it is; (b) consolidate the existing second mortgage in a new (cash-out refinance) first mortgage, leaving nonmortgage debt as it is; (c) consolidate both nonmortgage debt and the second mortgage in a new (cash-out refinance) first mortgage; (d) consolidate existing nonmortgage debt in a new (cash-out refinance) second mortgage, leaving the first mortgage as it is; or (e) do nothing.

The calculators provide two types of information about each option. One is the total monthly payment, which consists of mortgage payments, mortgage insurance premiums if any, and nonmortgage debt payments if any. Borrowers on tight budgets must be concerned with the monthly payment, but it should not be the major determinant of their choice. It fails to reflect differences in tax savings or debt reduction as between the options.

The second type of information the calculator provides about all the options is their **Time Horizon Cost** over a period specified by the user. If the user's time horizon is, say, five years, the total cost of each option is the sum of the upfront refinancing costs and monthly payments over five years, including lost interest, less the tax savings and reduction in total debt over that period.

Life After Consolidation: Borrowers who consolidate should use any monthly savings to accelerate the pay-down of principal on their mortgage(s). Even better is to shorten the term on the new mortgage(s) so that the new payment is close to the old payment.

Unfortunately, many borrowers interpret a payment-reduction consolidation as a license to take on more nonmortgage debt. A few years later, they look to consolidate again. If their house has appreciated enough, they may be able to, but sooner or later they run out of equity. Then they write me letters like this one:

We kept adding to our second mortgage to pay off credit card debt . . . the rate is now up to 13.75% . . . we don't have enough equity to break even if we sell . . . we feel trapped.

They trapped themselves. Don't let it happen to you.

Debt Elimination *A variety of scams that promise borrowers that for a modest investment, the scamster will get their debt reduced or eliminated.*

Deed in Lieu of Foreclosure *Deeding the property over to the lender as an alternative to having the lender foreclose on the property.*

See **Payment Problems/*Position of the Lender*/Permanent Problem.**

Default *Failure of the borrower to honor the terms of the loan agreement.*

Lenders usually view borrowers delinquent 90 days or more as in default. *See* **Payment Problems.**

Deferred Interest

Same as **Negative Amortization.**

Delinquency *A mortgage payment that is more than 30 days late.*

Demand Clause *A clause in the note that allows the lender to demand repayment of the balance in full.*

A demand clause is even better (for the lender) than an acceleration clause. An acceleration clause allows the lender to call the loan if the borrower violates some contractual provision, such as a requirement that the loan must be repaid upon sale of the property. A demand clause allows the lender to demand repayment for *any reason.* For example, the lender can force you to accept a higher rate by threatening that if you don't agree, the loan will be called.

The lender asking for a demand clause will no doubt disavow any intention of behaving in such a manner. But you don't put your head on a chopping block just because the executioner promises not to cut it off.

The Truth in Lending Disclosure has a statement that reads "This loan has a demand feature," which is checked yes or no. Some lenders will check yes even though the note has an acceleration rather than a demand feature (*see* **Acceleration**). Nonetheless, if it is checked yes, you want to examine the relevant sections of the note.

Desecuritization

Desecuritization *Reversing the securitization process by converting a security back into individual loans.*

Securitization converts large numbers of individual loans into security issues. Desecuritization converts the securities back into individual loans. The objective of both is the same: to enhance value. The first works during normal periods; the second makes sense during a crisis period, though to my knowledge, it has never been done.

Securitization enhances value during normal periods because a single type of loan can be converted into a variety of securities with different characteristics fashioned to meet the diverse needs of investors. For example, a pool of 30-year fixed-rate mortgages can be transformed into a security issue subdivided into subissues that vary in their duration (how long before the investor gets her money back), their exposure to risk of default as indicated by credit quality ratings, and their sensitivity to changes in market interest rates.

Where investor demand for 30-year fixed-rate mortgages is limited, the diverse securities fashioned from a pool of such mortgages could appeal to a wide range of investors. With securitization, the whole is worth more than the sum of its parts.

The breakdown of financial markets during the financial crisis, associated with high default rates on loans in pools supporting securities, reversed the equation. The total value of any mortgage security issue on which the AAA-rated pieces had been downgraded fell well below the sum of the values of the individual loans, assuming those loans could somehow be disentangled from the security.

For example, assume 20% of a portfolio of 1,000 mortgage loans defaults and each default costs 50% of the balance. Because the 200 loans that default do not affect the value of the 800 that don't, the decline in the total value of the portfolio, measured as the sum of the individual mortgage values, is only 10%. But if the loans are in a security issue, every piece of that security may be contaminated by the defaults. The overall decline in value could be 30% or even 60%; we have no way of knowing because markets largely shut down.

Desecuritization could unlock that value, but it requires a way for one investor to acquire control of 100% of a security issue. The investor who owns it all can dispose of the security and own the individual loans. To make this possible, the government would have to enact legislation that would make it possible to override the maze of private contracts involved in a securitization. This never became part of the government's program for dealing with the financial crisis.

Direct Lender *A term that small lenders sometimes use to distinguish them-selves from mortgage brokers.*

Disaster Myopia *A hypothesis designed to explain why decision makers in com-petitive industries often behave as if low-probability hazards that would cause major loss have zero probability of occurrence.*

See **Subprime Market/*Rise and Decline*/Disaster Myopia**.

Discount Mortgage Broker *A mortgage broker who is compensated entirely by the lender rather than by the borrower.*

The implication, that the broker's services are a bargain, is entirely untrue. If anything, the opposite is true: borrowers tend to pay more for broker's services when brokers are paid by lenders because under those conditions borrowers are either unaware of the cost, or unconcerned, or both. They pay for the broker's services in the interest rate, which hits them down the road rather than at the closing table.

In general, borrower resistance to broker fees is much weaker when the fees appear to be paid by the lender. And increasingly, brokers seek their compensation entirely in this way. The so-called discount brokers have merely formalized the process.

There is nothing wrong with a borrower electing to pay for the bro-ker's services with a higher rate rather than cash, provided that this is a deliberate selection. For a borrower with a short time horizon who won't be paying the high rate very long, paying with a higher rate makes sense. On the other hand, a borrower who expects to have the mortgage a long time and has the cash will do better using it to pay the broker and to pay points. Discount brokers don't offer this option.

See **Yield-Spread Premium**.

Discount Points

Same as **Points**.

Discretionary ARM *An ARM on which the lender has the right to change the interest rate at any time, for any reason, by any amount, subject only to a requirement that the borrower be notified in advance.*

The discretionary ARM is at the opposite pole from **Indexed ARMs** on which rate adjustments are completely rule based.

Discretionary ARMs were long the standard mortgage in the United Kingdom and in other English-speaking countries that imported it from the United Kingdom, such as India and South Africa. They never caught on in the United States, where the indexed ARM prevails.

Discriminatory Mortgage Pricing *The practice of charging higher mortgage prices to African Americans and Hispanics than to whites who are otherwise identical.*

Obviously discrimination is also possible based on age, sex, or whatever, but the only credible evidence for it applies to race. I have looked at the studies that find that racial minorities generally pay more, and they ring true. Why does it happen?

Mortgage Price Determination: In the great majority of mortgage transactions, mortgages prices are determined in a two-stage process. Stage 1 is the distribution of posted prices to loan officers and mortgage brokers dealing with borrowers. Stage 2 is the determination of final prices paid by the borrower.

Mortgage prices are delivered by fax or (increasingly) over the Internet in the form of rate sheets. These sheets are voluminous both because each loan program must be priced separately and because pricing has become so complex. Prices vary with the borrower's credit, purpose of loan, type of property, type of documentation, state location of property, and other factors. *See* **Rate Sheets**.

Posted Prices Are Free of Discrimination: Posted prices do not vary with race, which would be blatantly illegal. Neither do prices vary with proxies for race, such as property location. Minorities are much more heavily concentrated in center cities than in suburban areas, for example, so mortgage pricing based on this distinction could be discriminatory. However, lenders do not make such distinctions in their pricing. Most lenders in their pricing use only states. Some divide large states such as California into regions, but the regions don't correspond to any racial divisions.

I have looked at the price sheets of hundreds of lenders, both wholesale and retail. I have never seen one that had even a whiff of discriminatory treatment of minorities. Lenders may commit many sins, but discrimination against minorities is not one of them.

The unequal treatment of minorities occurs at the second stage, where posted prices are converted into final prices to the borrower.

Final Prices Have a Discretionary Component: In the wholesale market, lenders deliver wholesale prices to brokers, who add a markup to derive the retail prices offered to borrowers. If the posted price is 6% and zero points, for example, a broker might offer the loan at 6% and 1.5 points, the 1.5 points being the markup.

Within very wide limits, brokers have complete discretion over the final price, subject only to their ability to induce borrowers to pay it. They are independent contractors who price as they please. Some wholesale lenders place limits on markups, but these limits are absurdly high. Since there are many wholesale lenders, and brokers move easily from one to another, any one lender attempting to enforce more rigorous constraints on markups would quickly lose brokers.

In the retail market, lenders deliver retail prices to their loan officer employees (LOs). The lender's markup, including the LO's commission, is already included in these prices. However, LOs have limited discretion to charge more than the posted prices "in order to take advantage of market opportunities" and to charge less "in order to meet competition." Such price deviations are termed "overages" and "underages," respectively. But overages exceed underages by a wide margin. *See* **Overage**.

Discrimination Arises from Discretionary Pricing: The great majority of brokers and LOs are "equal opportunity overchargers." They charge what the market will bear, without regard to race or color. The perception of many of them is that minorities are easier to take advantage of than whites. To the extent that this is true, a market in which loan providers at the point of sale charge as much as they can get away with affects minorities disproportionately. The result is the same as if there were deliberate discrimination.

The Market Segmentation Theory: A related explanation for why minorities pay more for their mortgages than whites is that minorities receive more of their loans than whites from high-price lenders. It would be illegal for high-price lenders to target minorities, but they may well do more high-powered soliciting than other lenders; and if minorities are more vulnerable to solicitations, they will end up dealing with those lenders in disproportionate numbers. This is why I constantly advise borrowers of every color not to respond to solicitations.

The Community-Group Approach to Unequal Treatment of Minorities: Community groups don't accept my contention that discrimination arises from discretionary pricing by loan officers and mortgage brokers at the point of sale, because it takes lenders off the hook. Brokers and loan officers are a much less attractive target for them than lenders. A study by the Center for Responsible Lending (CRL) concedes that posted prices are free of bias, but claims that lenders influence the final prices in indirect ways that can be discriminatory. In my opinion, none of their arguments withstand close scrutiny (see "Why Do Minorities Pay More for Mortgages" on my Web site).

Community groups also don't like the idea that loan officers and brokers are out to skin everyone but are more successful with minorities. This conclusion can be interpreted to mean that the victims are partially responsible for their own mistreatment.

In my view, this interpretation is sometimes unavoidable. Borrowers are victimized primarily because they are ill informed; and given that the information that would protect them is widely available, they bear some responsibility for not finding and using it.

When my article on this topic appeared in the press, I received numerous letters complaining about Hispanic loan officers and brokers who took advantage of the Hispanic borrowers who sought them out. I have not verified these reports, but it would hardly be surprising if it were true. I would expect Hispanic loan providers would be equal opportunity overchargers, just like their white compatriots, except that they find easier pickings in the Hispanic community.

Documentation Requirements *A lender's requirements regarding how information about income, assets, and employment must be provided by the applicant and how it will be used by the lender.*

Documentation Requirements

The standard approach is called "full documentation." Both income and assets are disclosed and verified, and income is used in determining the applicant's ability to repay the mortgage. Formal verification requires the borrower's employer to verify employment and the borrower's bank to verify deposits.

In some cases, in order to save time, lenders will accept copies of the borrower's original bank statements, W-2s, and paycheck stubs. This is called **Alternative Documentation.**

During a long period ending in 2007, when loss rates on defaulted mortgages were very low, other types of documentation evolved in the market. These made it possible for consumers to qualify who were unable to meet standard requirements.

Stated Income–Verified Assets: Income is disclosed, the source of the income is verified, but the amount is not verified. Assets are verified and must meet an adequacy standard such as six months of stated income and two months of expected monthly housing expense.

Stated Income–Stated Assets: Both income and assets are disclosed but not verified. However, the source of the borrower's income is verified.

No Ratio: Income is disclosed and verified but not used in qualifying the borrower. The standard rule regarding housing expenses—that the borrower's housing expense cannot exceed some specified percentage of income—is ignored. Assets are disclosed and verified.

No Income: Income is not disclosed, but assets are disclosed and verified and must meet an adequacy standard.

Stated Assets or No Asset Verification: Assets are disclosed but not verified; income is disclosed, verified, and used to qualify the applicant.

No Asset: Assets are not disclosed, but income is disclosed, verified, and used to qualify the applicant.

No Income–No Assets: Neither income nor assets are disclosed.

While these categories became fairly well established in the market, there were numerous differences between individual lenders in the details. For example, under a stated income program some lenders did and some lenders did not require that applicants sign a form authorizing the lender to request the applicant's tax returns from the IRS in the event the borrower defaulted. Similarly, lenders differed in the amount of assets they required.

Documentation Requirements

The proliferation of different documentation programs reflected a realization by lenders that many consumers with the potential for homeownership were shut out of the market by excessively rigid documentation requirements. It also dawned on lenders that documentation could be viewed as a risk factor that could be priced or offset by other risk factors.

Full documentation is the least risky to the lender, no income–no asset is the most risky, and the others are in between. If the documentation is riskier, lenders will charge more, require risk offsets, or both. The most important risk offsets are large down payments and high credit scores.

The change in attitudes toward documentation requirements expanded the market. Here are examples of borrowers who would not have qualified under full documentation requirements:

- Jones is a personal trainer with no fixed place of business who makes good money but can't document it. He can document his mutual funds, and his CPA can verify his self-employed status, so Jones qualifies under a stated income–verified assets plan.

- Smith is in the same business and uses the same CPA as Jones, but an uncle is gifting him with the cash he needs. Since Smith cannot document assets, he pays a little more under a stated income–stated asset program.

- King can document income and assets but wants to allocate 58% of her income to housing expenses, which far exceeds conventional guidelines. King qualifies under a no ratio loan.

- Queen is leaving her job to move to a new city where she has no job and will buy a house when she gets there with money from the sale of her existing house. She has no income and cannot document assets because her old house won't be sold until after closing on the new one. Nevertheless, she qualifies under a no income–no asset program. If she has a contract of sale on the old house before closing on the new one, she will be able to document assets and can qualify under a no income program.

After the financial crisis erupted in 2007, these alternative forms of documentation largely disappeared, and the market returned to full documentation. In 2009, neither Jones, nor Smith, nor King, nor Queen would qualify for a loan.

Doubling Down on Mortgage Payments *A rapid mortgage payoff scheme where the borrower adds an extra payment each month equal to the principal payment that month.*

Purportedly, this cuts the life of the mortgage in half. When I tested this using an extra-payment spreadsheet from my Web site, I assumed a 15-year loan at 6% and made extra principal payments equal to the principal portion of the monthly payment.

I quickly realized that there are two ways this can be done. One way is to make extra payments equal to the *original schedule of principal payments*. When I did it this way, the loan paid off in 100 months, not 90.

However, if I based the extra payments on an *actual schedule that reflects the impact of prior extra payments*, payoff occurred in 91 months—just a tad past the halfway mark. While the required amount has to be recalculated every month, this is easy to do if you download the first of my extra-payment spreadsheets and update it every month.

The merit in this approach is that you don't require anyone's permission, and having a concrete goal such as cutting the life of the loan in half is one way to discipline yourself to save.

The downside of the scheme is that you must increase your savings every month over the previous month. For example, on my $100,000 loan at 6% for 15 years, the required savings would rise from $344 in month 1 to $833 in month 90. This might work well for some, but for many if not most borrowers, it would not.

Borrowers who want to cut the life of their mortgage in half can do it in many ways. For example, the four savings plans shown below would all pay off my $100,000 15-year 6% mortgage in 90 months. They are thus alternatives to the double amortization plan with its rising extra payment.

- A flat additional monthly payment of $539 starting in month 1.
- A flat additional quarterly payment of $1,624 starting in month 3.
- A flat additional annual payment of $7,021starting in month 12.
- A combination of flat additional payments of $300 a month starting in month 1 and $3,000 a year starting in month 6.

The four plans were derived from my calculators 2a and 2c, which you can use to develop your own plan. It should meet your own goals, which might be more or less ambitious than shortening the mortgage term by half. And it should be based on a realistic appraisal of the amount and timing of the savings you will be able to generate.

Down Payment *The difference between the value of the property and the loan amount, expressed in dollars or as a percentage of value.*

For example, if the house is valued at $100,000 and the loan is for $80,000, the down payment is $20,000, or 20%.

Down Payment and LTV: In percent, the down payment is 1 minus the LTV—the ratio of loan to value. In the example, the LTV is 80%, and 1 – LTV is 20%. Lender requirements are always expressed in terms of a maximum LTV rather than a minimum down payment because maximum LTV does not generate questions about what a down payment is.

Suppose the house in the example is purchased for $100,000 and the borrower has $20,000 for the down payment, but not the $3,000 needed for settlement costs. The settlement costs are therefore added to the loan amount, raising it to $83,000. The LTV is now 83%, and the borrower will be obliged to pay for mortgage insurance.

The borrower may say, "Hold on. I'm putting down the same $20,000 as before." However, the mortgage insurance requirement is set as a maximum LTV of 80% rather than a minimum down payment of 20%, so the argument is over before it begins. In reality, the down payment is $17,000, or 17%.

Sale Price Versus Appraised Value: Home purchasers who pay less for a home than its appraised value frequently question whether they can use the difference as their down payment. They cannot. The rule is that the property value used in determining the down payment and the LTV is the sale price or appraised value, *whichever is lower.* The only exception to this is when the seller provides a gift of equity to the buyer, as discussed below.

Gift of Equity: Gifts of equity arise when a house is sold for less than its market value, almost always to a family member. In this case, the lender recognizes that the house is being priced below market and will accept the appraisal as the value. Most lenders in such cases require two appraisals, and they take the lower of the two.

Gifts of equity should be structured to avoid gift tax liability, which arises on gifts from a single donor in excess of the maximum per recipient per year, which in 2009 was $13,000. The maximum gift in 2009 free of tax liability was $13,000 × D × R, where D is the number of donors and R the number of recipients. For example, if the donors are a couple gifting a family of four, they can provide a total gift of $104,000 without tax consequences. Donors who want to gift more than the amount calculated from the formula should talk to a tax advisor.

Cash Gifts: Lenders will accept cash gifts for some part of the down payment, but usually not for all of it. While the rules vary for different programs, it is common to require that the borrower contribute 3% of the down payment.

Lenders require a donor to sign a gift statement affirming that the funds provided are a gift rather than a loan. The lender wants assurance that the transfer of funds imposes no repayment obligation that could put the mortgage loan at risk. Sometimes, however, borrowers induce friends or family members who do not want to make gifts to lend in the guise of a gift.

For example, a house purchaser needs the equity in her current house to make the down payment on a new one, but she must close on the new one before the old one is under contract. Because there is ample equity in the old house, the buyer asks a friend or family member to lend the money needed for the down payment, to be repaid when the old house is sold.

This is a bad idea. Not only is it a fraud against the lender; it also involves risk to the donor. Contingencies that could result in not being repaid include a sharp drop in the value of the old house before it is sold or the sudden death of the home purchaser.

The homebuyer in this situation should be advised to take out a home equity loan on the old house, which can be repaid when it is sold. A home equity lender has a lien on the house and has diversified its risk over many loans. The lender pretending to be a donor has neither.

Land as Down Payment: Many people acquire land in order to build on it later, and the land serves as part or all of the down payment. If the land has been held for some time, the lender will appraise the completed house with the lot, and the difference between the appraisal and the cost of construction is viewed as the down payment.

For example, if the builder charges $160,000 for the house and the appraisal comes in at $200,000, the land is assumed to be worth $40,000. A loan of $160,000 in this case would have a down payment of 20%, or an LTV of 80%.

If the land was purchased recently, however, the lender will not value it for more than the purchase price. If the price was only $30,000 in the above example, the lender will value it at $30,000, and the down payment will only be 15.8%, or an LTV of 84.2%.

Home Seller Contributions: Home sellers often gift buyers, raising the price by enough to cover the gift. The purpose is to improve the buyer's ability to purchase the house by reducing the required cash. The practice is legitimate, provided it is done openly and conforms to the guidelines of lenders and mortgage insurers. For it to work, the appraiser must confirm that the house is worth the higher price.

For example, Jones offers his house to Smith for $200,000, which Smith is willing to pay. But under the best financing terms available to Smith, he needs $12,000, which he doesn't have.

So Jones and Smith agree that Jones will raise the price of the house to $206,000 and Jones will gift Smith $6,000. Assuming the appraiser goes along, the amount of cash required of Smith drops from $12,000 to $6,360, making the purchase affordable (see the table below). Jones gets his price and Smith gets his house, so everyone is happy—except, perhaps, the lender, because the equity protecting the loan is smaller.

Appraisals often ratify sale prices, whether justified or not. If the house is actually only worth the original offer price of $200,000, the buyer has only $180 of real equity—the difference between the original property value and the higher loan amount—rather than $6,180. Less equity means greater loss for the lender if the loan goes into default.

For this reason, lenders and mortgage insurers limit the size of seller contributions. The smaller the down payment requirement, the more critical the issue becomes. On conventional loans (loans not insured by the federal government), it is common to restrict seller contributions to 3% of sale price with 5% down and to 6% with 10% or more down.

Down Payment

How a Seller Contribution Reduces the Buyer's Required Cash		
	Before	**After**
Sale price	$200,000	$206,000
Appraised value		$206,000
Loan amount	$194,000	$199,820
Down payment (3%)	$6,000	$6,180
Total cash required	$12,000	$6,360
Down payment (3%)	$6,000	$6,180
Settlement costs (3%)	$6,000	$6,180
Gift from seller	0	$6,000
Buyer's stated equity	$6,000	$6,180
Buyer's real equity	$6–$12,000	$180–$6,180

Contributions Under FHA: On FHA loans, individual sellers can contribute up to 6% of the price to the buyer's settlement costs, but nothing to the down payment. However, until 2008, FHA allowed approved nonprofit corporations to offer down payment assistance using funds provided by sellers. The combination of direct seller contributions to settlement costs on FHAs and indirect contributions through down payment assistance programs could add up to 9–10% of the sale price. In 2008, however, Congress terminated down payment assistance programs funded by home sellers, because they had resulted in significant losses to FHA.

Investing in a Larger Down Payment: A larger down payment is an investment that yields a return that consists in part of the interest rate on the money you aren't borrowing. If you put an additional $10,000 down, for example, you are borrowing $10,000 less, and you save the interest that you would have paid on it. But there may be other savings as well that make the return higher than the interest rate on the loan.

First, most borrowers pay points or other loan fees expressed as a percentage of the loan amount. If you borrow $10,000 less, you save not only the interest but the upfront fees on the $10,000. Fees of fixed-dollar amounts don't affect the return because they aren't reduced when the loan amount is reduced.

Down Payment

A second possibility is that the larger down payment reduces or eliminates mortgage insurance, which must be purchased when the down payment is less than 20% of property value. In such event, the return on the larger down payment includes not only the savings in interest and points but also the savings in mortgage insurance that is eliminated by the larger down payment.

For this to happen, the larger down payment must reduce the loan past an LTV **Pricing Notch Point (PNP)**. For example, reducing the LTV from 93 to 90% will reduce the mortgage insurance premium because 90% is a PNP, but a reduction from 93% to 91% will not change the premium.

Still a third possibility is that the larger down payment reduces the interest rate by bringing the loan amount past a loan amount PNP. On conventional loans, in 2009, there were two loan amount PNPs, one for $417,000 applicable everywhere and a second larger one in high-cost counties. See **Pricing Notch Point (PNP)/Loan Amount and LTV PNPs**.

The rate of return on increases in down payment that bring the loan amount past a PNP was higher after the financial crisis than before because of the larger perceived risk on smaller down payments. For example, 85% loans that are otherwise prime carried a mortgage insurance premium of 0.7% in 2009 compared with 0.56% in 2005. As a result, the rate of return on the down payment increase required to make it an 80% loan rose from 9.84% to 11.55%.

Readers can make such calculations using calculator 12a, "Rate of Return on Larger Down Payment," on my Web site. The calculator allows you to adjust the mortgage insurance premium, the interest rate, or both in response to an increase in down payment.

No-Down-Payment Loans: The availability of no-down-payment loans (NDPs) is a mixed blessing. Some families become successful homeowners with the help of NDPs. Others, who shouldn't be homeowners, are enticed to try and fail.

NDPs have high default rates. This has been a finding of every study of mortgage defaults that I have ever seen. One reason is that homeowners who borrow the full value of their property have less to protect should economic adversity strike. If they lose their job or if property values decline temporarily, they lose less from a default than borrowers with equity.

A second reason is that borrowers unable to accumulate a down payment have not demonstrated budgetary discipline and the ability to plan ahead. People able to save money every month before they buy a home are much more likely to meet their monthly mortgage obligations afterward.

Why do lenders make NDPs? When this was written in 2009, they weren't, except on the occasional VA or USDA loan. But before the financial crisis, when property values were rising, NDPs were available on conventional loans at a price; and during the bubble period that immediately preceded the crisis, they became increasingly important.

Rising values create equity in houses that were initially mortgaged to the hilt. In recent years, furthermore, lenders have become more confident in their ability to assess the willingness and capacity of borrowers to repay their mortgages. Using credit scoring and other tools, they judged that it was safe to give less weight to an applicant's ability to accumulate a down payment. Lenders tried to protect themselves, furthermore, by charging a higher rate on NDPs. The rate included a "risk premium" to cover the losses lenders expected from higher delinquencies and defaults.

The premiums, however, turned out to cover only a small fraction of the losses incurred in NDPs during the crisis period. In the face of declining home values, no rate premium would be enough.

Securities as Down Payment: Some investment banks offer home loan plans where they accept the deposit of securities in place of a down payment. If you purchase a house for $200,000, for example, the bank will lend you the entire $200,000, provided you deposit securities worth $40,000 with them. For the bank, the securities provide essentially the same protection against default as a down payment, while discouraging the customer from shifting the account to another bank.

These plans delay the accumulation of equity in the house indefinitely. The customer begins with no equity, and if the payment only covers the interest for the first 10 years, which is a common feature, the only equity buildup is from appreciation in the value of the property. The theory behind this is that the consumer's overall wealth will grow more rapidly if the maximum amount is invested in securities.

In the example, the consumer is in effect borrowing an additional $40,000 to invest in securities. Whether this turns out to be a good idea or a bad idea depends on the yield earned on the securities relative to the mortgage rate. It doesn't make sense to borrow $40,000 at 7% to invest in government bonds yielding 5.5%. It may make sense for consumers investing in common stock, which might yield 10% or more over a long period.

"Dual Apper" *A borrower who submits applications through two loan providers, usually mortgage brokers, without their knowledge.*

Home purchasers sometimes submit more than one loan application as a way of protecting themselves against the hazards inherent in committing to one loan provider before the price is locked. Double apping strengthens their bargaining position in negotiating the lock price. I don't recommend it, however.

Mortgage brokers despise dual appers because they force the broker to do a lot of work and then bid for the loan or lose it. Being midway through the process with a resentful broker is not a happy prospect. If you run into a major roadblock, a resentful broker may not be willing to go the extra mile to remove it.

There is an alternative to double apping that protects you better, is fair to the broker, and avoids wasted effort. Demand to know the price before the work begins. While the price of the mortgage cannot be set in advance, the price of the broker's services can.

Upfront Mortgage Brokers (UMBs) quote a fee for their services up front. Separating the price of the broker's services from the price of the mortgage eliminates gamesmanship by the broker and the need for double apping. *See* **Upfront Mortgage Broker.**

Dual Index Mortgage *A mortgage on which the interest rate is adjustable based on an interest rate index, and the monthly payment adjusts based on a wage and salary index.*

Dual index mortgages are not written in the United States, but they are common in Mexico.

Due-on-Sale Clause *A provision of a loan contract stipulating that if the property is sold, the loan balance must be repaid.*

A mortgage containing a due-on-sale clause is not assumable. This prevents a home seller from transferring responsibility for an existing loan to the buyer when the interest rate on the old loan is below the current market.

See **Assumable Mortgage.**

Effective Rate *The interest rate adjusted for intrayear compounding.*

Because interest on a mortgage is calculated monthly, a 6% mortgage actually has a rate of 0.5% per month. Assuming monthly payments are continually reinvested at 0.5%, the investor earns an annual return of 6.17%. This is termed the "effective rate," while 6% is termed the "nominal" rate. Similarly, a 6% bond on which interest is paid quarterly has an effective rate of 6.14%.

80/10/10, 80/15/5, and 80/20/0 Loan Plans *Combination first mortgages for 80% of the sale price or value, second mortgages for 10, 15, and 20%, and down payments of 10, 5, and 0%.*

See **Second Mortgage/*Using a Second to Avoid Mortgage Insurance*.**

Equity *In connection with a home, the value of the home less the balance of out-standing mortgage loans on the home.*

Equity Grabbing *A type of predatory lending where the lender intends for the borrower to default so the lender can grab the borrower's equity.*

See **Predatory Lending/*Predatory Practices*/Equity Grabbing.**

Escrow *An agreement that specified monies or property be segregated pending the completion of some action.*

Escrow Abuse *Not crediting the borrower's mortgage payment because the escrow payment is deemed short.*

Sometimes, lenders notify borrowers of an increase in escrow payment, and for a variety of possible reasons, the borrower makes the old payment.

Most borrowers would assume that the servicer would credit the interest and principal payment as usual, deposit the escrow funds into the escrow account, even though it was short, and send another message to the borrower to remedy the shortage or face some kind of penalty. In fact, what often happens is that the entire mortgage payment is placed in an "unapplied" or "suspense" account where it sits in limbo until the next payment is made. The borrower is charged a late fee, and a 30-day delinquency notice is sent to the credit bureaus.

If the servicer does not send out monthly statements, which many do not, the borrower may have no idea about what is going on. The next month's regular mortgage payment will also be deposited into the suspense account, which now has enough to cover one full payment, including the increased amount demanded for escrow. But the borrower incurs a second late charge and a second 30-day delinquency report.

At this point the account may be sent to the collections department, where a pre-foreclosure notice is generated and a demand letter is sent to the borrower, who now suddenly finds himself liable for a series of costs manufactured for the occasion. These may include fees to cover a broker's price opinion, property inspection fees, legal fees, statutory foreclosure costs, and a new high-cost hazard insurance policy that covers the lender only.

To cure the default, the borrower must pay the full amount necessary to bring the account current. If this is not possible, the result will be foreclosure.

I don't know how widespread this practice is, but I know it is not uncommon. *Bottom line:* If you receive a notice of an escrow payment increase, pay it, even if you know it is wrong. Then, send a qualified written request to the servicer disputing the charge, following the procedures outlined in **Servicing/*Recourse***.

Escrow Account *In a home mortgage transaction, a deposit account maintained by the lender and funded by the borrower, from which the lender makes tax and insurance payments for the borrower as they come due.*

Lenders generally require escrow accounts. The rationale is that it prevents a weakening in the protection provided to the lender by the property. If the taxes are not paid, the tax authority could place a lien on the property that would have a higher priority than the lender's lien. Similarly, if the house burns down or is flooded, the lender's protection goes with it if the insurance premiums have not been paid.

Escrow Account

Size of the Account: To assure themselves that there will always be enough money in the account, lenders ask for more than they actually need as a "cushion." In years past, many of them maintained unreasonably large cushions. To deal with that, the Department of Housing and Urban Development (HUD) issued a ruling that placed a ceiling on the size of escrow accounts, which in turn limited the amount the lender could ask the borrower to deposit at closing.

The rule is that the deposit cannot exceed the amount needed to prevent the balance from falling below an amount equal to two months' worth of tax and insurance payments at its lowest point during the year. While HUD does not do a lot of enforcing, my impression is that all but a handful of lenders follow the HUD rules. If you want to check the calculation, I explain how to do it on my Web site; see "How Do I Figure Escrows?"

Reasons for Avoiding Escrows: The least important reason borrowers may want to avoid escrow is to capture the interest earnings on the account for themselves. The amounts involved are small. I explain how to measure the interest earnings on my Web site in "Should I Escrow?"

The more important reason is to establish control over the payments. Lenders require escrow to assure that the payments will be made, and borrowers may want to avoid escrow for the same reason. Lenders occasionally screw up, and when this happens, it can be a nightmare for the borrower. *See* **Servicing/Recourse**.

Ways to Avoid Escrow: Most lenders will waive escrow requirements if the borrower makes a down payment of 20% or more. The logic of this waiver is that if the borrower has that much equity in the house, it is safe for the lender to rely upon the borrower's self-interest to pay the taxes and insurance premiums.

So if you intend to put down 20% or more and you don't want to escrow, let the loan officer know up front that you will not be escrowing.

If you intend to put down less than 20%, it becomes more complicated. In most states, lenders are willing to waive escrows for a fee—usually 1/4 to 3/8 of a point. However, in a few states, lenders are barred from charging a waiver fee, which means that they may be less willing to waive escrows.

If you are already escrowing, getting rid of it is not easy. You must convince the lender that it is in the lender's interest to eliminate the requirement in your case.

If the lender is a depository institution servicing its own mortgages, your best shot is to appeal as a customer of the firm. If it isn't too costly, depositories usually want to satisfy their customers or potential customers. Increasingly, however, loans are being serviced not by lenders but by servicing agents working for lenders.

Servicing agents make most of their money from servicing fees paid by lenders and from the interest earnings on escrow accounts. When a loan they are servicing is refinanced, however, the income on this loan ceases unless the agent is the one making the new loan. If the servicing agent understands that if you cannot terminate your escrow account, you intend to refinance your mortgage with another lender, you will get the agent's attention. After all, it is better to lose only the escrow interest than to lose both the escrow interest and the servicing fee.

Fallout *Loan applications that are withdrawn by borrowers, because they have found a better deal or for other reasons.*

Fannie Mae *One of two federal agencies that purchase home loans from lenders. The other is Freddie Mac.*

See **Secondary Mortgage Markets/*Fannie Mae and Freddie Mac*.**

Fee Escalation *The process of increasing and finding new lender fees as a loan moves toward the closing date.*

See **Settlement Costs/*Fees Paid to Lender*/Lender Fees Expressed in Dollars**.

FHA Mortgage *A mortgage on which the lender is insured against loss by the Federal Housing Administration, with the borrower paying the mortgage insurance premiums.*

What FHA Does: By insuring lenders against loss in the event that borrowers default on their loans, FHA encourages lenders to make loans that they might otherwise view as too risky.

FHA Mortgage

FHA began operations in the depths of the depression of the 1930s when lenders had stopped making new loans altogether because a sizable proportion of existing loans were in default. As the country worked its way out of the depression, the FHA settled into the principal role it has today: helping a segment of the low-and-moderate-income population become homeowners who otherwise might not make it because they have shaky credit or can't come up with the cash needed for the down payment.

Some FHA programs are subsidized. For example, a special program of mortgage insurance for members of the armed forces is subsidized by the armed forces, while special programs for older declining urban areas and for displaced households are partially subsidized by FHA through insurance premiums that don't cover losses. Its standard (Section 203b) program, however, was designed from the beginning to be self-supporting out of the insurance premiums paid by borrowers.

When, during the late 1980s, rising defaults eroded the reserves that FHA maintains to pay losses under this program, the insurance premiums were raised substantially to restore the reserves to an adequate level. At the time this book was written in 2009, losses were up once again, and there was talk of raising the premiums.

Fluctuations in FHA's Market Share: The importance of FHA in the home mortgage market has changed markedly over the years. This has been due less to changes in the FHA itself than to changes in the broader market in which it operates.

In the early 1990s, FHA had about 15% of the home purchase market. In subsequent years through 2006, FHA lost business to the growing subprime market, which took many borrowers who could have gone FHA. In addition, FHA lost business to the prime conventional market, which developed and aggressively merchandised option ARMs and interest-only products, as well as reduced documentation underwriting, none of which FHA offered. In 2006, FHA's share of the purchase market had fallen to less than 4%.

Then came the financial crisis. With home prices declining and defaults rising, the subprime market largely disappeared; option ARMs declined to a trickle; and documentation requirements on prime conventional loans were substantially tightened. In addition, FHA loan limits were raised materially in 2008 and 2009. In early 2009, FHA's market share of new purchases was back to about 15%, and its share of refinances was substantially higher.

FHA Mortgage

FHA Loan Limits: The loan limits on FHA loans effective until year-end 2010, established on a county basis, were the same as those applicable to Freddie Mac and Fannie Mae. On a one-family house, they ranged from $271,050 to $729,750 in 76 higher-price counties. Loan limits on two- to four-family houses are higher. On HECMs (reverse mortgages), the maximum was raised to $625,500 through 2010. The limits by state and county can be found at https://entp.hud.gov/idapp/html/hicostlook.cfm.

Underwriting Requirements: These have always been more liberal than those on conventional loans, though they change over time. In 2009, FHA's 3.5% down payment compared favorably with 5–10% on most conventional loan programs. Zero-down loans, which were widely available in the conventional sector during the go-go years 2000–2006, had largely disappeared. The only generally available zero-down loans were VAs and USDA loans in rural counties.

On cash-out refinances, FHA required borrowers to have equity of 15%, compared with the 20% required on conforming conventional loans.

FHA borrowers in some cities, counties, or states have access to special programs that eliminate the need for a down payment by offering second mortgages at favorable terms. Usually, no payments are required on the second until the house is sold. The public agencies offering these programs have their own eligibility rules that are independent of FHA.

In 2009, FHA accepted credit scores of 620 compared with the required 680 on conforming conventional loans. FHA was also more flexible on maximum ratios of housing expense plus debt payments to income and more forgiving of past mistakes. FHA will forgive a Chapter 7 bankruptcy after only two years and a foreclosure after three years.

Mortgage Insurance Premiums: FHA borrowers pay a monthly mortgage insurance premium of 1/2% per year (0.55% on loans with less than 5% down) and an upfront premium of 1.75%, which is almost always included in the loan amount. All FHA borrowers must purchase mortgage insurance. In contrast, most conventional loans have only a monthly premium which is higher than the FHA monthly premium, but there is no upfront premium, and mortgage insurance is not required at all of borrowers who put 20% or more down. Because of the higher mortgage insurance premiums, an FHA will be more costly to a borrower when the rate, points, and other fees are the same.

The FHA Market Niche: In 2009 when this was written, conforming conventional loans required private mortgage insurance (PMI) if the down payment or homeowner equity was less than 20%, while the PMI companies would not provide insurance to any borrower with a credit score below 680. The core FHA market niche, therefore, consisted of borrowers who could not meet the 20% equity requirement (but could meet the modest FHA requirement) and who had credit scores below 680—down to 620, which was as low as FHA would go.

Some loan officers steer borrowers into FHA loans although they would do better with conventional loans. Either the loan officers specialize in FHAs and don't want to lose a sale, or they can earn a higher fee on an FHA, or both. If you can put 5% down and have a FICO score of 680 or higher, don't let anyone steer you to an FHA without considering alternatives.

FHA Loans Are Assumable: Both FHA and VA loans have the advantage that they can be assumed by a qualified buyer. If a house is to be sold with an FHA or VA mortgage carrying a rate well below the current market, the seller can enhance its marketability by allowing the buyer, who must be approved by the agency, to assume the old mortgage. Conventional loans carry due-on-sale clauses that require the loan to be repaid when the house is sold. *See* **Assumable Mortgage**.

FHA and House Quality: Homebuyers often assume that FHA's involvement as the mortgage insurer protects them against defects in the house. It doesn't. FHA has been bedeviled by this problem since it began operations in 1934.

The assumption that FHA protects the homebuyer is reasonable. FHA requires that properties be appraised and that homes meet certain "minimum property requirements." In 1999, furthermore, FHA adopted a new set of rules regarding appraisals that it trumpeted in PR releases as a Homebuyer Protection Plan. The fact is, however, that FHA does not guarantee the value or condition of a home. FHA appraisals are to protect FHA, and homebuyers should protect themselves by ordering a home inspection.

In 2000, FHA developed a form that all purchasers of existing houses taking an FHA mortgage must sign before the date of the sales contract. The form is entitled "For Your Protection: Get a Home Inspection." Immediately above the signature, it reads:

I understand the importance of getting an independent home inspection. I have thought about this before I signed a contract with the seller for a home.

FICO Score

See **Credit Score**.

Financing Points *Including points in the loan amount.*

See **Points/*Financing Points***.

First Mortgage *A mortgage that has a first-priority claim against the property in the event the borrower defaults on the loan.*

For example, a borrower defaults on a loan secured by a property worth $100,000 net of sale costs. The property has a first mortgage with a balance of $90,000 and a second mortgage with a balance of $15,000. The first mortgage lender can collect $90,000 plus any unpaid interest and foreclosure costs. The second mortgage lender can collect only what is left of the $100,000.

Fixed-Rate Mortgage (FRM) *A mortgage on which the interest rate remains unchanged throughout its life.*

Fixed Rate Versus Fixed Payment: Usually, the term "FRM" also means that the payment is fixed for the life of the loan and pays off the balance over the term. This should be (but usually isn't) called a "level-payment fully amortizing FRM" to distinguish it from other types of loans that have a fixed rate but not a fixed payment.

For example, one of the earliest types of fixed-rate mortgages was repaid with equal monthly payments of principal plus interest. If the loan was for $300,000 at 6% and the term was 300 months, then the payment in month 1 would be $1,000 of principal plus $1,500 of interest for a total $2,500. Each month the total payment would decline because interest would be calculated on a lower balance. This was the standard type of mortgage in New Zealand for many years, despite the obvious disadvantage of high payments in the early years.

A fixed-rate mortgage can also have a rising payment. The version in the United States is called a "graduated payment mortgage," or GPM. GPMs appeared in the early 1980s and are still available from a few lenders. *See* **Graduated Payment Mortgages**.

Fixed-Rate Mortgage (FRM)

The interest-only version of a fixed-rate mortgage also does not have fixed payments. Borrowers begin paying only the interest, which declines if they voluntarily pay any principal, until the end of the interest-only period. At that point, the payment jumps, and it becomes a level-payment fully amortizing FRM. *See* **Interest-Only Mortgage**.

Calculating the Fully Amortizing Payment: As noted, the term "FRM" without any modifiers means a mortgage with a fixed rate and level payments that fully pay off the balance. For example, on a $300,000 30-year 6% FRM, the monthly payment is $1,798.66. If the borrower makes that payment every month for 30 years, the 360th payment will reduce the balance to zero.

Where does that $1,798.66 figure come from? It is calculated from an algebraic formula; those interested can find it in **Mortgage Equations**. The much easier way is to use a financial calculator such as an HP19B or an online calculator such as my Monthly Payment Calculator (7a). Technophobes can buy a book of monthly payments at a bookstore.

Rising Principal Payments Over Time: On an FRM, the composition of the payment between principal and interest changes every month. At the beginning, it is mostly interest, but the principal portion gradually rises over time. In the example, the principal payment in month 1 is $299, in month 12 it is $316, and in month 60 it is $401.

This feature, where borrowers make the same payment every month but the saving component of the payment increases every month, is powerful but underappreciated. Some borrowers don't recognize that debt repayment is saving, and many of those who do recognize it as such think that they aren't earning any return on it. I am frequently asked whether they would not do better putting their money in a bank account earning 3% than repaying their mortgage.

In fact, a principal payment of $100 on a 6% mortgage earns the same return as a $100 bank deposit that pays 6%. The deposit earns $6 a year in interest, while the principal payment reduces interest payments by $6 a year. The effect on the borrower's wealth is the same.

Of course, if you can earn 10% on your money, paying down a 6% mortgage is not the best choice. The recent popularity of interest-only loans, and option ARMs that allow borrowers to pay less than the interest, has been encouraged by the notion that borrowers can earn a return higher than the mortgage rate by investing their money elsewhere. In my view, however, most borrowers cannot earn a return above the mortgage rate without taking unacceptable risk.

Different Terms on FRMs: FRMs come with different terms, ranging generally from 10 to 40 years, with the 15- and 30-year FRMs being the most popular. In contrast, ARMs are almost all 30 years. This means that discussions of how to select the mortgage term apply almost entirely to FRMs.

Flexible-Payment ARM

Same as **Option ARM**.

Float *Allowing the interest rate and points on a loan in process to vary with changes in market conditions, as opposed to "locking" them.*

Floating may be mandatory until the lender's lock requirements have been met. After that, the borrower may elect to lock the rate and points at any time but must do so a few days before the closing.

Allowing the rate to float exposes the borrower to market risk and also to the risk of being taken advantage of by the loan provider. *See* **Locking/ Choosing When to Lock**.

Float-Down *A rate lock plus an option to reduce the rate if market interest rates decline during the lock period.*

See **Locking/*Clarifying a Lender's Lock Policies*/What Happens If the Market Price Drops After the Loan Is Locked but Before It Is Closed?**

Forbearance Agreement *An agreement by the lender not to exercise the legal right to foreclose in exchange for an agreement by the borrower to a payment plan that will cure the borrower's delinquency.*

See **Payment Problems/*Position of the Lender*/Temporary Problem**.

Foreclosure *The legal process by which a lender acquires possession of the property securing a mortgage loan when the borrower defaults.*

See **Payment Problems/*Position of the Lender*/Permanent Problem**.

40-Year Mortgage *A mortgage with a term of 40 years.*

See **Term**.

Freddie Mac *One of two federal agencies that purchase home loans from lenders. The other is Fannie Mae.*

See **Secondary Mortgage Markets/*Fannie Mae and Freddie Mac***.

Fully Amortizing Payment *The monthly mortgage payment which, if maintained unchanged through the remaining life of the loan at the then-existing interest rate, will pay off the loan at term.*

See **Amortization/*The Fully Amortizing Payment***.

Fully Indexed Rate *On an ARM, the current value of the interest rate index plus the margin.*

See **Adjustable-Rate Mortgage (ARM)/*The Fully Indexed Rate***.

Generic Prices *Prices that assume a more or less standardized set of transaction characteristics that generally command the lowest prices.*

Generic prices are distinguished from transaction-specific prices, which pertain to the characteristics of a specific transaction. See **Nichification/*Generic Price Quotes***.

Gift of Equity *A sale price below market value, where the difference is a gift from the sellers to the buyers.*

Such gifts are usually between family members. Lenders will usually allow the gift to count as a down payment. *See* **Down Payment/***Gift of Equity***.

Good Fairy Syndrome *A belief that somewhere out there is a good fairy who will solve all our financial (and other) problems.*

Con men and scamsters understand the power of the good fairy syndrome. They realize that some people will buy into any claim, no matter how absurd or contrary to common sense, if it awakens their latent belief in the good fairy.

I see the good fairy syndrome lurking in many of the questions I get from readers, and in the advertising spam that provokes these questions. How else, except from a gut belief in a good fairy, can one explain why borrowers would pay $3,500 to someone they don't know and never heard of, who claims to be able to have their mortgage paid off? I could fill this book with other illustrations.

The good fairy does not limit her beneficence to the mortgage market. At least weekly, a letter comes in from abroad offering to transfer large sums to my bank account, with me getting to keep multiple millions. The good fairy is an accomplice to every con game that works.

One of the reasons I dislike lotteries is that they strengthen the good fairy syndrome. Lotteries are a bad gamble because the prize is almost always less than the amount wagered, but since someone always wins, lotteries legitimize the good fairy. This has to strengthen the impulse to rely on her in other areas where no one wins but con artists.

There are no data on trends in the incidence of fraud, so it is not possible to verify that the growth of lotteries in the United States has encouraged fraud by stimulating reliance on the good fairy. However, a survey of consumer fraud by the Federal Trade Commission in 2004 indicated how pervasive the problem is. The survey indicated that "nearly 25 million adults in the United States—11.2% of the adult population—were victims of one or more of the consumer frauds covered by the survey during the previous year. More than 35 million incidents of these various frauds occurred during the year."

Good Fairy Syndrome

The FTC survey, furthermore, only covered types of fraud that are relatively easy to define, such as "Purchased credit card insurance" or "Billed for internet services you did not agree to purchase." Losses on these types of frauds often don't amount to much. Mortgage frauds and medical frauds were not covered, probably because they are more difficult to define. Yet both are widespread, and the losses associated with them are often very large indeed.

Another indicator of how widespread is belief in the good fairy is the pervasive unwillingness of consumers to pay for information. Most people prefer to have their financial advisors (mortgage brokers, financial planners, security brokers, etc.) get paid by the providers of financial services that the advisors select for them, rather than paying the advisors themselves. This prejudices the validity of the information, of course, and this costs consumers dearly. But it allows them to pretend to themselves that the advisors are good fairies.

As a high school teacher, what brief lessons about finance should I give my students?

I was tempted to give a list of substantive lessons, such as how interest rates and credit scores are determined. This kind of information, however, if not used, is soon forgotten. Besides, it isn't ignorance that leads to bad financial decisions, it's "knowing" what isn't true.

Here is my list of the three most important principles that students—and all other consumers—should know:

1. There is no such thing as a good fairy. It is this belief, rather than ignorance of financial matters, that makes people gullible and vulnerable to fraud.

2. Don't respond to solicitations. This is a direct corollary of principle 1, since those who solicit are never good fairies. While not all those who solicit are rogues, all rogues solicit, which means the odds are against you when you respond.

3. Don't be afraid to pay for information. This is another corollary of principle 1; since those who have the information you need are not good fairies, you should expect to pay a fair price for it.

Good Faith Estimate (GFE) *The form that lists the settlement charges the borrower must pay at closing, which the lender is obliged to provide the borrower within three business days of receiving the loan application.*

See **Settlement Costs/Good Faith Estimate**.

Government National Mortgage Association (GNMA) *A federal agency that guarantees mortgage securities that are issued against pools of FHA and VA mortgages.*

See **Secondary Mortgage Markets/*Ginny Mae***.

Grace Period *A number of days, usually 10 to 15, that a borrower is allowed to be late in making the mortgage payment without suffering any penalty.*

Graduated Payment Mortgage (GPM) *A mortgage on which the payment rises by a constant percentage for a specified number of periods, after which it levels out over the remaining term and amortizes fully.*

How a GPM Works: As an example, the mortgage payment on a $200,000 FRM for 30 years at 6% is $1,199. Stretched over 40 years, the payment would be $1,100. But the initial payment on a 30-year GPM at 6.50%, on which the payment rises by 7.5% a year for 5 years, is only $941. The interest rate on the GPM is fixed, just as it is on a standard FRM.

The quid pro quo for the low initial payment is a larger payment later on. The payment on the GPM rises for 5 consecutive years, reaching $1,351 in month 61, where it stays for the remainder of the term.

The initial payment on a GPM does not cover the interest. The difference, termed **Negative Amortization**, is added to the loan balance. In the example, the loan balance peaks at $202,905 in month 36 before it starts down. Not until month 61 does the balance fall below $200,000. This rising balance is a feature that lenders don't like, and it is why they charge a higher rate for GPMs than for FRMs.

Alternative Types of GPMs: Other GPMs have different rates of payment increase over different periods. One has a 3% graduation rate over 10 years instead of 7.5% for 5 years. Assuming the same 6.5% rate, the initial payment would be higher at $1,031, rising to $1,388 in month 121. Negative amortization, however, is smaller, peaking at $200,908 in month 24.

GPMs Versus Temporary Buy-Downs: The GPM is not the only type of mortgage with rising payments. FRMs with temporary buy-downs also carry lower payments in the early years. For example, the payments in the first 2 years on an FRM with a 2-1 buy-down are calculated at rates that are 2% and 1% lower than the rate on the FRM. On a 6% 30-year FRM of $200,000, the first-year payment would be $955, rising to $1,074 in year 2 and to $1,199 in years 3–30. And the buy-down loan amortizes as it would without the buy-down—there is no negative amortization! *See* **Temporary Buy-Down**.

For a temporary buy-down to work, however, someone must fund the required buy-down account. Withdrawals from this account supplement the payments made by the borrower in years 1 and 2 so that the lender receives the same payment ($1,199) throughout. The $4,436 required for the buy-down account must be provided by either the borrower or the home seller. GPMs don't require a buy-down account.

GPMs Versus Option ARMs: Rising payments are also available on many types of adjustable-rate mortgages, most notably on the flexible-payment or option ARM. Under its minimum-payment option, the first-year payment on this ARM is calculated at rates as low as 1.95%. On a $200,000 30-year loan, this amounts to $734, strikingly lower than the $941 on the 5-year GPM.

Increases in the ARM payment, furthermore, are limited to 7.5% a year for the first 5 years, just like on the 5-year GPM. In year 5, therefore, the ARM payment has risen to $980 as compared with $1,256 on the GPM.

In month 61, however, the chickens come home to roost. The GPM payment rises by 7.5% one more time, to $1,351, where it stays. The ARM payment increase, on the other hand, could be 7.5%, or it could be 75% or even higher, depending on what happens to interest rates.

The core difference between the GPM and the option ARM is that the borrower with a GPM knows in advance exactly how and when the payment will change. The ARM borrower, in contrast, is throwing the dice. A new eruption of inflation is bound to cause market rates to rise markedly, which will clobber all ARM borrowers, but especially those who make the minimum payment on an option ARM. *See* **Option Arm**.

GPMs carry risk to borrowers, who must be able to meet the scheduled rise in payments, but the risk is known and at least partly within their control.

Graduation Period *The interval over which the payment increases on a GPM.*

Graduation Rate *The percentage increase in the payment on a GPM.*

Hazard Insurance *Insurance purchased by the borrower and required by the lender, to protect the property against loss from fire and other hazards.*

Hazard insurance is also known as "homeowner insurance," and is the second "I" in **PITI**.

Historical Scenario *The assumption that the interest index to which the interest rate on an ARM is tied follows the same pattern as in some prior historical period.*

In meeting their disclosure obligations in connection with ARMs, some lenders show how the mortgage payment would have changed on a mortgage originated some time in the past. That is not very useful. Showing how a mortgage originated *now* would change if the index followed a historical pattern would be useful, but nobody does it.

Home-Account *A multilender Web site with unique borrower-protection features.*

The writer has associated himself with this venture because it promised to incorporate features that he considered important, which could be delivered on his own Web site. The major features, which at this writing were still under development, are as follows:

Preapplication Counsel on Borrower Status: The site locates the client in one of four categories: category A qualifies for the best conventional prices, B qualifies for conventional financing but not the best prices, C qualifies for FHA financing, and D doesn't qualify. It also shows exactly where the client who is not an A falls short. It could be too low a credit score, too much debt, too small a down payment, insufficient cash reserves, or some combination of these.

This information might induce a non-A client to take a detour, delaying the loan while working to improve her credentials. If she takes the detour, Home-Account will provide concrete suggestions on how to do it.

Use of Total Horizon Cost (THC) to Find the Best Mortgage Program: Home-Account provides the client with a list of all mortgage programs for which the client qualifies, along with the THC of each program and each program option. On ARMs, THC is calculated on several assumptions regarding interest rate changes after the initial rate period expires. *See* **Total Horizon Cost**.

Use of Total Horizon Cost (THC) to Find the Best Rate-Point Combination on the Preferred Mortgage Program: Borrowers will be given the opportunity to compare THCs at different combinations of interest rate and points on their preferred mortgage program.

Selection of the Lender Who Has the Best Price on the Preferred Mortgage: In the early stages of the program, Home-Account will select the lender offering the best price. When information becomes available for assessing lender performance, that information will be provided to borrowers who can then use it, in conjunction with price data, to make their own selections. The performance data will cover the locking process, post-locking price adjustments, and periods required to close.

Rate Locks Are as of the Time the Lock Is Requested: In 2009, a tightening of underwriting requirements and problems in connection with appraisals (*see* **HVCC**) caused widespread delays in getting final approval of loans on which borrowers had requested rate locks. At best, this forced many borrowers to allow their price to float until the lender had completed the approval process. At worst, after the delay, the borrower was locked at the requested price if the current market price was lower and at the current price if it was higher.

On Home-Account, however, lenders can lock immediately based on approval by Home-Account. If the lender wants to be 100% sure and delays the lock until final approval, the lock is at the price prevailing on the day of the lock request.

Homebuyer Protection Plan *A plan purporting to protect FHA homebuyers against property defects.*

But it doesn't. *See* **FHA Mortgage/FHA and House Quality**.

Home Equity Conversion Mortgage (HECM) *A reverse mortgage program administered by FHA.*

See **Reverse Mortgage/FHA's Home Equity Conversion Mortgage (HECM).**

Home Equity Line

Same as **Home Equity Line of Credit (HELOC).**

Home Equity Line of Credit (HELOC) *A mortgage set up as a line of credit against which a borrower can draw up to a maximum amount, as opposed to a loan for a fixed-dollar amount.*

For example, using a standard mortgage you might borrow $150,000, which would be paid out in its entirety at closing. Using a HELOC instead, you receive the lender's promise to advance you *up to* $150,000, in an amount and at a time of your choosing. You can draw on the line by writing a check, using a special credit card, or in other ways.

Most HELOCs are second mortgages and are used to fund intermittent needs, such as paying off credit cards, making home improvements, or paying college tuition. However, an increasing number of HELOCs are first mortgages used to refinance an existing first mortgage.

Interest Calculated Daily: Because the balance of a HELOC may change from day to day, depending on draws and repayments, interest on a HELOC is calculated daily rather than monthly. For example, on a standard 6% mortgage, interest for the month is 0.06 divided by 12, or 0.005, multiplied by the loan balance at the end of the preceding month. If the balance is $100,000, the interest payment is $500.

On a 6% HELOC, interest for a day is 0.06 divided by 365, or 0.000164, which is multiplied by the average daily balance during the month. If this is $100,000, the daily interest is $16.44, and over a 30-day month, interest amounts to $493.15; over a 31-day month, it is $509.59.

Draw Period and Repayment Period: HELOCs have a draw period during which the borrower can use the line and a repayment period during which it must be repaid. Draw periods are usually 5 to 10 years, during which the borrower is only required to pay interest. Repayment periods are usually 10 to 20 years, during which the borrower must make payments on the principal equal to the balance at the end of the draw period divided by the number of months in the repayment period. Some HELOCs, however, require that the entire balance be repaid at the end of the draw period, so the borrower must refinance at that point.

Low Upfront Cost: A major advantage of a HELOC over a standard mortgage in a refinancing is a lower upfront cost. On a $150,000 standard loan, settlement costs may range from $2,000 to $5,000, unless the borrower pays an interest rate high enough for the lender to pay some or all of it. On a $150,000 credit line, costs seldom exceed $1,000 and in many cases are paid by the lender without a rate adjustment.

High Exposure to Interest Rate Risk: The major disadvantage of the HELOC is its exposure to interest rate risk. All HELOCs are adjustable-rate mortgages (ARMs), but they are much riskier than standard ARMs. Changes in the market impact a HELOC very quickly. If the prime rate changes on April 30, the HELOC rate will change effective May 1. An exception is HELOCs that have a guaranteed introductory rate, but these hold for only a few months. Standard ARMs, in contrast, are available with initial fixed-rate periods as long as 10 years.

HELOC rates are tied to the prime rate, which some argue is more stable than the indexes used by standard ARMs. It would be more accurate to say that the prime rate does not change frequently by small amounts, as other rate indexes do, but it is far from stable. For example, in 2001, it changed 11 times and ranged between 4.75% and 9%. In 1980, it changed 38 times and ranged between 11.25% and 20%.

In addition, most standard ARMs have rate adjustment caps, which limit the size of any rate change. And they have maximum rates 5–6% above the initial rates, which in 2009 put them roughly at 8 to 11%. HELOCs have no adjustment caps, and the maximum rate is 18% except in North Carolina, where it is 16%.

Shopping for a HELOC: Shopping for a HELOC is simpler than shopping for a standard mortgage, if you know what you are doing. The major reason is that important HELOC features are the same from one lender to another. All HELOCs are indexed to the prime rate, the rate adjusts on the first day of the month following a change in the prime rate, and there are no rate adjustment caps.

The critical feature of a HELOC that is *not* the same from one lender to another, and which should be the major focus of smart shoppers, is the *margin*. This is the amount that is added to the prime rate to determine the HELOC rate. *Many if not most lenders do not volunteer the margin unless they are asked.*

Here is what can happen when you don't ask. Borrower X, who provided me with his history, was offered an introductory rate of 4.5% for three months. He was told that after the three months the rate "would be based on the prime rate." At the time the loan closed, the prime rate was 4%. Three months later, the prime rate was still 4%, but the rate on his loan was raised to 9.5%. It turned out that the margin, which the borrower never asked about, was 5.5%!

Warning: Do not assume that the difference between your HELOC start rate and the prime rate is the margin. It may or may not be. Ask. Bear in mind, as well, that the margin varies with credit score, ratio of total mortgage debt to property value, documentation, and other factors. You need the margin on *your deal*, not the margin they are advertising which is their *best deal*.

Other HELOC Features: If the HELOC will be used to meet future contingencies rather than to refinance an existing mortgage, the shopper needs to know whether there is a minimum draw at closing or a minimum average loan balance. Lenders don't make any money unless the HELOC is used, but they are not always forthcoming about this. Borrowers who are uncertain about future usage don't want to be forced to borrow money they won't need.

Last and least important are the fees. Upfront fees are the same types as on standard mortgages, except that HELOC lenders seldom charge points, and third-party fees tend to be small and are often paid by the lender. In addition, there are some uniquely HELOC charges that you should factor in. These include an annual fee, usually $25–$75 and often waived the first year, and a cancellation fee, perhaps $350–$500, which is usually waived if the account stays open for 3 years.

Truth in Lending (TIL) on a HELOC: The required TIL disclosure on HELOCs is a travesty. Borrowers must be given an APR, but it is the same as the interest rate. Among other things, it does not reflect points or other upfront costs, as the APR on standard loans does. The borrower described above was given an APR of 4.5% early on, and when his rate jumped to 9.5%, he was told that his new APR was 9.5%. TIL does not require disclosure of the margin.

Shopping Checklist: Make sure the figures you get apply to *your deal*.

1. Introductory rate and period

2. Margin

3. Minimum draw

4. Required average balance

5. Upfront lender fees

6. Upfront third-party fees

7. Annual fee

8. Cancellation fee

Home Equity Loan

Same as **Second Mortgage**.

Home Keeper *A reverse mortgage program administered by Fannie Mae, terminated in 2008.*

Homeowner's Equity

See **Equity**.

Homeowners Insurance *Insurance purchased by the borrower, and required by the lender, to protect the property against loss from fire and other hazards. It is the second "I" in* PITI.

Homeowners Insurance as a Settlement Cost: Homeowners insurance appears on the Good Faith Estimate as an estimated amount, and the actual amount is shown on the HUD-1, which is the closing document that lists all settlement costs.

It is not a mortgage cost, but lenders require that their "minimum insurance requirements" be met before they will fund a loan. The house is their collateral, and they don't want to lose it to a fire or other catastrophe.

The insurance requirements vary from lender to lender, but on a house purchase, most require that the premium be paid for the first year at closing. If the borrower is maintaining an escrow account, an additional amount equal to several months of premiums must be paid to fund the account.

Homeowners Insurance

Shopping for Homeowners Insurance: Homeowners insurance is a lot easier to shop for than a mortgage because premiums change only occasionally, and so the price you are quoted is very likely the price you will pay.

Shoppers should be aware that carriers today have access to databases that combine claims data from many companies. If you have been making numerous small claims, all the carriers you shop will likely be aware of it. It is still worth shopping, however, because the carriers use different risk evaluation systems.

In shopping for the lowest premium, you must be very careful to compare apples with apples. The principal factors you must hold constant in soliciting quotes from different carriers are the deductible and the coverage.

The deductible is the loss amount that is the homeowner's responsibility, e.g., $1,000. Only losses above that amount are insured. Higher deductibles carry lower premiums.

The coverage dictates the maximum loss the policy will pay. There are four levels of coverage, called "actual cash value" (lowest coverage), "replacement cost," "extended replacement cost," and "guaranteed replacement cost" (highest coverage, but not necessarily available). Higher coverage carries higher premiums.

Carry a High Deductible: I have the highest deductible my carrier offers, and if it offered a larger one, I would take it. I live in a heavily wooded area, and every other year or so, a large tree falls that I must have removed. Even if the cost exceeds my deductible, I don't make a claim because it will raise my premium. The number of claims a homeowner makes figures importantly in setting the premium.

Homeowners insurance should not be used as a way to budget expenditures for minor mishaps, such as my falling trees. Even if small claims did not impact the premium, the carriers price deductibles so advantageously that it pays homeowners to self-insure for small mishaps.

If the typical homeowner took the largest deductible, banked the saving in premium, and used the account to pay for what would have been claims under a smaller deductible, the savings account would grow over time. The saving in premiums using the large deductible would more than cover the claims under the small deductible.

Home Owners Loan Corporation (HOLC) *A federal government agency established by Congress in 1933 to help families avoid having their homes foreclosed.*

HOLC refinanced loans of borrowers with mortgages in default or held by distressed institutions. It refinanced about 20% of all qualifying home mortgages in the country, liquidating itself in 1951 at a slight profit to the government. Many observers proposed using the same model to deal with the housing and mortgage crisis that erupted in 2007, but other approaches were adopted instead.

Homeownership Accelerator (HOA) *An adjustable-rate mortgage, usable as a demand deposit or a HELOC, that is designed to provide payment flexibility and to encourage rapid pay-down of the balance.*

HOA as a Deposit Account: An HOA can be used as if it were a checking account. A borrower's paycheck, instead of being deposited in a bank account to earn little or no interest, is used to pay down the mortgage balance. The borrower thus earns the mortgage rate starting the day of deposit.

As the borrower spends money, by writing checks, withdrawing cash from an ATM, or using a bill-pay service, the mortgage balance rises. Even if the balance at the end of the month is the same as at the beginning, the average balance—and therefore the interest charge—is lower.

HOA as a Line of Credit: Both HOA and a home equity line of credit (HELOC) accrue interest daily and adjust the interest rate frequently—monthly on the HOA, anytime on the HELOC. Borrowers can draw up to a specified maximum amount at any point during an initial 10-year draw period, with repayment required over the ensuing 20 years.

But there are important differences. HOA is a first lien and is used to purchase properties and to refinance existing loans. A HELOC is usually a second lien and is used for other purposes, such as making home improvements and consolidating other debts. A HELOC cannot be used as a deposit.

Perhaps the most important difference is that an HOA borrower has no required payment and can even withdraw funds during the repayment period, so long as the current balance is below the maximum balance. A

HELOC borrower must make a payment every month and cannot make withdrawals during the repayment period.

The HOA maximum is unchanged during the first 10 years, unless the borrower exercises a one-time option to increase it. During the 20-year repayment period, the maximum balance declines every month by 1/240 of the amount at the beginning of the repayment period.

The interest rate risk is also much lower on the HOA. The maximum HOA rate is 5–6% over the initial rate, whereas HELOCs have no contractual maximums; they are limited only by state usury ceilings, which are substantially higher.

HOA as a Permanent Mortgage: HOA is an adjustable-rate mortgage (ARM) with monthly rate adjustments. Monthly adjustments make the HOA more sensitive to market changes in both directions than hybrid ARMs on which the initial rate is fixed for up to 10 years.

The HOA rate is fully indexed, meaning that it equals the current value of the rate index plus the margin, starting in month 1. In most rate environments, the HOA rate will begin above the start rate on hybrid ARMs.

HOA as an Early Payoff Tool: HOA is overhyped as an early payoff tool, because the prospect of paying off early captures people's attention. However, while the intramonthly interest savings described earlier are real, unless a borrower has a business with heavy cash flows that can be run through the HOA, they don't add up to much. For everyone else, paying off a 30-year loan in 10 or 15 years requires extra payments, and you don't need HOA to make extra payments. The flexibility of the HOA, however, makes it easier.

HOA as a Flexible Planning Tool: Flexibility is the major virtue of the HOA. Borrowers with money that they might use to pay down the mortgage, but don't because they might need it again, don't have to make that choice. They can use it, and if they need it again, they can draw it out. Borrowers with highly unstable incomes can make a large payment when they are flush and can skip making payments when they are not.

HOA and the Financial Crisis: HOAs stopped being offered in the fall of 2008 and were revived about a year later. The sole investor, GMAC Mortgage, got into trouble during the crisis and was unable to fund them any longer. GMAC's problems had nothing to do with its holding of HOAs, on which the payment experience was extremely good, but it took a year to find a new investor.

Despite the excellent payment record, the new version carries more conservative terms than the original version. The margin was raised from 2.25% to 3.25%, the ceiling rate became 6% over the start rate rather than 5%, the maximum LTV ratio fell from 90% to 75%, and the required FICO score went from 680 to 720.

Home Valuation Code of Conduct (HVCC) *A rule adopted by Fannie Mae and Freddie Mac in 2009 that the agencies thenceforth would only purchase mortgages that were supported by an "independent" appraisal.*

Objective: The objective of HVCC was to insulate the appraisal process from influence by any of the parties with an interest in the outcome. During the 2000–2006 period of rising home prices, reports emerged that lenders were pressuring appraisers to generate appraisals that would validate the prices home purchasers were agreeing to pay. Under HVCC, mortgage brokers and Realtors could no longer have any contact with appraisers, and lenders had to obtain appraisals in some manner that prevented them from exercising any control.

Bad Timing: While the motivation for this well-intentioned rule emerged from the housing bubble, the rule became effective in the middle of the worst housing market since the 1930s. With house prices declining, the upward bias in appraisals that had prevailed during the bubble had morphed into a downward bias. Many deals were not getting done because appraisals were coming in too low, and HVCC seriously aggravated the problem.

Emergence of Appraisal Management Companies: To protect themselves from liability under HVCC, most lenders began ordering appraisals from appraisal management companies (AMCs), which intermediate between the lender and the appraiser. The AMC selects and pays the appraiser, receives and evaluates the appraisal, and passes it to the lender, who has no direct contact with the appraiser.

Because AMCs operate nationally but do not have appraisers everywhere, more appraisals are being done by appraisers who are not familiar with the local market. Appraisers working for AMCs are also paid less per appraisal than independents, which may induce them to invest less time. Less knowledge by appraisers means more scope for bias, and in a declining price market, the prevailing bias is toward lower values.

Intermediation by AMCs also lengthened the period required to complete purchase transactions. People involved in the process told me that it might add an extra week. In an increasing number of cases, the paperwork didn't get done either by the contracted due date or before the buyer's mortgage lock expired, either of which might derail the transaction. HVCC also prevented the loan officers, mortgage brokers, and Realtors who work with borrowers from pressuring appraisers to get a deal done in time to meet a deadline.

Loss of Information: Under HVCC, the loan officers, brokers, and Realtors who fashion deals for consumers could no longer keep their clients informed about the status of an appraisal because they were no longer in the loop. Further, they no longer had access to informal value opinions from the appraisers with whom they worked. Such opinions allowed them to abort house purchases and refinances that clearly would not fly because of inadequate property value. With this source of information closed to them, deals that previously would have been screened out went through the system to be rejected, imposing needless costs on everyone involved.

Appraisals Can Be Used Only Once: HVCC pretty much eliminated the ability of a borrower to use the same appraisal with multiple loan providers. Before HVCC, mortgage brokers could use one appraisal with any of the wholesale lenders with which they dealt, and lenders sometimes accepted appraisals ordered by others. Under HVCC, brokers are out of it, and lenders using AMCs will not accept appraisals ordered by other lenders because they cannot be sure that the other lenders are following the HVCC rules. The upshot is that borrowers often have to pay for more than one appraisal.

In sum, the HVCC "cure" for the appraisal problem of overvaluation was implemented in a market where the problem had become undervaluation, and HVCC made that problem much worse. It is an object lesson in how not to regulate.

Housing Bank *A government-owned or government-affiliated lender that makes home loans directly to consumers.*

With minor exceptions, government in the United States has never loaned directly to consumers, but housing banks have been widespread in many developing countries. In the first two decades after World War II, about 50 housing banks were formed in the same number of countries. At various times over the years, I have had occasion to visit and consult with institutions of this type in Iran, Ethiopia, Indonesia, Pakistan, Portugal, Thailand, Brazil, and Fiji.

With one exception, these housing banks have been a disaster. Some have been terminated, while others are looking to privatize.

One of the major problems of the housing banks has been high default rates. In some cases, half or more of the borrowers don't repay their loans. Chronically high default rates reflect poor loan selection practices and poor collection practices after the loans are made.

With private lenders, the dominant criteria used to determine whether or not to make a loan is the likelihood of repayment. With government lenders, politics and favoritism are often involved in a major way. This is especially likely when loan rates are below the market and therefore a bargain, which is often the case.

Housing banks were set up on the premise that the government's only investment was the required initial capitalization. After that, the bank would administer a "revolving" loan fund, where loan repayments plus interest provided the funds for new loans. But because repayment experience was so bad, the housing banks have needed continuing cash infusions by the government. This is a major reason why governments have become disillusioned.

When housing banks operate side by side with private banks, the housing banks are subject to "adverse selection." The private banks that turn down loan applicants because of bad credit histories refer the applicants to the housing bank.

Housing banks also do very poorly at loan collections. In many cases, their loan collections systems are so poor that borrowers who stop paying do not receive a delinquent notice for six months or longer, by which time it may be too late to remedy the situation.

In dealing with delinquent borrowers, furthermore, housing bank officials usually shrink from exercising the ultimate sanction, which is to take away the house. It isn't their money, so why should they take the political heat? As a consequence, borrowers learn that they can get away with not paying, and word gets around. In many cases, the distinction between a loan and a government grant becomes blurred.

The Housing Bank of Thailand is the exception to these comments because it has been well managed, its loan default rates have been comparable to those of private banks, and it has grown without need for continuing investment by the government. The secret of its success is that the government granted it virtually complete autonomy to operate in essentially the same manner as a private bank. The only major difference has been that dividends have been paid to the government rather than to private shareholders.

Housing Bubble *A marked increase in house prices fueled partly by expectations that prices will continue to rise.*

One would expect that house markets would be less vulnerable to bubbles than financial markets because the cost of buying houses in order to resell them is very high. Costs include sales commissions, on both the purchase and sale, and the costs of carrying the property until the sale. Nonetheless, steep price increases and the expectation of more to come can overcome sales commissions and carrying costs.

Housing bubbles of varying sizes in different markets occurred during 2000–2006, especially toward the latter part of the period. These bubbles were self-reinforcing. Rising home prices made mortgages safer to investors, which led to a relaxation of underwriting standards, which increased housing demand, which put greater upward pressure on house prices. During the period January 2000 to July 2006, house prices rose on average about 106%, but in some areas the increase was twice as large.

One area in which the bubble was most pronounced was southwest Florida, from where I received numerous eyewitness reports.

Bubbles in New Construction: One report pointed out that on new construction, it was possible to speculate on a price increase without incurring any transaction costs at all, and without even having to qualify for a loan!

> *Here is how it works. Borrower A puts down a $10,000 deposit to reserve a condo unit at $300,000 . . . 12 months later, with 2 months to go before completion, A sells her reservation to B for $450,000. B gets a loan and purchases the condo, with A shown on the closing documents as a lien holder. A never has to qualify and walks away with $150,000 on a $10,000 deposit . . .*

Bubbles are powered by easy credit, with lenders willing to assume that house price appreciation will continue taking loans away from lenders who want to remain conservative.

Housing Bubble

I'm a mortgage broker and the Realtors in this area won't give me the time of day because my terms are not competitive. I need 5% investment loans and the best I can offer is 10% . . . Do you know a lender who can help me be competitive?

The system also provided an array of mortgage choices for speculative buyers looking for price appreciation. These included the option ARM, an adjustable-rate mortgage designed to maximize a borrower's buying power by providing exceptionally low payments in the early years. *See* **Option ARM**.

Looking for advice on financing a $500,000 home that I know will appreciate to $700,000 in 3–4 years, or an $800,000 estate that will appreciate to $1.2 million . . . This will be a second home. I will flip it in 3–4 years . . . I'm leaning toward an option ARM that will calculate my starting payment at 2%, with only 7.5% increases the first 5 years . . .

This buyer was convinced her property would appreciate markedly, so she stretched her buying power to the limit. The more expensive the house, the more money you make. This is the mindset of a housing bubble buyer.

Bubbles in Existing Homes: Some homeowners used the growing equity in their homes as a way to live beyond their means. They would build up credit card debt, then consolidate the debt into their mortgages through a cash-out refinance. The consolidation, by extending the term of the credit card debt, reducing the rate, and making the interest tax deductible, would reduce the borrowers' total monthly payments. They could then start building up their credit card debt all over again.

This process could continue only so long as their houses appreciated. As soon as appreciation stopped, they were stuck with total debt service costs that might be unmanageable or with negative equity in their houses or perhaps both.

Bubbles last only until the expectation of continued price appreciation comes into serious question. When prices stopped rising in 2006, speculative buyers and owners living on their equity had a rude awakening, as did the lenders and investors who had financed them.

Mortgages Become Riskier: As the housing bubble expanded during 2000–2006, the mortgage mix became increasingly risky. Average credit scores declined, and an increasing proportion of new loans were subprime. Average down payments declined, with a rising proportion having zero down. Limited documentation became increasingly common. And a rising share of new mortgages carried an interest-only payment option or allowed negative amortization. When the bubble finally burst, default rates were scaled with vintage—those originated in 2007 had the highest default rates, those from 2006 the next highest, and so on.

Housing Expense *The sum of the monthly mortgage payment, property taxes, and hazard insurance.*

Housing expense is sometimes referred to as "PITI," standing for principal, interest, taxes, and insurance. It also includes mortgage insurance if any; and on condominiums, it includes homeowners association fees.

Housing Expense Ratio *The ratio of housing expense to borrower income.*

This ratio is one factor used in qualifying borrowers. *See* **Qualification/ Meeting Income Requirements/Expense Ratios**.

Housing Investment *The amount invested in a house, equal to the sale price less the loan amount.*

The House Investment Decision: Lenders impose the upper limit on how much a household can spend for a house. When borrowers push the limit, it becomes costly because such borrowers are viewed as more risky to the lender. Small down payments require a higher interest rate or mortgage insurance.

Does a household accumulate more wealth over time by pushing its buying power to the limit? While such an aggressive policy involves taking on more debt at a higher cost, it also generates larger capital gains—3% appreciation on a $200,000 house is twice as much as 3% on a $100,000 house.

Consider two buyers who both have $20,000 in cash, have enough income to meet all lender requirements, are in the same tax bracket, and can borrow at 7% for 30 years and zero points. However, one is "aggressive," purchasing a $150,000 house, borrowing $130,000, and paying a mortgage insurance premium of 0.53% for 10 years. The other buyer is "cautious," purchasing a $100,000 house and borrowing $80,000, thus avoiding mortgage insurance. Which buyer accumulates more wealth over time?

The major component of wealth is the value of the house. This is affected by the assumed rate of price appreciation. Higher price appreciation benefits the aggressive buyer more than the cautious one.

From this must be deducted the balance of the mortgage. Both the rapidity with which the loan balance is reduced and the size of the monthly mortgage payment are affected by the mortgage interest rate. Since the aggressive buyer borrows more than the cautious buyer, higher mortgage rates hurt the aggressive buyer more than the cautious buyer.

We must also deduct the amount paid each month for interest, principal reduction, mortgage insurance, and the lost interest on this amount. This is affected by the assumed "investment rate," which is the rate the buyers could have earned if they had invested this money elsewhere. Since the monthly payments are larger for the aggressive buyer, higher investment rates hurt the aggressive buyer more than the cautious buyer. On the other hand, interest is tax deductible, so that higher tax rates work in the opposite direction.

The tables below show how long it takes, if ever, for the greater price appreciation enjoyed by the aggressive buyer to offset the effects of the higher costs. For example, if the investment rate is 5% and the buyers are in the 15% tax bracket, the aggressive buyer never catches up if the appreciation rate is 5% or less. At a 6% rate of appreciation, the aggressive buyer catches up in 25 years. Shifting to a tax rate of 35%, the aggressive buyer would catch up in 3 years.

These numbers suggest that in a "normal" environment, an aggressive purchase policy is difficult to rationalize from a wealth perspective. No buyer should expect 6% appreciation in an environment in which the mortgage rate is 7%; yet 6% appreciation is needed to justify an aggressive policy. On the other hand, no account is taken of the benefits to the aggressive buyer from living in a more expensive house.

Readers can assess their own situations using the spreadsheet used to compile these tables. It is on my Web site.

How Long It Takes an "Aggressive" Buyer to Accumulate More Wealth Than a "Cautious" Buyer Using a 7% 30-Year Mortgage					
Income Tax Rate of Buyer 15%					
	Investment Rate				
Property Appreciation Rate	Zero	2.5%	5%	7.5%	10%
3% or lower	Never	Never	Never	Never	Never
4%	20 years	Never	Never	Never	Never
5%	12 years	20 years	Never	Never	Never
6%	7 years	11 years	25 years	Never	Never
7%	2 years	3 years	7 years	Never	Never
8%	1 month	1 month	1 month	1 month	26 years
9%	1 month	1 month	1 month	1 month	7 years
Income Tax Rate of Buyer 35%					
	Investment Rate				
Property Appreciation Rate	Zero	2.5%	5%	7.5%	10%
2% or lower	Never	Never	Never	Never	Never
3%	25 years	Never	Never	Never	Never
4%	14 years	28 years	Never	Never	Never
5%	7 years	12 years	Never	Never	Never
6%	1 year	1 year	3 years	Never	Never
7%	1 month	1 month	1 month	1 month	23 years
8%	1 month	1 month	1 month	1 month	11 years
9%	1 month	1 month	1 month	1 month	1 month
Note: The aggressive buyer pays a mortgage insurance premium of 0.53% for 10 years.					

HUD-1 Form *The form a borrower receives at closing that details all the payments and receipts among the parties in a real estate transaction, including borrower, lender, home seller, mortgage broker, and various other service providers.*

Hybrid ARM *An ARM on which the initial rate holds for some period, during which it is "fixed rate," after which it becomes adjustable rate.*

In some sense, all ARMs are hybrids because the initial rate is always preset. In practice, the term is generally applied to ARMs with initial rate periods of three years or longer.

Indexed ARMs *Adjustable-rate mortgages on which the interest rate is mechanically determined based on the value of an interest rate index.*

Indexed ARMs are distinguished from **Discretionary ARMs**, in that the first provides the lender with *zero* discretion in setting future interest rates, while the latter provides the lender with *complete* discretion. All ARMs discussed in **Adjustable-Rate Mortgage** are indexed ARMs, which is the only kind used in the United States.

Initial Interest Rate *The interest rate that is fixed for some specified number of months or years at the beginning of the life of an ARM.*

    See **Adjustable-Rate Mortgage (ARM)/***How the Interest Rate on an ARM Is Determined**.*

Initial Rate Period *The number of months for which the initial interest rate holds on an ARM.*

    See **Adjustable-Rate Mortgage (ARM)/***How the Interest Rate on an ARM Is Determined**.*

Interest Accrual Period *The period over which the interest due the lender is calculated.*

Assume a 6% mortgage with a $100,000 balance. If the interest accrual period is a year, as it is on some loans in the United Kingdom and India, the interest for the year is 0.06($100,000) = $6,000. If interest accrues monthly, as it does on most mortgages in the United States, the monthly interest is 0.06/12($100,000) = $500. If interest accrues biweekly, as on a few programs in the United States, the biweekly interest is 0.06/26($100,000) = $230.77. And if interest accrues daily, as it does on HELOCs and some other mortgages in the United States, the daily interest is 0.06/365($100,000) = $16.44.

The interest accrual period may or may not correspond to the payment period. On the annual accrual mortgages in the United Kingdom, payments are made monthly. On most monthly accrual mortgages in the United States, payments are also made monthly, but in some cases payments are made biweekly. On biweekly accrual mortgages, payments are made biweekly. On daily accrual mortgages, payments are made monthly or biweekly.

Given the same stated annual interest rate, as 6% in the example, shorter accrual periods result in higher interest earnings over a year because of reinvestment of prior interest. *See* **Effective Rate**.

Interest Cost (IC) *A comprehensive and time-adjusted measure of loan cost to the borrower.*

IC on a Mortgage: IC is what economists call an "internal rate of return." It takes account of all payments made by the borrower over the life of the loan relative to the cash received up front. On a mortgage, the cash received up front is the loan amount less all upfront fees paid by the borrower. On an ARM, IC captures the effect of interest rate changes on the monthly payment and the balance, but future rate changes must be assumed.

Formula: IC is (i) in the formula below:

$$L - F = P1 + P2/(1 + i)^2 +. . . (Pn + Bn)/(1 + i)^n$$

where:

L = Loan amount

F = Points and all other upfront fees paid by the borrower

P = Monthly payment

n = Month when the balance is prepaid in full

Bn = Balance in month n

IC Versus APR: IC differs from APR in the following ways: IC is measured over any time horizon, whereas APR assumes that all loans run to term. IC may be measured after taxes, whereas APR is always measured before taxes. On an ARM, IC can be calculated on any interest rate scenario, whereas APR always uses a no-change scenario.

While the IC is a better measure than the APR, it has some disadvantages relative to the THC.

See **Time Horizon Cost**.

Interest Due *The amount of interest, expressed in dollars, computed by multiplying the loan balance at the end of the preceding period times the annual interest rate divided by the interest accrual period.*

On a monthly accrual mortgage, interest due is computed by multiplying the loan balance at the end of the preceding month times the annual interest rate divided by 12. Interest due is the same as the interest payment except when the scheduled mortgage payment is less than the interest due, in which case the difference is added to the balance and constitutes negative amortization.

Interest-Only Mortgage (Option) *An option attached to a mortgage, which allows but does not require the borrower to pay only the interest for some period.*

A mortgage is "interest-only" if the scheduled monthly mortgage payment—the payment the borrower is required to make—consists of only interest. Borrowers have the right to pay more than interest if they want to. If the borrower exercises the interest-only option every month during the interest-only period, the payment will not include any repayment of principal. The result is that the loan balance will remain unchanged.

For example, if a 30-year fixed-rate loan of $100,000 has an interest rate of 6.25%, the standard payment is $615.72. This payment is "fully amortizing," meaning that if it is continued and the rate does not change, the loan will pay off at maturity. The interest-only payment, however, is only $520.84. The $94.88 difference is principal repayment.

Interest-Only in the 1920s and Now: If a loan is interest-only until maturity, the loan balance will be the same at maturity as it was at the outset. Back in the 1920s, loans of this type were the norm. Borrowers typically refinanced at term, which worked fine so long as the house didn't lose value and the borrower didn't lose her job.

But the depression of the 1930s caused a large proportion of these loans to go into foreclosure. Lenders stopped writing them and switched to fully amortizing loans.

When interest-only loans were revived in this century, most were interest-only for a specified period, usually 5 to 10 years. At the end of that period, the payment was raised to the fully amortizing level.

Types of Borrowers for Whom Interest-Only Mortgages Are Suitable: Interest-only mortgages are for borrowers who have a good reason for preferring the lower initial required payment and are prepared to deal with the consequences. Here are some possible reasons:

Pay Principal When Convenient: Borrowers with fluctuating incomes may value the flexibility the IO mortgage gives them. When their finances are tight, they can make the IO payment; and when the borrowers are flush, they can make a substantial payment to principal. This only works for borrowers who are disciplined enough to make principal payments when they aren't obliged to.

Buy More House: It is common for families to begin with a "starter house" and then move into a more expensive house as their incomes rise. This process of "trading up" carries high transaction and moving costs. These costs can be avoided by skipping to the second house now. In the short term, this will cause a cash flow strain, but the IO mortgage may make it manageable.

This only works for borrowers who are comfortable with the risk that the expected higher income won't materialize. There is the further risk that if home prices decline, they will suffer a larger loss. This was the fate of many who bought during the peak-price years of 2005–2006.

Invest the Cash Flow: For most homeowners, paying down mortgage debt is the most effective way to build wealth. Nonetheless, some may build wealth more rapidly by investing excess cash flow in financial assets rather than paying down their mortgage. For this to succeed, their return on investment must exceed the mortgage interest rate, since that is the rate they earn when they repay their mortgage.

Possible examples are young borrowers with long time horizons who invest in common stock or in their own businesses. But I don't recommend it as a wealth-building strategy for most borrowers, because most borrowers can't earn returns on investment that exceed their mortgage rate without taking undue risks.

Interest-Only Mortgage (Option)

Allocate Cash Flow to Second Mortgage: A borrower with a high-rate second mortgage might prefer an IO option on his first mortgage so he can pay down the balance of the high-rate mortgage first. This makes sense, especially if the second mortgage is an ARM that carries the risk of rate increases in the future.

Payment Responsive to Principal Reduction: On many but not all IO loans, whether fixed or adjustable rate, the monthly mortgage payment will decline in the month following a principal payment. This is the only type of mortgage that may have this feature. On a standard FRM, the payment never changes in response to extra payments, while on ARMs, the payment doesn't change until the next rate adjustment.

Some borrowers find this feature extremely convenient. For example, a home purchaser who must close before his existing house is sold may want to use the proceeds of the sale, when it occurs, to reduce the payment on the new mortgage.

On some IOs, a principal payment reduces the payment in the following month, on others the payment doesn't change until the anniversary month, and on still others it does not change until the end of the IO period. Borrowers who are contemplating an interest-only loan, and who find immediate payment adjustments in response to extra payments a highly desirable feature, should ask about it. Don't be surprised if the broker or loan officer doesn't know the answer.

IO Hazards: The major hazard is being deceived into believing that an interest-only mortgage has special desirable features that in fact it doesn't have. All the deceptions noted below have been reported to me by borrowers.

Deception 1: Countless borrowers have told me that an IO carries a lower interest rate. The fact is that lenders almost always charge *higher* rates on loans that carry an IO option, relative to an identical loan that does not have the option. Lenders view the IO as riskier, because after any period has elapsed, the loan with the IO option will have a larger balance. If a loan is riskier to the lender, it will have a higher price.

The deception arises from comparisons of apples and oranges. Most interest-only loans are adjustable-rate mortgages (ARMs), and ARMs have lower rates than fixed-rate mortgages (FRMs). ARMs with the IO option may have lower rates than FRMs, but that is because they are ARMs, not because they are IOs.

Interest-Only Mortgage (Option)

Deception 2: An interest-only loan allows the borrower to avoid paying for mortgage insurance. Not so. Since loans with an IO option are riskier to the lender, the option cannot cause the disappearance of mortgage insurance. On the contrary, mortgage insurers charge higher premiums on IOs.

The deception arises from the fact that lenders can always elect to purchase mortgage insurance themselves and charge the borrower for it in the rate. If they do this on an IO, then the borrower does not have to pay mortgage insurance on the IO. But the inference, that this makes the IO less costly to the borrower, is patently false.

Deception 3: On an ARM with an interest-only option, the quoted interest rate is fixed for the interest-only period. This may or may not be the case. On a 10/1 ARM, both the interest-only period and the initial rate period will be 10 years. But a 3/1 ARM on which the initial rate holds for only 3 years may well have a 10-year interest-only period.

Deception 4: It is less costly to amortize an interest-only loan than the same loan that is not interest-only. This is probably the most ridiculous of all the assertions about IOs, but some variant of it keeps popping up in my mail. Furthermore, some of this mail comes from loan officers and brokers who believe it and preach it to borrowers.

Assume two loans that are identical—they even have the same rate, but one has an IO option and the other doesn't. On one, the borrower must make the fully amortizing payment, while on the other, his twin brother must pay only interest for the first 10 years. Now let's assume further that the twin with the IO has a change of heart, deciding that he never wants to owe more than his twin brother. He therefore makes the same fully amortizing payment as his brother. His loan will amortize in exactly the same way. There is nothing in the IO option that affects the way a loan amortizes.

My example assumed the interest rates on the two mortgages were the same. In fact, because IOs are riskier to the lender, they are priced higher. This means that if the twin with the IO made the same payment as the twin without it, because his IO carries a higher rate, it would amortize more slowly.

Any reader who wants to compare the amortization of an IO with that of a fully amortizing mortgage can do it with a spreadsheet called "Keeping Track of Payments on Interest-Only (IO) Mortgages" on my Web site.

Interest Payment *The dollar amount of interest paid each month.*

The interest payment is the same as interest due so long as the scheduled mortgage payment is equal to or greater than the interest due. Otherwise, the interest payment is equal to the scheduled payment.

Interest Rate *The rate charged the borrower each period for the loan of money, by custom quoted on an annual basis.*

A mortgage interest rate is a rate on a loan secured by a specific property.

Calculating the Interest due from the Interest Rate: The interest rate is used to calculate the interest payment the borrower owes the lender. Since the interest payment is calculated monthly, the rate must be divided by 12 before it is used to calculate the payment.

Assume a 6% $100,000 loan. In decimals, 6% is 0.06, and when divided by 12, it is 0.005. Multiply 0.005 times $100,000, and you get $500 as the monthly interest due.

Interest Rate Versus Total Interest Payments as Cost Measures: Some loan officers encourage borrowers to view total interest payments, rather than the interest rate, as the measure of cost they seek to minimize. This is a mistake. The lower the interest rate borrowers pay, the better off they are. Interest payments, in contrast, depend not only on the rate but also on the loan amount and the maturity.

Some borrowers bamboozled by this argument pay a higher interest rate or fees for a biweekly mortgage that cuts their interest payments. But the lower interest payments on a biweekly are due to a shortening of the term, which results from making an extra monthly payment every year. *See* **Biweekly Mortgage**.

Quoted Rates Versus Actual Rates: Not everybody can borrow at the rates quoted in the media, which are based on numerous favorable assumptions: that the applicants' credit is good, they have enough income to qualify, they can fully document their income and assets, they will occupy the house as their primary residence, and on and on. If a particular applicant doesn't meet all the assumptions, her rate will be higher. *See* **Nichification**.

Determinants of Mortgage Rates: A major determinant of all interest rates is inflation. Rates paid by prime borrowers on 30-year FRMs reached

15% in 1981 when the inflation rate was unusually high (for the United States). During 2000–2009, the rate was generally below 6% because the inflation rate was very low.

A second factor that affects mortgage rates is the efficiency of the housing finance system. In most respects, the U.S. system is more efficient than those in most other countries. As a result, mortgage rates to prime borrowers in the United States are only 1–1.5% above long-term government bond yields. In many other countries, the spread is twice as large or more.

Predicting Mortgage Rates: The general level of interest rates is not predictable, but specific interest rates that lag the general market may be. Before the development of secondary mortgage markets, mortgage rates had some degree of predictability because they lagged bond yields by anywhere from two to eight months.

Today, however, the mortgage market is thoroughly integrated into the broader capital market. A large proportion of all mortgages are placed in pools against which mortgage-backed securities (MBSs) are issued. MBSs trade actively in the market and are considered close substitutes for bonds. This means that MBS yields and bond yields change together. Since lenders base their rates to borrowers on MBS yields, there is no longer a leading indicator of mortgage rates.

Interest Rate Adjustment Period *The frequency of rate adjustments on an ARM after the initial rate period is over.*

The rate adjustment period is sometimes but not always the same as the initial rate period. As an example, using common terminology, a 3/3 ARM is one in which both periods are three years, while a 3/1 ARM has an initial rate period of three years after which the rate adjusts every year. *See* **Adjustable-Rate Mortgage (ARM)/*How the Interest Rate on an ARM Is Determined***.

Interest Rate Ceiling *The highest rate possible under an ARM contract; same as "lifetime cap."*

It is often expressed as a specified number of percentage points above the initial interest rate. *See* **Adjustable-Rate Mortgage (ARM)/*How the Interest Rate on an ARM Is Determined***.

Interest Rate Decrease Cap *The maximum allowable decrease in the interest rate on an ARM each time the rate is adjusted.*

It is usually one or two percentage points. *See* **Adjustable-Rate Mortgage (ARM)/***How the Interest Rate on an ARM Is Determined*.

Interest Rate Floor *The lowest interest rate possible under an ARM contract.*

Floors are less common than ceilings. *See* **Adjustable-Rate Mortgage (ARM)/***How the Interest Rate on an ARM Is Determined*.

Interest Rate Increase Cap *The maximum allowable increase in the interest rate on an ARM each time the rate is adjusted.*

On ARMs with initial rate periods of 5–10 years, the first cap is likely to be 5%. On annual adjustments, it is usually 2%. *See* **Adjustable-Rate Mortgage (ARM)/***How the Interest Rate on an ARM Is Determined*.

Interest Rate Index *The specific interest rate series to which the interest rate on an ARM is tied, such as "Treasury Constant Maturities, One-Year" or "Eleventh District Cost of Funds."*

See **Adjustable-Rate Mortgage (ARM)/***ARM Rate Indexes*.

Internet Mortgages *Mortgages delivered using the Internet as a major part of the communication process between the borrower and the lender.*

Three types of mortgage Web sites are discussed in this book. *See* **Lead-Generation Site**, **Referral Site**, *and* **Single-Lender Web Site**.

Investment Property *In the home loan market, a home purchased to rent out.*

Investor *In the home loan market, a borrower who owns or purchases a property to rent out as an investment rather than for occupancy.*

Jumbo Mortgage *A mortgage larger than the maximum eligible for purchase by the two federal agencies, Fannie Mae and Freddie Mac.*

Mortgages eligible for purchase by the agencies are **Conforming Mortgages.** The permanent conforming loan maximum was $417,000 during 2006–2009. In 2008, as part of the government's program to combat the financial crisis, higher maximums were set for selected high-cost counties, ranging up to $729,750. Loans larger than $417,000 that were eligible for purchase in high-cost counties came to be called "conforming jumbos," because the agencies charged higher prices on them than on conforming loans of $417,000 or less. Authority for conforming jumbos was scheduled to expire at year-end 2010.

Junk Fees *A derogatory term for lender fees that are expressed in dollars rather than as a percentage of the loan amount.*

See **Settlement Costs/*Fees Paid to Lender*/Lender Fees Expressed in Dollars**.

Late Fees *Fees assessed by lenders when payments are late.*

Late fees are usually 4 or 5% of the payment. A borrower with a 6% mortgage for 30 years who pays a 5% late charge every month raises her interest cost over the life of the loan to 6.46%.

Late Payment *A payment made after the grace period stipulated in the note, usually 10–15 days.*

Lead-Generation Site *A mortgage Web site designed to provide leads to lenders.*

A "lead" is a packet of information about a consumer who may be in the market for a loan. Lenders and mortgage brokers pay for leads, and these sites are an important source of them.

Prospective borrowers fill out a questionnaire covering the loan request, property, personal finances, and contact information. The sites use this information to select the lenders to whom the information is sent. Lenders then prepare offers to the borrower based on the same information.

Lead-Generation Site

Lender Screening: Lender selection by lead-generation sites should be valuable to borrowers with one or more challenging features, such as poor credit, incomplete documentation, or little cash. Such borrowers can avoid wasting time soliciting lenders who won't deal with them.

Lender screening also provides some protection against falling into the hands of rogues—lenders or mortgage brokers out to extract as much revenue as possible from every customer. The sites have every reason to bounce a lender who attracts multiple complaints from borrowers. They could do a lot more, as noted below.

Promoting Lender Competition: Lead-generation sites are sometimes called "auction sites" because they purport to provide a group of lenders, usually up to four, who will bid for the borrower's business. Selecting from among lenders provided by an auction site, however, is as difficult for most borrowers as selecting among any other group of lenders.

The sites don't require that the initial price quotes provided by their lenders be sufficiently complete to allow borrowers to make intelligent choices. It is no easier to get settlement cost data or get the complete specs on an ARM from these lenders as from any others. Neither do the sites protect borrowers against "sharp practices" by lenders during the period between initial price quotes and the time when the price is "locked." Nor do they prevent sharp practices after the lock.

Guidelines for the Most Effective Use of Lead-Generation Sites

- Decide beforehand whether you want a fixed- or adjustable-rate mortgage, as well as your preferred loan term, down payment, and points. If you are uncertain about any of these, do some homework.

- Fill out the questionnaire as accurately and completely as you can. That information is used to match you with the lenders most likely to be interested in your loan.

- Mortgage price information comes from the lenders who contact you, not from the site. The amount of price information they give you may depend on what you ask for. Remember that on fixed-rate mortgages you need the interest rate, points, and dollar fees. While some lenders are not in the habit of providing their dollar fees in initial price quotes, you can insist upon it.

- If you are interested in an ARM, you need to know more than the rate, points, and loan fees. *See* **Adjustable-Rate Mortgage (ARM)/ Information Needed**.

- Receiving price quotes over the telephone is looking for trouble. Ask lenders to e-mail or fax their prices to you.

- The interest rate and points quoted by a lender apply only to the day you receive them. The prices that really matter are those quoted to you on the day you "lock" the loan with the lender. The lock means that the lender is committed to the prices. Lender locking requirements vary widely, ranging from very little, to a signed application, to a signed application plus a nonrefundable payment. You are entitled to know at the outset exactly what each lender's requirements are and how long it should take if you do everything expected of you. Ask!

- Since you selected the lender based on the initial price quote but it is the locked price that you are going to pay, you have a right to know how the lender will set the price on the day you lock. The lock price should be the same as the price the lender is quoting to new customers on the identical loan on the same day. Ask if the lender has a Web site that contains up-to-date prices that you can use to monitor your price day by day. If it does not, ask the loan officer how he intends to demonstrate that you have received the correct price.

- Unlike rates and points, other lender fees are not market driven. Unless you change one or more of the loan characteristics, there is seldom a good reason for these fees to change between the time you receive the initial price quote and the time you close. Some lenders will guarantee their fees in writing if you ask. Lenders can't guarantee the fees of third parties, but they may be willing to include appraisal fees and credit charges in a guarantee because they order them and know how much they cost.

Emergence of Lead Generators That Warrant Lender Performance: The development of the leads market has not benefited borrowers materially because lead generators accept virtually no responsibility for the actions of loan providers. The most that they do is to display ratings based on borrower reports of their experience. Yet lead generators have the potential to transform the home loan market for the better.

The trick is to provide borrowers with an array of invaluable decision supports and transaction protections, including selection of the best product and the best lender offering that product, such that the conversion rate from lead to closing hits 50% or more. This will provide the lead generator with the clout required to induce lenders to follow the lead-provider's standards of behavior, I am working with a new firm called Home-Account to develop such a system. *See* **Home-Account**.

Leads

See **Mortgage Leads**.

Lease-to-Own Purchase *A transaction in which a hopeful homeowner-to-be leases a home with an option to buy it within a specified period at an agreed-upon price.*

Contract Features of a Lease-Purchase: A lease-purchase has five major provisions: purchase price, rent, option period, option fee, and rent premium.

Purchase Price and Rent: Both the price and the rent are market determined, yet subject to negotiation just as in a straight purchase or rental transaction. Because they are combined in one deal, trade-offs between them are possible to meet the particular preferences of the parties. For example, if the seller views the likelihood of the buyer exercising the option as very low, he might be willing to trade off a lower price for a higher rent.

Option Period: This is the period within which the purchase option can be exercised. Buyers generally prefer a long option period because it provides more time to build equity and repair credit. A long period can boomerang on them, however, if they are not able to exercise the option, since they lose the rent premium they have been paying all the while, in addition to the option fee. Sellers generally prefer a short option period, but if it is too short, the house won't be sold.

Option Fee and Rent Premium: The option fee is an upfront payment by the buyer, usually 1–5% of the price, paid up front. The rent premium is an increment to the rent that is paid monthly. Both are credited to the purchase price, but if the purchase option is not exercised, the buyer loses both.

The option fee and rent premium are viewed differently by buyers and sellers. To the buyers, the fee and premium are part of the equity in the house they will soon own. Fully anticipating that they will exercise the option, the only cost is the interest they would otherwise have earned. To sellers, however, these payments are the best guarantee that their houses will sell; if they don't sell, the payments are retained as income. That the benefit to the seller generally exceeds the cost to the buyer makes the lease-to-own deal a possible win-win.

Lease-to-Own Purchase

Using a Lease-Purchase to Buy: The lease-purchase offers homeownership opportunities to consumers who have little cash or poor credit but who are prepared to bet on themselves. The bet is that before the option period expires, they will qualify for the mortgage they need to exercise the purchase option. During the option period, they have the opportunity to rebuild their credit and accumulate equity while living in the house.

The development of the subprime market, in which consumers with poor credit or no cash could obtain loans, might have lessened interest in lease-purchase; it is hard to say. The subprime market provided an alternative route to homeownership for the credit impaired, but it also stimulated a lot of them, who otherwise would have stayed renters, to consider the possibility of ownership.

On the other hand, the financial crisis, and the marked tightening of underwriting requirements that followed it, substantially increased interest in lease-to-own because it made many hopeful buyers-to-be ineligible for mortgage financing. Following the crisis, the article on lease-to-own on my Web site rocketed to the top of my page rankings by readership.

Consumers who need to rebuild their credit rating during the option period should understand that paying their rent on time won't do it. Rent payment information is not used in compiling credit scores. While Fair Isaac, the company that developed credit scoring, has added an "expansion" score based on "nontraditional credit data," at this writing the score did not include rent payment information from individual homeowners. Lease-purchase buyers who need a higher credit score must focus on their credit cards and loans.

Even though it is costly, the right *not* to exercise the purchase option is of value to buyers. If there is something seriously wrong with the house, neighborhood, or neighbors, the money left behind on a lease-purchase is much smaller than the cost of an outright purchase followed by a sale.

Dangers to Buyers: On October 2, 2005, Bob Mahlburg, an investigative reporter for the *Sarasota Herald-Tribune*, published an article on a substantial lease-to-own program in Florida that had generated numerous complaints. Over a five-year period hundreds of deals were executed under this program but only a handful of purchases. In fact, there were more evictions than purchases.

The contract used in this program made it all too easy for the seller to avoid having to sell when it was more profitable to evict the tenant and do another deal with another hopeful buyer. The moral: buyers should read the contract very carefully to make sure they are confident they can live up to all the terms, such as paying the rent on time, every time.

Using a Lease-Purchase to Sell: Most home sellers want a cash sale, but for those prepared to hang on to the property awhile longer, the benefits of a lease-purchase can be compelling. Bob Bruss, who was an expert's expert on lease-purchases before his untimely death in 2007, said that in this market, there were always more buyers than sellers—he had been both. In his experience, buyers generally paid top dollar, perhaps including some assumed future appreciation.

To be sure, the deal may fall through, but in that case the seller gets to pocket the option fee and rent premium. The seller also enjoys the tax deduction on his mortgage interest payments during the option period.

Lender

See **Mortgage Lender**.

Lender-Pay Mortgage Insurance (LPMI) *Mortgage insurance on which the premiums are paid by the lender rather than the borrower.*

From a system perspective, lender-pay mortgage insurance (LPMI) has marked advantages over borrower-pay mortgage insurance (BPMI). Under BPMI, the borrower purchases the policy and pays the premiums, but the lender selects the insurer. This arrangement gives the lender referral power and a preference for higher rather than lower premiums. Higher premiums permit larger kickbacks to the lenders for the referral of business to the insurers.

While direct kickbacks are illegal under the Real Estate Settlement Procedures Act (RESPA), there are numerous ways to legalize them. One that has become common among large lenders is to establish a reinsurance affiliate that shares the premiums on insurance sold to the lender's customers.

With an LPMI system, in contrast, the lender pays the premium and charges the borrower for it in the rate. Since lenders compete for borrowers in terms of rate, their incentive is to pay as little as possible for the insurance. The increment to rate that borrowers must pay in an all-LPMI system would be smaller than the insurance premium they pay in an all-BPMI system.

The system that exists in the United States is mixed, with BPMI dominating but LPMI available to lenders who want to use it for competitive reasons. These lenders pass through the premium to the interest rate, which simplifies the deal and makes the premium deductible to the borrower by converting it into interest.

A mixed system with a small number of insurers will not generate the benefits of an all-LPMI system because the insurers will maintain prices on LPMI that do not undercut those on BPMI. The market awaits a new entrant offering only LPMI.

LIBOR *The London Interbank Offer Rate, which is the interest rate offered for U.S. dollar deposits by large banks in London.*

Rates are quoted for 1-month, 3-month, 6-month, and 12-month deposits.

LIBOR ARM *An ARM that uses a **LIBOR** rate as the index to which rate adjustments are tied.*

Before the financial crisis, **LIBOR** ARMs were attractively priced to A-quality borrowers because of their appeal to foreign investors. During a short period during the financial crisis, **LIBOR** rates spiked because of a loss of confidence in many banks. The spread between one-month **LIBOR** and one-month Treasuries rose from 0.38% in January 2007 to 2.18% in December 2007. **LIBOR** ARM borrowers whose rates adjusted during that period suffered a rude shock. However, it didn't last. In July 2009, the spread was down to 0.19%.

Lien *A claim against a property that encumbers it until the discharge of a debt.*

Loan Amount *The amount the borrower promises to repay, as set forth in the loan contract.*

The loan amount may exceed the original amount requested by the borrower if points, mortgage insurance, or other upfront costs are financed—that is, included in the loan.

Loan Discount Fee *The term used to describe points on the Good Faith Estimate.*

Loan Flipping *The process of raising cash periodically through successive cash-out refinancings.*

This is a scam initiated by mortgage brokers that victimizes wholesale lenders, with the connivance of borrowers. *See* **Mortgage Scams and Tricks/ Strictly Broker Scams/Successive Refinancings Using Rebate Loans**.

Loan Officers *Employees of lenders or mortgage brokers who find borrowers, sell and counsel them, and take applications.*

Loan officers employed by mortgage brokers may also be involved in loan processing. In the case of a one-person mortgage broker firm, that person is both the broker and the loan officer.

While loan officers are employees, they act more like independent contractors. They are compensated largely, if not entirely, on a commission basis. The typical commission rate is 1/2 of 1% of the loan amount, and successful loan officers earn six-figure incomes.

Both lenders and mortgage brokers post prices with loan officers to be offered to consumers. The loan officers usually have limited discretion to reduce the price if necessary to meet competition, and they may have full discretion to raise the price if they can. The difference between the posted price and the price charged the consumer is called an **Overage**, and the loan officer usually gets a share of it.

Loan Provider *A mortgage lender or mortgage broker.*

Loan-to-Value Ratio (LTV) *The loan amount divided by the lesser of the selling price or the appraised value.*

The LTV and down payment are different ways of expressing the same facts. *See* **Down Payment/*Down Payment and LTV*.

Locking

Locking *An option exercised by the borrower, at the time the loan application has been approved or later, to "lock in" the rates and points prevailing in the market at that time.*

When lenders "lock," they commit to lend at a specified interest rate and points, provided the loan is closed within a specified "lock period." For example, a lender agrees to lock a 30-year fixed-rate mortgage of $200,000 at 7.5% and 1 point, good for 30 days.

Note that the type of mortgage is specified in the lock. If the borrower decides to change the loan type after the lock, the lender will allow it only at the higher of the lock price or the current price. That makes it important for borrowers to know exactly what they want before they request a lock.

The Need for Locking: The need for locking arises out of two special features of the home loan market: volatility and process delays. Volatility means that rates and points are reset each day, and sometimes within the day. Process delays refer to the lag between the time when the terms of the loan are negotiated and the time when the loan is closed and funds disbursed.

If prices are stable, locking isn't needed even if there are process delays. If there are no process delays, locking isn't needed even if prices are volatile. It is the combination of volatility and process delays that creates the need for locking.

For example, Smith is shopping for a loan on June 5 for a house purchase scheduled to close July 15. Smith is comfortable with the rates and points quoted on June 5, but a rate increase of 1/2% within the following 40 days could make the house unaffordable, and Smith doesn't want to take that risk. Smith wants a lock, and lenders competing for Smith's loan will offer it.

Cost of Locking to Lenders: If locks were equally binding on lender and borrower, locks would not cost the borrower anything. While lenders would lose when interest rates rose during the lock period, they would profit when interest rates fell. Over a large number of customers they would break even.

In practice, however, borrowers are not as committed as lenders. The number of deals that don't close, known as "fallout," increases during periods of falling rates, when borrowers find they can do better by starting the process anew with another lender. Fallout declines during periods of rising rates.

Locking

This means that locking imposes a net cost on lenders, which they in turn pass on to borrowers. The cost is included in the points quoted to borrowers, which are higher for longer lock periods. The lender who quoted 7.5% and 1 point for a 30-day lock, for example, might charge 1.25 points for a 45-day lock.

Lender Control over Lock Costs: Lenders could control lock costs by requiring borrowers to pay a significant commitment fee in cash, which is forfeited if they walk from the deal. The problem is that borrowers don't like large commitment fees, and lenders and mortgage brokers don't want to place themselves at a competitive disadvantage by requiring them. Commitment fees are seldom more than $400 and are credited to settlement costs at closing.

To control lock costs, most lenders refuse to lock until borrowers demonstrate commitment to the deal by completing one or more critical steps in the lending process. This may include submitting a completed application and paying for an appraisal and credit report. When underwriting requirements are liberal, some lenders will lock based on submission of only an abbreviated lock request form. When underwriting requirements are restrictive, more lenders will require that the loan be approved before locking.

Lenders who make it difficult to lock will have lower fallout and may therefore offer better prices, but the locking delays that arise from their requirements impede effective shopping. Lenders who make it easy to lock have large fallout costs, but they allow borrowers to shop and lock in a short period.

The onset of the financial crisis in 2007 put a serious crimp in the operations of easy-locking lenders. *See* **Locking Following the Financial Crisis**, *which follows.*

Legalistic Ways of Controlling Lock Costs: A less savory way for lenders to control lock costs is to load the loan approval with conditions that allow the lender to back out. Every lock is conditioned on the borrower being approved for the loan, and approval is frequently subject to conditions. Most of these are completely reasonable, for example, the removal of a lien on the property. But some conditions are designed to allow the lender to exit the lock lawfully.

An interesting one was reported to me by a puzzled borrower. Her commitment letter stated that if the loan application, which the lender had approved, was rejected by the investor to whom the lender intended to sell the mortgage, the lender's lock was no longer valid. This borrower was alert, caught the condition, and asked me what I thought about it. I told her that it was the lender's responsibility, not hers, to determine whether she met the investor's requirements. The lender removed the condition.

Many lenders would rather protect themselves with contractual escape clauses than charge a nonrefundable fee because they know that most borrowers don't read contracts but fees drive them away. Other things being the same, smart borrowers should prefer lenders who charge a nonrefundable lock fee. Lenders who protect themselves from being gamed in stable- and declining-rate markets are more likely to honor their locks in a rising-rate market.

Lock Costs on Mortgage Brokers and Correspondent Lenders: Lock costs do not fall on mortgage brokers and correspondent lenders because they do not assume the risk of higher rates. It is the wholesale lenders to whom they deliver the loans who bear the risk, because they will own the mortgages that decline in value when market rates rise.

Nonetheless, the wholesalers expect that their brokers and correspondent lenders will effectively implement the wholesaler's policies designed to control lock costs, and they will cut off funding for any that fail. The key statistic the wholesaler uses for this purpose is "fallout": the percent of locked loans that are not delivered. If the fallout rate is too high, the loan provider will be cut off.

Choosing When to Lock: Borrowers developing a lock strategy should forget about trying to guess the direction of interest rates. Interest rates are not predictable.

The first thing borrowers should consider is their capacity to take the risk of a rise in market rates. If they barely qualify at today's rates and an increase would knock them out of the market or force them to accept other unfavorable terms, they should lock ASAP.

If they can withstand a rise in rates and are confident that the loan provider will offer the true market price when they finally lock, there is a benefit in delaying it. As noted above, the price is lower for shorter lock periods because the lender takes less risk with a shorter lock. This means that if market interest rates don't change, the lock price will fall as the lock period shortens.

Borrowers can only capture this benefit, however, if the market price quoted to them, when they finally do lock, is accurate. Borrowers will know that the price is accurate if they can access the price on the lender's Web site or are dealing with an "Upfront Mortgage Broker." (Upfront Mortgage Brokers give you the best price quoted by their wholesale lenders and will show you the price sheets.) They won't know, and should expect the worst, if the market price on the lock day is what the loan provider says it is over the telephone. In that event, "lock ASAP" remains the best advice.

This is particularly the case with home purchasers, who lose the ability to walk away from their loan provider as the closing date approaches. Borrowers who are refinancing can always change loan providers if they get a fast shuffle on the lock day.

Is the Borrower Committed Under a Lock? I have changed my position on this question. Originally my view was that borrowers were committed. Now my view is that borrowers can't be held to a commitment they don't make. If lenders lock at their own risk to get the borrower's business, lock jumping is just another cost of business.

The prevailing practice of brokers and lenders is to leave the borrower's commitment under a rate lock unstated. They want borrowers to consider themselves committed by rate locks. However, they fear that if they ask the borrower for a written acknowledgment of commitment, the borrower might be frightened into the arms of another loan provider who doesn't require it. This is the same reason that loan providers don't require a commitment fee that borrowers would lose if they jump the lock.

If the borrower's commitment under a rate lock is left ambiguous, then the borrower is entitled to interpret that ambiguity as he pleases. In other words, lock jumping is OK, unless the borrower acknowledges in writing that it is not OK.

Clarifying a Lender's Lock Policies: If a borrower is dealing directly with a lender, rather than through a broker (see below), it is a good idea to find out the lender's locking rules and procedures beforehand. This is not easy because very few volunteer the information; the borrower must ask. Here are the questions:

What Are the Requirements to Lock? In most cases, the lender will require that a purchaser have a contract of sale and that the loan application has been approved. Approvals take longer after the financial crisis than before, making the two questions that follow very relevant.

What Happens If the Market Price Rises Before Approval? Generally, the lender will be willing to lock only at the new higher price. This is a major source of frustration for borrowers, some of whom think they have been victimized by a "bait and switch." Actually, they have been victimized by price volatility and delays in getting loans approved, but because lenders seldom warn borrowers that this can happen, the borrower's misinterpretation is natural.

What Happens If the Market Price Falls Before Approval? A lender who locks at the current price when that price is higher than the one prevailing on the lock request date should do the same when the current price is lower. My surmise, however, is that in most cases, lenders lock at the higher price on the lock request date, just because they can. Borrowers are unlikely to object if they are locked at the price they requested. It is ironic that borrowers perceive themselves as victimized most often when prices rise after the lock request, whereas the reality is that they are victimized most often when prices decline.

What Are the Fees to Lock? Lenders usually charge from $300 to $600 to lock, often to cover the cost of credit check and appraisal. Borrowers lose these charges if they walk from the deal, but if they stay, most lenders will credit the charges to settlement costs at closing, Verify that that is their policy.

What Is Covered by the Lock? I once encountered a case where the lender locked the interest rate but not any fees, which is ridiculous. It is the equivalent of locking the price of a box of doughnuts but not the number of doughnuts in the box.

Locks *should* cover the rate, points, and all other lender fees. The prevailing practice, however, is to lock only the rate and points. This permits unscrupulous lenders to escalate fees as the loan moves toward closing. This type of skullduggery is especially common on purchase transactions that have a firm closing date. *See* **Settlement Costs/*Fees Paid to Lender/* Lender Fees Expressed in Dollars**.

Borrowers should insist on all lender fees being included in the lock. Lenders know what their fees are, and if they have no intention of practicing fee escalation, it costs them nothing to lock them all.

What Happens If the Market Price Drops After the Loan Is Locked but Before It Is Closed? If the borrower is committed to the lock (*see **Is the Borrower Committed Under a Lock?***), nothing happens, and the loan process continues to closing. If the borrower is not committed, she may decide it pays to opt out and begin anew with another loan provider.

Some lenders, recognizing that borrowers may cancel when rates drop, offer a "float-down." Where a lock freezes the rate and points, a float-down freezes them only in the event that market rates increase. If rates decrease, the rate under a float-down will also decline, though probably not by the full amount of the market decline.

Since a float-down carries more value to the borrower than a lock, and is more costly to the lender to provide, it carries a higher price. For example, a lender who charges 1 point to lock the interest rate for 45 days might charge 1.5 points for a 45-day float-down.

The exact terms of float-downs vary from lender to lender. Questions to ask include "When can I exercise," "How often can I exercise," "Is there any minimum price reduction for exercise," and" How is the current market price communicated to me?"

This last question is critical. If the market price is what the loan provider says it is over the telephone, the borrower is vulnerable to being scammed. To avoid being scammed, borrowers should ask the lender to agree to show the price sheet with the relevant price circled, at the borrower's request, anytime within the exercise period. A Web site that clearly identifies the price niche into which the deal falls is even better.

What Happens If the Lock Expires Before the Loan Closes? Lenders will say that if the delay is their fault, the lock period will be extended at no cost to the borrower, but if the delay is the borrower's fault, the borrower will be charged for a lock extension. Borrowers should be told what they are held responsible for and what the charges for an extension are.

It is reasonable for lenders to hold borrowers responsible for providing requested documentation promptly, for prompt accommodation of appraisal inspections, and for obtaining a subordination agreement from the second mortgage lender if there is one.

For some tips on how to prevent a lock expiration, *see* **Lock Expirations**.

What Happens If the Borrower Wants to Change the Mortgage? A lock applies to a particular mortgage program. If a borrower wants to change the program, most lenders will allow it only at the higher of the current price of the new mortgage and the price of that mortgage on the original lock date.

Using a Mortgage Broker: A mortgage broker can be enormously useful in helping a borrower navigate through the locking process. Unfortunately, brokers can play Dr. Jekyll or Mr. Hyde in the locking process. Among other things, Dr. Jekyll explains the lock process to the borrower, including the borrower's obligations, and passes through the lock statement as soon as it is received from the lender. Dr. Jekyll also uses his experience

Locking

and judgment to explain the cost and risk of a longer versus a shorter lock period, but leaves the final decision to the borrower. *See* **Mortgage Brokers/*How to Identify a Good Broker*.**

Mr. Hyde, in comparison, plays games designed to increase his fee. In contrast to Dr. Jekyll, who charges a set fee for his services and passes through the price from the lender, Mr. Hyde's fee is unstated and expansible. He has an incentive to select the shortest possible lock period because the price saving will go to him rather than the borrower. If the borrower loses the lock because the loan doesn't get closed in that period, Mr. Hyde will blame the lender, Realtor, appraiser, or title agency—anyone but himself.

The worst game played by Mr. Hyde is telling the borrower the loan is locked when it isn't. If rates go down, Mr. Hyde can get a better price than the one promised to the borrower and keep the difference himself. If rates go up, Mr. Hyde has an array of excuses for losing the lock, most of which involve blaming the lender. That's why borrowers should accept no excuses for not being provided with the lock statement from the lender. *See* **Mortgage Scams and Tricks/*Strictly Broker Scams*/Charging for a Lock Without Locking with the Lender.**

Locking Following the Financial Crisis: The financial crisis that erupted in 2007 increased the importance of rate locks to borrowers, at the same time making locks less dependable. The greater need for locks arose out of increased market volatility. Overnight mortgage rate changes of 0.25% were no longer unusual. Locks became less dependable because they took longer to execute and the market could change while the borrower was waiting.

When underwriting requirements are liberal and enforcement lax, lenders can lock based on preliminary information with little risk, and only occasionally will the borrower not be approved. When underwriting requirements tighten, as they did with a vengeance during the crisis, the risk of disapproval increases to the point where lenders feel the need to verify data on credit, property value, and income before issuing a lock. Appraisal delays associated with the **Home Valuation Code of Conduct (HVCC)** aggravated the problem. Longer periods needed for approval mean longer periods during which borrowers are exposed to the risk of a rate increase.

Ideally, delayed locks should be issued at the prices prevailing when the lock was requested, not the prices on the lock day. This would require that lenders archive their prices. It would also require that the borrower's commitment be strengthened; otherwise the fallout from a decline in market rates, and in lock costs to lenders, would be larger.

Lock Commitment Letter *A letter from a lender verifying that the price and other terms of a loan have been locked.*

Borrowers who lock through a mortgage broker should always demand to see the lock commitment letter.

Lock Expiration *What happens when a loan cannot be closed within the lock period.*

When locks expire, lenders typically will extend the lock period only if interest rates have not increased. If rates are higher, they will relock at the higher rate.

The only situation where a lender will extend a lock when interest rates have risen would be where the lender accepts responsibility for the delays that caused the lock expiration. This does not happen very often. Typically, there are too many people involved in the process for the lender to assume full responsibility. These include the borrower, mortgage broker, appraisers, escrow agents, and Realtors.

Deals that don't get done on time are more likely to be refinances than home purchases. Lenders generally give purchasers a priority. Delayed refinancings can be rescheduled, but not completing purchase mortgages on time can jeopardize the deals, at high cost to buyers. It could also jeopardize lenders' relationships with real estate brokers, upon whom many depend for borrower referrals.

Recourse: When interest rates spiked in July–August 2003, my mailbox was suddenly flooded with messages from frustrated borrowers whose locks had expired. In some cases borrowers held the broker responsible, in other cases the lender, but they all ended with the same question to me: "What is my recourse?"

In cases where the broker informed the borrower in writing that the loan was locked but did not lock with the lender, it would be relatively easy to prove the broker's culpability. (If the broker told the borrower the loan was locked but did not commit it to writing, it would be one recollection against another.)

Obtaining a court judgment and then collecting from a broker, however, is another matter. It might work against some substantial broker firms, but many brokers are individual operators who may be here today and gone tomorrow.

Lenders who allowed locks to expire by deliberately slowing down the process are more attractive targets for a lawsuit, but proving their culpability in any individual case is difficult. Lenders can claim that the borrower should have selected a longer lock period or that the borrower was slow in meeting the lender's reasonable requests for information. They can also claim that unforeseen circumstances for which they are not responsible slowed down the process. Hence, filing an individual suit against a lender is not likely to provide redress. The better approach is to focus on prevention.

Prevention: Here are some tips for minimizing the likelihood of a lock expiration:

- When you select the lock period at the beginning, ask how long the lender's current turnaround time is. Lenders usually report this to their loan officers and mortgage brokers every day. During a refinance boom, it makes sense to add 15 days more than you think you need.

- Be sure you know all the documents needed by the broker or lender, and assemble them so they can be produced when needed.

- Be available to answer questions or provide additional documents during the entire period the loan is in process, and respond to questions in a timely manner.

- Stay on top of the loan officer or mortgage broker, who should be the chief coordinator of all the players. In interviewing them at the outset, seek assurance that they have the time to handle your deal effectively.

Lock Failure *The inability of a lender to honor a mortgage price that the lender had guaranteed.*

Locks are a type of insurance sold to borrowers, similar in some respects to homeowners insurance. Both protect the borrower against an adverse event that could cause heavy loss if it occurred. The difference is that the adverse event that triggers homeowners insurance is usually isolated and random, whereas the adverse event that triggers lock insurance— a rise in interest rates—affects every locked loan in lenders' pipelines. A rise in interest rates can force a lender who is not adequately hedged into insolvency.

Most lenders protect themselves against a major hit to their profitability from rising rates. Either they lock the price with the lender to whom they will sell the loan, or they hedge by executing transactions that will increase their profits when rates increase. A lender who is fully hedged would not be affected by a rise in rates, but since hedging is costly, few lenders are fully hedged.

A long period of declining interest rates weakens the lock system. Hedging during such a period is money down the drain, so lenders are tempted to do less of it. And a few may actually adopt a "go-for-broke" policy where they don't hedge at all. They look to make as much money as they can during the low-rate period, and they go out of business when it ends, leaving failed locks behind. Indeed, a significant proportion of the failed locks in 2003 can be traced to one large lender who evidently pursued such a policy. When it closed its doors, hundreds of borrowers were left stranded.

Lock failures are rare, and there isn't a lot that borrowers can do to protect themselves. They can't monitor a lender's financials, and neither can a broker. What a borrower can do is select a lender with tough lock requirements. Lenders who turn away business in stable- or declining-rate markets by making it difficult for lock jumpers are demonstrating that they expect to be around for a long time. *See* **Lock Jumper**.

Lock Jumper *A borrower, usually refinancing rather than purchasing a home, who allows a lock to expire when interest rates decline after the lock in order to lock again at a lower rate.*

See **Mortgage Scams and Tricks/***Scams by Borrowers***/Lock Jumping**.

Lock Period *The number of days for which any lock or float-down commitment holds.*

The longer the lock period, the higher the price to the borrower.

Lowballing *The widespread practice by loan originators of quoting prices they have no intention of delivering.*

See **Mortgage Scams and Tricks/Other Scams by Loan Providers/ Lowballing**.

Mandatory Disclosure *The array of laws and regulations dictating the information that must be disclosed to mortgage borrowers, along with the method and timing of disclosure.*

Mandatory Disclosure as a Regulatory Option: Disclosure rules can be viewed as a relatively benign alternative to price controls and contract controls for protecting borrowers. Where price controls usually restrict the supply of loans and contract controls reduce borrower options, mandatory disclosures at worst increase lender costs, which are passed on to borrowers. At best, mandated disclosures help borrowers make better decisions.

Making Disclosure Rules Work: Perhaps the most important principle of effective disclosure, which has been grossly violated in the United States, is to limit mandated disclosures to the absorptive capacity of consumers. The greater the volume of disclosures, the less the likelihood that the borrower will find what is important. Disclosing everything is no more helpful to the borrower than disclosing nothing.

How much borrowers can absorb depends partly on how much time they have available and how much pressure they are under to move it along. If they can read documents at their leisure before the closing, their capacity is much greater than if everything is dumped on them at the closing, leaving the other participants tapping their fingers impatiently.

Disclosure Principles: Setting limits requires principles regarding what to disclose. Lenders need not be required to disclose provisions that benefit borrowers, so there is no need to mandate them. Lender arguments that disclosures should be "balanced" should be resisted. Mandated disclosures should be focused on provisions that are disadvantageous to borrowers, with special emphasis on potential future hazards that borrowers could easily overlook. Lenders can always balance mandated disclosures with their own.

In addition to "balance," lenders seek to avoid compliance ambiguity, and on this issue their expertise should be respected. The legal liability imposed on lenders by ambiguously framed disclosure requirements helps lawyers, not borrowers.

Accountability: Adherence to sound disclosure principles is extremely difficult if responsibility for it is divided, as it has been in the United States. The two most important mortgage disclosures, the Good Faith Estimate and Truth in Lending, have been the responsibility of HUD and the Federal Reserve Board for three decades, and as of 2009, there was still no way of reconciling the information on one with the information on the other. With two entities involved, neither is accountable for the sum total of disclosures, or for keeping disclosures up to date. That is why I favor the proposal advanced in 2009 to create a Consumer Protection Agency that would take over responsibility for all disclosures to consumers.

See **Truth in Lending** *and* **Good Faith Estimate**.

Also see **Adjustable-Rate Mortgage (ARM)/*Mandatory Disclosures***.

Manufactured Home *A home built entirely in a factory, transported to a site, and installed there.*

Manufactured homes are distinguished from "modular," "panelized," and "precut" homes. Manufactured houses usually are built without knowing where they will be sited, and they are subject to a federal building code administered by HUD. The other types of factory-built housing are not assembled until the site is identified, and they must comply with the local, state, or regional building codes that apply to that site.

Because of efficiencies in factory production, manufactured houses cost significantly less per square foot than housing constructed on-site. Manufactured housing is an important source of affordable housing, especially in the South and in rural areas.

There are major differences within the manufactured housing market, so much so that it makes sense to think of two different markets. A major difference is that one segment is shut out of the mainstream mortgage market and the other segment isn't.

The Deprived Market: Many purchasers of manufactured housing must find loans in a parallel market, which is much like the unsecured personal loan market. Lenders in this parallel market assume that loss rates on manufactured house loans will be high, as they are on personal loans, and they price them accordingly. They view manufactured houses as poor collateral that provides them with little protection.

Manufactured Home

One reason for this view is that manufactured houses can be moved. Before the HUD building code went into effect in 1976, manufactured houses were called "mobile homes," and this term is still widely used. Even though few ever leave their first site, they remain tarnished by the image of mobility.

Lender concern that the collateral can disappear is well grounded when the house sits on rented land, which is the case for about half of all manufactured houses. Most leases are short, and if the landowner decides that it is more profitable to use the land in some other way, the manufactured house owner must move it or leave it. Since the cost of moving is very high, and in many cases the property is worth little more than the debt, owners sometimes just walk away. The lender's collateral ends up in the trash heap.

In the deprived market, few owners of manufactured houses have built equity the way owners of site-built houses do. A major part of the appreciation in the value of site-built houses is due to rising land values. If you don't own the land, you don't realize this benefit. Furthermore, many purchasers of manufactured houses began with no or negative equity, putting nothing down and including settlement costs (and sometimes furniture and insurance) in the loan.

Manufactured houses in the deprived sector also seem to have more defects than site-built homes. Because they are geared to low-income purchasers, the materials used have often been inferior. Sometimes mishaps occur in moving houses from factory to site, and sometimes the installation is defective.

Getting defects in a manufactured house fixed can be a hassle because responsibility is divided and finger-pointing is common. The factory owner says the mover did it, the mover says the installer did it, and the installer says it happened at the factory.

The Healthy Market: In this part of the market, buyers of manufactured houses have them installed permanently on their own land, and they qualify for mainstream mortgage financing. It is even possible to qualify under a lease, provided the lease is long enough and affords adequate legal protections to the house owner and lender.

The quality of houses in this segment is good. Quality has been improving generally since Congress passed the Manufactured Housing Improvement Act (MHIA) in 2000. The act provided an improved system for keeping the HUD building code up to date, and it required states to improve the quality of installation and to set up dispute resolution programs.

In California, some developers have used manufactured housing in lieu of on-site construction, marketing and financing them in the same way. This avoids many of the problems referred to above that have tarnished the industry.

Guidelines: Here are some guidelines for avoiding the deprived market.

Do Not Buy a Home from a Dealer in a Package That Includes Installation, Site, and Financing: Tempting as it may be, one-stop shopping in this market is a surefire recipe for overpaying and not getting what you want. Take it one step at a time. It is easiest to compare the houses offered by different dealers if the price applies only to the house. Bundling muddies the waters.

Find the Site First: Before I did anything else, I would decide where I want my house and whether I wanted it on rented or owned land. If your credit is good and you have enough cash to buy your own plot, you will be eligible for mainstream mortgage financing. The savings in financing costs and in rent, if converted into a "present value," will probably be well in excess of the cost of the land.

If you rent because you can't find a plot or don't have the cash to buy one, but your credit is good, you may still be eligible for mainstream financing. This requires that you obtain a proper lease, which is one that has a term of at least five years and provides the other legal protections required by lenders.

Freddie Mac will buy mortgages on manufactured houses secured by leaseholds in some but not all states. Freddie's requirements are complicated, and you may need a lawyer to determine whether any particular lease is in compliance.

If you can't purchase a plot or obtain an eligible lease, you will be obliged to settle for personal loan-type financing, paying 2–3% more. Even so, you will want to pay careful attention to the lease terms, which can vary widely. If you accept a monthly term, or the landlord's right to approve a purchaser, you will be at the landlord's mercy. Before you sign, talk to residents of the park about their experience.

Get a Warranty on Installation: Installation of manufactured houses remains trouble-prone. The dealer may want to include installation in the price. That is one type of bundling that makes sense, provided the dealer assumes responsibility with a strong warranty. If the dealer includes installation in the price but will not provide an adequate warranty, either ask for a price without installation or walk.

If you buy the house without installation, you have to hire an installer yourself. This is no small matter, which is why so few buyers do it. The MHIA requires states to develop installation programs that include installation standards, training and licensing of installers, and inspections, but compliance has been spotty. Ask local owners for recommendations, ask installers for references, and make sure they are insured.

Arrange Your Own Financing: The dealer will try to package financing into the deal. He can get you approved fast and easily, which is an attractive lure. If you can qualify for mainstream financing, however, you will do better to find your own loan. If you don't qualify, it might not matter.

Margin *On an ARM, an amount that is added to the interest rate index to obtain the interest rate charged the borrower after the initial rate period ends.*

On prime loans, margins generally are in the 2–3% range; on subprime loans they were 4–6%.

See **Adjustable-Rate Mortgage (ARM)/***How the Interest Rate on an ARM Is Determined*.

Market Niche *A particular combination of loan, borrower, property, and transaction characteristics that lenders use in setting prices and underwriting requirements.*

See **Nichification**.

Maturity *The period until the last payment is due.*

The maturity is usually but not always the same as the period used to calculate the mortgage payment. *See* **Term**.

Maximum Combined Loan-to-Value Ratio (CLTV) *The maximum allowable ratio of combined first and second mortgage loans to property value on any loan program.*

Maximum Loan Amount *The largest loan size permitted on a particular loan program.*

For programs where the loan is targeted for sale to Fannie Mae or Freddie Mac, the maximum will be the largest loan eligible for purchase by these agencies. On FHA loans, the maximums are set by the Federal Housing Administration and vary by state and county. On other loans, maximums are set by lenders.

Maximum Loan-to-Value Ratio *The maximum allowable ratio of loan to value (LTV) on any loan program.*

These are set by FHA on FHA loans, by VA on VA loans, by Fannie Mae and Freddie Mac on loans they purchase, and by mortgage insurers or lenders on other conventional loans. Before the financial crisis, the ratios could range up to 100%, and in some cases they went above 100%. After the crisis, maximums were generally scaled down, and the conditions required to qualify for the higher ratios were tightened.

Maximum Lock Period *The longest period for which the lender will lock the rate and points on any program.*

Before the financial crisis, the longest lock period on most programs was 90 days; some went to 120 days and a few to 180 days. After the crisis, it was difficult to find a lock period exceeding 60 days.

It is extremely important that the lock period selected be long enough to cover your home purchase closing. On a refinance, the period must be long enough for the loan to be processed. This can vary widely, depending on the lender's workload. Discuss the time required with the broker or lender.

Minimum Down Payment *The minimum allowable ratio of down payment to sale price on any loan program.*

If the minimum is 10%, for example, it means that you must make a down payment of at least $10,000 on a $100,000 house or $20,000 on a $200,000 house.

The minimum down payment ratio is equal to 1 minus the maximum LTV. If the maximum LTV is 95%, for example, the minimum down payment is $1 - .95 = 0.05$, or 5%.

Monthly Debt Service *Monthly payments required on credit cards, installment loans, home equity loans, and other debts, but not including payments on the loan applied for.*

Monthly Housing Expense

Same as **Housing Expense**.

Monthly Total Expense

Same as **Total Expense**.

Mortgage *A written document evidencing the lien on a property taken by a lender as security for the repayment of a loan.*

The term "mortgage" or "mortgage loan" is used loosely to refer both to the lien and to the loan. In most cases, the lien and the loan are defined in two separate documents: a mortgage and a note.

Mortgage Auction Site

Same as **Lead-Generation Site**.

Mortgage-Backed Security (MBS) *A security on which the cash flows from a pool of mortgage collateral are passed through to the investor.*

The pass-through occurs with a delay of 30 to 45 days and includes scheduled payment of principal and interest, which is guaranteed, plus prepayments as received. MBSs issued by private firms in the United States are not liabilities of the issuer. MBSs issued by Danish mortgage banks are.

See **Secondary Mortgage Markets/*Types of MBS* and** **Danish Mortgage System/*Mortgage Banks*.**

Mortgage Bank

Same as **Mortgage Company**.

See **Mortgage Lender/*Mortgage Banks Versus Portfolio Lenders*.**

Mortgage Bond *A bond collateralized by a pool of mortgages which is a liability of the issuer.*

The cash flows on a mortgage bond may be those on the collateral pool which are passed through to the investor, as in Denmark. Or the cash flows on the bond may be set independently of the cash flow on the mortgage collateral, as was the case with mortgage bonds issued by savings and loan associations in the United States during the 1980s.

Mortgage Broker *An independent contractor who offers the loan products of multiple lenders, called wholesalers.*

Mortgage brokers do not lend. They counsel borrowers on any problems involved in qualifying for a loan, including credit problems. Brokers also help borrowers select the loan that best meets their needs and shop for the best deal among the lenders offering that type of loan. Brokers take applications from borrowers and lock the rate and other terms with lenders. They also provide borrowers with the many disclosures required by the federal and state governments.

In addition, brokers compile all the documents required for transactions, including the credit report, property appraisal, verification of employment and assets, and so on. Not until a file is complete is it handed off to the lender, who approves and funds the loan.

How Brokers Make Money: The lenders that mortgage brokers deal with quote a "wholesale" price to the broker, leaving it to the broker to add a markup in order to derive the "retail" price offered the consumer. For example, the wholesale price on a particular program might be 7% and zero points, to which the broker adds a markup of 1 point, resulting in an offer to the customer of 7% and 1 point. But if the broker adds a 2-point markup, the customer would pay 7% and 2 points.

Mortgage Broker

Note: In the United Kingdom, Canada, and some other countries, lenders quote retail prices to brokers and pay the broker fee. *See **Mortgage Brokers in the United Kingdom** below.*

What determines the markup? Most have a target, sometimes in points (say 1.5 to 2), sometimes in dollars (say $3,000), which they try to adjust to the anticipated workload. Some brokers set the markup in each case as high as they can get away with. An unsophisticated customer who shows no inclination to shop the competition will be charged more than a sophisticated customer who makes clear an intention to shop.

Indeed, mortgage brokers often rationalize the high markups they charge some customers on the grounds that these are needed to offset the excessively small markups they are forced to accept on other deals. Some borrowers do turn the tables on mortgage brokers by threatening to bail out of a deal after most of the work has been completed unless the mortgage broker agrees to cut the price.

How Much Brokers Make: A survey taken in 1998 of about 1,000 broker firms found that the average income per loan was $2,443, which was 2.02% of the average loan amount of $120,744. This is gross income—none of the brokers' expenses are deducted.

A study I did covering 774 loans brokered in December 2000 and January 2001 provides more detailed information on factors affecting mortgage broker income. The brokers covered are larger firms employing multiple loan officers, and they operate in relatively upscale markets. Their average income per loan was $3,191, which was 2.10% of the average loan of $152,031.

Brokers make more money on large loans than on small ones. For loans of $80,000 and less, the brokers averaged $1,600 per loan. For loans greater than $225,000, they averaged $5,453 per loan. Income per loan was higher on FHA loans than on conventional loans. For example, on loans between $80,000 and $110,000, brokers averaged $3,234 on FHAs and $2,093 on conventionals.

Advantages of Dealing with Brokers: Borrowers with special needs do better dealing with a broker. No one lender offers loans in every market niche. For example, many lenders won't offer loans to borrowers with poor credit, borrowers who can't document their income, borrowers who can't make any down payment, borrowers who want to purchase a condominium as an investment, borrowers with very high existing debts, borrowers who need to close within 72 hours, or borrowers who reside abroad.

The list goes on and on. But there are lenders in every one of these niches; and brokers, who deal with multiple lenders, can find them when needed.

After the financial crisis, this advantage of dealing with a broker became less pronounced because many of the niches disappeared. Important examples are loans to subprime borrowers and to borrowers unable to document their income. This was one factor underlying the decline in the market share of brokers after the crisis.

In addition, brokers are experts at shopping the market. Brokers are far better positioned than consumers to select the best deal available from competing lenders on the day the terms of the loan are locked. In addition, brokers keep lenders honest on lender fees specified in dollars, sometimes called "junk fees." Some retail lenders view these fees as an added source of revenue because borrowers often don't know what they are at the time they select the lender. But wholesale lenders don't play this game.

Lenders quote wholesale prices to brokers because of the work that brokers do for them that lenders would otherwise have to do themselves. While there are no published statistics on the wholesale-retail price difference, informed observers say that it averages about 1.5 points.

The price savings to the borrower thus consist of the wholesale-retail price spread plus the savings from better shopping. On the other side of the ledger is the broker's fee. If the price savings exceed the fee, the borrower pays less dealing with a broker.

Disadvantages of Dealing with Brokers: A lender will honor a mistake in the customer's favor made by one of its employees, but it won't honor a mistake made by a mortgage broker. In addition, some borrowers find comfort in dealing with a large lender with a recognizable name. Brokers are not known nationally, although they may be well known locally, especially by the real estate agents from whom they receive referrals.

It is not at all clear that an unsophisticated borrower is more likely to be taken advantage of by a broker than by a lender. Predators come from both groups. Lender predators may actually be more difficult to spot because they are subject to less rigorous disclosure rules than brokers. Nonetheless, there are some unscrupulous brokers, and it is very difficult for borrowers to distinguish them from the scrupulous ones.

How to Identify a Good Broker: Loan officers who are employed by a single lender operate very much like brokers except they provide the programs of only one lender. Much of what I say below applies as much to them as to brokers.

Mortgage Broker

Good Brokers Are Selected: Good brokers enjoy referrals from previous customers, Realtors, and others, including me, whereas poor brokers must constantly solicit. It is not the case that good brokers never solicit, but the odds are in the borrower's favor if the borrower does the selection. A good rule is not to respond to solicitations.

Good Brokers Are Financial Planners: Mortgages should fit properly into a household's overall financial situation and goals, which often involves challenging questions, such as "What is the best type of mortgage?" and "Should I pay points?" While brokers don't have to take a test measuring their skills as planners, some clues arise in their interactions with borrowers, and in particular on how they respond to questions.

A good sign is that before offering any opinions, the broker quizzes you about your financial status and plans. Another good sign is that the broker takes a little time to educate you in response to questions by indicating what the answer to your question depends on; e.g., whether you should pay points depends heavily on how long you expect to have the mortgage. An even better sign is that the broker indicates a specific analytical tool he will use to answer the question, such as a specific calculator or spreadsheet. A bad sign is that the broker assumes the answer before you have asked the question.

Good Brokers Find the Best Mortgage Rate and Points: You can't take this for granted because it can be tedious work. Brokers get their prices from wholesalers in the form of very complicated price sheets, all of which are formatted differently, making comparisons difficult. Further, while pricing the loan, the broker must also be mindful of getting the loan approved. A good sign is that before quoting a price, the broker first quizzes you about loan size, down payment, loan purpose, type of property, use of property, state, credit score, and documentation of income and assets. A bad sign is when the broker quotes a price without knowing these things; it indicates that he is **Lowballing**.

Good Brokers Minimize Fees Imposed on Borrowers: In dealing with the lender and third parties, good brokers represent the borrower. They will prevent any fee escalation by lenders and will seek out the best possible prices for third-party charges such as title insurance. A good sign is the broker's willingness to discuss and provide assurances on both topics.

Good Brokers Steer Borrowers Through Rate-Lock Minefields: Locking the rate with the lender can be a major challenge, especially in a volatile market. A good broker will protect the borrower against volatility; a bad one will try to exploit it for her own profit.

Mortgage Broker

A good sign is that the broker explains the locking process to the borrower, including the borrower's obligation, and advises the borrower on the pros and cons of locking for a longer as opposed to a shorter period, while allowing the borrower to make the final decision. A bad sign is that the broker does not discuss the length of the lock period required. A critically bad sign is that the broker fails to deliver the lock statement from the lender, which probably means the broker has not locked but is speculating for a larger payoff at the borrower's risk.

Good Brokers Are Masters of Detail: Mortgages have many details that must be attended to before a loan can close. Overlooking even one can delay the closing, which could be costly to the borrower. Good brokers avoid this danger using the same tool that is standard for airplane pilots about to take off, and increasingly standard in hospital intensive care units: a checklist. This is a low-tech device that has been shown to save lives, and it can also save a mortgage.

A good sign is a willingness of the broker to show you her checklist, but don't expect to keep it. Another good sign is the broker indicating how you will be kept informed of progress, either volunteering the information or in response to a question.

A Good Broker Operates Transparently: The broker who keeps you in the dark is the one most likely to sacrifice your interests for her payday. This is particularly true regarding the broker's own fee, which good brokers will spell out and commit to writing. Doing this is part and parcel of the broker acting as the borrower's agent.

The Broker as the Borrower's Agent: One strategy I recommend for finding a good broker is to select one who is willing to work as your agent. The prevailing practice is for brokers to operate as independent contractors.

A broker operating as an independent contractor adds a markup to the wholesale prices received from lenders, quoting a retail price to the borrower. The borrower doesn't know what the markup is. But if you retain a broker as your agent, you pay the broker a fee agreed upon in advance, which includes your payment and any compensation the broker receives from the lender. The broker passes through the wholesale prices, which are disclosed to you, without any markup.

Implementing this strategy requires finding a broker prepared to work as your agent for an agreed-upon fee. Upfront Mortgage Brokers, listed at www.upfrontmortgagebrokers.org, prefer to work in this way. But many other brokers would also be willing to if customers requested it.

Successful implementation requires that the broker's compensation from your transaction be stipulated at the outset, in writing, signed by the broker and by you. This avoids misunderstandings or surprises. The document should state:

The total compensation to [name of broker], including any rebates from the lender, will be _____. A separate processing fee will be _____.

See **Upfront Mortgage Broker**.

Mortgage Brokers in the United Kingdom: The pricing of broker services is much more transparent in the United Kingdom than in the United States. This greater transparency is closely related to differences in the way that lenders price mortgages.

The prices quoted by lenders in the United Kingdom are the retail prices available to borrowers through brokers. These prices are viewed as public information, and some lenders advertise them in various media and on their Web sites. An eligible borrower who seeks out such a price knows that he can obtain that price from any broker dealing with that lender. The broker's fee is paid for and set by the lender and is likely to be the same for all transactions of a given type.

As a result, brokers in the United Kingdom cannot engage in opportunistic pricing, charging what the traffic will bear, as many brokers do in the United States. While they perform the same functions, the average broker fee in the United Kingdom is less than half of what it is in the United States.

Impact of the Financial Crisis: The market share of mortgage brokers in the United States was much lower after the financial crisis than before. Underwriting requirements had tightened severely across the board, reducing the number of special market niches, access to which is part of a broker's stock in trade. (*See* ***Advantages of Dealing with Brokers***.) In addition, FHA loans had become much more important, and many brokers could not meet FHA requirements for loan originators. Further, under the new appraisal rules established by the ***Home Valuation Code of Conduct (HVCC)***, brokers could no longer order appraisals or contact appraisers.

Mortgage Company *A mortgage lender that sells all the loans it originates in the secondary market.*

See **Mortgage Lender/*Mortgage Banks Versus Portfolio Lenders***.

Mortgage Equations

Mortgage Equations *Equations used to derive common measures used in the mortgage market, such as monthly payment, balance, and APR.*

Fully Amortizing Payment: The following formula is used to calculate the fixed monthly payment (P) required to fully amortize a loan of L dollars over a term of n months at a monthly interest rate of c. (If the quoted rate is 6%, for example, c is 0.06/12, or 0.005.)

$$P = L[c(1 + c)^n]/[(1 + c)^n - 1]$$

Balance After a Specified Period: The next formula is used to calculate the remaining loan balance (B) of a fixed-payment loan after p months.

$$B = L[(1 + c)^n - (1 + c)^p]/[(1 + c)^n - 1]$$

Annual Percentage Rate (APR): The APR is what economists call an "internal rate of return" (IRR), or the discount rate that equates a future stream of dollars with the present value of that stream. In the case of a home mortgage, the formula is

$$L - F = P_1 + P_2/(1 + i)^2 + \ldots (P_n + B_n)/(1 + i)^n$$

where

i = IRR

L = Loan amount

F = Points and all other lender fees

P = Monthly payment

n = Month when the balance is paid in full

B_n = Balance in month n

This equation can be solved for i only through a series of successive approximations, which must be done by computer. Many calculators will also do it provided that all the values of P are the same.

The APR is a special case of the IRR, because it assumes that the loan runs to term. In the equation, this means that n is equal to the term and B_n is zero.

Note that on ARMs, the payments used to calculate the APR are those that would occur under the assumption that the index rate does not change over the life of the loan.

Future Values: Many of my calculators measure financial results in terms of "future values"—the borrower's net wealth at the end of a specified period. The future value of a single sum today is

$$FV_n = S(1 + c)^n$$

where

FV_n = Value of the single sum after n periods

S = Amount of the single sum now

c = Applicable interest rate

n = Length of the period

The future value of a series of payments of equal size, beginning after one period, is

[EQ]

$$FV_n = P[(1+c)^n - 1]/c$$

where P is the periodic payment and the other terms are as defined above.

Mortgage Grader *An online mortgage broker operation that offers fee transparency and the ability to price loans on the site, but that is cumbersome to use.*

Mortgage Insurance *Insurance protecting the lender against loss on a mortgage in the event of borrower default.*

In the United States, all FHA and VA mortgages are insured by the federal government. On other mortgages, the general practice is to require mortgage insurance from a private mortgage insurer when the loan amount exceeds 80% of property value. Borrowers usually pay the insurance premium, but in some cases lenders pay the premiums and charge borrowers for it in the rate. *See* **Private Mortgage Insurance**.

Mortgage Insurance Premium *The upfront and periodic charges that the borrower or lender pays for mortgage insurance.*

There are different mortgage insurance plans with differing combinations of monthly, annual, and up-front premiums.

Mortgage Leads

Mortgage Leads *Packets of information about consumers who might be in the market for a mortgage, compiled mainly by specialist firms that sell them to loan providers who solicit the consumers.*

Leads have value based on the likelihood of their becoming closed loans. If you were attracted by an ad such as "mortgage rates as low as 1%" and filled out a questionnaire about yourself in response, you are a lead.

The questionnaires ask about the things that matter to a lender in assessing a loan, including income, employment, credit, house price, and loan amount. They also ask for identifying information including telephone numbers and e-mail addresses. The more information, the more valuable the lead, but lead generators are fearful of asking for so much that the prospect gets discouraged and aborts the process.

Leads Before the Internet: Before the Internet, leads were usually generated by loan providers themselves, poring over public records to find borrowers who might want to refinance. The public records would show homeowners who had mortgages carrying interest rates above the current market. The pitch to the lead was basic and often persuasive. For example, "You have an 8% mortgage. I can get you one for 6.5%, which will save you $X a month."

When interest rates rose, this type of lead activity largely disappeared. While refinancing for the purpose of raising cash ("cash-out") continued, there was no easy way to identify in advance which borrowers might be interested.

Internet-Generated Leads: With the development of the Internet, the lead business changed dramatically. Most leads are now generated not by loan providers but by lead specialists who may know very little about mortgage lending. When they say, "We don't care how bad your credit is," they are telling the truth; they don't care because they are not the ones who will lend you money. Of course, the loan providers who buy their leads do care.

The leads business has become specialized because the skills required to harvest large numbers of leads at very low cost on the Internet have little to do with mortgage lending. The effective lead generators are skilled at developing marketing pitches, at the placement of ads in search engines, and at finding ways to slip their direct e-mail messages past the surveillance of spam filters.

Where leads in the era before the Internet only targeted borrowers who could refinance into a lower rate, Internet-based leads cover a wide range of possible consumer concerns. For example, consumers with lots of nonmortgage debt might be enticed with "Pay off high-interest credit cards" or "Consolidate into one lower payment." Consumers struggling to make their mortgage payments might succumb to "Payment options starting at 1%." Borrowers with adjustable-rate mortgages who are worried about rising future payments might be receptive to "Rates are rising. Lock in a fixed rate today." Consumers anxious about their credit may be mollified by "Credit not perfect? No problem" or "You have been approved up to 577K at 3.92%."

Whether the loan providers to whom the leads are sold will be able to deliver on these promises is largely irrelevant to the lead generators. The purpose of their message is to generate leads, period. I am reminded of the wonderful ditty by Tom Lehrer about the rocket scientist Wernher Von Braun: " 'Once the rockets go up, who cares where they come down. That's not my department,' says Wernher Von Braun."

Borrowers Responding to Solicitations Face Adverse Selection: Lead generators have no responsibility to borrowers and offer no warranties about the loan providers to whom they sell leads. Since the "bad guys" in the industry get few referrals from satisfied customers and business contacts, they are much more dependent on leads than the "good guys." And that means that consumers who become leads, and who respond to the loan providers who contact them, face adverse selection. In responding to a solicitation, their chance of getting a predator is greater than if they opened the yellow pages to "mortgages" and threw a dart at the listings.

Lead-generation Web sites, which do their own solicitations of borrowers, may provide them with some limited protections. *See* **Lead-Generation Site**.

How Leads Differ from Referrals: The major difference between a lead and a referral is that a lead generator does not recommend a loan provider, whereas a referrer does. Lead providers accept no responsibility to the borrower for the actions of the loan provider, whereas referrers may accept some responsibility.

The lack of responsibility of lead generators reflects the largely impersonal nature of this market. Lead generators typically sell to any loan providers willing to pay their price. Leads are often sold to more than one loan provider, and there may be an intermediary between the lead generators and the loan providers. If a loan turns out badly for the borrower, there are seldom any recriminations for the lead generator, which is remembered by the borrower, if at all, as a glitzy Web site with no face.

In contrast, a real estate agent who refers a borrower to a loan provider will typically have a relationship with the loan provider. If the loan sours, the borrower will know and likely blame the agent making the referral. As a result, the agent has a long-term business interest in the borrower having a favorable experience with the recommended loan provider.

A referral system has its weaknesses, but it does provide some protections to borrowers, where existing leads systems offer none. It is ironic, therefore, that under RESPA, payments for referrals are illegal but paying for leads is not. The legal definition of a referral, however, is not altogether clear.

Lead Fees and Referral Fees Under RESPA: My interpretation of the difference between a legal lead fee and an illegal referral fee, which I know is shared by many others, is that the first is a payment for information about a borrower, while the second is a payment for information about a borrower that results in a closed loan. When I expressed this view in an article, two lawyers familiar with RESPA wrote to tell me that I was wrong, though they did not agree between themselves.

One said that the key difference is whether or not the payment is made to a professional engaged in the real estate business. In this view, payments to professionals are illegal referral fees, no matter how they are made. On the other hand, "If you or I were to go into the business of selling names of potential borrowers to lenders, the payments for our services would not be a RESPA violation, even if made on the basis of closed loans."

The second lawyer said that the difference is whether or not the party receiving the payment has affirmatively influenced the selection of the loan provider. This says that if I sell information about a potential borrower to a predatory lender, so long as I don't tell the potential borrower anything about the lender, it is a legal lead. If I direct the potential borrower to a lender whom I recommend because of her integrity and good pricing, it is an illegal referral.

Neither definition provides a defensible rationale for leads being legal and referral fees illegal.

Mortgage Lender *The party advancing money to a borrower at the closing table in exchange for a note evidencing the borrower's debt and obligation to repay.*

Retail, Wholesale, and Correspondent Lenders: Lenders who perform all the loan origination functions themselves are called "retail lenders." Lenders who have certain functions performed for them by mortgage brokers or correspondents are called "wholesale lenders." Many large lenders have both retail and wholesale divisions. Wholesale lenders will have different departments to deal with correspondent lenders and mortgage brokers. The division of functions is shown in the table that follows.

Correspondent lenders are typically small and depend on wholesale lenders to protect them against **Pipeline Risk**. A correspondent lender locks with a wholesale lender at the same time that it locks a price for a borrower.

Mortgage Banks Versus Portfolio Lenders: Mortgage banks sell all the loans they make in the secondary market because they don't have the long-term funding sources necessary to hold mortgages permanently. They fund loans by borrowing from banks or by selling short-term notes, repaying when the loans are sold.

Mortgage banks dominate the U.S. market. In 2002, of the 10 largest lenders, 9 were mortgage banks and only 1 was a portfolio lender. In 2009, it was 10 of 10. However, all of the large mortgage banks are affiliated with large commercial banks.

Function	Retail Lender	Wholesale Lender	Correspondent Lender	Mortgage Broker
Find and counsel customers	X		X	X
Take application	X		X	X
Process loan	X		X	X
Lock loan terms	X	X	X	
Assume price risk	X	X		
Underwrite loan	X	X	X	
Close and fund loan	X	X	X	

Portfolio lenders include commercial banks, savings banks, savings and loan associations, and credit unions. They are sometimes referred to as "depository institutions" because they offer deposit accounts to the public. Deposits provide a relatively stable funding source that allows these institutions to hold loans permanently in their portfolios.

Mortgage banks often offer better terms on fixed-rate mortgages than portfolio lenders, while the reverse is more likely for adjustable-rate mortgages. It would be a mistake to place too much reliance on this rule, however, because the variability within each group is very wide.

Mortgage Marvel *A multilender Web site that is useful for borrowers shopping credit unions and community banks.*

The weakness of the site is that it does not provide enough information to make selections, forcing the borrower to go to the individual lender sites to compare prices.

Mortgage Modification *Revision of the loan contract to make it more manageable to a borrower who has or soon will have a problem making the payment.*

Modifications became a major policy issue during 2007–2009 when foreclosures rose to levels not seen since the depression of the 1930s. The modifications were seen as a method for keeping people in their homes, while reducing losses to investors relative to the alternative of foreclosure.

Definition: Modifications can be very modest or quite extensive. Adding delinquent interest to the loan balance and recalculating the payment over the remaining term—which results in a payment increase—is a "modification." Writing down the loan balance by 40% and reducing the payment by 40% is also a "modification." During the crisis period, there were many modifications of the first type, very few of the second. Public policy supported an in-between approach. *See* **The Government's Making Home Affordable Program**.

Bias Favoring Borrowers in Default: Under the voluntary modification programs adopted by loan servicers, priority was given to borrowers already in default. Servicers are contractually obliged to modify only if it is in the financial interest of the investors who own the mortgages or the securities issued against the mortgages. A modification is in the financial interest of the owner if the loss on it is smaller than the loss on a foreclosure. But if a loan is in good standing, the presumption is that it will remain in good standing, so no loss will be incurred.

Furthermore, the number of borrowers in trouble quickly outstripped the capacity of servicers to deal with them, forcing servicers to set priorities. A plausible way to set priorities was in terms of the degree of urgency of the problem. This placed borrowers who were current at the bottom of the list, if they were even placed on the list at all.

This tendency was reinforced by the fear of free riders. Many borrowers who didn't need them would apply for a modification if they could get one without hurting their credit. By only considering modifications for borrowers who are already delinquent, the servicer reduces the number of free riders.

The Issue of Borrower Savings: A major issue that arises with borrowers who can no longer make payments out of current income, but can make them for some period out of savings, is whether they should. I have advised borrowers with reduced income but good prospects of recovery to make the payment out of savings, avoiding a hit to their credit. If their prospects of recovery were poor, however, I suggested husbanding their savings, which would move them up on the servicer's priority list for a modification. While it also moves up the hit to their credit, that would happen anyway as soon as their savings were exhausted.

The Government's Making Home Affordable Program: Borrowers who needed a modification did best if they qualified for one under Making Home Affordable (MHA)—the federal government's assistance program. Borrowers did not have to be in default to qualify, and if they stayed current on the modified loan, they received $1,000 a year from the government in the form of balance reductions for up to five years. This program took a long time to get untracked because of servicer problems (see below), and it was still in ramp-up mode when this was written.

Assistance: Contracts of eligible borrowers are modified under MHA to reduce the expense ratio to 31%. This is done primarily through temporary interest rate reductions, following procedures detailed by the government.

In most cases, borrowers who apply for a modification and who are eligible under the MHA program will be modified under that program. Servicers have special financial incentives to place eligible borrowers in the program. The government compensates the servicer as well as the borrower.

Qualification Requirements: To qualify, borrowers must occupy the property as their primary residence, have a first mortgage of no more than $729,750 (the maximum is higher on two-, three-, and four-family houses), and have housing expenses that exceed 31% of gross before-tax income.

Housing expenses consist of the mortgage payment of principal and interest, property taxes, homeowners insurance, flood insurance, and association or condominium fees, but not mortgage insurance. The borrower must be able to document expenses and income and be willing to sign Treasury Form 4506, which authorizes the servicer to request a copy of the borrower's tax return. Eligibility is not affected by the property value or by a second mortgage.

The Liquid Asset Requirement: There is also a vague requirement that "borrowers must also represent and warrant that they do not have sufficient liquid assets to make their monthly mortgage payments." Exactly what constitutes a "liquid asset," or how much can be held without becoming ineligible, is not stated. On this thorny issue, the government punted to the loan servicers.

Modification Not a Remedy for Prolonged Unemployment: Modification was a remedy for borrowers who were faced with rising payments they could not meet or who had a partial reduction in income. But they still had to be able to meet the payment on a modified loan that was worth more to the investor than a foreclosed loan. In most cases, unemployment insurance would not provide sufficient income to justify a modification.

Borrower Frustration with Poor Response of Servicers: Many borrowers seeking modifications have been frustrated by the poor response of their servicer. Borrowers complain that it takes forever, and sometimes it is impossible to reach the counselor with whom they had their initial contact. They may have to begin again with someone else, who may not be able to find their file and who may tell them a different story than the previous counselor.

If the borrower has not submitted all the proper forms, each one filled out correctly, the file is likely to be put aside, which the borrower may not know about unless she inquires and is lucky enough to speak to someone who knows. Files put aside often get lost, which means that the borrower has to submit the entire file again, without necessarily knowing what was wrong with the previous submission.

Servicer Inefficiency: Servicers over the years focused their systems development on reducing the costs of dealing with borrowers who paid. Those with payment problems were few in number and could be handled by a relatively small staff. When the number of problem cases exploded, the servicers were overwhelmed.

Most responded by substantially expanding their counseling staffs, but the systems needed for the staffs to work effectively were lacking. One observer noted that most servicers have inadequate call routing for in-bound calls; have inadequate mail, fax, and image facilities; lack systems for tracking files; require excessive numbers of hand-offs in the decision process; and manage largely in a firefighting crisis mode.

Mortgage Payment *The payment of principal and interest made by the borrower, usually including an escrow payment for taxes and insurance and sometimes including a mortgage insurance premium.*

Mortgage Payment Insurance (MPI) *An alternative type of mortgage insurance under which the insurer, instead of reimbursing the lender for the net loss on a mortgage after foreclosure, would continue the monthly payments until the foreclosure process is completed, at which point it would repay the unpaid balance plus foreclosure costs.*

With my colleague Igor Roitburg, I developed a proposal for using MPI as a tool for dealing with the financial crisis and for strengthening the system against similar episodes in the future. See the relevant articles on my Web site under "Public Policy," and also see "Mortgage Payment Insurance and the Future of the Housing Finance System" in *Prudent Lending Restored*, edited by Yasuyuki Fuchita, Richard J. Herring, and Robert E. Litan (The Brookings Institution, 2009).

Mortgage Price *The interest rate or rates and upfront fees paid to the lender and mortgage broker.*

Some upfront charges are expressed as a percentage of the loan, and some are expressed in dollars. The price includes the total of each type.

On a fixed-rate mortgage (FRM), one interest rate is preset for the life of the loan. On an adjustable-rate mortgage (ARM), the rate is preset for an initial period, ranging from a month to 10 years, and then can change. For ARM shoppers who are uncertain about how long they will be in their house, the price includes ARM features that affect the ARM rate after the initial rate period ends. These include the "margin," "maximum rate," "rate adjustment period," and "rate adjustment caps."

The "margin" is the amount that is added to the index used by the ARM in determining the rate after the initial rate period ends. In a stable-interest-rate environment, the ARM rate will become the index plus margin, called the "fully indexed rate." Both the index and the margin are specified in the ARM contract.

The "maximum rate" is the highest rate permitted by the ARM contract. It tells shoppers how high the ARM rate can go in a rising rate environment.

The "rate adjustment period" and "rate adjustment caps" indicate how often the rate is changed and the maximum amount of any change. Hence, they indicate whether any rate increases at the end of the initial rate period will be abrupt or gradual.

Mortgage Price Quotes *Rates and points quoted by loan providers.*

You cannot safely assume that mortgage price quotes are always timely, niche adjusted, complete, or reliable.

Timeliness: Most mortgage lenders change their prices daily, generally in the morning after secondary markets open, and sometimes they will change them during the day as well. This is a major problem for shoppers using traditional distribution channels, since prices collected from lender 1 on Monday and from lender 2 on Tuesday will not be comparable if the market has changed in the meantime.

Prices advertised in newspapers are out of date when they are read. A newspaper that publishes price information in its Monday edition, for example, is reporting Friday's prices. On Monday when the paper hits the street, lenders have already posted new prices.

The Internet can ease the pain of shoppers trying to stay abreast of the market. On Monday morning when the newspapers are reporting Friday's prices, some Web sites are reporting Monday's prices. In addition, it is easy to compare prices of different lenders on the Internet, so having to repeat the process on successive days is not a burden.

Mortgage Price Quotes

Not all mortgage Web sites provide current data, however. Some of the prices posted on the Internet are even more out of date than those in the newspapers. Almost always, however, the date of the quote is given, so you can ignore those that are not current. If the date is not given, you can assume the quote is not current.

Niche-Adjusted: Most mortgage price quotes are based on the most favorable assumptions possible about your niche. For a list of such assumptions, *see* **Nichification/*Generic Price Quotes***. If your deal does not correspond to these assumptions, the price you ultimately receive will be higher.

Niche-adjusted prices are available from a loan officer by volunteering the information needed to determine the correct price. Usually, the loan officer will ask you to fill out an application in the process, which makes it difficult to shop. The easier way to shop niche-adjusted prices is at Web sites that offer a "customized" price. To receive it, you must first fill out a form that provides the required information about your deal, but you don't have to apply. Multiple Web sites can be shopped in one sitting. **Upfront Mortgage Lenders** allow you to shop anonymously, but most others don't.

Completeness: Most price quotes consist of rate and points only. They omit fixed-dollar fees, and on ARMs they also omit features that affect the ARM rate after the initial rate period ends. *See* **Mortgage Price**.

Complete price quotes are available on sites of **Upfront Mortgage Lenders**.

Reliability: A reliable price quote is one that, assuming the market does not change, the loan provider intends to honor when you lock.

Some loan providers offer lowball quotes they have no intention of honoring. The objective is to rope you in. They figure that once you are in the application process, they have a good chance of landing you as a borrower.

If you are purchasing a house, the cost of terminating the process with one loan provider and starting again with another becomes increasingly high as you move toward the home closing date. Your bargaining power recedes with the passage of time.

I know a mortgage broker who aims to make at least a 1.5-point markup on all loans but includes only a 0.5 point markup on prices he quotes over the telephone. When he lands a customer, he finds a way to recover the point (or more) before the loan terms are locked.

For example, suppose market interest rates rise after the initial quote, with the original wholesale quote of 8.25% and 1 point now having risen to 8.25% and 1.5 points. The broker tells you, "Sorry, the market has gone against us. The loan you want is now at 8.25% and 3 points." The broker makes an extra point by pretending that the increase in market rates was larger than it was.

Conversely, if the wholesale quote falls to 8.25% and zero points, the broker can make her 1.5-point markup by providing you with the terms originally quoted. The broker merely ignores the decline in market rates.

How do these brokers get away with it? Loan providers legally can't be held to a price quote. Since the market is volatile, yesterday's price may not apply today. All loan providers warn borrowers that price quotes aren't firm until they are locked.

You can attempt to forestall this trickery by monitoring changes in the market after you get a price quote, but probably you won't get far. The broker will point out that your market information is general and does not accurately describe the specific segment of the market relevant to your loan. Only the broker has that information. You will probably lose this argument because you're fighting on the broker's turf, and you have a closing date on the near horizon.

It would be a different story if the broker agreed initially to share her market information with you. If the broker in my example revealed the wholesale lenders' price quotes, you would know exactly how the market relevant to you had changed. But then the broker would not be able to modify her lowball markup, which is why most brokers keep wholesale prices to themselves.

On the Internet, you are less vulnerable to lowball offers that disappear under the cloud of "market change adjustments." Loan providers who quote prices on the Internet can't tell you market rates rose by 1/2% between the day you applied and the day you locked unless they did, because their rates are posted for you and others to see on both days. An attractive alternative is to hire an Upfront Mortgage Broker to shop prices for you. (*See* **Upfront Mortgage Broker**.)

Mortgage Program *A bundle of mortgage characteristics that lenders view as relevant to pricing so that each program is separately priced.*

The characteristics used include whether it is an FRM, ARM, or balloon; the term; the initial rate period or the index on an ARM; whether it is

FHA insured or VA guaranteed; and if it is not FHA or VA, whether it is "conforming" (eligible for purchase by Fannie Mae or Freddie Mac) or "nonconforming."

Mortgage Referrals *Advice on where to go to get a mortgage.*

A borrower can always select a loan provider by throwing a dart at the yellow pages. A referral is of value if it raises the probability of a good outcome above that from throwing the dart. The four major sources of referrals are real estate sales agents, other borrowers, Internet referral sites, and builders.

Real Estate Sales Agents: Home purchasers accept more referrals from real estate sales agents than from all other sources combined. Sales agent referrals generally are to individual loan officers or brokers, as opposed to firms. An agent with great confidence in a loan officer will continue to refer clients even when the loan officer switches firms.

Sales agents have the same interest as buyers in completing trans-actions. Hence, they refer clients to loan providers who can generally be depended upon to close on time. This is the agent's major concern, and it is a concern of borrowers as well.

Sales agents have no comparable interest in the mortgage price or whether the borrower is placed in the right kind of mortgage. However, the agent doesn't want the price to be so far out of line or the service provided so abysmal that the borrower throws a fit and blames the agent. Hence, referrals from sales agents are significantly better than throwing a dart at the yellow pages.

Other Borrowers: Referrals from other borrowers are usually based on a single transaction. They are better than the yellow pages, but not much better. I have seen borrowers who were very pleased with their experience because they were not aware that they had seriously overpaid. I have also seen the reverse—borrowers who bad-mouthed their loan provider, who had done the best possible job under adverse circumstances, and who had earned very little on the deal. Before acting on a borrower referral, grill the borrower about the basis for her opinion.

Internet Referral Sites: These Web sites provide price information for a large number of lenders and mortgage brokers, usually listed by state. They also provide quick entree to the Web sites of each loan provider listed. In theory, a borrower can sort through the list of loan providers, identify those with the lowest prices, and visit the individual Web sites to make a final selection. In practice, I found that referral sites were no better than the yellow pages, and low-priced quotes are not to be trusted. *See* **Referral Site**.

Builder Referrals: Builder referrals are usually to a lender with whom the builder has a financial arrangement. Hence, they are suspect. In some cases, preferred lenders price loans above the market and kick back some of the excess to the builder. This makes builder referrals inferior to the yellow pages.

But builders can trap you into using their preferred lender. They do this by offering a price concession conditional on your using the preferred lender. The builder pads the house price, then offers back part of what has been taken from you. If you don't accept it, you lose even more. *See* **Mortgage Scams and Tricks/*Scams by Home Sellers*/Builder Concessions**.

Self-Referrals: Responding to self-referrals (solicitations) usually is a bad idea. Not all lenders who solicit are predators, but all predators solicit. Your chances of avoiding one are better if you throw a dart at the yellow pages.

Referrals Versus Leads: It is illegal to charge for a referral, but not for a mortgage lead. *See* **Mortgage Leads**.

Mortgage Scams and Tricks *Deceptive practices used by mortgage loan providers and other participants in the mortgage process.*

Locking Scams: Because locking the price of a mortgage is a critical step, it is not surprising that many scams arise in connection with locking.

Exploiting Approval Delay: Jones requests a lock on Monday, the loan provider won't lock until the loan is approved, which happens on Wednesday, but on Tuesday the price changes. If the price is lower, the loan provider locks at Monday's price. If the price is higher, the loan provider asks Jones if he wants to lock at the higher price. This became a widespread practice in the aftermath of the financial crisis because the time required to gain approval increased substantially.

A borrower can protect herself against this "tails I win, heads you lose" proposition by delaying the lock request until the lender is prepared to provide an immediate lock. This leaves the borrower exposed to the rate increase, but that is unavoidable, and by delaying, the borrower gets to take advantage of a price decrease.

Float Abuse: Doe believes interest rates will drop and, after being approved, decides to let the price "float" until three days before closing, when locking is mandatory. At that point, the lender should lock at the price that would be quoted to the applicant's identical twin if the twin walked through the door on the lock date as a new customer shopping the exact same deal. In practice, the quote may be higher because the applicant is at least partially committed while the twin is only shopping.

The obvious way to avoid this scam is to lock ASAP. The borrower determined to float can avoid being scammed by dealing with a lender whose Web site allows the borrower to price his loan on the site every day. The best are the **Upfront Mortgage Lenders**.

Lock Only Part of the Price: It is common practice to lock the interest rate and points, which leaves other lender fees out of the equation. This paves the way for **Fee Escalation**.

On ARMs, the lock can omit the margin, maximum rate, or adjustment caps, which should be part of the ARM program definition. However, sometimes the program definitions change.

Borrowers should insist that the lock include the total of all lender fees. On an ARM lock, borrowers should insist that all the relevant ARM features be in the lock or that they have a written description of the ARM that includes these features.

Deliberately Allow Locks to Expire in a Rising Market: When interest rates spiked in July–August 2003, my mailbox was flooded with complaints from borrowers who lost their locks. Their lenders could not get the loans processed in time. In as many as half of these cases, the borrower was at least partially at fault for not selecting a long enough lock period or for not providing needed documents on a timely basis. But in many other cases, it seems clear that the lender deliberately slowed the process so the lock would expire. I draw this inference from the flimsy excuses they provided the borrowers, who relayed them to me.

Also see ***Strictly Broker Scams*/Charging for a Lock Without Locking with the Lender**.

Other Scams by Loan Providers: Lenders and mortgage brokers may employ a number of tricks to increase their income from originating a loan, at the borrower's expense.

Lowballing: To draw customers, some loan providers will advertise lowball prices that they have no intention of honoring. Lowballing is endemic on referral Web sites that list lenders by name and price, because it is the only way to stand out against the competition.

Lowballers who succeed in roping in the client have numerous plausible explanations for why they can't deliver the promised price: the two standard ones are that the market price has increased since the lowball offer and that the borrower's qualifications are deficient in any of a dozen ways that disqualify the borrower for the best price. *See* **Mortgage Price Quotes/*Reliability*.**

Loan providers who advertise mortgage prices are not lowballers if they are prepared to lend to qualified applicants at those prices. However, borrowers should recognize that advertised prices are for A-grade deals for which only a minority of borrowers may qualify. Further, advertised prices in the written media are obsolete by the time they are read.

Borrowers might avoid lowballing if they give the loan providers from whom they are soliciting price quotes the information that is needed to determine the price. *See* **Qualification Requirements** *and* **Credit Score.** Borrowers who request a quick price over the telephone or by e-mail are inviting a lowball quote.

Pocket the Borrower's Rebate: Some unwary borrowers are steered into high-rate loans on which they should receive a rebate from the lender but don't. For example, the loan officer's price sheet shows 6% at zero points, 5.75% at 2 points, and 6.25% at a 2-point rebate. If the borrower is willing to pay 6.25% without argument, the rebate is retained by the loan provider. *See* **Overage**.

As with many scams, the best protection is having alternatives, though in this market that is not always feasible. Another approach is to be aggressively curious about the source of a price quote. Ask to see the schedule of rates and points on the fax price sheet or computer screen. If the loan provider insists on transcribing them to a separate piece of paper, ask point-blank if the price includes an overage.

Offer No-Cost Loans That Aren't: Some loan providers tout deals as "no cost" when the settlement costs are added to the loan balance. These deals should be referred to as "no cash." This is a scam if the borrower doesn't understand that he or she is borrowing more to pay the settlement costs. *See* **No-Cost Mortgage.**

Surreptitiously Change the Contract: Borrowers who accept whatever they are told may find that the note includes a provision favorable to the lender, about which the borrower has no knowledge. A favorite is a prepayment penalty, which increases the value of a loan by 1% or more. A loan provider who includes it in the contract without your knowledge can put the point in her pocket—rather than in yours, where it belongs. *See* **Prepayment Penalty/*Surreptitious Penalties*.**

Strictly Lender Scams.

Overpriced Simple Interest Biweekly: The biweekly mortgage meets the needs of some borrowers, either to help them budget or as a forced-saving device to pay off the loan early. (*See* **Biweekly Mortgage**.) Some lenders, however, promote the simple interest biweekly as a way of substantially accelerating the rate of payoff, compared with a standard biweekly. They offer to refinance borrowers into their simple interest biweekly at rates well above those the borrower is paying.

On a standard biweekly, an extra monthly payment is credited to the borrower's account after 12 months. On a simple interest biweekly, a half payment is credited to the borrower's account every two weeks. This does result in an earlier payoff and reduced total interest outlays. The advantage over a standard biweekly, however, is very small.

For example, on a 6% 30-year loan with biweekly payments, a borrower would be justified in paying only 6.063% for the monthly payment equivalent. This is the rate that would equalize the payoff date and total interest outlays. It is a far cry from the 8 or 9% that might be charged. Readers can make the same comparisons using the biweekly spreadsheets on my Web site. *See* **Biweekly Mortgage/*Simple Interest Biweeklies*.**

Deceive Borrowers Regarding ARMs: Because ARMs are complicated, the loan officers selling them tend to focus on one or two major features. In doing this, they sometimes cross the line between acceptable "puffery" and unacceptable deception. Expecting lenders to police the sales practices of loan officers is unrealistic. Indeed, some lenders provide their loan officers with tools that aid and abet deceptive practices.

For example, mortgage applicants have sent me exhibits prepared for them showing schedules of interest rates, monthly payments, and balances on obviously favorable assumptions regarding future interest rates. But the assumptions are not indicated. In one case, the footnote to the table says, "Actual results may vary . . . Consult your regulation Z."

At a minimum, ARM borrowers should have amortization schedules based on the assumption that (a) the index rate does not change and (b) the ARM rate increases by the maximum amount permitted by the note. These are "no-change" and "worst-case" scenarios. Borrowers can develop these schedules (and many others) themselves using calculator 7b or 7c on my Web site.

Pad the GFE: The Good Faith Estimate of settlement, or GFE, shows the borrower all the settlement costs connected to the loan. Until January 1, 2010, when a new GFE became effective, lenders were not bound to the numbers shown there, including their own charges. Further, there were no penalties for discovering new charges or increasing existing ones at the eleventh hour—which is exactly what some lenders did.

However, the new GFE makes fee padding difficult if not impossible. *See* **Settlement Costs/*Good Faith Estimate***.

Servicing Scams: My mailbox is stuffed with letters from borrowers complaining about their servicing. It is difficult, however, to distinguish poor service from scams. The basic problem is that servicing provides lenders with many opportunities to profit from their own mistakes.

For example, sometimes lenders don't pay taxes on time, but is it deliberate? Some lenders purchase hazard insurance on the borrower's house and add the premium to the loan balance, even though the borrower already has insurance. Were they really unaware that the borrower was already insured? Occasionally a lender won't credit borrowers for extra payments, for one reason or another.

If you believe you have been mistreated, you can't fire your servicer, but you can file a written complaint with the lender, addressed to Customer Service. Do not include it with your mortgage payment, which you should continue to make separately. State the following:

Your loan number.

Names on loan documents.

Property and mailing address.

This is a "qualified written request" under Section 6 of the Real Estate Settlement Procedures Act (RESPA).

I am writing because:

[Describe the problem and the action you believe the lender should take.]

[Describe any previous attempts to resolve the issue, including conversations with customer service.]

[If it is relevant to the dispute, request a copy of your payment history.]

[List a daytime telephone number.]

I understand that under Section 6 of RESPA you are required to acknowledge my request within 20 business days and must try to resolve the issue within 60 business days.

If this doesn't do the trick, you can file a complaint with HUD. You can also sue. According to HUD, "A borrower may bring a private lawsuit, or a group of borrowers may bring a class action suit, within three years, against a servicer who fails to comply with Section 6's provisions."

You can also file a complaint with the government agency that regulates the servicing agent. Here are Web sites you can use to contact these agencies:

- For national banks, www.occ.treas.gov/customer.htm.
- For federally chartered savings and loan associations, www.ots.treas .gov/contact.html.
- For state-chartered banks and savings and loans, www.lending professional.com/licensing.html.
- For mortgage banking firms, www.aarmr.org/lists/members-IE .html.

If you don't know the proper agency, you can send the complaint to the Consumer Protection Division of the state attorney general. The attorney general's office will forward it to the relevant state or federal agency.

All borrowers should periodically check their transaction history to make certain that (a) payments are always applied to the balance at the end of the preceding month, (b) tax and insurance payments from escrow are correct and there have been no double payments, (c) rate adjustments on ARMs are in accordance with the method stipulated in the note, and (d) there isn't anything in the history that looks "funny."

Any borrower who does not receive a complete transaction statement at least annually should periodically submit a "qualified written request" for one, using the form described above.

Borrowers should retain all servicing statements until the loan has been paid off and the lien has been removed from their property. If the servicing is sold by predator A to predator B and the complete file is not transferred to B, which has happened, a claim by the borrower covering the period the loan was serviced by A will require documentation from the borrower.

Strictly Broker Scams: Some scams are initiated only by mortgage brokers. The first one described below is directed against the borrower, the second against the lender.

Mortgage Scams and Tricks

Charging for a Lock Without Locking with the Lender: Locking the mortgage rate assures borrowers that the interest rate and points they have agreed to pay will be honored at closing, even if market rates rise in the meantime. Some mortgage brokers tell their clients that the interest rate has been locked with the lender when that is not the case. They substitute their lock for the lender's without informing the borrower.

Brokers do this to increase their markup. For example, a lender might quote 6% plus 0.5 point for a 10-day lock and 6% plus 1 point for the 60-day lock an applicant requires. The lying broker tells the applicant she is locked for 60 days at 6% plus 1 point. If the market doesn't change, the broker locks 10 days from closing at 0.5 point and pockets the other 0.5%.

Brokers rationalize this lie by saying that they are assuming the lock risk themselves and will deliver the "locked" rate and points to the borrower even if they have to take a loss. In a stable- or declining-rate market, they can get away with this, perhaps for years at a time.

But sooner or later interest rates will suddenly spike, and brokers locking at their own risk will not be able to deliver. For example, in the two-month period January–March 1980, mortgage rates jumped from 12.88% to 15.28%. A broker who locked for 60 days at 12.88% would have to pay a lender about 15 points to accept a loan with that rate in a 15.28% market. The broker would either go out of business or deny that a lock was given. (Broker locks are oral commitments.) The borrower would be left high and dry in either case.

Indeed, many nonlocking brokers deserted their customers following the much smaller rate increase that occurred in July–August 2003. Unlike lenders who can always come up with an excuse, a nonlocking broker who is challenged by a borrower cannot produce a lock commitment from a lender. About all the broker can do is apologize or run.

Broker locks are a deceitful practice because the borrower is led to believe that the lender is providing the lock. To protect himself, a borrower locking through a broker should insist on receiving the rate lock commitment letter from the lender identifying the borrower as the applicant. The borrower must demand this at the time of the lock, not after the lock fails.

Successive Refinancings Using Rebate Loans: This scam is directed toward wholesale lenders and requires the cooperation of venal borrowers who participate in it. The larger the loan, the more profitable the scam.

Lenders pay rebates on high-rate loans. For example, a lender who offers a 30-year FRM at 5.875% and zero points might pay a rebate of

4 points for a 7.5% loan. Lenders know that 7.5% loans have relatively short lives because borrowers refinance them as soon as they can. Nonetheless, the lender will recover the 4 points through the above-market rate in 30 months, and most such loans last longer than that. Or rather, they last longer unless there is a scam to pay off in 3 months.

On a loan of $350,000, the lender pays a rebate of 4% of $350,000, or $14,000. Over 3 months, the lender collects only about $1,400 in excess interest. The broker pays the borrower's closing costs of about $4,000 and $1,400 to cover the higher interest payment on the 7.5% loan for 3 months. The balance of $8,600 is split between them, with the broker keeping most of it. After 3 months, they do it again, but with a different lender in order to avoid disclosure.

I classify this as a broker scam because the broker initiates and executes it, but the broker requires a corrupt borrower as an accomplice.

Scams by Borrowers: Because borrowers are in the market only intermittently, they have less incentive and fewer opportunities than loan providers to develop and refine scams. Not surprisingly, those they come up with often don't work or even backfire on them.

"End Run" Around the Broker: Some borrowers believe they can beat the system by using a broker to find the right lender, then going directly to that lender. They think they can cut out the markup in this way. This is a sleazy practice because the broker won't be compensated for her time and for the use of her knowledge and expertise on the borrower's behalf. It is why even the most scrupulous brokers keep the identity of the lender concealed until an application has been submitted.

Nor does it work the way the borrower expects it to. Lenders who lend both directly to borrowers and indirectly through brokers have separate retail and wholesale departments. The borrower who dumps the broker to go directly to the lender will be directed to the retail department and be offered retail prices, which are higher. They could be higher than the price the borrower would have paid going through the broker.

Net Jumping: Net jumping involves using a broker's time and expertise to become informed and creditworthy, then jumping to the Internet to get the loan. Here's a broker's story.

When Jones came to me six months ago, his credit score wouldn't have qualified him to purchase a doghouse. But I worked with him while he disputed his credit report with the bureaus, and negotiated with collection agencies. His credit score went from D to A. While he was working with me, he learned his responsibilities as a future homeowner . . . Then he informed me that he was going to shop for a loan on the Internet.

Brokers could protect themselves against net jumping by charging a nonrefundable fee. Few do this, however, for fear it would place them at a competitive disadvantage.

Multiple Apping: Another borrower trick is to submit multiple applications through different brokers—two, three, or even more. All the brokers check credit, shop loan programs, and fill out the application, but only the one offering the best deal on the lock date will be compensated. The others waste their time.

Borrowers who submit multiple applications also waste their own time, but the practice is evidence of how difficult it is to shop traditional mortgage channels. Borrowers typically can't obtain a complete list of loan fees and charges until they submit an application, which encourages "shopping by application."

But multiple apping can boomerang. If the application runs into a major roadblock, a resentful broker may have little motivation to go the extra mile that may be needed to remove it.

Lock Jumping: Under a loan lock agreement, the lender and the borrower should be committed to the interest rate and other specified terms. Some borrowers, however, act as though the agreement only binds the lender. If interest rates rise prior to closing, the lender is committed to the rate specified in the agreement. But if rates decline, the borrower feels free to go to another broker and relock at a lower rate.

Borrowers who want both the benefit of a rate decline and protection against a rate increase should purchase a "float-down." It allows the rate to remain locked if market rates rise; but if market rates decline, the borrower can relock at a lower rate. A float-down costs a little more than a straight lock.

Unfortunately, in many cases borrowers are never put on notice that the lock commits them as well as the lender. Many brokers fear that if they mention the "C" word, they will lose the client. This makes lock jumping morally ambiguous.

Lock jumping is much more common among refinancers, who are more flexible on when they close than purchasers, who must close on a specified date. This means that lenders could largely eliminate lock jumping if they offered only float-downs to refinancers.

Mortgage Scams and Tricks

The Double House Purchase: A buyer who wants to buy two houses, but can qualify for a mortgage on only one, arranges to have them close on the same day. That way, the debt from one is not counted in the expense-to-income ratio of the other.

However, the application for whichever loan closed second would contain false information because it would not reveal the loan that closed first. This could be caught in a post-closing audit of either loan. It would also be caught if both loans ended up being serviced by the same entity. Since servicing is becoming increasingly concentrated in the hands of a few large players, the chances of that happening are not insignificant.

Scams by Home Sellers: Scams by home sellers are directed against lenders or borrowers.

Fictitious Down Payments: Down payment assistance programs are widespread and often involve gifts by home sellers offset by a price increase equal to the gift. The practice is legitimate, provided it is done openly and conforms to the guidelines of lenders and mortgage insurers. *See* **Down Payment/*Home Seller Contributions***.

Down payment assistance becomes a scam when it is done without the knowledge or permission of the lender. For example, buyer and seller agree on a price of $289,000, but the buyer cannot meet the down payment requirement of $15,000. So they agree to raise the price to $304,000 and for the seller to lend the borrower the $15,000 needed for the down payment. After the closing, the loan is forgiven. This is a scam because the lender is tricked into believing that the borrower has made a down payment when that is not the case.

For this scam to work, the appraisal of the property must come in at $304,000. The appraiser either is hoodwinked by the fictitious sale price or is a party to the scam.

The buyer is a party to the scam as well. For the loan to close, the buyer is obliged to lie about the source of the funds used for the down payment.

Assuming the deception is not caught and the loan goes through, it might be caught in a post-closing audit, in which event the lender could elect to call the loan. All mortgage loans contain an "acceleration clause," which allows the lender to demand immediate repayment if any information provided by the borrower turns out to be false.

Builder Concessions: Many builders have a financial interest in a lender to which they refer business. While the law prohibits builders from requiring buyers to use their preferred lenders, the builders can offer financial concessions contingent on using those lenders.

Since the builder will include the concession in the price of the house, buyers who agree to the price are going to find it difficult not to deal with the preferred lender. The lender can charge an above-market rate or points, but with the concession buyers are still better off than if they financed elsewhere.

Suppose, for example, the builder pads the sale price by $5,000 but offers a concession of $5,000 for using the preferred lender. If the lender prices the loan $3,000 above the market, the buyer using that lender is still ahead by $2,000.

The only way a buyer can avoid this trap is to refuse deals that tie concessions to use of a preferred lender. Offer the builder the asking price less the concession.

"Wrapping" a Mortgage: Home sellers sometimes have compelling reasons to avoid repaying their mortgage when they sell their house. The interest rate might be well below the current market rate. Or they might have a willing buyer who is unable to qualify for a new mortgage.

To keep the old mortgage going, the seller makes a mortgage loan to the buyer while continuing to make the payments on the old loan. For example, S, who has a $70,000 mortgage on her home, sells her home to B for $100,000. B pays $5,000 down and borrows $95,000 from S on a new mortgage. This mortgage "wraps around" the existing $70,000 mortgage because the lender-seller will make the payments on the old mortgage.

Wraparounds, like down payment gifts, are OK if the lender knows about them and agrees. They are a scam when used to circumvent restrictions on assuming old loans. The home seller who does this violates her contract with the lender and may or may not get away with it. In some states, escrow companies are required by law to inform a lender whose loan is being wrapped. If a wraparound deal on a nonassumable loan does close and the lender discovers it afterward, watch out! The lender will either call the loan or demand an immediate increase in interest rate and probably a healthy assumption fee.

Modification Scams: These are scams directed toward borrowers in trouble who need to have their loan contracts modified in order to make the payment more affordable. Modification scams became a growth industry in 2009, as the number of desperate borrowers on the way to foreclosure reached levels not seen since the depression of the 1930s.

The most common scam was simply to promise that for a modest upfront fee, which could be $3,000–$4,000, the scamster would deliver a modification. What the scamster actually delivers is excuses, and eventually they disappear.

A more sophisticated version preyed on borrowers who had requested a modification themselves and were turned down because they were not yet behind in their payments. As noted in **Mortgage Modification/*Bias Favoring Borrowers in Default*,** it is common practice for servicers to prioritize modification requests and place those who are still current on their mortgages at the bottom of the list.

The scamster works with an insider who provides a list of borrowers who had been turned down because they were in good standing. Contacting these borrowers, the scamster says, "I know you were refused a loan modification, but I can get it for you if you follow my instructions. My fee is $5,000 but you don't have to pay me until you actually receive the loan mod approval."

The scamster instructs the borrowers to become "distressed" by missing two payments, which makes them acceptable candidates. The bank insider sends the borrower's financials to the scamster, who resubmits the requests back to the servicer through the insider, who sees that they are accepted.

Mortgage Shopping *Trying to find the best deal on a mortgage.*

It isn't easy to do it right, as a summary of the major steps involved will demonstrate. This guide is based on the regulatory structure in November 2009. A HUD-revised Good Faith Estimate that became effective January 1, 2010 should make it a little easier. *See* **Settlement Costs/*Good Faith Estimate*.**

Step 1: Decide If You Are a Potential Shopper: Not everyone is a potential shopper. Some will do a lot better entrusting that responsibility to someone else. Read the following statements, giving yourself one point if a statement marked "1" best describes you, two points if a statement marked "2" describes you best, and 1.5 points if you are in between.

A1. I like to bargain and have no hesitancy in speaking up if I think someone is trying to take advantage of me.

A2. I avoid confrontation at all costs.

Mortgage Shopping

B1. I feel that I either know or have the capacity to learn as much about mortgages as I will need to know to take care of myself in the marketplace.

B2. I feel overwhelmed by the complexity of mortgages, and I don't have the time, energy, or desire to educate myself about them.

C1. When significant money is at stake, I like to control things myself.

C2. When significant money is at stake, I like to find someone I can trust to make critical decisions for me.

D1. I feel very comfortable using a computer.

D2. I am computer-phobic.

If your total score is above six, find a mortgage broker to be your agent in shopping for a mortgage. I recommend Upfront Mortgage Brokers (UMBs) because they are prepared to provide this service at a set fee, negotiated in advance. Once the fee is established, your interest and that of the broker are closely aligned. *See* **Upfront Mortgage Broker**.

Potential shoppers score six or lower. What follows is directed primarily at them.

Step 2: Decide Which Mortgage Features You Want: Before entering the market, shoppers should decide on the type of mortgage, term, points, down payment, and lock period.

You can't compare prices of different loan providers accurately unless you can specify exactly what you are shopping for. When you shop for an automobile, you decide beforehand that you want, e.g., a four-door Toyota Corolla with accessory package 101. You must do the same when you shop for a mortgage.

It is especially important to know exactly what you want before you lock the price. If you change your mind after you lock and market prices have risen in the meantime, many lenders will allow a change only at the higher price.

Step 3: Determine Your Market Niche: The interest rate and points on a mortgage vary with a number of borrower, property, and transaction features. Loan officers quoting prices will assume the features commanding the lowest price. *See* **Nichification/*Generic Price Quotes***.

For example, if you don't say anything about the property, the loan officer will assume it is a single-family detached house constructed on the site. If in fact it is a low-rise condominium unit, a four-family structure, or a manufactured house, the price will probably be higher. To obtain valid price quotes, shoppers must indicate all such deviations between their deal and the generic deal.

Make a list of your "niche adjustments"—all the deviations between your deal and the generic assumptions. Whenever you are soliciting price quotes, you offer the list.

Step 4: Formulate Your Price Selection Strategy: Selecting the best price on a mortgage is not like selecting the best price on a toaster. Mortgages have three (or more) price components, toasters only one.

Pricing Strategy on Fixed-Rate Mortgages (FRMs): Once you know your loan amount, convert all upfront charges into a single total dollar figure. Multiply all upfront fees expressed as a percentage of the loan times the loan amount. (This includes points, origination fee if there is one, and broker fee if it is defined as a percentage.) Add fixed-dollar fees charged by the lender and broker. For example, if the loan is for $150,000 at one point ($1,500), with lender fees of $800 and broker fees of $3,000, total dollars amount to $5,300.

Ignore the cost of title-related services and settlement services. If you are in an area in which it can pay to shop for them, you can do it after selecting the loan and lender. Also ignore any government charges, escrows, and per diem interest. You can't shop these. Hazard insurance you buy on your own.

When you have two price components—the interest rate and total dollars up front—there are two ways to make a selection decision. One way is to fix the interest rate (call it your "shopping rate") and ask for quotes on total dollars at that rate. It is convenient that interest rates are generally quoted in 1/8% increments.

You thus ask the loan provider, "If these are my mortgage features and niche adjustments, what are your points and total fees at (say) 5.875%?" You must be clear that "total fees" refers to payments to the lender and the broker, excluding payments to third parties, per diem interest, and escrows.

The best shopping rate for your purpose can only be found through trial and error. If you begin with a shopping rate that elicits larger total dollar quotes than you want to pay, for example, raise it. As your shopping rate goes up, the total dollar quotes will go down.

Mortgage Shopping

An alternative to soliciting total dollar quotes for a given shopping rate is to combine different rate and total dollars into a single measure of **Interest Cost (IC)**. Economists call this measure an "internal rate of return," or IRR. The annual percentage rate (APR), which is a mandatory disclosure, is an IRR. The problem with the APR is that it is calculated over the entire term of the loan, which makes it a biased measure for borrowers with short horizons.

If you know you will be in your house for 10 years or longer, you can use the APR because the error is small. Otherwise, you should compare interest costs over your own shorter time horizon. You can do that using calculator 9c on my Web site.

There is one way to shop a single price that has become popular in recent years. This is to shop for the lowest interest rate with zero settlement costs. The lender pays all costs, including third-party charges. This approach makes it almost as easy to compare mortgage prices as toaster prices. Just make sure all costs are covered except per diem interest and escrows, and nothing is added to the balance. *See* **No-Cost Mortgage**.

This is a great strategy if your time horizon is less than 5 years. The lender pays your settlement costs in exchange for higher interest payments, but these payments don't go on long enough to wipe out the benefit. After about 5 years, however, the higher interest payments convert the strategy into a loser.

Pricing Strategy on ARMs and Balloon Loans: Both ARMs and balloons have fixed rates for some initial period. For balloons, that period is almost always either 5 or 7 years. For ARMs, it can range from a month to 10 years.

If you know that you will be out of the house before the initial rate period ends, you can use the same price selection strategy as on an FRM. As far as you are concerned, it is an FRM. In using calculator 9c to measure interest cost, enter the initial rate period as the period you expect to stay in your house. The calculator will ignore what happens after that period.

The problem is that very few borrowers can be certain that they will be gone by the end of any initial rate period. Life has a bad habit of changing our minds. You should be aware of what can happen at the end of that period and factor that into your decision process.

In the case of balloon loans, that is not difficult. At the end of the initial rate period, you must refinance at the market rate prevailing at that time.

Since all balloons are equally bad in that regard, select the one that is the best deal over the initial rate period. The pricing strategy for a balloon thus turns out to be the same as that for an FRM.

ARMs, however, have built-in protections against rate increases after the initial rate period, and these may differ from one ARM to another. If two 5-year ARMs have the same interest cost over the 5 years, you want the one that exposes you to less risk of a rate increase at the end of 5 years.

Unfortunately, this is not easy to determine because it is affected by a number of ARM features that won't be provided to you in a comprehensible form unless you ask. Print out "Information Needed to Evaluate an ARM" from my Web site and have the lender fill it in for any ARM you are considering. You then have what you need to use calculators 7b or 7c and 9a or 9b. These calculators will tell you what will happen to your interest rate and monthly payment at the end of the initial rate period if (a) the interest rate index doesn't change, (b) the index goes through the roof (a "worst case"), or (c) the index follows any other future scenario you choose to examine.

Step 5: Solicit Price Quotes:

Validity: To be valid, mortgage price quotes must be:

- Complete, which means inclusive of lender and broker fees expressed in dollars, as well as those expressed as a percentage of the loan. On adjustable-rate mortgages (ARMs), it also means inclusive of information on features affecting the interest rate and payment when the initial rate period ends.

- Timely, which means that the prices are live at the time they are conveyed to the shopper.

- Niche adjusted, which means that the prices are adjusted for all the ways in which the shopper's transaction differs from the generic assumptions used by lenders in developing their best prices.

- Honest, which means that the loan provider would be willing to lock the rate and points quoted, rather than lowballing to get the business, and is willing to guarantee fixed-dollar fees.

Sources: One source of price quotes is individual loan officers recommended by your sales agent, if it is a purchase transaction, or by other borrowers. Provide them with your mortgage features and niche adjustments. If you are shopping an ARM, include the blank table on "Information Needed to Evaluate an ARM" from my Web site. Request that quotes include fixed-dollar fees and that they be e-mailed or faxed.

Mortgage Shopping

A second source of price quotes is Internet-based mortgage lead-generation sites. These sites ask you to fill out a questionnaire covering the loan request, property, personal finances, and contact information. (It is their version of your mortgage features and niche adjustments.) The sites use this information to select the lenders, usually up to four, to whom the information is sent. The selected lenders then send price quotes to you based on the same information, hopefully on the same day.

This is a quick and easy way to obtain up to four price quotes. However, the niche adjustments may or may not be complete, they may not ask you about your mortgage preferences, and they may not include information on fixed-dollar fees or on important ARM features. Hence, you probably will need to request a second round. The integrity of the quotes is no more verifiable than those you get by directly soliciting loan officers yourself.

A third source of price quotes is single-lender Internet sites. They are less convenient than auction sites since you can only get one quote per site. However, you choose your mortgage features, and the price quotes are more likely to be complete. Furthermore, if your loan is priced online, it is an honest price. They can't give you a lowball quote to snare your business, then raise the price when you lock, because you can monitor the price when you lock.

Single-lender sites vary greatly in the extent of their niche adjustments. The more questions they ask the user, the more complete the niche adjustment can be. However, many lenders are afraid to ask too many questions on their Web sites for fear the user will become discouraged and leave. The trick, therefore, is to determine whether the questions posed by a site have captured your particular niche adjustments. If you are buying a two-family house, for example, and you are asked about "Type of Property" with "Two-Family House" as one possible answer, then you know that they adjust for that.

To make it easier to shop single-lender sites, I developed the "Upfront Mortgage Lender" certification. The requirements include filling out a niche table, which allows a shopper to tell at a glance whether the niche into which the shopper falls is priced online by the lender. Complete pricing is also a requirement. At this writing, there were six UML Web sites. *See* **Upfront Mortgage Lender**.

Step 6: Select the Loan Provider: Lenders who price high often argue that service quality is equally important. "You wouldn't hire a lawyer or an architect based strictly on price, would you?" The problem with this argument is that there is very little reliable information available to borrowers on the service quality of loan providers. Furthermore, there is no reason whatever to believe that lenders who price high provide better service.

There is one particular service, however, that shoppers may want to consider in making their final selection. This is the lender's requirements for locking the price.

Some lenders refuse to lock until a borrower demonstrates commitment to the deal by completing one or more critical steps in the lending process, including an application. Other lenders will lock based on very little. We would expect that lenders who make it easy to lock would quote higher prices because they have higher lock costs. Some shoppers will lock with them as protection against a rate increase while they continue to shop for a better deal elsewhere. However, it doesn't always work out that way.

If two lenders have the same price, but one will lock you today while the other won't lock you for three days, you should go with the first. This is especially the case if you have no way to verify the validity of the changes in the market that occur over the three days.

Step 7: Lock the Price: Most borrowers lock as soon as possible, and you can't get into trouble doing that. Allowing the price to float until shortly before closing can be either a good gamble, meaning that the odds are in your favor, or a bad gamble. It has nothing to do with whether market interest rates go up or down over the period, because that is not predictable.

Allowing the price to float is a good gamble only if all the following conditions are met:

- You can afford the hit if market rates go up. If your income is only marginally adequate to qualify, it would be foolish to risk being disqualified by a rate increase.

- You can monitor your price day by day. In general, this is possible only if your specific deal is priced on the lender's Web site.

- The lender charges lower prices for shorter lock periods. This means that if the market is stable, your price will drop as the lock period shortens.

For example, you have 60 days to closing and the quote is 5% and 1 point for a 60-day lock, 0.875 point for a 45-day lock, 0.75 point for a 30-day lock, and 0.625 point for a 15-day lock. If you float until 5 days before closing and the market does not change, you save 0.375 point, the difference between the 60-day and the 15-day lock prices. Some mortgage brokers do this as a matter of course; i.e., they "lock" the borrower at their own risk at the 60-day price but don't lock with the lender until they can get the 15-day price.

This is a good gamble because you win if interest rates neither rise nor fall, but it remains a gamble because you lose if interest rates rise. If the lender charges the same price for a 15-day as for a 60-day lock, it is no longer a good gamble since you don't profit in a stable market. If you can't monitor your price, it is a bad gamble because you are then at the mercy of the lender to tell you what the market price is.

Locking the price should end the shopping process, but unfortunately it doesn't. When it comes to mortgages, "it isn't over till it's over." If you don't watch yourself, you can be victimized by "lender fee inflation" or by "contract chicanery."

Step 8: Cover Your Rear:

Lender Fee Inflation: When you lock the price of the loan, you are not locking the whole price. You are locking the market-sensitive part, consisting of interest rate and points. Lender fees specified in dollars are not market sensitive and are not locked. Further, such fees do not usually appear in media ads that show mortgage price and are seldom volunteered to shoppers. They are shown on the Good Faith Estimate of settlement (GFE), along with all other settlement costs. However, the GFE need not be provided to borrowers until 3 business days after receipt of an application. This is too late to help shoppers.

But it gets worse. Lenders are not bound by the numbers on the GFE, which are "good faith estimates." The GFE concept made some sense with regard to third-party services, such as title insurance. It never made any sense with regard to lender charges, however, because lenders know their own charges with certainty. The GFE has thus provided a cloak behind which some rogue lenders extract additional fees from unsuspecting borrowers. See **Mortgage Scams and Tricks/Strictly Lender Scams/Pad the GFE**.

This is not a problem if you are dealing with a mortgage broker. Brokers know the fees of each lender they deal with and will not tolerate lenders taking advantage of their clients. Fee inflation puts no money in brokers' pockets. The problem arises in dealing with lenders.

Upfront Mortgage Lenders include their fixed-dollar fees in their price quotes and guarantee that these will be the fees charged at closing. If they can do it, any lender can, and the lender will if shoppers demand it. Just make sure you get it in writing.

Note: A substantially revised Good Faith Estimate became effective January 1, 2010, and indications are that it will put a stop to fee escalation. *See* **Settlement Costs/Good Faith Estimate**.

Contract Chicanery: The mortgage note is a contract between the lender and the borrower, but ordinarily the borrower does not see the contract until the closing, and few read it even then. Generally this is not problematic, but it can be if the lender slips something in that disadvantages the borrower, without the knowledge of the borrower. This is contract chicanery.

When this happens, the offensive provision is likely to be in a rider to the contract. Judging from my mailbox, the most common such rider is a prepayment penalty. The inducement is a significant enhancement in the value of the note, part of which will probably go into the pocket of the loan officer.

It is remarkably easy to prevent this from happening. There is a line on the Truth in Lending (TIL) form you are given after you submit your application that says, "If you pay off your loan early, you [ ] may [ ] will not have to pay a penalty." If there is a check in front of "may," it means that your loan does have a prepayment penalty, no maybes about it. If you have not agreed to a prepayment penalty, this is when you should catch it.

I also see contract chicanery in connection with adjustable-rate mortgages (ARMs). In the typical case, the borrower is sold an ARM based on one or two features and never confronts the remaining features that are included in the note. Unlike a prepayment penalty, which must come to light if the borrower tries to refinance, disadvantageous ARM features can remain undetected indefinitely. To prevent this, collect all the relevant information about the ARMs for which you shop.

Mortgage Spam *Outrageously false claims from a mortgage tooth fairy delivered by e-mail.*

Until I learned how to control it, I used to find about 100 letters when I logged onto my computer in the morning, of which about 75 would be spam. The largest category consisted of those that wanted to enhance my sexual capacity, but those looking to interest me in a mortgage ran a close second. Some of them made my blood boil.

A spamster I once spoke to told me why mortgage spam makes outrageous claims. "The more outrageous the claim," he said very matter-of-factly, "the higher the response rate." This is why we read about "2.95% mortgages," "poor credit not a problem," "we cut your payment by 45%," "buy the home you couldn't dream you could afford," "you are approved," and on and on.

These claims, like those for enhancing my sexuality, are all fantasy. Most of the people who make the claims aren't loan providers and have no say regarding mortgage prices or the borrower approval process. Mortgage lenders and brokers initiate very little mortgage spam.

Most mortgage spam comes from lead-generation sites that are in the business of compiling information on potential mortgage borrowers, then selling it to lenders or brokers. The sole purpose of the enticing messages is to induce you to fill out a questionnaire. A completed questionnaire is a lead, for which loan providers will pay $40 or more, depending on how much information it contains. *See* **Mortgage Leads**.

This is a very easy business to enter. All you need is a Web site with a questionnaire for potential borrowers to fill out; a deal with a spam distributor to spread your outrageous claims as widely across the Internet as possible; and deals with loan providers, or with a lead wholesaler, to sell the leads.

If you fill out the questionnaire of a mortgage spamster, you will be solicited by one or more loan providers. You will know nothing about them, but they will know a lot about you. Having paid good money for that information, they are highly motivated to land you as a client. To accomplish that, some of them may make promises that are as phony as those of the spamster who enticed you into the process.

Mortgage Suitability *The doctrine that loan providers should be responsible for assuring that mortgages are suitable for the borrowers to whom they are offered.*

The doctrine is based on analogy to the securities industry. The argument is that a federal suitability rule has worked there, so why not with home mortgages?

Proponents of a suitability standard believe it is the answer to a raft of problems besetting the home mortgage market, including:

- Borrowers selecting mortgages that are excessively risky
- Borrowers selecting mortgages that are not affordable

Mortgage Suitability

- Borrowers receiving no tangible benefit from refinancing

- Borrowers being steered into any of the above by loan originators

I discuss only the first, with particular reference to option ARMs (OAs), because it matches the securities market problem most closely. An analogous treatment of the other problems can be found on my Web site.

The Problem of Bad Mortgage Selection: The following is a composite of many letters from borrowers who took out OAs in 2005 and 2006, which were sent to me during the crisis years that followed.

I took this loan because the monthly payment was much lower than any of the alternatives . . . The interest rate was only 1% because I qualified for a special program . . . I was led to believe that it would last for five years . . . I realize now that it didn't and that my loan balance has been going up every month . . . I am afraid that next year my payment is going to increase so much I won't be able to afford it . . . How do I get out of this mess? Do I have recourse against the loan officer (broker) who talked me into it?

OAs along with interest-only mortgages (IOs), which have some similar features, were marketed to borrowers who were attracted by the lower initial payments. In all too many cases, however, the borrowers didn't understand why the payments were lower, and they were not prepared for the risks of higher payments in the future.

Bad mortgage selection was a minor problem until the later stages of the housing bubble, when the volume of OAs and IOs exploded. The marketing of these mortgages was often based on deception. The most blatant piece of deceit, which I saw time and time again, was to lead or allow the borrower to believe that the very low quoted rate on an OA held for five years, when it actually held for one month. Because of their horrendous default rates, OAs stopped being offered in 2007. IOs continued to be available but at stiffer terms.

Suitability as a Remedy: If lenders were held liable for making unsuitable mortgages, they would have to delegate operating responsibility to those who deal directly with borrowers: loan officers and mortgage brokers, whom I will call "loan originators," or LOs. Their role is analogous to that of security brokers.

Short-Run Versus Long-Run Financial Interest: Both LOs and security brokers have a financial stake in their clients taking a mortgage or purchasing a security. Judging that a mortgage or security is not suitable for a client costs them money in the short run. However, the short-term interest of brokers in selling unsuitable securities is usually overruled by their long-term interest in maintaining a roster of satisfied clients. While transaction-oriented operators looking for the fast buck exist, some of them operating out of the proverbial boiler rooms, they are on the periphery of the industry.

In the home mortgage market, in contrast, client-oriented LOs are the minority group. The great majority are transaction oriented—they sell loans. To force LOs to follow a suitability standard, lenders would have to hire an army of inspectors, and there is no one to ride herd on most mortgage brokers, who are independent contractors.

Information Required to Determine Suitability: Determining the suitability of an investment or a mortgage requires balancing the objectives of the client against the risk of the instrument. In the case of investments, this is relatively easy because the client's objective can almost always be framed in terms of risk versus return.

The objectives of mortgage borrowers, in contrast, are diverse and complex and often not known by the LO. Here are five objectives that have been reported to me by borrowers who have selected OAs:

- Reduce cash outflow to invest the excess in securities.
- Reduce cash outflow to pay down a second mortgage.
- Reflecting unstable income, pay principal when convenient.
- Qualify to purchase more house.
- Reduce current payment to avoid default.

I sometimes get involved in an exchange with borrowers on whether their particular objectives are worth the risk, and sometimes I express my opinion to them quite forcefully. I would not want the legal right to overrule them, however, because I am not that smart.

Let's look at the first because it is the case most analogous to the securities market model, and it illustrates clearly why the model can't be extrapolated to home mortgages.

Many borrowers told me that they took an IO or OA so they could invest the saving in monthly cash flow relative to other mortgages. Given this objective, whether or not the mortgage is suitable for the borrower depends on whether (a) they have the discipline required to invest the savings every month rather than spend it and (b) they have access to investments that will yield a return higher than the mortgage rate without taking excessive risk.

An LO typically has no knowledge of the securities a mortgage borrower plans to acquire. Contrast that to a securities broker, who knows the risk of the investments being offered to his client because the broker himself is offering them. Furthermore, the mortgage loan provider has no special expertise for analyzing the wisdom of the borrower's decision and no special insight into whether the borrower is a disciplined investor.

The upshot is that making lenders responsible for mortgage suitability is not a manageable way of dealing with the problem that some borrowers select mortgages unsuitable for them.

A Better Remedy Is Selective Disclosure: Given the way in which mortgages are sold, a new disclosure added to the morass of existing disclosures can be effective only if it hits mortgage shoppers between the eyes and cannot be swept aside by loan officers and mortgage brokers. My proposal is the following very simple rule:

Whenever a shopper is quoted a monthly payment, he must also be shown the highest monthly payment possible on that loan and the month it would be reached, assuming the borrower always makes the minimum payment allowed.

This rule focuses on the primary motivation for taking IOs and OAs: the lower initial payment. The rule would put borrowers on their guard, which is what a disclosure rule is designed to do.

The lender and broker trade groups will find this proposal unacceptable—because it emphasizes the negative. They argue that mandatory disclosures should be "balanced," showing the good news as well as the bad. But potential borrowers are besieged with good news from the media and their loan providers. To be effective, mandatory disclosure has to be negative because it is designed as a corrective to an onslaught of hype.

Negative Amortization *A rise in the loan balance when the mortgage payment is less than the interest due.*

Negative amortization is sometimes called "deferred interest." *See* **Adjustable-Rate Mortgage (ARM)/***How the Monthly Payment on an ARM Is Determined***/Negative Amortization ARMs**.

Negative Amortization Cap *The maximum amount of negative amortization permitted on an ARM, usually expressed as a percentage of the original loan amount (e.g., 110%).*

See **Adjustable-Rate Mortgage (ARM)/*How the Monthly Payment on an ARM Is Determined*/Negative Amortization ARMs**.

Negative Equity *Mortgage balances that exceed house value.*

The concept was not in the first edition of this book because it was so rare. When home prices began to decline in mid-2006, however, negative equity became increasingly common and brought with it a chain of adverse consequences.

Psychic Burden and Default: Many borrowers find it difficult to make their mortgage payments when they know that the portion of their mortgage payments that goes to principal only serves to reduce the amount of their negative equity. They can't start building positive equity until they cross the zero-equity threshold, which may seem very far away. If making the payment is a struggle every month, having negative equity may cause the borrower to lose it. Negative equity encourages default.

Loss of Mobility: Negative equity can also prevent a borrower from moving. Sometimes a homeowner loses a job and has to move to another area to find a new one. To sell a house, good title must be conveyed to a buyer, which means that all existing liens, including HELOCs and any tax or mechanic's liens, must be paid off.

If the house cannot be sold because the owner can't pay off all the liens, the owner either stays put or becomes a renter in the new area and a landlord in the old one.

Liens Are Not Transferable: Owners cannot escape the immobility trap by transferring an existing lien to another property. When negative equity was at its peak in 2009, I was asked frequently whether a second mortgage could be transferred to the new house the borrower hoped to purchase. The answer is no; liens apply to a particular property and can't be transferred to another property without the permission of the lender, which the lender never gives.

Sources of Negative Equity: Homebuyers who make no down payment—their loan or loans equal 100% of the purchase price—have negative equity when they move in. If they had to sell immediately, they could not repay the loans out of the sales proceeds because of the transactions costs. The sales commission alone runs 3–6% of the price.

Most homebuyers realize this but expect that price appreciation will bail them out. Price appreciation is like a tooth fairy; you need do nothing except put your house under the pillow, and come morning (or next year), as if by magic, you have equity. Except that sometimes the tooth fairy of price appreciation is replaced by her evil twin, price depreciation, as was the case during 2006–2009.

There isn't much a borrower with negative equity can do. You hunker down, pay your mortgage on time, pray that nothing happens that will force you to move, and wait for the good fairy of appreciation to reappear. If she doesn't, you may be forced to build equity the old-fashioned way, by paying down your mortgage.

Negative Points *Points paid by a lender for a loan with a rate above the rate on a zero-point loan.*

For example, a lender might quote the following prices: 8%/0 points, 7.5%/3 points, 8.75%/–2.5 points. Negative points, often referred to as "rebates," are used to reduce a borrower's settlement costs. When negative points are retained by a mortgage broker, they are called a "yield-spread premium." *See* **Points/*Points and Rebates as Borrower Options***.

Net Branch *A facility offered by some lenders to mortgage brokers where de jure the brokers become employees of the lender, but de facto they retain their independence as brokers.*

One of the advantages of this arrangement to brokers is that they need not disclose yield-spread premiums received from lenders.

Net Jumping *Using a broker's time and expertise to become informed and creditworthy, then jumping to the Internet to get the loan.*

See **Mortgage Scams and Tricks/*Scams by Borrowers*/Net Jumping**.

Nichification *Proliferation in the number of loan, borrower, property, and trans-action characteristics used by lenders to set mortgage prices and underwriting requirements.*

Nichification is unique to the United States and reflects the importance of secondary markets there. Any characteristic identified by investors in the secondary market as affecting risk or cost is priced in the secondary market and then in the primary market. The following is a partial list of factors used in pricing or in setting qualification requirements.

Transaction Characteristics

- Loan amount
- Desired lock period (in days)
- Down payment (as percentage of property value)
- Term
- Prepayment penalty (if any)

Borrower Characteristics

- Credit score
- Ratio of borrower income to monthly housing expense
- Ratio of borrower income to total housing expense

Property If Not Single-Family Detached

- Two family
- Three family
- Four family
- Co-op (building is owned by a cooperative association in which members own shares)
- Condominium (borrower owns unit in a project in which some facilities are owned in common)
- Condominium more than four stories high
- Manufactured (house was not built on site)
- Attached (twin, triplex, row)
- Planned unit development (house is located in a PUD with a home-owners association that charges dues)

Nichification

Loan Purpose If Not Purchase for Permanent Occupancy

- Purchase second home (vacation home)

- Refinance

- Cash-out refinance (loan is larger than old loan balance by an amount larger than the settlement costs)

- Investment (home is being purchased to rent out)

Documentation If Not Standard

- Alternative documentation (borrower wants to provide payroll and bank statements rather than wait for verification of information from employer and bank)

- Documentation for self-employed (borrower wants to use special documentation requirements available for the self-employed)

- No income verification (borrower doesn't want reported income to be verified by the lender)

- No asset verification (borrower doesn't want reported assets to be verified by the lender)

- "No docs" (borrower doesn't want reported income or assets to be verified by the lender)

- No income ratios (borrower doesn't want income to be used in determining qualification)

- Streamlined refinance (borrower wants the reduced documentation requirements available on refinances only)

Special Borrower Features

- Nonoccupant coborrower (one of the borrowers won't be living in the house)

- Subordinate financing (there will be a second mortgage on the property when the new loan is made)

- Nonpermanent resident alien (borrower is employed in the United States but is not a U.S. citizen or permanent resident)

- Nonpermanent nonresident alien (borrower is not a U.S. citizen and is not employed in the United States)

- Waiver of escrows (borrower wants to be responsible for payment of taxes and insurance)

Nichification

Numbers of Niches: The number of potential niches is extremely large because of combinations of niche characteristics. Pricing technology offered by the company with which I was once involved allowed lenders to enter up to *40 million prices for each loan program*. A second loan program could have a different 40 million. While no one lender used any significant part of this capacity, in combination the lenders using the system priced for several million niches at least.

Impact of the Financial Crisis on Nichification: The tightening of underwriting requirements that followed the financial crisis resulted in some reduction in the extent of nichification. The largest shrinkage occurred in documentation, where six of the seven types of alternative documentation listed above were eliminated. Yet the market remained heavily nichified.

Implications for Mortgage Shopping: First, shoppers need to understand that no lender operates in every niche, and the narrower the niche, the fewer the lenders. In a survey of 15 national lenders that I once did, I found that all 15 made investor loans on 30-year fixed-rate mortgages. However, only 9 of them made investor loans to borrowers who were doing a cash-out refinance, and only 4 were also willing to waive standard loan documentation requirements. On adjustable-rate mortgages, furthermore, the number fell to 2.

Second, the lender offering the best deal in one niche is very unlikely to be the one offering the best deal in another niche. In a study of 13 lenders operating in 19 niches that I did some time ago, I found that 12 of them offered the best deal in at least 1 niche. Further, no one of the lenders offered the best deal in more than 3 of the 19 niches.

Third, nichification is a major reason why mortgage brokers have become such a major part of the market. Since mortgage brokers deal with multiple lenders, they are well positioned (as consumers are not) to identify the lenders who operate in a particular niche and to select the best of the available deals. The reduced market share of brokers after the financial crisis partly reflected reduction in the number of market niches.

Finally, in collecting price data from loan providers, shoppers must be sure that they have provided each loan provider with the information required to place them in the correct market niche. Otherwise, the shopper does not know whether the prices apply or not.

Generic Price Quotes: Casual mortgage shoppers who ask loan providers for "their rate and points" will receive a generic price quote: one based on a series of favorable assumptions. Here are typical assumptions underlying generic price quotes:

- The transaction is a home purchase or no-cash refinance.

- The loan amount is below the conforming loan limit ($417,000 in 2009) and larger than some minimum, such as $50,000, which can vary.

- There will not be a second mortgage on the property when the loan closes.

- The property is single family, detached, and constructed on the site.

- All coborrowers will occupy the house as their permanent residence.

- The FICO score of all coborrowers is above some level, often 720–740.

- The borrowers can document that they have enough cash for the down payment and closing costs.

- The borrowers can document that they have sufficient income to meet the maximum income-expense ratios on the program selected.

- The borrowers are U.S. citizens or permanent resident aliens.

Any deviations from these assumptions will call for a higher price.

No-Asset-Verification Loan   *A documentation requirement where the applicant's assets are not disclosed.*

See **Documentation Requirements**.

No-Change Scenario *On an ARM, the assumption that the value of the index to which the interest rate is tied does not change from its initial level.*

No-Cost Mortgage *A mortgage on which all settlement costs except per diem interest and escrows are paid by the lender and/or the home seller.*

A no-cost mortgage should be distinguished from a "no-points mortgage," which will have other settlement costs, and a "no-cash-outlays mortgage," on which settlement costs are added to the loan balance. Calling the latter "no cost" is extremely deceptive.

A true no-cost mortgage is one where the interest rate is high enough to command a rebate from the lender that covers the closing costs (except for per diem interest and escrows, which borrowers always pay). In general, no-cost mortgages make sense only for borrowers who expect to hold their mortgages for no more than five years. A borrower with a longer time horizon and with the cash to pay settlement costs ought to avoid the no-cost option.

Lenders demand a high interest rate for rebates because they assume they won't enjoy it very long. The average life of high-interest-rate loans is short. A borrower who pays the high rate for a long time gets a bad deal. It is akin to a healthy person buying life insurance from a company that mainly insures diabetics and smokers and prices its insurance accordingly.

The critical number for potential borrowers is the "breakeven period" (BEP) for a no-cost loan, relative to the same loan with a lower rate on which the borrower pays the costs. Over periods shorter than the BEP, the no-cost loan has lower costs. Beyond the BEP, the no-cost loan has higher costs. The BEP can be calculated in any real situation using calculators 11a and 11b on my Web site.

One important side benefit of no-cost mortgages is that shopping for them is relatively easy. The shopper needs quotes on only one price dimension—the interest rate. *See* **Mortgage Shopping/*Step 4: Formulate Your Price Selection Strategy*/Pricing Strategy on Fixed-Rate Mortgages**.

NOHOs *Consumers who are not cut out to be homeowners.*

The Distinguishing Characteristic of NOHOs: It is not their income, their mobility, or where they live—rather, it is *how* they live, which is week to week or month to month, depending on how often they are paid. Typically, they have nothing left at the end of the period, and if they run out early, they often borrow at high interest rates.

When they purchase durables, such as a TV set, NOHOs price the purchase in terms of the monthly payment, which they attempt to fit into their weekly or monthly budget. They are payment myopic. *See* **Predatory Lending/*Targets of Predators*/Payment Myopic**.

NOHOs never get ahead of the game, and if they run into an emergency that costs money, they are in trouble. Because homeownership is rife with such emergencies, they should not be homeowners.

NOHOs

NOHOs sometimes write me about buying a house because they have heard that owning is cheaper than renting. They would buy a house in the same way they would buy a TV set, by seeing if they can afford the monthly payment. They have no savings but have heard that it is possible to get a loan for 100% of the sale price. I try to discourage them by explaining the hidden costs and risks of homeownership and by pointing out that as owners, they rather than the landlord are responsible for everything that goes wrong.

NOHOs During the Bubble: The bubble period 2000–2006 was extremely friendly to NOHOs. This was when lenders were offering 100% financing and turning a blind eye to the adequacy of borrower incomes. It is possible that more NOHOs became homeowners during this period than in the prior two centuries.

NOHOs After the Bubble: Even if the bubble had not been followed by a financial crisis, the foreclosure rate among NOHOs would have been horrendous. Any bump in the road is enough to throw homeowning NOHOs in the ditch. A common bump in the road is property taxes. A NOHO who wrote me was in serious trouble almost immediately after buying a house because the property tax estimate by the lender turned out to be $200 a month too low. The NOHO said she would not have purchased the house had she known the correct figure. The reason for writing me was to solicit advice on how to sue the lender.

More often, NOHOs can manage the tax when they move in but can't manage a future tax increase. Of course, property taxes are known to rise, if not this year then next; it doesn't take a lot of foresight to expect it. But foresight is in short supply among NOHOs.

Down Payment Requirements and Down Payment Assistance: During most of our history, NOHOs had to rent, primarily because they did not have the down payment lenders required to finance a purchase. The down payment requirement usually screens out NOHOs because NOHOs can't save for a down payment. However, NOHOs can slip through the down payment screen if somebody other than the borrower puts up the down payment and the lender (or insurer) accepts it.

Many NOHOs get FHA mortgages through this escape hatch. The FHA down payment requirement is only 3.5%, but in 2008, borrowers provided their own down payment on less than half of all new FHA loans. In the other cases, down payment assistance was provided by (in order of importance) nonprofit entities, family, state and local government agencies, and employers.

I am not making a blanket condemnation of down payment assistance programs. Not everyone who can't make a down payment is a NOHO, and our society seems to have a weak spot for "first-time homebuyers." But providing down payment assistance to first-time homebuyers allows the NOHOs among them to slip in.

Perhaps the least harmful source of down payment assistance is family members, for whom assistance is a vote of confidence by those who usually know the borrower best. The most harmful are the nonprofit entities that get their money from home sellers. The reason is that the home sellers who provide the assistance raise their prices in order to get it back. These programs were made illegal by Congress in 2008, but legislation to revive them was pending when this was written in 2009.

No-Income Loan *A documentation requirement where the applicant's income is not disclosed.*

See **Documentation Requirements**.

Nominal Interest Rate *A quoted interest rate that is not adjusted for intrayear compounding.*

A quoted rate of 6% on a mortgage, for example, is nominal. Adjusted rates are called "effective." See **Effective Rate**.

Nonconforming Mortgage *A mortgage that does not meet the purchase requirements of the two federal agencies, Fannie Mae and Freddie Mac, because it is too large or for other reasons, such as poor credit or inadequate documentation.*

Nonpermanent Resident Alien *A noncitizen with a green card employed in the United States.*

Nonpermanent resident aliens are subject to somewhat more restrictive qualification requirements than U.S. citizens. Permanent resident aliens are not.

No-Ratio Loan *A documentation option where the applicant's income is disclosed and verified but not used in qualifying the borrower.*

The conventional maximum ratios of expense to income are not applied. *See* **Documentation Requirements**.

No-Surprise ARM *An ARM that provides payment certainty at the cost of term uncertainty.*

The Accordion ARM: The only way to create absolute payment certainty on an ARM is by making the term uncertain. This is an "accordion loan": the borrower knows exactly what his payment will be through the life of the loan, but he doesn't know how long he will have to pay. If rates go up, he pays for a longer period; and if they go down, he pays off more quickly. At various times, a few small depositories have offered accordion ARMs, but they have never attracted much business.

The reason is that the accordion loan won't work if the initial term on the ARM is 30 years, because that doesn't leave enough room for a term extension. A practical limit on the term would be 40 years, and an extension from 30 to 40 years offsets only a small increase in the interest rate early in the life of the loan.

If the 30-year ARM rate is 6%, for example, extending the term to 40 years (with no change in payment) will offset an immediate rate increase only to 6.70%. Since other ARMs allow rate increases of 5% or more, a maximum increase of 0.7% is unacceptable to lenders.

To be workable, the initial term on an accordion loan must not exceed 15 years. A term extension from 15 to 40 years would offset an immediate rate increase from 6 to 9.93%. If the increase were delayed for 3 years, it could be as high as 11.65%. Lenders find this acceptable, which is why the accordion loans that have been offered have had initial terms of 12–15 years. But this makes the payment substantially higher than it would be at 30 years, which limits acceptability to borrowers.

Graduating the Payment on an Accordion ARM: To make the accordion mortgage more affordable, the payment could be graduated as on a graduated payment mortgage (GPM). This is what I have called a "no-surprise ARM."

On the most popular GPM, for example, the payment increases by 7.5% a year for 5 years before leveling off. The same principle could be applied to the no-surprise ARM. Then lenders would have the rate protection provided by the short initial term, and borrowers would have a more affordable initial payment.

I have modeled the no-surprise ARM but have not been able to stir up any interest in it by lenders.

Note *A document that evidences a debt and a promise to repay.*

A mortgage loan transaction always includes a note evidencing the debt and a mortgage evidencing the lien on the property.

100% Loan *A loan with no down payment.*

See **Down Payment/*No-Down-Payment Loans***.

125% Loan *A mortgage loan for 125% of property value.*

Since such loans are only partly secured, they have many of the characteristics of unsecured loans, including relatively high interest rates. A drawback is that borrowers have difficulty refinancing 125% loans and can't sell their house without defaulting unless they can come up with the additional cash required to pay off the 125% loan. After the financial crisis, 125% loans largely disappeared.

Opportunity Cost *The value of the option not selected.*

For example, the opportunity cost of prepayment is the interest that could be earned had the money used for prepayment been used to acquire financial assets. Similarly, borrowers who take out a new mortgage have an interest opportunity cost on the cash they invest up front, as well as on the monthly payments.

See **Time Horizon Cost**.

Option ARM *An ARM on which borrowers have options on how large a payment they will make, including interest only and a "minimum" payment that is usually less than interest only.*

Option ARM

A majority of borrowers elect the minimum-payment option, which results in a growing loan balance and large payment increases in the future.

Identifying an Option ARM: Ask the loan provider if the rate adjusts monthly and if negative amortization is allowed. If the answer to both questions is yes, you almost certainly have one. The names that an option ARM goes by are all over the lot and include "1 Month Option Arm," "12 MTA Pay Option ARM," "Pick a Payment Loan," "1-Month MTA," "Cash Flow Option Loan," and "Pay Option ARM."

Advantages of an Option ARM: The main selling point of an option ARM is the low minimum payment in year 1. It is calculated at the interest rate in month 1, which can be as low as 1%, and it rises by only 7.5% a year for some years.

The low initial payment entices some borrowers into buying more costly houses than they would have otherwise or tempts them to use the monthly payment savings for other purposes, including investment. Loan providers often have a list of ways to use the cash flow savings. What they are less likely to give you is a sense of the risks you will face down the road.

The Risks of an Option ARM: For those electing the minimum-payment option, the major risk is "payment shock"—a sudden and sharp increase in the payment for which they are not prepared.

The rule that the minimum payment can rise by no more than 7.5% a year has two exceptions. The first is that every 5 or 10 years the payment must be "recast" to become fully amortizing. It is raised to the amount that will pay off the loan within the remaining term at the then current interest rate—*regardless of how large an increase in payment is required.*

The second exception is that the loan balance cannot exceed a negative amortization maximum, which can range from 110 to 125% of the original loan balance. If the balance hits the negative amortization maximum, which can happen before 5 years have elapsed if interest rates have gone up, the payment is *immediately* raised to the fully amortizing level.

Either the recast provision or the negative amortization cap can result in serious payment shock.

Protecting Yourself Against Risk of Payment Shock: There are three things you can do.

Measure the Risk: You can do this yourself using calculator 7ci on my Web site. It will show you what will happen to the payment on *your* option

ARM if interest rates follow any of a number of future scenarios selected by you. An important side benefit is that the calculator lists the information you need, which you want for shopping purposes anyway.

Minimize the Risk by Shopping for the Lowest Margin: The margin on your loan is the amount added to the interest rate index to get your rate. Since the margin affects the rate in months 2–360, it is the most critical price variable on an option ARM. The lower the margin, the lower your cost and your vulnerability to payment shock. *Note:* The margin is not a required disclosure, so don't expect that it will necessarily be volunteered.

Minimize the Risk by Taking the Highest Initial Payment You Can Afford: The higher your initial payment, the smaller the potential payment shock down the road. Since the initial payment is determined by the interest rate in month 1, you should select the *highest rate* that results in a payment with which you are comfortable. Asking for a higher rate sounds a little strange, but remember, the quoted rate holds only for 1 month.

Who Should Take an Option ARM? Choose one if your time horizon is short and you want to maximize your homebuying capacity. Because of the low initial rates and payments, borrowers can usually qualify for a larger loan using an option ARM. Since payments will be substantially higher in later years, you should confidently expect your income to rise in the future.

The option ARM is also a refinance option if your income has dropped and the alternative to lower payments is default.

I usually advise against using this instrument to generate cash flow savings to invest because few people have access to safe investments that yield more than the cost of an option ARM.

Borrowers Should Shop for Option ARMs: Shop not for the rate, because that holds only for 1 month, but for the *margin*, because that is what determines your rate after the first month. Your second priority should be the *maximum rate*. Your third priority should be *total lender fees*.

The good news about monthly ARMs is that lenders don't reprice them every day as they do other mortgages, which makes comparison shopping much easier. You don't need a rate lock, but ask the loan provider to specify the margin, maximum rate, and fees on paper.

Option ARMs During the Housing Bubble and the Crisis That Followed: Option ARMs were a favorite instrument of speculators during the housing bubble of 2002–2007, and their volume ballooned. When house prices began to decline in 2007, however, the combination of rising payments and negative equity caused a precipitous rise in defaults. In 2008 and 2009, no new option ARMs were written.

Option Fee *An upfront fee paid by a buyer under a lease-to-own house purchase, usually 1–5% of the price.*

The fee is credited to the purchase price when the option is exercised, but lost if it is not. *See* **Lease-to-Own Purchase**.

Origination Fee *An upfront fee charged by some lenders, expressed as a percentage of the loan amount.*

It is the same as points except that points vary with the interest rate and the origination fee does not.

Overage *The difference between the price posted to its loan officers by a lender or mortgage broker and the price charged the borrower.*

Loan officers who work for lenders or mortgage brokers receive updated prices from their head office every morning. These consist of rates and points for different loan programs. They are the "posted prices."

The loan officer who executes a deal at the posted price gets paid a commission that may be 0.5–0.7% of the loan amount. On a $100,000 loan, the commission might be $500–$700. But if the loan officer can induce the borrower to pay more than the posted price, the commission rises. It now includes an overage.

For example, the posted price on a particular loan is 5% and zero points, but the loan officer induces the borrower to pay 5% and 1 point. That point is the overage. It is worth $1,000 on a $100,000 loan, and the loan officer might get half. An overage can double the loan officer's commission.

Overages are heavily concentrated on high-rate loans with negative points, or "rebates." For example, the lender posting a price of 5% and zero points might also quote 5.25% and –1.5 points. Loan officers push higher-rate plus rebate combinations because they can collect an overage without taking any cash out of borrowers' pockets. If the loan officer in the example above quotes 5.25% and zero points to the borrower, the 1.5

point rebate becomes the overage. The borrower pays for the overage in the interest rate for the next 5 or 10 years, but that's down the road.

Overages associated primarily with rebate loans are an abuse practiced by lenders and mortgage brokers alike. The only difference is that mortgage brokers who retain rebates from lenders leave a trail in the Good Faith Estimate of disclosure, where it can be discovered by the borrower, although usually too late to do anything about. Rebates retained as overages by loan officer employees of lenders disappear without a trace.

Defenders of overages argue that they merely reflect the wheeling-and-dealing characteristic of many markets. They point out that sometimes borrowers turn the tables, forcing loan officers to cut the price below the posted price, which results in an "underage." The automobile market works essentially the same way.

The weakness of this argument is that almost everyone who buys an automobile understands that wheeling and dealing is part of the game, but many mortgage borrowers don't. They are innocents. That's why the number of underages is minuscule compared with the number of overages.

To avoid overages, borrowers must either confront the loan officer or switch to a distribution channel where there are no overages. Confrontation means letting the loan officer know that you know that mortgage prices are not engraved in cement and that you have explored or intend to explore other options. If you find this disagreeable, either retain an Upfront Mortgage Broker (UMB) to act as your agent in shopping for a loan or deal with an Upfront Mortgage Lender, which do not allow employees to deviate from posted prices.

Also see **Loan Officers** *and* **Mortgage Scams and Tricks/***Other Scams by Loan Providers***/Pocket the Borrower's Rebate**.

Par Price *In the secondary mortgage market, a price of $100.*

Par Rate *In the primary mortgage market, the interest rate on a mortgage at zero points.*

Partial Prepayments (or Paying Off Early) *Making a payment larger than the fully amortizing payment as a way of retiring the loan before term.*

Partial Prepayments (or Paying Off Early)

Making Extra Payments as an Investment: Suppose you add $100 to the scheduled mortgage payment. This makes the loan balance at the end of the month $100 less than it would have been without the extra payment. In the months that follow, you save the interest on that $100. Since the interest payment that you would have made is determined by the interest rate on your mortgage, the yield on your $100 investment in prepayment is equal to that rate.

Absent any prepayment penalty, principal repayment yields a return equal to the interest rate on the loan. A prepayment penalty would reduce that yield.

Factoring Taxes into the Equation: Many borrowers want to reduce the yield on mortgage repayment by the amount of the lost tax saving. If the borrower is in the 36% tax bracket, for example, her after-tax yield on an 8% mortgage is $(1 - 0.36) \times 8$, or 5.12%.

If the yield on the mortgage repayment is being compared with the yield on other taxable investments, however, it doesn't matter whether the yield is measured before tax or after tax. If mortgage repayment is compared with a 6% taxable bond, for example, the before-tax comparison is 8% versus 6%, while the after-tax comparison is 5.12% versus 3.84%. The conclusion, that mortgage repayment earns the higher return, remains the same.

On the other hand, if the alternative investment is tax exempt, you should compare only after-tax yields.

Partial Prepayments Versus Other Investments: To determine whether paying more principal is a good investment, the yield should be compared with the yield on alternative investments, with allowance for differences in default risk. An investment in mortgage repayment carries zero default risk.

Mortgage repayment will always carry a higher return than other riskless investments—insured certificates of deposit and U.S. government securities. However, investments that shelter income, such as contributions to a 401(k) plan, will usually generate a higher after-tax return than mortgage repayment. In addition, a diversified portfolio of common stock may yield 10% or more over a long time horizon, provided the borrower is prepared for the risk of short-term fluctuations in portfolio value.

Seniors Versus Juniors: Investing in mortgage repayment is generally smarter for a senior than for anyone else. Many seniors no longer have income to shelter; even those that do have a lower after-tax return because the tax deferment period is short. Furthermore, where a diversified portfolio of common stock is a prudent risk for people in their 30s or 40s, it is less prudent for those in their 70s or older. A single stock market tumble could crack their nest egg. For this reason, mortgage repayment is a preferred investment for many older investors.

This does not necessarily mean, however, that they should repay the entire mortgage balance at one fell swoop, as explained below. The partial-prepayment decision and the repayment-in-full decision are very different.

Partial Prepayment Versus Repayment in Full: Whether to allocate excess cash flow to mortgage repayment is a relatively easy decision because borrowers get to change it every month if they want. They prepay if the mortgage rate is higher than the rate that can be earned *this month* on newly acquired financial assets. Next month, the investment rate could be higher and the decision different.

Whether to repay the entire mortgage balance by liquidating financial assets, in contrast, is a single, irrevocable decision. Either the assets are liquidated to pay off the mortgage or they aren't.

While the principle, that the decision should be based on comparison of the mortgage rate and the investment rate, is the same, borrowers can't adjust to future changes in the investment rate. They have to look ahead and anticipate what these changes might be as well as how long they will be around.

To help deal with this problem, I developed a spreadsheet that allows borrowers to enter any scenario for future interest rates and compare their wealth in every future month in the two cases: where they liquidate their assets to repay the mortgage at the outset and where they retain both the mortgage and the assets. The spreadsheet is available on my Web site.

For example, assume the mortgage rate is 6% while the current investment rate is 2%, but the borrower assumes that in 2 years it will jump from 2 to 7% and stay there. The spreadsheet shows that for the first 67 months, the borrower's wealth would be greater in the case where he repaid the mortgage. After 67 months, this person's wealth is greater in the case where he didn't. The borrower then must decide whether he is likely to be around for more than 67 months.

In general, the sooner interest rates increase, the larger the increase when it happens, and the longer the borrower expects to live, the weaker the case for liquidating assets to pay off the mortgage. Seniors having to make this decision may find it instructive to play with the spreadsheet.

Partial Prepayments (or Paying Off Early)

Mechanics of Paying Early: To repay early, just increase the amount of your monthly check. With the exception noted below, you don't have to tell the lender to apply the extra payment to principal. There isn't anything else the lender can do with it except steal it, and if he wants to steal it, nothing you write on the check will stop him.

For example, if the regular monthly payment is $600 of which $500 is interest, the other $100 is used to reduce the loan balance. If you make a payment of $650, the loan balance will decline by $150. Since the interest has already been paid, the additional $50 is used to reduce the balance by the same amount.

The lender's computerized servicing system does this automatically. Of course, if your lender's account records are maintained by a guy who is sitting on a stool and has a quill pen and sports a green eye shade, you may have to watch what he does.

But don't make an extra payment equal to the exact amount of your regular payment without telling the lender what you want done with it. If your monthly payment for April is $600, for example, and you send in a check for $1,200, the lender does not know, unless you tell him, whether you wish to reduce the principal by another $600 or to make your May payment early. If you intend it as a reduction of principal but don't inform the lender, the lender may interpret it as the May payment sent early, in which case the lender gets the interest on the $600 during April instead of you.

Excepting simple interest mortgages, the benefit of early prepayment is *not* affected by when it is received within the month, though the lender may require that it be received before the end of the grace period. Thus, $100 received by the lender on either May 1 or on May 10 reduces the loan balance on May 1, on which the interest payment due June 1 is calculated, by $100. On simple interest mortgages, however, extra payments reduce the balance on the day they are received and posted.

Effect of Early Payment on Monthly Payments: Extra payments to principal affect different types of mortgage differently.

FRMs: On an FRM, extra payments shorten the period to final payoff but do not affect the monthly installment payment. This is sometimes a source of frustration to borrowers who come into a sizable amount of money that they would like to use to reduce their installment payment burden. They can't do it except by refinancing the reduced loan balance.

Partial Prepayments (or Paying Off Early)

On balloon mortgages, the monthly installment payment is not affected either. However, the balance that must be rolled over at the end of the 5- or 7-year rollover period is lower than it would be otherwise. And this means that the new installment payment is lower than it would be otherwise.

ARMs: On ARMs, prepayments result in lower monthly payments whenever the rate is adjusted. Where it is difficult to reduce the monthly payment on an FRM, it is difficult to shorten the payoff period of an ARM. The reason is that every time the mortgage payment is recalculated to reflect changes that have occurred in the interest rate, the calculation assumes that the loan will pay off in the period remaining of the original term.

For example, if the interest rate on a 30-year ARM is adjusted after 5 years, the payment for year 6 would be calculated over 25 years. Hence, any additional principal payments made during the first 5 years would result in a lower monthly payment, but no change in the payoff period.

It is possible to shorten the payoff period of an ARM by making extra payments, but you must increase the extra payment at every payment adjustment date to offset the decline in the scheduled payment resulting from prior prepayments. This is a pain, but spreadsheets on my Web site can ease the pain substantially. Each time the rate changes, the borrower can find the extra payment required for a target payoff date at the new rate. The spreadsheets can also be used to monitor the lender's calculations.

Repayment Opportunities During Financial Crisis: The financial crisis during 2007–2009 reduced the yield on very low-risk assets, including prime mortgages, making refinance attractive to borrowers who qualified. At the same time, however, the crisis reduced the number who qualified for prime terms by reducing the value of their homes, while increasing the premiums on the mortgage insurance they had to purchase if their loan balances exceeded 80% of current property value.

For example, a reader who had taken an 80% loan a few years earlier at 6.125% could refinance at 5.125%, but because of the decline in her property value, the refinance would require mortgage insurance that would wipe out much of the benefit.

This situation created a very attractive investment in partial prepayment combined with a rate-lowering refinance. The borrower in my example had to come up with $18,000 to pay down the balance to 80% of the current appraised value. Relative to remaining with her current mortgage, the $18,000 investment would yield 18% over 5 years. The return includes the lower payment over the 5 years plus the smaller loan balance at the end of the period.

Partial Prepayments (or Paying Off Early)

The return on investment is not very sensitive to how long the borrower has the mortgage; it will be a little higher if the period is shorter and a little lower if it is longer. If the loan runs to term, the return would be 16.6%.

The return *is* sensitive to the required size of the investment. The smaller the investment in prepayment required to get to the 80% mark, the higher the return.

The crisis also increased the yield spread between conforming and jumbo loans, increasing the return on partial prepayment that brings the loan balance down to the conforming maximum. For example, a reader with a jumbo balance of $809,000 could refinance it at 5%, or he could pay down the balance to $729,000 and refinance at 4.375%. I calculated the yield on the required $80,000 investment to be 10.4% over 5 years. If the investment required to convert the new loan from jumbo to conforming was $40,000 instead of $80,000, the rate of return over 5 years would be 15.4%.

Note: I did all these calculations on a hand calculator with financial functions. These calculators are available today for about $20; look for the telltale symbols: N, I, PV, PMT, and FV. Here is how to calculate the rate of return in the jumbo case:

Calculate the payment and balance after 5 years on the $809,000 jumbo at 5% for 15 years.

Enter: 180 in N

    5 in I

    −809000 in PV

    0 in FV

Solve for PMT = 6397.53

Enter: 60 in N

Solve for FV = 603167 (balance after 5 years)

Repeat the process for the $729,000 conforming loan at 4.375% for 15 years. The payment is 5,530.34, and the balance after 5 years is 536,734.

Calculate the difference in payment and balance between the two cases. The payment on the conforming loan is 867.19 lower, and the balance is 66,433 lower. These are the components of the return on the $80,000 investment in loan repayment.

Partial Prepayments (or Paying Off Early)

To calculate that return over 5 years:

Enter: 60 in N

   –80000 in PV

   867.19 in PMT

   66433 in FV

Solve for I = 10.40%

Figuring the Payoff Month: Calculators 2a, 2b, and 2c on my Web site will help borrowers who want to pay off early. Calculator 2a is for those who want to know when their loan will pay off and how much interest they will save if they allocate a certain amount to extra payments. Calculator 2b is for borrowers who want to know how much extra they must pay to pay off their loan within a specified period. Calculator 2c is for borrowers who want to know when their loan will pay off and how much interest they will save if they shift to a biweekly payment schedule.

Monitoring the Lender: Many borrowers worry about whether or not lenders have properly credited them for partial prepayments. While I don't think that any lenders misappropriate payments, mistakes happen, and it is a good idea to keep an eye out for them. A few lenders have begun to provide borrowers with access to their payment history on the Internet, but it will be a while before this becomes standard practice.

Meanwhile, you can use two Excel spreadsheets I developed for just this purpose that are accessible on my Web site. The spreadsheets can be saved to your computer so you can maintain a permanent record of your mortgage.

The spreadsheets show an entire amortization schedule for an FRM or an ARM, with an empty column for prepayments. The ARM version also has a column for the interest rate. When you enter an extra payment, the entire schedule is recalculated. The resulting balance can then be compared with the balance shown in the lender's statement.

Closure at Payoff: After the mortgage is fully paid, you should receive a "satisfaction of mortgage" from the lender, along with your note. This is the evidence you need that your loan has been paid off.

If you don't receive these documents, contact the lender, but give him a few weeks at least. You must also make sure that the lender has filed the satisfaction of mortgage with the county where your mortgage was registered so that it no longer appears on your property record. Check with the county, but give the lender at least six weeks.

If your taxes are escrowed, you must also notify the tax office or offices that henceforth tax notices should be sent directly to you.

Also see **Biweekly Mortgage**.

Pay-Down Magic *Belief that there is a special way to pay down the balance of a home mortgage faster, if you know the secret.*

Since many if not most borrowers don't fully understand how mortgage amortization works, they are susceptible to wishful thinking–type myths. As a mortgage counselor, I hear these myths frequently. Most make no sense at all, such as those that advocate early payment of specific future principal payments. A few, however, have some foundation in fact.

Making a Large Extra Payment as Soon as the Loan Closes: According to my respondents, two books promote this as a way to pay off a loan early and save lots of interest. Instead of borrowing $190,000, they suggest you borrow $200,000 and immediately repay $10,000. If the loan is for 30 years at 6%, doing it their way will result in a payoff in 316 months instead of 360 and a saving of $32,042 in interest. These numbers are correct.

The reason for the early payoff and interest savings is that if you borrow $200,000 and immediately repay $10,000, your monthly mortgage payment is calculated on $200,000 rather than $190,000, making it $60 higher. This additional $60 a month is the entire secret. You will get exactly the same result by borrowing $190,000 and making the payment for $200,000.

This does not mean that the two alternatives are equivalent. If you borrow $200,000 and immediately repay $10,000, you have a required payment of $1,199. If you borrow $190,000, your required payment is $1,139, and the extra $60 is optional. Which is better depends on whether you prefer the discipline of having to make the higher payment or the flexibility of having it optional.

Borrowing the larger amount also increases all the settlement costs that depend on the loan amount, including points and origination fees, title insurance, and per diem interest. These will be calculated on $200,000 rather than $190,000. In addition, you will pay another full month's interest on $200,000 if the lender's accounting system does not recognize an extra payment before the first installment payment is due.

The upshot is that, in an apples-to-apples comparison where the monthly payment is the same, borrowing $200,000 and repaying $10,000 immediately will cost more than the alternative of borrowing $190,000.

Refinancing into a Simple Interest Biweekly: While the "magical" device described above costs little to those who act on it, the same cannot be said for this one. I have found borrowers who were bankrupted by it. It is a biweekly mortgage with daily interest accrual, as described in **Mortgage Scams and Tricks/*Strictly Lender Scams*/Overpriced Simple Interest Biweekly**.

In the merchandising of this scam, loan officers paint a magical aura around the way their mortgages pay down. They use words like "reamortize" to connote a unique process that saves borrowers money despite the higher interest rate. In fact, every borrower I have encountered who has taken one of these mortgages has been duped.

Payment Adjustment Cap *Limit on the size of payment change on an adjustable-rate mortgage.*

See **Adjustable-Rate Mortgage/*How the Monthly Payment on an ARM Is Determined*/Negative Amortization ARMs**.

Payment Adjustment Interval *The period between payment changes on an ARM, which may or may not be the same as the interest rate adjustment period.*

Payment Period *The period over which the borrower is obliged to make payments.*

On most mortgages, the payment period is a month, but on some it is biweekly. It is not necessarily the same as the **Interest Accrual Period**.

Payment Power *A Fannie Mae program that allows a borrower to skip up to 2 mortgage payments in any 12-month period and up to 10 over the life of a loan.*

A skipped payment results in an additional loan, equal to the payment plus a healthy access fee tacked on to the balance. As an emergency source of funds, it is much more costly than accessing a home equity line of credit (HELOC). It is much inferior to the **Homeownership Accelerator**.

Payment Problems *When a borrower has difficulty making the scheduled payment.*

Many homeowners faced with payment problems do nothing, allowing the problem to overwhelm them when it hits. That is not smart. When you know a tidal wave is coming, you should minimize the damage by preparing for it the best way you can.

Position of the Lender: A good place to start is by understanding the position of the lender. A game plan for survival should be based on a realistic view of what the lender is likely to be willing to do.

Temporary Problem: When a borrower is unable to pay but the problem is temporary, the lender has an interest in finding a way to help the borrower ride it out. A tool for this purpose is a forbearance agreement combined with a special repayment plan.

A forbearance agreement means that the lender suspends or reduces payments for a period, usually less than six months, although it can go longer. At the end of the period, the repayment plan kicks in. The borrower agrees to make the regular payment plus an additional agreed-upon amount that will cover all the payments that were not made during the forbearance period. The repayment period is usually no longer than a year.

When successful, the borrower is brought current after a lapse, and the lender suffers no loss. However, a lender will consider this approach only if convinced that the borrower's problem is temporary. The burden of proof is on the borrower.

Permanent Problem: If the borrower's problem is permanent, the lender's objective is to minimize loss. The ultimate remedy is foreclosure, where the lender goes through a lengthy legal process to acquire possession of the house. The lender then sells the house to recover the loan balance, unpaid interest, and expenses—provided there is sufficient equity in the property to cover it all.

Lenders often do not come out whole on a foreclosure, and they do not like forcing people out of their homes. They look for alternatives to foreclosure that will cost them less, but they don't want to be scammed by borrowers in the process.

If a borrower's income has been reduced to the point where she can't pay the current mortgage but could pay a smaller amount, the lender might consider a **Mortgage Modification**. This could be a lower interest rate, a longer term, a different loan type, a reduction in the loan balance, or any combination of these.

A lender is likely to be most receptive to a loan modification where the borrower has little equity in the house but wants to keep living there. With no equity, foreclosure would be costly. But the lender must be convinced that the borrower's inability to pay is completely involuntary.

When foreclosures mushroomed during 2007–2009, modifications became a preferred remedy, and the federal government introduced a special program to encourage them. *See* **Mortgage Modification/***The Government's Making Home Affordable Program***.

If the borrower's inability to pay is long term and the borrower is resigned to giving up the house, the lender will consider several alternatives to foreclosure. If the borrower has a qualified purchaser who will take title in exchange for assuming the mortgage, the lender may allow it. This is called a **Workout Assumption**.

Alternatively, the lender might allow the borrower to put the house on the market and accept the sale proceeds as full repayment, even though it is less than the loan balance. This is called a **Short Sale**.

If the borrower is unable to sell the house, the lender might accept title to the house in exchange for discharge of the debt. This is called a **Deed in Lieu of Foreclosure**.

Note that neither a short sale nor a deed in lieu, when they don't fully cover the loan balance plus expenses, necessarily leave the borrower unencumbered. Depending on how the agreement is worded and on the laws of the state, the lender may retain the right to pursue a judgment in the future for any deficiency.

Knowing what a lender *can* do is useful, but it does not tell you what a particular lender *will* do in any specific situation. Lenders differ in how they respond to payment problems. It may depend on whether they own the loan or merely service it. It may depend on who answers the phone. It will certainly depend on the borrower's behavior.

The Borrower's Game Plan: Borrowers having payment problems should develop a game plan before they become delinquent, based on a realistic understanding of the position of the lender. While some actions you can take on your own, such as selling your house, other actions have to be negotiated with the lender.

Payment Problems

Document Your Loss of Income. This will position you to demonstrate to the lender that your inability to pay is involuntary, should this be necessary later on. This is always necessary in obtaining a modification.

Estimate Your Equity in the House. Your equity is what you could sell it for net of sales commissions, less the balance of your mortgage. This will help you develop a strategy for dealing with the lender.

Determine Whether Your Financial Reversal Is Temporary or Permanent. A temporary reversal is one where, if you are provided payment relief for up to 6 months, you will be able to resume regular payments at the end of the period and repay all the payments you missed within the following 12 months. You must document the case for the reversal being temporary. If you cannot make a persuasive case that the change in your financial condition is temporary, the lender will assume it is permanent.

Your game plan should take account of whether or not you have substantial equity in the house and whether the change in your financial status is temporary or permanent.

Best Strategy When You Have Substantial Equity: If you have substantial equity in your house, the least costly action to the lender may be foreclosure. While foreclosure is costly, the lender is entitled to be reimbursed from the sales proceeds for all foreclosure costs plus all unpaid interest and principal.

While foreclosure makes the lender whole, it is a disaster for you. Your equity is depleted, you incur the costs of moving, and your credit is ruined. Hence, you must avoid foreclosure, if necessary by selling your house.

If your financial reversal is temporary and you can persuade the lender of this, the lender may be willing to suspend payments for a period, followed by a repayment plan. The lender will probably prefer to keep your loan, rather than foreclose on it, but only if convinced it is a good loan. The burden of proof is on you in this situation to demonstrate that temporary payment relief will really work.

If your financial reversal is permanent, sell the house before you begin accumulating delinquencies. This way, you at least retain your equity and your credit rating.

Obtaining full value for your home may take some time—you don't want to be forced into a fire sale. If delinquency is looming, take out a home equity line of credit to keep your payments current.

Best Strategy When You Have Little or No Equity: If you have little or no equity, your bargaining position is actually stronger because foreclosure is a sure loser for the lender.

If your financial reversal is temporary and you want to remain in your house, it will be easier to persuade the lender to offer payment relief.

If your financial reversal is permanent, but not major, the lender may be favorably disposed to a contract modification that will permanently reduce the payments.

If your financial reversal is permanent and major, the lender probably will be willing to accept either a short sale or a deed in lieu of foreclosure. In both cases your debt obligation may be fully discharged. They do appear on your credit report, but are not as bad a mark as a foreclosure.

The lender will turn a wary eye on borrowers with negative equity who have the means to continue making payments but would like to rid themselves of their negative equity through short sale or deed in lieu. While these options are less costly to the lender than foreclosure, lenders view borrowers as responsible for their debts, regardless of the depletion of their equity. How they respond depends on how convinced they are that the borrower's problems are truly involuntary and on whether they think they could collect more if they go after the borrower for the deficiency.

Payment Rate *The interest rate used to calculate the mortgage payment.*

The interest rate and the payment rate are often the same, but they need not be. They must be the same if the payment is fully amortizing (*see* **Amortization/*The Fully Amortizing Payment***). If the payment rate is higher than the interest rate, the payment will be more than fully amortizing, and if continued, the loan will pay off before term. If the payment rate is below the interest rate, the payment will be less than fully amortizing, and if continued, the loan will not be fully paid off at term.

Payment Shock *A very large increase in the payment on an ARM that may surprise the borrower.*

See **Adjustable-Rate Mortgage (ARM)/*How the Monthly Payment on an ARM Is Determined*/Negative Amortization ARMs**.

The term is also used to refer to a large difference between the rent being paid by a first-time homebuyer and the monthly housing expense on the purchased home.

Payoff Month *The month in which a zero loan balance is reached.*

The payoff month may or may not be the loan term.

Per Diem Interest *Interest from the day of closing to the first day of the following month.*

To simplify the task of loan administration, the accounting for all home loans begins as if the loan were closed on the first day of the month following the day the loan is closed. For example, if the loan is closed and the money disbursed on May 15, the clock begins ticking on that loan as if it were closed on June 1, with the first payment due July 1. But since the lender actually advanced the money on May 15, the lender expects to be paid interest for the period between May 15 and June 1. That payment is the "per diem interest," which is due at closing.

If the loan in the example above was $100,000 and the interest rate 6%, the per diem interest would be $100,000 × 0.06/365 × 17, or $279.

In some cases, especially when a loan is closed early in the month, the lender is willing to rebate interest to the borrower for those few days and collect the first payment a month earlier. If the loan above were closed May 3, for example, the lender would pay three days of interest at closing and collect the first monthly payment on June 1.

Permanent Buy-Down

Same as **Points**. *Also see* **Temporary Buy-Down/***Temporary Versus Permanent Buy-Downs*.

Piggyback Mortgage *A combination of a first mortgage for 80% of property value and a second for 5, 10, 15, or 20% of value, designated as 80/5/15, 80/10/10, 80/15/5, and 80/20/0, respectively.*

See **Second Mortgage/***Using a Second to Avoid Mortgage Insurance*.

Pipeline Risk *The lender's risk that, between the time a lock commitment is given to the borrower and the time the loan is closed, interest rates will rise and the lender will take a loss on selling the loan.*

See **Locking/*Cost of Locking to Lenders***.

PITI *Principal, interest, taxes, and insurance.*

These are the components of the monthly housing expense. *See* **Qualification/*Meeting Income Requirements*/Expense Ratios**.

PMI

See **Private Mortgage Insurance**.

Points *An upfront cash payment required by the lender as part of the charge for the loan, expressed as a percentage of the loan amount; e.g., "3 points" means a charge equal to 3% of the loan amount.*

When points are negative, the lender credits the borrower or the mortgage broker. Negative points are termed "rebates." When retained by a mortgage broker, they are termed "yield-spread premiums."

Points and Rebates as Borrower Options: The points-rebate system is unique to the United States. It offers borrowers more options at the cost of greater complexity. The following is a typical schedule for a 30-year fixed-rate mortgage:

5.375% and 2.75 points

5.50% and 2.0 points

5.625% and 1.375 points

5.750% and 0.75 point

5.875% and 0.125 points

6% and 0.5 rebate

6.125% and 1.0 rebate

6.25% and 1.5 rebate

6.375% and 2.0 rebate

6.5% and 2.3755 rebate

For borrowers who have the cash and expect to remain in their house for a long time, paying points to reduce the rate makes economic sense. The benefit from the lower rate extends over a long period. In addition, borrowers who have difficulty qualifying because their income is low relative to their monthly housing expense may pay points to reduce their monthly payment.

In contrast, borrowers with a short time horizon do better with high-rate–rebate combinations because they don't pay the high rate very long. In addition, borrowers who are short of cash prefer to pay interest rates high enough to command rebates, which can be used to cover their settlement costs.

Sharpening the Rate-Point Decision: Borrowers who are neither cash short nor income short can sharpen the decision process using one of the calculators on my Web site. Calculators 11a and 11b, covering FRMs and ARMs, respectively, compare the future costs of a low-rate–high-points combination with those of a high-rate–low-points combination over any period specified by you. These calculators also show the "breakeven period," which is the minimum period you must hold the mortgage to come out ahead with the low-rate–high-points combination.

A different approach to the decision is to look at the payment of points as an investment that yields a return that increases the longer you stay in your house. This return can be compared with the return on other investments available to you. This approach is used in calculators 11c and 11d.

Paying Points Versus Making a Larger Down Payment: An advantage of viewing the payment of points as an investment decision is that it allows you to compare the return from paying points with the return from increasing the down payment. (You can find the latter using calculator 12a.)

Factors Affecting the Return: In both cases, the borrower makes an upfront cash outlay and receives a stream of income in the future. With a larger down payment, the income is the reduction in monthly payment that results from the smaller loan and mortgage insurance premium. With points, the income is the reduction in monthly payment that results from the lower interest rate. The better investment is the one that yields the higher return over the period you retain the mortgage.

Points

The return on investment in points is extremely sensitive to how long you stay in the home. For example, if you are in the 25.5% tax bracket, pay 4 points to reduce the rate on a 30-year fixed-rate mortgage from 6 to 5%, and stay in your house for 3 years, your after-tax return is a negative 12.6%. But if you stay for 15 years, your return is a positive 16.4%.

In contrast, the return on an investment in a larger down payment declines over time, though not very much. If you increase your down payment from 5% of the property value to 10%, for example, which reduces the mortgage insurance premium on a 6% 30-year FRM from 0.78% to 0.52% of the loan amount, the after-tax return over 3 years is 10.0%; over 15 years it is 8.8%.

Note that in this example, the larger down payment reduced the loan-to-value ratio past a **Pricing Notch Point (PNP)** of 10%. If the borrower only has enough excess cash to get to 8%, the mortgage insurance premium would not change, and the return on investment would be only 6%. This raises the possibility that the borrower may find it profitable to invest in both. *See* **Investing in Both** *below*.

Hence, in general, if your time horizon is short, you should invest in a larger down payment, and if it is long, you should invest in higher points. But how long is "long"?

In most cases the crossover point where the returns are the same occurs in 8 years or less. However, the crossover point is affected by a number of factors, including your tax bracket, PMI premiums, the rate reduction you receive for a given increase in points, and appreciation of your house, which affects how long you'll carry PMI. The beauty of calculators 11c, 11d, and 12a is that they take account of all the specifics of your own particular situation.

Investing in Both: Since the return on investment in a larger down payment is highest when the loan-to-value ratio is reduced to a **Pricing Notch Point (PNP)**, it may be profitable to increase the down payment *and* pay points. For example, if the borrower in the example above has enough excess cash to increase the down payment from 5 to 12%, the best scheme is to go to 10% and use the remaining cash to pay points.

Financing Points: Points can be included in the loan amount, but usually it isn't a good idea if you can avoid it. In most cases, financing the points lengthens the breakeven periods, as illustrated in the table below. The first number in each cell assumes the borrower pays the points in cash, while the number in parentheses assumes the points are financed.

Points

Breakeven Periods in Months on a 30-Year Mortgage Used for Purchase: 6% at 0 Points Versus 5% at 4 Points			
Savings Rate	Tax Rate 0%	Tax Rate 28%	Tax Rate 40%
0%	49 (63)	49 (85)	49 (103)
5%	56 (59)	55 (80)	54 (99)
10%	68 (55)	63 (75)	61 (94)

Financing points lengthens the breakeven period if the savings rate—the rate the borrower could earn on cash not used to pay points—is below the rate on the high-rate–low-points mortgage. This usually is the case. On purchase transactions, furthermore, financing points spreads the tax deduction over time, whereas points paid in cash are deductible in the year paid. Financing points is worthwhile only where the savings rate is above the mortgage rate and the tax rate is low.

The breakeven periods when points are financed could be even longer than those shown in the table if financing the points brings the loan amount past a loan size PNP or past a loan-to-value ratio PNP. Most loan originators will not allow a borrower to make this mistake, but it does happen.

Points and Mortgage Shopping: It is a good idea to decide what you want to do about points before you shop. If you want to pay points to reduce the rate, you shop rate based on a specified number of points. This has the added advantage of letting loan officers know that you know what you are doing.

If you want a rebate, the best strategy is to shop for a **No-Cost Mortgage**, which means a rebate high enough to cover all settlement costs except escrows and per diem interest. This has the added advantage of protecting you against getting whacked with additional settlement costs at closing.

Selecting a loan provider while the rate-point combination is undecided is a bad mistake. Because of the wide variability in pricing points, the lender offering the lowest points at one rate is not necessarily the same as the lender offering the lowest points at a different rate.

Furthermore, once you are too far along in the process to back out, the price in points to lower the rate, or the price in rate to increase the rebate, may be "off the sheet"—meaning that the loan officer may take advantage of the opportunity to make a few extra dollars by giving you a worse deal than the one shown on her price sheet.

Portable Mortgage *A mortgage that can be moved from one property to another.*

Ordinarily, you repay your mortgage when you sell your house and take out a new mortgage on the new home you purchase. With a portable mortgage, you transfer the old mortgage to the new property.

An Innovation in 2003: Portable mortgages were talked about for a long time, but did not appear until 2003, when they were introduced by E*TRADE Mortgage. E*TRADE offered the portability option on 30-year fixed-rate mortgages only, at an interest rate 3/8% higher than the rate on the identical mortgage without the option. Borrowers had to be purchasing single-family homes as their permanent residence (refinancing didn't qualify), they had to have squeaky-clean credit, and they had to provide full documentation.

When the second edition of this book was written in 2009, E*TRADE was struggling to survive very heavy losses, and portable mortgages were no longer being offered. As far as I could determine, E*TRADE's portable mortgages had little or nothing to do with the company's problems. Because the portable mortgage is a useful product that may appear again, I decided to retain the analysis below from the first edition.

Benefits to the borrower: There are two. One is that it avoids the costs of taking out a new mortgage. This cost must be set against the cost of paying 3/8% more in rate, which rises the longer the period between the first purchase and the second. The breakeven period comes out to roughly 4 years on a $150,000 loan. If you expect that you won't be buying your next house within 4 years, the cost saving on the future mortgage won't cover the cost penalty imposed by the 3/8% rate premium. The period is a little shorter on a larger loan, longer on a smaller loan.

The second benefit is that it allows you to avoid any rise in market interest rates that occurs between the time you purchase one house and the time you purchase the next one. Since World War II, mortgage rates have been as low as 4% and as high as 18%. When rates are about 6%, there is clearly much greater potential for rise than for decline. If rates increase, the portable mortgage protects you; and if they decrease, you can get the benefit by refinancing. There is no prepayment penalty.

Borrowers who confidently expect to move within 5 or 6 years and fear that a major spike in rates could seriously crimp their plans may find the 3/8% rate increment a reasonable insurance premium. It is less valuable for borrowers who expect to move every 3 years since the transfer option can only be used once.

Portability is also less valuable for borrowers who expect to trade down when they move. Since they will need a smaller mortgage at that point, the rate protection is not worth as much. However, E*TRADE will recalculate the payment if the new mortgage is more than $10,000 smaller than the old one.

Borrowers who trade up cannot increase the original loan. E*TRADE will give them a second mortgage at the market rate on first mortgages at that time, but the sum of first and second mortgages cannot exceed 80% of property value. The borrower will have to pay settlement costs on the second—the same costs that a new borrower would have to pay at that time. Borrowers trading up could well find that they would do better getting a second mortgage from another lender.

Borrowers with the excellent credit needed to qualify for a portable mortgage should be confident that they can maintain that record. Borrowers in bankruptcy or behind in their payments cannot exercise the transfer option. In such a situation, they would have paid the 3/8% rate increment for nothing.

Portfolio Lender *A lender that holds the loans it originates in its portfolio rather than selling them.*

See **Mortgage Lender/*Mortgage Banks Versus Portfolio Lenders*.**

Posted Prices *The mortgage prices delivered by lenders to loan officers and mortgage brokers, as opposed to the final prices paid by borrowers.*

See **Rate Sheets**.

Preapproval *A written opinion by a lender that a prospective homebuyer has the income, assets, and credit to carry the mortgage required to purchase a house of some assumed value, prior to the identification of the specific property that will be purchased.*

A preapproval is *more* than a prequalification, because the lender verifies the financial information provided by the potential borrower and checks her credit. But a preapproval is *less* than an approval because the property value is preliminary and won't be definitively established until there is a purchase contract. Furthermore, a preapproval may not specify a mortgage interest rate, and if it does specify a rate, it is not binding on the lender.

Since the borrower's mortgage-carrying capacity depends on an interest rate that is not yet known, and since the price of the house is preliminary, a preapproval has a lot of slack. It is usually adequate, however, for the purpose for which it is intended. That purpose is to convince a home seller that a prospective buyer has the means to make the purchase and should therefore be taken seriously.

Lenders offer preapprovals in the hope that the purchaser will view the preapproval as the first step in obtaining a loan. It is a way of generating a promising lead. However, borrowers should not view it that way. It would be a mistake to select a lender for no other reason than that the lender had issued you a preapproval. On the other hand, there is no reason to exclude that lender from your search for a loan provider, especially if your experience with the preapproval was favorable.

Predatory Lending *A variety of unsavory lender practices designed to take advantage of unwary borrowers.*

Predatory lending covers much the same ground as **Mortgage Scams and Tricks/*Scams by Loan Providers***. The difference is that the term "predatory lending" has been associated with practices in the subprime market that specifically target unsophisticated and vulnerable borrowers. Scams operate across a wider spectrum and usually don't leave quite as much human wreckage in their wake.

Predatory Practices: The two most important types of predatory lending are "equity grabbing" and "price gouging."

Equity Grabbing: This is lending that is intended by the lender to lead to default by the borrower so the lender can grab the borrower's equity.

Equity grabbing may be associated with cash-out refinancing to cash-dazzled customers. In one case, a borrower with significant equity in her home refinanced a low-interest-rate loan into one carrying a high interest rate plus heavy fees, with the fees included in the new loan. The inducement was the cash, more than the borrower had ever seen at one time. But the borrower was saddled with a larger repayment obligation that she couldn't meet, resulting in default and loss of the home.

Home improvement scams work in a similar manner. Gullible home-owners are sweet-talked into contracting for repairs for which they are overcharged, and then the cost of the repairs plus high loan fees are rolled into a mortgage that they cannot afford. Default follows, and the borrower loses the home.

Equity grabs are extremely difficult to regulate away because they represent an abusive application of legitimate activities. Most borrowers who do a cash-out refinance retain their equity, and this is true as well for most of those who take out home improvement loans. There are no remedies that won't curb legitimate transactions, except perhaps for counseling directed at potential victims. But people can't be compelled to seek counsel or to listen when they receive it.

The home price declines during 2006–2009 reduced equity grabbing by eliminating the equity in millions of homes. You are safe from equity grabbers if you have nothing to grab.

Price Gouging: This is charging interest rates and fees that are excessive relative to what the same borrower would have paid had he shopped the market effectively. It also includes packaging related services, such as credit life insurance, which are overpriced and made to appear as if they are required.

A large number of the newspaper columns I write are designed to help potential borrowers avoid price gouging. Informed borrowers who shop, even if it is only to check prices on the Internet, are very unlikely to be gouged.

Still, there are many uninformed borrowers who don't shop, and government ought to protect them if there were ways to do it that didn't seriously harm other borrowers. Unfortunately, the regulatory reaction to price gouging is to set maximum prices, which prevents borrowers from being gouged only by depriving other borrowers of access to credit altogether. The trade-off between protection and harm becomes increasingly unfavorable as the market widens to provide market access to more and more consumers. As offensive as price gouging is, price controls are not a good remedy.

Targets of Predators: To educate myself on what makes a victim, I studied 51 case histories of households victimized by mortgage lenders. The histories were provided by ACORN, which has been in the forefront of the struggle against predators. While every case is different, victims share certain features that make them vulnerable to predators.

Predatory Lending

Passive: Perhaps the most pervasive characteristic of victims by far is that they are passive. They don't select a loan provider; the loan provider selects them. In more than half the cases compiled by ACORN, the victims were solicited by the lenders. In most of the remaining cases, the victims approached a lender they knew from prior experience, either their own or that of someone they knew.

Borrowers who passively go with a loan provider who solicits them run a high risk of getting a predator. While not all lenders who solicit are predators, all predators solicit. This means that a borrower would do better by throwing a dart at the loan providers listed in the yellow pages than by responding to a solicitation.

Borrowers who allow themselves to be selected by loan providers stay selected. Passive borrowers don't shop alternatives. They also don't ask as many questions as they should, which is one of the reasons they usually end up confused about the transaction.

Confused: In almost all of the case histories provided by ACORN, the borrower was confused about one or another feature of the transaction. In some cases, borrowers were under the impression that they were getting unsecured loans rather than mortgages. In many cases, they purchased credit life insurance under the impression that it was required. Often, they thought that they were paying a lower interest rate than was in fact the case. The total amount of fees packed into the loan balance usually surprised them. A large number did not know that their contract included a prepayment penalty until years later when they went to prepay.

Why so much confusion? Victims often don't read documents; or if they do read them, they are afraid to ask questions about what they don't understand. The "plain English" movement has not impacted mortgage documents, although there isn't a segment of the economy that needs it more.

Predators thrive on confusion, which provides a smoke screen for their shenanigans. To a predator, a reading-challenged borrower is an invitation to take advantage in every possible way. And mortgages provide lots of ways.

Confusion and passivity go hand in hand and must be overcome together. It is the loan provider's responsibility to eliminate confusion. If he doesn't do it, walk out the door.

Indebted: Victims are often heavily in debt and therefore vulnerable to the siren call of debt consolidation. Debt consolidation was the primary motivation in about two-thirds of the ACORN cases.

Predatory Lending

The argument is compelling: make one lower payment, and enjoy tax benefits besides. While these advantages can be real, they tend to disappear in dealing with a predator. Sometimes the payment is higher rather than lower, because of the stiff interest rate. Even if the payment is lower, the borrower's equity is depleted by the inclusion of large upfront fees in the loan. Consolidate debts with a predator, and you end up worse off than you were before.

Consumers who have accumulated too much short-term debt have an option other than debt consolidation. They can instead work out a debt management plan with a credit counselor. In exchange for agreeing to take on no new debt and to pay off the old debt within a prescribed period, the counselor can get the creditors to agree to a reduction in interest rates. The consumer makes one payment to the agency, which in turn pays the creditors.

A debt management plan is protection against falling into the hands of a predator. It also avoids one of the perils of a successful debt consolidation, which is that it paves the way for a new credit binge.

Cash Dazzled: Many victims are cash dazzled—the prospect of pocketing a significant sum of money causes a complete lapse of judgment. They ignore where the money is coming from and what it is costing them.

Cash-dazzled victims are prime candidates for cash-out refinancing—refinancing into loans that are larger than the outstanding balance of the old loans. Frequently, the new loan has a higher interest rate than the old one, and the refinancing fees are added to the loan balance. Some borrowers will refinance again and again, a practice known as "flipping," until they have used up all their equity.

There are many legitimate cash-out refinance transactions. They become predatory when the cash-dazzled victim agrees to terms that are far more costly than the borrower could have obtained by shopping alternative sources.

The worst rip-off is cash-out refinancing of zero interest loans, a problem that has plagued the Habitat for Humanity program. The Coalition for Responsible Lending estimated that 10% of all Habitat borrowers between 1987 and 1993 subsequently refinanced their zero interest loans into loans carrying rates of 10–16%. Borrowers who did this were paying interest costs of 60% and up for the cash in their pockets. Cash-dazzled victims don't see it.

Payment Myopic: Victims often base decisions solely on the affordability of monthly payments; they are payment myopic. They don't consider interest costs or how the decisions will affect the equity in their homes.

Here is the kind of deal that payment-myopic, cash-dazzled borrowers find irresistible. The borrower has paid down her 8% loan to $100,000 and has only 12 years to go. She is offered a 30-year loan for $110,000 at 9%. The monthly payment would fall from $1,082 to $885, and she puts $10,000 in her pocket tax free. What a deal!

Of course, 5 years down the road, she would have owed only $69,449 had she stayed with her original mortgage. With the new mortgage she will owe $105,468—even more if there are upfront fees included in the new loan, which is almost always the case. Payment-myopic borrowers don't look down the road.

Prepaid Finance Charges *Fees paid to the lender as reported on the Truth in Lending form.*

These fees are subtracted from the loan amount to obtain the **Amount Financed**.

Prepayment *A payment made by the borrower over and above the scheduled mortgage payment.*

If the additional payment pays off the entire balance, it is a "prepayment in full"; otherwise, it is a "partial prepayment." *See* **Partial Prepayments**.

Prepayment Penalty *A charge imposed by the lender if the borrower pays off the loan early.*

The charge is usually expressed as a percentage of the loan balance at the time of prepayment or a specified number of months' interest. Some part of the balance, usually 20%, can be prepaid without penalty. Usually, the penalty declines or disappears as the mortgage ages. For example, the penalty might be 3% of the balance net of the exclusion within the first year, 2% in the second year, and 1% in the third year.

A penalty may or may not apply to prepayment resulting from a home sale. A penalty that applies whether the loan is prepaid because of a sale or because of a refinancing is referred to as a "hard" penalty. A penalty that applies only to a refinancing is a "soft" penalty.

Advantage of a Prepayment Penalty for Prime Borrowers: Prime borrowers can usually negotiate a lower interest rate in exchange for accepting a prepayment penalty. Investors who buy loans from lenders in the secondary market are willing to accept a lower rate in exchange for a prepayment penalty. The benefit of the penalty to them is that it discourages refinancing if interest rates decline in the future. Lenders will then pass the benefit on to knowledgeable borrowers who ask for it.

Whether it is a good deal depends on the rate reduction and the size and scope of the penalty. I would consider a 1/4% reduction in rate in exchange for a 2–3% penalty during the first three to five years, payable only on a refinancing, as a good deal. It would be an exceptionally good deal for someone who expects to be in the house a long time.

Penalties on Loans to Subprime Borrowers: In contrast to prime loans, where penalties are an option, penalties were required on most subprime loans. Lenders demanded them because the risk of refinancing was higher on subprime loans than on prime loans. Subprime borrowers profit from refinancing if their credit rating improves, even when the general level of mortgage rates does not change. Because of high origination costs and high default costs, subprime lending was not profitable if the good loans walked out the door after only two years. Of course, looking back, what destroyed the subprime market was defaults, not prepayments.

Surreptitious Penalties: During the heavy refinance periods after 1998, I received hundreds of letters from borrowers who claimed that they were unaware that their loan carried a prepayment penalty until they went to refinance it. In many cases, they alleged that the loan officer had explicitly told them that there was no penalty.

Considering that the penalty must be in the note and also in the Truth in Lending Disclosure Statement (TIL), both of which are signed by the borrower, how could they not have known?

My best guess, and it is just a guess, is that about half of them did know, but preferred to forget. But that leaves half who were hoodwinked.

It is all too easy, because so many borrowers are so overwhelmed with documents that they sign without reading. Or they read, but what is important in the document doesn't register. It is extremely easy to overlook a prepayment penalty on the TIL.

Prepayment Penalty

"Prepayment" lies at the bottom of the TIL, the last piece of information on a long form. It reads as follows:

PREPAYMENT: If you pay off your loan early, you

[ ] *may* [ ] *will not have to pay a penalty*

[ ] *may* [ ] *will not be entitled to a refund of part of the finance charge*

This is a strange set of choices. The negative is definite—"you . . . will not have to pay a penalty"—but the affirmative is qualified. The dictionary says that "may" refers to "a possibility"; "may" and "may not" thus mean exactly the same thing. Use of the word "may" suggests falsely that there may not be a penalty. It would not be surprising if this misleading phraseology put borrowers off their guard.

Since either a mortgage loan has a prepayment penalty clause or it doesn't, the disclosure should be rephrased as follows:

PREPAYMENT: Your loan

[ ] *does* [ ] *does not have a prepayment penalty clause*

The second line under "Prepayment" on the existing TIL form indicates whether or not, in the event of early payment, the lender will refund "part of the finance charge." There is no good reason for this being here. Lenders *never* refund fees to borrowers, and even if they did, borrowers need not be warned about the possibility of lender generosity.

What this item does is cause confusion. Because this confusing and wholly unnecessary statement is placed immediately below the already weak notice of a prepayment penalty, it weakens the penalty notice further by diluting the borrower's attention. The effectiveness of disclosure declines as the amount of other information with which it is packaged rises. The borrower trying to figure out what the refund option means is not concentrating on the penalty option.

It is thus readily understandable why many borrowers signed a TIL but were later surprised to find that they were subject to a prepayment penalty.

As this was written in 2009, changes in TIL were being considered and hopefully will include a better way of disclosing a prepayment penalty. A new **Good Faith Estimate** that became effective January 1, 2010, discloses any penalty very clearly.

Prequalification

Same as **Qualification**.

Price Gouging *Charging unwary borrowers interest rates and fees that are excessive relative to what the same borrowers could have found had they effectively shopped the market.*

See **Predatory Lending/*Predatory Practices***.

Pricing Notch Point (PNP) *A loan amount, loan-to-value ratio, or credit score at which the interest rate, points, or mortgage insurance premium changes.*

For example, if the interest rate on a $417,000 loan is 4.75% but the rate on a loan for $417,001 is 5.375%—these were wholesale rates on 30-year FRMs at zero points on September 18, 2009—$417,000 is a PNP.

Importance of PNPs: Since the increase in price that results from crossing a PNP applies to the entire loan, not just to the increment, the increment is extremely costly. While no one would borrow $417,001, a person might borrow $500,000. In that case, the $83,000 increment in the example above would cost 8.5%, after taking account of the higher rate on the $417,000.

Loan Amount and LTV PNPs: On conventional loans, in 2009, there were two loan amount PNPs. One was $417,000, called the "conforming loan limit," which was the largest loan that could be purchased by Fannie Mae and Freddie Mac before conforming jumbos were authorized. It remained the limit in counties in which jumbos were not authorized.

The second PNP, called the "conforming jumbo limit," varied by county up to $729,750 and was scheduled to expire at the end of 2010. If a county had a conforming jumbo limit of $729,750, it meant that the agencies could purchase mortgages up to that amount from that county. Since the agencies charged a higher rate on the jumbos, the jumbo limit was another PNP.

PNPs in the ratio of loan amount to property value are generally 80, 85, 90, 95, and 97%. In the crisis market that developed after the housing bubble burst in 2007, 75% also became a PNP.

PNPs and Financing Closing Costs: PNPs become relevant most often in connection with two issues faced by borrowers. One is whether or not to finance closing costs, since doing so increases the loan amount and could breach a PNP. As an example, if closing costs on a $400,000 loan are $8,000 and the LTV is 80–83% of value, financing the closing costs won't affect the price because the ratio will remain below 85%. The cost of borrowing the additional $8,000 is the interest rate and points on the $8,000. But if the initial LTV was 84%, adding the $8,000 would bring the ratio above 85%, raising the price on the $400,000. That would make the cost of the $8,000 astronomical.

PNPs and the Down Payment/Prepayment Decision: The other situation where PNPs are important to borrowers is where they have the capacity to make a larger down payment or to pay down the balance preparatory to a refinance. If the larger down payment or prepayment penetrates a PNP, the return on investment will be very high. The financial crisis increased these returns by widening the price spreads between PNPs and by eroding borrower equity. Here is an example from my mailbox.

My credit is excellent, my income is adequate, my rate is 6.125%, and I qualify for a refinance at 5.125%. However, the value of my house has declined from 360K to 280K and we owe 242K. My lender says that for us to refinance we need mortgage insurance, which was not required when we took out the loan originally.

If this borrower can come up with $18,000 to pay down the balance to $224,000, that balance would be 80% of the current appraised value, and no mortgage insurance would be needed. Relative to remaining with her current mortgage, the $18,000 investment would yield 18% over 5 years, 16.6% over 30 years, with no risk.

Similar logic applies if a partial prepayment converts a jumbo into a conforming loan. Because the crisis has increased the yield spread between them, the return on an investment in prepayment can earn a sizable return for a refinancing borrower. In a case I looked at, a prepayment of $80,000 that would have been required to convert a jumbo into a conforming loan yielded 10.4% over 5 years; if only $40,000 was required, the return would rise to 15.4%.

FICO scores have their own PNPs, which are not as well known as loan amount or LTV PNPs and which may differ some from lender to lender, but they are equally important. A typical set would be 800, 780, 720, 700, 680, 660, 640, and 620. As an illustration, the interest rate closest to zero points on a 30-year FRM of $340,000 used to purchase a $400,000 home, as quoted by a major lender on September 17, 2009, was 4.875% at 800, 5.125% at 720, 5.375% at 660, 5.5% at 640, and 5.75% at 620.

Primary Mortgage Market *The market in which borrowers transact with lenders to create a new mortgage, as opposed to the secondary market, where existing mortgages and mortgage-backed securities are purchased and sold.*

Primary Residence *The house in which the borrower will live most of the time, as distinct from a second home or an investor property that will be rented.*

The loan application asks whether applicants intend to occupy the property as their primary residence. Lenders offer better terms to homebuyers who view the home as their primary residence. The lenders have found that when borrowers have financial trouble, they will struggle harder to save their primary residence than a vacation home or a property held as an investment.

Principal *The portion of the monthly payment that is used to reduce the loan balance.*

See **Amortization**.

Principal Limit *The present value of a house, given the elderly owner's right to live there until she dies or voluntarily moves out, under FHA's reverse mortgage program.*

See **Reverse Mortgage/FHA's Home Equity Conversion Mortgage (HECM)/ The Net Principal Limit**.

Private Mortgage Insurance (PMI) *Mortgage insurance provided by private mortgage insurance companies (PMIs).*

As distinguished from mortgage insurance provided by the government under FHA, VA, and USDA.

Insurance Premiums: Premiums are most often quoted as annual rates that are paid monthly. To obtain the monthly premium in dollars, the quoted figure is multiplied by the loan balance and divided by 1,200. If the premium rate is 0.92 and the loan is for $100,000, for example, the monthly premium is $92,000 divided by 1,200, or $76.67.

Private Mortgage Insurance (PMI)

The premiums charged by different companies are either identical or so close that the difference isn't worth bothering with.

Before the crisis, insurance premiums varied primarily by type of mortgage, down payment, and term. After the crisis, premiums (as well as the availability of PMI at any price) were tied to the credit score and other factors that affect risk—essentially the same factors used by lenders. For example, in late 2009, most PMIs required a FICO score of 680 or higher.

Alternative Premium Plans: There are a number of ways of paying for PMI, but several of them are historical relics and rarely used. Today, the majority of policies carry the monthly premiums illustrated above.

An attractive alternative to the monthly premium plan is the financed upfront premium, where a one-time premium is included in the loan amount. In late 2009, I priced monthly and one-time premiums on a $360,000 loan in Pennsylvania to a prime borrower. The monthly premium was $216. The upfront premium was $12,168: this would increase the loan by that amount, and it would increase the payment on a 5% 30-year FRM by only $65.32. Further, $50.70 of the additional payment is additional interest that is tax deductible. Mortgage insurance premiums are deductible through 2010, but beyond that, nobody knows.

The downside of the financed upfront premium plan is that the borrower will have a higher loan balance when the loan is repaid. However, loan repayment in the early years results in a partial refund of the premium. The refund is about 90% after 1 year, 50% after 6 years, and zero after 12 years.

Unfortunately, few borrowers are aware of this attractive alternative because most lenders don't offer it. Fannie Mae and Freddie Mac require lenders to obtain special authorization to use this program on loans that are sold to them. Most lenders prefer to avoid this inconvenience, and they aren't pressed because few customers are aware of the option.

PMI Versus Piggybacks: Prior to the financial crisis, most borrowers who could not put 20% down had a choice. They could buy mortgage insurance, or they could take a second mortgage "piggyback" for the loan amount required above 80%. I developed my calculator 13a that allowed a borrower to determine which option would be less costly. The crisis destroyed the piggyback market, however, leaving PMI the only game in town.

Deductibility of PMI Premiums: Until 2007, the IRS maintained that mortgage insurance premiums were not deductible. In this, they were inconsistent.

Private Mortgage Insurance (PMI)

Interest payments on home mortgages are deductible, and no distinction is made by the IRS between the portion of the interest payment that represents compensation for the time value of money and the portion that represents compensation for risk. If a low-risk borrower pays 7%, for example, while a high-risk borrower pays 9%, the entire interest payment of the high-risk borrower is deductible. However, if the lender charges both borrowers 7% but requires that the high-risk borrower purchase mortgage insurance, with the mortgage insurer now collecting the 2% or its equivalent, the IRS will not allow the 2% to be deducted. That is inconsistent.

The IRS classifies mortgage insurance premiums as payments by borrowers for services provided by the lender, similar to an appraisal fee, and as a general matter such payments are not deductible. The problem with this position is that the lender is not in fact providing any service in connection with mortgage insurance. The mortgage insurance premium is a payment for risk, in exactly the same way that the 2% rate increment charged the high-risk borrower is a payment for risk. Apart from possible differences in price, the borrower doesn't care whether the lender receives the payment and takes the risk or the mortgage insurance company receives the payment and takes the risk.

In 2007, Congress made PMI premiums deductible for specified years. At this writing, deductibility holds through 2010. What will happen after that is not clear.

Why Do Borrowers Pay the Premiums? It is more historical accident than anything else. When the modern PMI industry began in the late 1950s, many states had legal ceilings on interest rates. If lenders paid for mortgage insurance and passed on the cost to borrowers as a higher interest rate, they might have bumped up against those ceilings. If the borrower paid the premium, this potential roadblock was avoided.

Unfortunately, a borrower-pay system is much less effective than a lender-pay system. When the borrower pays, lenders have little interest in minimizing insurance costs to the borrower because these costs do not influence a consumer's decision regarding the selection of a lender. Insurers do not compete for the patronage of consumers, but for the patronage of the lenders who select them. Such competition is directed not at premiums but at the services provided by the insurers to the lenders. Its effect is to raise the costs to insurers and ultimately the cost borne by borrowers.

For the potential advantages of a lender-pay system, *see* **Lender-Pay Mortgage Insurance**.

Private Mortgage Insurance (PMI)

Mortgage Insurance Versus Higher Rate: Some lenders purchase mortgage insurance themselves so they can offer a higher interest rate in lieu of PMI. The sales pitch is that interest is tax deductible, whereas PMI premiums may not be. The other side of the coin, however, is that the borrower must pay the higher interest rate for the life of the mortgage, while mortgage insurance is terminated at some point.

Calculator 14a on my Web site provides a cost comparison of the options. It takes account of the borrower's tax bracket, the period the borrower expects to be in the house, the PMI premium, the rate increment to avoid the premium, and the number of years until PMI terminates.

Terminating PMI: Until 1999, borrowers could terminate PMI only with the permission of the lender. Because borrowers paid the premiums, however, lenders had no financial incentive to agree. Some lenders allowed PMI termination under certain specified conditions. Others had more stringent conditions. Still others did not allow it at all. Many borrowers, furthermore, were unaware of the possibility of terminating insurance and paid premiums for years longer than necessary.

What Congress should have done to deal with this problem was mandate that lenders pay PMI premiums. If lenders paid for mortgage insurance and passed on the cost in the interest rate, lenders would decide when to terminate based on whether or not they felt the insurance was still needed. This would also have reduced the cost of PMI, for reasons indicated above. Instead, Congress in 1999 elected to do it the hard way, by enacting mandatory termination rules. Unfortunately, the rules are unavoidably complicated.

Under federal law, lenders are required to cancel PMI on loans made after July 29, 1999, when amortization has reduced the loan balance to 78% of the value of the property at the time the loan was made. Cancellation is automatic. Loans made before July 29, 1999, are not covered by the law.

In addition, under the 1999 law, lenders must terminate insurance *at the borrower's request* when the loan balance hits 80% of the original value. Borrowers who take the initiative can thus terminate earlier than those who wait. However, the lender need not comply if the property has a second mortgage or has declined in value. Furthermore, the borrower cannot have had a payment late by 30 days or more within the year preceding the cancellation date or cannot have been late by 60 days or more in the year before that.

Loans sold to Fannie Mae or Freddie Mac, however, are subject to the termination rules of the agencies regardless of when the loan was made.

And these rules are more favorable to homeowners because they are based on the current appraised value of the property rather than the value at the time the loan was made.

Under the rules of the agencies:

- Borrowers can terminate after 2 years if the loan balance is no more than 75% of current appraised value, and they can terminate after 5 years if it is no more than 80%.

- Borrowers must request cancellation and obtain an appraisal acceptable to the agencies and to the lender.

- The ratios required for termination are lower if there is a second mortgage, if the property is held for investment rather than occupancy, or if the property is other than single family.

- The agencies will not accept termination if a payment has been 30 days late within the prior year or 60 days late in the year before that.

Loans made before July 29, 1999, and not sold to Fannie or Freddie, remain subject to the termination rules of the lender. However, California, Connecticut, Maryland, Minnesota, Missouri, New York, North Carolina, Oregon, Texas, and Virginia also have termination rules.

The best strategy for borrowers is to assume that they are subject to the liberal Fannie or Freddie rules. After 2 years, they should begin periodically to estimate the current value of their house. Web sites offering tools that can help include HomeGain.com, DataQuick.com, and Zillow.com.

When it appears that the agencies' requirements have been met, contact the lender and ask whether the mortgage is held by one of the agencies. If it is, confirm the ratio of balance to current value that permits termination in your case, and ask about acceptable appraisers.

If the loan isn't held by one of the agencies, ask the lender for a written statement of its own termination policy. If the loan was made after July 29, 1999, follow the most liberal of the lender's rules, federal law, or state law if the property is in one of the states listed above. If the loan was made before July 29, 1999, you are stuck with the lender's rules or possibly state law.

PMIs During the Financial Crisis: PMIs are the only major player in the home loan market that has not been blamed for contributing to the financial crisis.

Private Mortgage Insurance (PMI)

- Lenders and investment bankers drastically relaxed their underwriting standards in response to the euphoria associated with rapidly rising home prices during 2000–2006. They approved loans that could not possibly be repaid without an indefinite continuation of house price inflation.

- Bank regulators ignored the breakdown of underwriting standards until it was much too late to take effective action.

- Mortgage brokers and loan officers encouraged borrowers to buy more house than they could afford and to accept toxic mortgages that they did not fully understand.

- Consumers allowed themselves to be seduced into buying houses they couldn't afford, into purchasing second and third homes on speculation, and into depleting their existing equity through cash-out refinances, in order to maintain lifestyles they could not sustain.

- Rating agencies provided AAA and AA ratings to securities issued against pools of new types of extremely risky loans when they had no adequate statistical basis for estimating potential losses on the loans.

- Fannie Mae and Freddie Mac invested in such securities and relaxed their underwriting standards, taking large losses and weakening their capacity to be a source of strength during the crisis period.

- The Federal Reserve kept interest rates low well past the point where it should have raised them, and as a regulator, was asleep at the same switch as were all the other regulatory agencies.

The PMIs did not fully participate in the euphoria and excess that preceded the crash. They did insure some risky loans that would not have been acceptable to them earlier, but for the most part they stuck to their guns. In large part, this was probably attributable to the unique regulatory structure under which they operate.

PMIs must place half of their premium inflow in contingency reserves that can't be touched for 10 years except to meet unusually large losses. This encourages the companies to set premiums based on estimates of losses over long periods, so premium rates change infrequently. This dampens the temptation to make a lot of money in a short period by taking advantage of ebullient markets. PMIs can't record artificially inflated incomes that fail to reflect high future losses and then pay themselves as if the recorded income were valid, as lenders and investment banks can.

During the crisis, the PMI industry did exactly what it was set up to do, which is to cover losses to lenders during a period of stress, out of reserves that it had accumulated during periods of prosperity. If lenders had reserved half of the excess interest they collected during the go-go years as the PMIs did, they also could have met their losses out of reserves rather than by depleting their capital.

Processing *Compiling and maintaining the file of information about a mortgage transaction, including the credit report, appraisal, verification of employment and assets, and so on.*

Mortgage brokers usually process the loans they handle. The processing file is handed off to underwriting for the loan decision.

Purchase Money Mortgage *A mortgage offered by a housebuyer as partial payment for the house.*

See **Seller Financing**.

Qualification *The process of determining whether a prospective borrower has the ability to repay a loan.*

Qualification Versus Approval: A qualified borrower is one who has the financial capacity to repay. An approved borrower is one who has both the financial capacity to repay and the willingness to repay. The borrower's willingness to repay is assessed largely by the applicant's past credit history. Qualified borrowers may ultimately be turned down because, while they have demonstrated the capacity to repay, a poor credit history suggests that they may be unwilling to pay.

Meeting Income Requirements: Lenders ask two basic questions about the borrower's ability to pay. First, is the borrower's income large enough to service the new expenses associated with the loan, plus any existing debt obligations that will continue in the future? Second, does the borrower have enough cash to meet the upfront cash requirements of the transaction? The lender must be satisfied on both counts.

Expense Ratios: Lenders assess the adequacy of the borrower's income in terms of two ratios that have become standard in the trade. The

Qualification

"housing expense ratio" is the sum of the monthly mortgage payment, including mortgage insurance and condominium fees, property taxes, and hazard insurance, divided by the borrower's monthly income. The "total expense ratio" is the same except that the numerator includes the borrower's existing debt service obligations. For each of their loan programs, lenders set maximums for these ratios, such as 28 and 36%, which the actual ratios must not exceed.

Debt Service: The debt service portion of total expenses includes alimony but not income taxes, which doesn't make a lot of sense. It also does not include student loans if repayment is deferred for a year or longer, although the underwriter can elect to include it if the amount involved is very large or the borrower's credit is weak. If there are coborrowers, the debts of both must be included.

Variations in the Ratios Among Loan Programs: Maximum expense ratios may vary from one loan program to another. Hence, an applicant only marginally over the limit may need to do nothing more than find another program with higher maximum ratios.

Variations in Ratios with Other Transaction Characteristics: Within any program, maximum expense ratios may vary with other characteristics of the transaction. For example, the maximum ratios are often lower (more restrictive) if the property is two to four family, co-op, condominium, second home, manufactured, or acquired for investment rather than occupancy. On the other hand, if the applicant makes a down payment larger than the minimum, or has a high credit score, the maximum expense ratios may be higher.

Applicant's Ability to Get the Maximum Ratios Raised: The maximum ratios are not carved in stone. The following are illustrative of circumstances where the limits may be waived:

- The borrower is just marginally over the housing expense ratio but well below the total expense ratio—29 and 30%, for example, when the maximums are 28 and 36%.

- The borrower has an impeccable credit record.

- The borrower is a first-time homebuyer who has been paying rent equal to 40% of income for 3 years and has an unblemished payment record.

Reducing Expense Ratios by Extending the Term: If expense ratios exceed the maximums, one possible option is to reduce the mortgage payment by extending the term. If the term is already 30 years, the best way to do that is to select a mortgage with an interest-only option. *See* **Interest-Only Mortgage (Option)**.

Using Excess Cash to Reduce Expense Ratios: Borrowers paying more than the minimum down can shift the excess over the minimum to reduce expense ratios. They can pay points to reduce the interest rate, pay off other debt, or fund a temporary buy-down. Except for the last, however, the impacts are quite small. They won't work at all, furthermore, if the reduced down payment increases the mortgage insurance premium.

The mortgage insurance premium categories, defined in terms of the ratio of down payment to property value, are 5 to 9.99%, 10 to 14.99%, and 15 to 19.99%. An applicant putting down 10, 15, or 20% cannot reduce the down payment without moving into a higher mortgage insurance premium category. But an applicant putting down 7.5, 12.5, 17.5, or 22.5% can.

The most effective way to reduce expense ratios is to use a temporary buy-down, which some lenders allow on some programs. With a temporary buy-down, cash is placed in an escrow account and used to supplement the borrower's payments in the early years of the loan. *See* **Temporary Buy-Down**.

Income Used to Qualify: Lenders disregard income that is viewed as temporary, such as overtime or bonuses. But sometimes income from such sources can be expected to continue. The burden of proof is on the applicant to demonstrate this. The best way to do this is to show that the income has in fact persisted over a considerable period in the past.

Borrowers who intend to share their house with another party can also consider making that party a coborrower. In such a case, the income used in the qualification process would include that of the coborrower. Of course, the coborrower would be equally responsible for repaying the loan. This works best when the relationship between the borrower and the coborrower is permanent.

Lenders will not take account of anticipated growth in income, even if it is highly probable, such as in the case of a physician just out of medical school. They are not going to base a loan on anticipated income that may or may not materialize. And they will not include income from a job the borrower is confident of getting but doesn't have.

Lenders include investment income if it can be documented as relatively stable. This includes income from property, such as the income

Qualification

obtained when a homebuyer elects to rent rather than sell an existing home. Lenders in this situation will assume that some part of the rental income (usually 75%) will remain after paying for utilities, maintenance, etc. From this, they subtract the mortgage payment, taxes, and insurance. If the difference is positive, they add it to income, but if it is negative, they add it to debt service payments.

Getting Fired Before the Loan Closes: If this happens, the applicants should tell the lenders immediately because the lenders will get the bad news anyway when they send out an employment verification request. If the lenders hadn't been told, they will be annoyed at having their time wasted and probably won't be as helpful as they might have been otherwise.

Is an ARM Needed to Qualify? Because the interest rate used to qualify applicants is generally lower on an ARM than on an FRM, some borrowers need an ARM to qualify. Yet some borrowers who appear to require an ARM in fact could qualify with an FRM using one or more of the approaches discussed above. It just takes a little more work by the loan officer. If the loan officer is lazy or is primarily interested in selling ARMs, the effort may not be made.

Meeting Cash Requirements: More borrowers are limited in the amount they can spend on a house by the cash requirements than by the income requirements. Cash is needed for the down payment and also for points and other fees charged by the lender, title insurance, escrows, and a variety of other charges. Settlement costs vary from one part of the country to another and, to some degree, from deal to deal. *See* **Settlement Costs**.

Down Payment Requirements: Down payment requirements depend on the type of program, loan amount, property characteristics, and borrower's credit rating. The financial crisis tightened the requirements for obtaining a conventional loan with 5% down, though loans at 5% down were still available to some borrowers in some areas. The FHA required 3.5% down. The VA and USDA continued to accept zero-down loans to veterans and purchasers in rural areas.

In general, down payment requirements are higher whenever a transaction has characteristics that lenders view as risky. The million-dollar loan has a high requirement, for example, because it is secured by an expensive house that may have unique features that appeal to a limited number of potential buyers and is therefore subject to much greater price variability than a less expensive house. For similar reasons, lenders will usually require a larger down payment if the borrower has a poor credit record, is purchasing a house as an investment rather than for occupancy, wants to refinance for an amount significantly larger than the existing balance, and so on.

Sources of Funds for Down Payment: In general, lenders prefer that borrowers meet the down payment requirement with funds they have saved. This indicates that the borrower has the discipline to save, which bodes well for the repayment of the loan. Other sources of funds may be problematic.

Gifts and secured loans are acceptable but only within limits. On conventional loans having down payments of less than 20% of property value, at least 5% of the down payment must come from the applicant's own funds. (There are some special programs for which the "own-funds" requirement is only 3%.) The balance can come from a gift or a secured loan. With a 20% down payment, the entire amount can come from gifts or secured loans.

Secured loans must be reported as existing debt, and the payments on them are included in total housing expenses. If this total as a percentage of income exceeds the lender's guidelines, a secured loan may not work where a gift would work.

Lenders want to be sure that an alleged gift is really a gift. If it comes from a family member, they may ask that member to sign a gift affidavit. The concern is that the gift is really an unsecured loan and that if the borrower gets into financial difficulty, she will give first priority to paying off the family member.

If the gift is from the home seller, the concern is that the sale price has been correspondingly inflated. This would mean that the equity in the property is less than it appears. For this reason, lenders tend to set a limit on "gifts" by sellers, which are typically referred to (more accurately) as "seller contributions." *See* **Down Payment/*Home Seller Contributions***.

Qualifying Self-Employed Borrowers: The system is somewhat more complicated and onerous for self-employed borrowers. It does work, but it does not work as well after the financial crisis as it did before the crisis.

The major problem with lending to the self-employed is documenting an applicant's income to the lender's satisfaction. Applicants with jobs can provide lenders with pay stubs, and lenders can verify the information by contacting the employer. With self-employed applicants, there are no third parties to verify such information.

Qualification

Consequently, lenders fall back on income tax returns, which they typically require for 2 years. They feel safe in relying on income tax data because any errors will be in the direction of understating rather than overstating income. Of course, they don't necessarily feel safe that the W-2s given them are authentic rather than concocted for the purpose of defrauding them. For this reason, they will require that the applicant authorize them to obtain copies directly from the IRS.

The support it provides to self-employed loan applicants is an unappreciated benefit of our income tax system. It may not be fully appreciated, of course, by applicants who have understated their income. In countries where virtually no one pays income taxes because cheating is endemic, tax returns are useless for qualifying borrowers.

The second problem with lending to the self-employed is determining the stability of reported income. For this purpose, the lender wants to see an income statement for the period since the last tax return and in some cases a current balance sheet for the business.

The two government-sponsored enterprises, Fannie Mae and Freddie Mac, have developed detailed guidelines for qualifying self-employed borrowers. Lenders looking to sell such loans to the agencies must follow the guidelines. The problem is that implementation can be complicated and time consuming, especially when the declared income comes from a corporation or a partnership. If you own 25% or more, you are considered as "self-employed."

Until the financial crisis, most lenders offered reduced documentation loans to self-employed applicants who cannot demonstrate 2 years of sufficient income from their tax returns. (*See* **Documentation Requirements**.) These programs varied from lender to lender, but they all provided less favorable pricing or tougher underwriting requirements of other types. Lenders invariably required larger down payments and perhaps a better credit score or higher cash reserves. In addition, they may have limited the types of properties or types of loans that were eligible. Nonetheless, reduced documentation programs allowed many self-employed who could not document adequate income with their tax returns to become homeowners.

The financial crisis put an end to that. Full documentation became the rule for every borrower, including the self-employed. In 2009, I encountered case after case of frustrated self-employed applicants who had very high credit scores and lots of equity in their properties but who could not qualify for a loan.

Qualification Rate *The interest rate used to calculate the mortgage payment used to qualify a borrower.*

The rate used in qualifying borrowers may or may not be the initial rate on the mortgage. On FRMs with **Temporary Buy-Downs**, the qualifying rate is the "bought-down" rate. On ARMs, the borrower may be qualified at the **Fully Indexed Rate** rather than the initial rate.

Qualification Ratios *Requirements stipulated by the lender that the ratio of housing expense to borrower income and the ratio of total expense to borrower income cannot exceed specified maximums.*

See **Qualification/*Meeting Income Requirements*/Expense Ratios**.

Qualification Requirements *Standards imposed by lenders as conditions for granting loans, including maximum ratios of housing expense and total expense to income, maximum loan amounts, maximum loan-to-value ratios, and so on.*

Qualification requirements are less comprehensive than underwriting requirements, which take account of the borrower's credit record.

Rate

See **Interest Rate**.

Rate-Point Breakeven *The period you must retain a mortgage in order for it to be profitable to pay points to reduce the rate.*

See **Points/*Sharpening the Rate-Point Decision***.

Rate-Point Options *All the combinations of interest rates and points that are offered on a particular loan program.*

On an ARM, rates and points may also vary with the margin and interest rate maximum.

Rate Protection *Protection for a borrower against the danger that rates will rise between the time the borrower applies for a loan and the time the loan closes.*

Rate protection can take the form of a lock, where the rate and points are frozen at their initial levels until the loan closes, or a float-down, where the rates and points cannot rise from their initial levels but they can decline if market rates decline. In either case, the protection only runs for a specified period. If the loan is not closed within that period, the protection expires, and the borrower will have to either accept the terms quoted by the lender on new loans at that time or start the shopping process anew. *See* **Locking**.

Rate Sheets *Tables of interest rates and points for different loan programs distributed by lenders to their loan officers or mortgage brokers.*

Distribution of Rate Sheets: Each morning, retail lenders distribute rate sheets to their loan officer employees, and wholesale lenders distribute theirs to all their approved mortgage brokers and correspondent lenders. The prices shown on rate sheets are those the lender is willing to accept at the time the sheet is distributed. They are sometimes referred to as **Posted Prices**. The prices hold for the day, unless they are replaced by a new rate sheet issued later in the day. Rate sheets are distributed by fax or (increasingly) over the Internet.

Coverage of Rate Sheets: Usually they cover the lender's major loan programs only, because complete coverage would make them voluminous. Lenders vary in the number of programs included. If brokers or loan officers are looking for a program not covered by the rate sheet, they have to call the lender representative who handles such questions.

Meaning of "Loan Program": A loan program is a category of loan that is relatively homogeneous with regard to its major features and underwriting rules. Each loan program is separately priced.

A loan program offered by every lender is "Conforming 30-Year Fixed," which refers to 30-year fixed-rate mortgages that meet the eligibility requirements of Fannie Mae and Freddy Mac, the two federal agencies that purchase mortgages. "Conforming 15-Year Fixed" is a separate program with its own pricing.

Lender Commitment to Prices: Lenders stand willing to lock the prices on the rate sheet if the lock is requested before a specified cutoff time and if the shopper has met all the lender's requirements to lock. These almost always include submission of a completed application and may also require approval of the application.

On the other hand, a price taken off a rate sheet and quoted to a shopper by a loan officer or mortgage broker is not binding. If the shopper comes back the next day, the quote could be different.

Borrower Access to Rate Sheets: Borrowers seldom see them. Keeping such critical information under wraps gives the loan provider a negotiating advantage. In addition, rate sheets are quite complicated, and few loan providers want to take the time required to explain them. This is especially true of mortgage brokers, who receive different rate sheets, no two of them alike, from every wholesale lender with whom they do business.

Rate Sheets and Mortgage Broker Fees: The rate sheets distributed to mortgage brokers by a wholesale lender show the lender's wholesale prices. The broker's fee is the markup over those prices and is not shown on the sheet.

Rebate

Same as **Negative Points**.

Recast Clause *A contract provision that adjusts the payment on an ARM periodically to make it fully amortizing.*

See **Adjustable-Rate Mortgage (ARM)/*How the Monthly Payment on an ARM Is Determined*/Negative Amortization ARMs**.

Referral Fees *Payments made by service providers to other parties as quid pro quo for referring customers.*

For example, a real estate agent is rewarded by a title insurance agent or a lender for sending a potential borrower to the agent or lender. The reward, whatever form it takes, is a referral fee.

Referral Fees Arise from Referral Power: Referral power is the ability to direct a client to a specific vendor. Referral power is based on information possessed by the referrer, the authority of the referrer, and the ignorance of the client. The real estate broker, for example, has information about the reliability of loan providers, and may have authority in the eyes of the borrower, who is often ignorant about loan providers

While referral fees arise out of referral power, not everyone with referral power collects a fee for making referrals. For instance, it is not the practice for physicians to collect a fee for a referral.

Why Referral Fees Are Considered a Bad Practice: One reason is the widespread prejudice that charging for something that takes no effort, or almost none, is like being paid for nothing. We undervalue information.

The second and more compelling reason for the hostility to referral fees is the fear that payment for referrals will degrade the quality of the information. If a real estate agent collects referral fees from lenders, for example, does he send borrowers to the best lenders or to the ones willing to pay the referral fee? This is a legitimate concern.

The third reason is a concern that referral fees raise the cost to the client. It seems plausible that if service providers have to pay referral fees, they are going to charge more in order to cover that cost. This is the major concern with regard to referral fees in the home mortgage market. It overlooks that a service provider who is barred from paying referral fees has to find another way to market to those with referral power, and the alternative could well be more costly.

Why Referral Fees Are Pervasive in the Home Mortgage Market: The major reason is that referral power pervades this market. Real estate and mortgage transactions involve a large number of diverse players who sell services that consumers are required to purchase. Since they are in the market very seldom, consumers typically don't know who all the players are or even what they do. They are thus heavily dependent on referrals from those who have this knowledge. Referral power in this market is based largely on the ignorance of consumers.

Realtors and builders have referral power on home purchase transactions, referring consumers to lenders and title agencies. Lenders and mortgage brokers usually select the credit reporting agency on purchases, and they select all third-party service providers on a refinance except the appraiser. Lenders always select the mortgage insurer. Before the financial crisis, lenders and brokers selected the appraiser, but after the crisis many lenders operate through an **Appraisal Management Company** and brokers are shut out of the selection process altogether. *See* **Home Valuation Code of Conduct (HVCC)**.

Referral Fees

Referral Fees Do Not Raise Settlement Service Prices to Consumers:
Referral power raises prices to consumers, not referral fees. When there is referral power, service providers compete not for the favor of consumers but for the favor of the referral agents. Such competition raises the costs of service providers, which are passed on to the consumer.

If we had a magic wand that immediately eliminated all referral fees but left referral power intact, it is as likely that prices to the consumer would rise as it is that they would fall. To service providers, referral fees are a marketing expense. Remove them and service providers would have to find other ways to market themselves to the same referrers.

Why Referral Fees Are Illegal Under RESPA: The rationale of the restrictions imposed by the Real Estate Settlements Procedures Act (RESPA) is that "kickbacks or referral fees . . . tend to increase unnecessarily the costs of certain settlement services . . ." [RESPA, Section 2601 (a)].

But Congress was wrong about that. Settlement costs are raised by referral power, not by referral fees, and RESPA fails to address referral power. Not surprisingly, therefore, the RESPA prohibition of referral fees has not reduced settlement costs at all, a fact acknowledged by HUD, which has the unpleasant task of enforcing RESPA.

RESPA Has Not Prevented Referral Fees: There are too many referral agents—and too many ways they can receive something of value from service providers. HUD would require an army of examiners to shut down the practice, and it has never had such an army. While it has taken enforcement actions against some major players, small players continue to operate below HUD's radar screen. The enforcement actions have encouraged larger players to find legal ways to exploit their referral power.

RESPA Allows Interindustry Affiliations: RESPA does not prevent a firm in one industry from entering another industry, even when the express purpose is to exploit referral power. For example, Realtors or lenders can establish their own title company and refer business to that company, whose income would not be considered referral fees. Indeed, there are firms that will put any lenders or Realtors in the title insurance business by creating a title agency for them, which can be a joint venture or an entity wholly owned by the referrer. These firms guarantee that the title companies they create are RESPA compliant.

Since the capital investment required to create a title agency is considerable, this option is available only to firms able to generate a volume of referral business large enough to justify the investment, Smaller firms have to choose between observing the law at their loss or violating it.

Alternative Approaches to High Settlement Costs: Since making referral fees illegal has not worked, what would?

Allow Service Packaging: One approach is to suspend the prohibition of referral fees for any firm that combines a mortgage loan and all settlement services connected to it in one package offered at a single guaranteed price. Lenders who were packagers, for example, instead of referring customers to title insurers and the like, would negotiate the best prices they could with each service provider so that they could offer competitively-priced packages to consumers.

This approach was proposed by HUD in 2002. I supported it, even though the details were devilishly complicated; but most industry groups didn't, and their opposition killed it.

Require Service Consolidation: The best approach, which would sidestep RESPA altogether, is to enact a legal rule that is as simple as it is obvious: any third-party service required by lenders must be paid for by lenders. If lenders paid the charges, they would be included in the rate, of course, but it would cost borrowers far less than now. Competition by third-party providers to sell lenders would force the prices down, and rate competition by lenders would force them to pass the savings on to borrowers.

Scrap the RESPA Prohibition on Referral Fees: This is a second-best approach that has the virtues of simplicity and (likely) industry support. The prohibition was misguided to begin with and never reduced settlement costs, which was the rationale for enacting it. What the RESPA prohibition has done is to encourage wasteful affiliations, the sole purpose of which is to legally sanitize referral fees.

Referral Site *A mortgage Web site that shows mortgage prices posted by participating lenders, in some cases hundreds of them.*

Referral sites are similar to newspapers in that lenders and brokers pay for the privilege of posting their mortgage prices on the site. However, they provide more information than newspapers. At least some of the price information on referral sites, furthermore, is posted on the day the user looks at the screen, whereas all price information in newspapers is obsolete when it is published. Some referral sites are Bankrate.com, BestRate.com, CompareInterestRates.com, Interest.com, and LoanPage.com.

When I looked at these sites in 2003, I found that they did not provide all the data needed by shoppers to select the lenders quoting the best prices, especially in the case of ARMs. Further, the Web sites of some of the listed lenders were poor and showed prices that differed from those on the referral site.

When I checked back in 2009, the five sites named above were providing more information about a smaller number of lenders with better Web sites. But LoanPage.com and Interest.com required personal information about the shopper, indicating that they had gone into the business of selling leads. While the other three were improved, the data they showed on ARMs remained incomplete.

Refinance *Paying off an old loan while simultaneously taking a new one.*

Borrowers refinance for four major reasons:

- To reduce their financing costs. For this to work, the new interest rate must be lower.

- To reduce the risk of rising costs in the future. This involves refinancing an ARM into an FRM.

- To reduce the mortgage payment. If the rate isn't reduced in the process, the financing cost will rise.

- To raise cash as an alternative to a second mortgage. The use to which the cash is put is another issue.

Refinancing to Lower Financing Cost: A necessary though not a sufficient condition for reducing financing cost by refinancing is that the interest rate on the new loan be lower than the rate on the existing loan. Purveyors of a simple interest biweekly mortgage are fond of saying that their mortgage reduces financing costs even though the interest rate on the new loan is higher, but this is based on the bogus premise that financing cost is measured by total interest payments. *See* **Mortgage Scams and Tricks/ Strictly Lender Scams/Overpriced Simple Interest Biweekly**.

Valid measures of financing cost include **Interest Cost**, the present value of all costs, or the future value of all costs. In each case, costs are measured separately for the old loan and the new loan, over the period that is the borrower's best guess as to how long the loans being compared will be outstanding. I use future values because I have found it easier for readers to understand.

Refinance

Future Value of Costs and Gains: Calculator 3a on my Web site shows all the costs over a specified period of an existing and a new mortgage side by side. It also shows the breakeven period, which is the *minimum* length of time the borrower must hold the new mortgage to make the refinancing pay. So if you are confident that you will have the mortgage longer than the breakeven period, you know the refinance pays.

The first edition of this book included extensive tables of breakeven periods, but for this edition, we ran out of space. Never mind, the calculator is better; not only do you find out what the breakeven period is, but you also find out why it is what it is.

The components of the future value of costs and gains, which are calculated separately for the existing mortgage and the prospective new one, are as follows:

Points and other closing costs paid up front

Plus total monthly payments of interest, principal, and mortgage insurance during period

Plus lost interest on upfront and monthly costs during period

Minus tax savings on points and interest

Minus reduction in loan balance

Equals future value of net costs at period end

A side benefit from using a calculator is that it forces you to collect all the information that affects the profitability of a refinance.

Avoid This Common Rule of Thumb: Loan officers often calculate a breakeven period by dividing the cost of the loan by the reduction in the monthly mortgage payment. For example, if it costs $4,000 to refinance and the monthly payment falls by $200, the breakeven would be 20 months.

This rule of thumb does not take account of differences in how rapidly you pay down the balance of the new loan as opposed to the old one, it does not allow for differences in tax savings, and it ignores differences in lost interest on upfront and monthly payments. All these factors are taken into account by the calculator.

Financing Upfront Costs: Lenders ordinarily allow refinancers to fold the settlement costs into the loan amount without classifying it as a "cashout." For example, if the balance on the old loan is $100,000 and settlement costs including the lender's fees are $3,750, the new loan could be for $103,750.

Refinance

Financing the settlement costs, however, almost always reduces the gains from refinancing because the borrower must pay interest on the costs at the mortgage rate. It is also possible that financing the costs will flip the loan amount past a **Pricing Notch Point (PNP)**, increasing the rate or the mortgage insurance premium. Calculator 3a includes a financing option and automatically captures any PNPs.

No-Cost Refinance: A no-closing-cost loan is one where the interest rate is high enough to command a rebate from the lender that covers the closing costs. This is very different from a no-cash-outlay loan, where closing costs are added to the loan balance. Note that even with a legitimate no-cost loan, borrowers should always expect to pay per diem interest and escrows at closing.

The no-cost option is for borrowers who are sure to have the mortgage for no more than 5 years. Their plan is to sell the house or pay off the remaining balance within that period. For further discussion, *see* **No-Cost Mortgage**.

Refinancing Versus Contract Modification: Many borrowers wonder why their lender won't lower the rate on their existing loan, avoiding the settlement costs on a new loan. Such contract modifications do occur, but not very often. In most cases, the lenders to whom borrowers send their payments don't own the loans. They are the servicing agents of the owners. Ordinarily, owners will not grant servicing agents the right to modify the interest rate. Owners fear that agents would agree to rate reductions too readily in order to retain their servicing income, which is not affected by a reduction in the interest rate.

Even a servicing agent who owns the loan will not necessarily volunteer a rate reduction. The lender's objective is to drop the rate only if necessary to prevent the borrower from refinancing with another lender. Borrowers who understand this will take the initiative to let the lender know their intentions. The best way to do this is to request a payoff statement. This tells the lender that you have begun a refinance process with another lender.

Don't Confuse "Better Off" with "Best": The fact that a refinancing lowers your cost doesn't mean you should do it. Another mortgage may be available that would save you even more. If you are happy with your savings at a rate below the rate on your existing mortgage but above the market rate, the loan officer will be happy too.

Refinance

Refinance Versus Extra Payments: Many borrowers get confused over how the decision to make extra payments bears on their decision to refinance. It is complicated, but here are some guidelines:

- Ignore extra payments made in the past; that's water over the dam.

- Looking ahead, consider first whether you want to repay your loan in full. Repayment is an investment on which the yield is the rate at which you could refinance with no upfront costs. (If you can refinance your current loan at 6%, for example, you earn 6% by paying it off.) Compare this with the returns on your investment alternatives. If you repay in full, the process ends.

- If you elect not to repay in full, consider whether refinancing pays if you make the extra monthly payments that you can afford. Extra payments reduce the benefit from refinancing. You factor them into your analysis, using my refinance calculators, by shortening the term of your new mortgage. If you plan to refinance into a 15-year loan, for example, but extra payments would result in payoff in 10 years, you use 10 years as the term. You can determine the payoff period from any extra payments using my calculator 2a. If refinancing is beneficial assuming extra payments, you refinance—end of process.

- If refinancing is not profitable with the extra payments, do the analysis again without the extra payments. If refinancing remains unprofitable, you don't refinance. But if refinancing is profitable without the extra payments, you must decide whether to refinance without extra payments or to make extra payments without refinancing.

Refinancing When You Have Two Mortgages: Two mortgages complicate the refinance decision. You can refinance the first alone (provided the second mortgage lender allows it; *see* **Subordination Policy**), you can refinance the second alone, you can refinance both into two new mortgages, and you can refinance both into one new mortgage.

You can analyze the first three possibilities using my calculator 3a and the fourth using 3b. You must obtain price quotes on a new first for the amount of the balance on the existing first, on a new second for the amount of the balance on the existing second, and on a new first for the amount of the balance on both existing loans.

Effect of Prior Refinances on the Current One: When interest rates drop, some homeowners who had refinanced earlier are discouraged from refinancing again, for reasons that make no sense.

Refinance

Some homeowners assume that there must be a waiting period before they are allowed to refinance again. This is not the case.

Of course, lenders hate serial refinancing with a passion, but it is a cost of doing business. While loan contracts may discourage refinancing with a prepayment penalty, in jurisdictions where such penalties are allowed, that is a different issue.

Some homeowners are reluctant to refinance the second time because it means they "have to start all over again." One borrower commented that "I have already paid 5 months of the term and am reluctant to give that up."

But she gives up nothing. In the 5 months she had the loan, she reduced the balance by an amount equal to the five principal payments she made. If she refinances, it will be on this lower balance, so her savings remain intact.

It is true that if she refinances into another 30-year loan, she will be staring at 360 new payments. Lenders won't write a loan with a term of 355 months. That is easily remedied, however, by making a small increase in the monthly payment, sufficient to pay off in 355 months.

Some borrowers are reluctant to refinance a second time because they haven't yet recovered the costs of the previous refinance. For example, one borrower told me that she had paid $4,500 to refinance 8 months ago and she wanted to wait 17 months to refinance again because it would take that long for her savings to cover the $4,500.

But the $4,500 is gone and should not affect her current decision. My calculator 3a, which can be used to determine whether or not it pays to refinance now, must be given information about a number of things, including the interest rates on the current and new loans and the points and other costs of the new loan. But the costs incurred on the previous refinance are not there, because they are irrelevant to whether another refinance pays.

Refinancing May Cost More Than a Purchase Loan: One would think that if the borrower, property, and loan are the same, a loan used to purchase a home would be priced the same as a cost-reduction refinance. Historically, this is in fact the case most of the time. During the prolonged refinance boom in 2000–2003, however, refinancing loans began to be priced higher than purchase loans.

The boom stretched to the limit the capacity of lenders to process loans. Reluctant to add more employees when the boom could fizzle out at any time, lenders preferred to lengthen the processing period and let borrowers queue up for longer periods. But purchasers often have closing dates they must meet, and lenders strive to give them priority over refinancers. Pricing refinance a little higher is one way to do this because it cuts the number of refinancers in the queue.

Another factor was at work as well. It costs lenders more to lock the interest rate on refinance loans than on purchase loans. In the past, this was never important enough to cause a difference in pricing, but that also changed during the refinance boom.

If loan applicants who lock always went to closing, over time, lenders would gain as much from rate declines as they lost from rate increases. But in practice borrowers do not always close, and the fallout, as it is called, is larger when rates are falling. Some applicants are "lock jumpers." They lock, and if rates subsequently decline, they find another loan provider and lock again at a lower rate. Locking thus imposes a net cost on lenders.

This cost is larger on refinancings than on purchases because lock jumping is more common among refinancers. Borrowers who are refinancing usually are flexible on when they close. Most purchasers, in contrast, must close on a specific date and don't have time to restart the process with another lender.

The prolonged refinance boom increased the number of refinancing lock jumpers. An unusually large number of borrowers refinanced multiple times within just a few years, learning the ropes in the process. One thing they learned is how to lock-jump. This widened the difference in lock cost to lenders between refinancings and purchase loans.

In late 2009, I checked again, and the price difference had disappeared.

Refinancing to Reduce the Risk of Rate Increases: A borrower with an ARM may want to refinance into an FRM in order to avoid future rate and payment increases.

Information Needed for the Decision: To properly assess this decision, the borrower needs five pieces of information: (1) the current rate on the ARM, (2) the period until the next ARM rate adjustment, (3) the current fully indexed rate on the ARM, (4) rate caps on the ARM, and (5) the rate and other terms on the FRMs available in the current market.

Most borrowers know the ARM rate they are currently paying, the time when the rate will adjust, and the rate caps, but few know the current fully indexed rate (FIR). This is the most current value of the interest rate index used by the ARM plus the margin. The index used and the margin are both shown in the note, while the current value of the index is available at www.mortgage-x.com/general/mortgage_indexes.asp.

The importance of the FIR is that it is the best available predictor of how your ARM rate will change. At the next adjustment date, the new ARM rate will reset to equal the index value at that time, plus the margin, subject to the caps, which prevent a very large change.

This generalization has to be modified slightly for four indexes: COFI, CODI, COSI, and MTA. Because these indexes lag the market, the best estimate of what they will be when your ARM rate is adjusted is their projected value 12 months ahead, not their value today. The mortgage-x site referred to above provides such projections for you.

The relevant FRM rate is the one you can command in today's market without incurring any refinance costs. Shop for a no-cost refinance at one of the Upfront Mortgage Lenders.

Making the Refinance Decision: Borrowers with an ARM can find themselves in any of four possible situations:

1. **Both the ARM Rate and the FIR Are Higher Than the FRM Rate:** This means that the borrower would profit from refinancing immediately. She would also profit after the next ARM rate adjustment unless the index fell by enough to bring the new ARM rate below the FRM rate. *Case for refinance:* Very strong.

2. **Both the ARM Rate and the FIR Are Below the FRM Rate:** This means that refinancing is a loser now, and will to be a loser after the next ARM rate adjustment unless the index increases enough to bring the new ARM rate above the FRM rate. *Case for refinance:* Weak, except for the most risk-averse borrowers.

3. **The ARM Rate Is Below While the FIR Is Above the FRM Rate:** This means that the borrower would lose money by refinancing the ARM now, but the situation probably will be reversed at the next ARM rate adjustment. *Case for refinance:* Strong, but unless the borrower is very risk averse, it makes sense to wait until shortly before the next rate adjustment.

   This is the most common situation. Some borrowers get spooked into hasty action by fear that rates will be higher in the future, which could happen; but rates could also be lower. My advice is not to give up the clear benefit of holding the ARM until the rate adjusts unless

Refinance

the current FRM rate is about the maximum the borrower can afford. In that case, the reward from hanging onto the ARM until the rate adjusts is outweighed by the risk.

4. The ARM Rate Is Above While the FIR Is Below the FRM Rate: This means that the borrower would profit from refinancing the ARM now, but the situation probably will reverse itself after the next rate adjustment. *Case for refinance:* Murky.

It is clear that if the borrower refinances in this case, it should be done immediately. What is not clear is whether the short-term savings from getting rid of the high-priced ARM now justifies giving up a lower ARM rate in the future. A calculator analysis can help clarify the issue.

An ARM-into-FRM Calculator: My calculator 3e is designed for this purpose. Here are some of the major factors the calculator uses:

Time Horizon: In general, the longer the borrower expects to remain in the house, the stronger the case for the refinance. More bad things can happen to the ARM over a longer period.

ARM Features: Refinance is a less attractive option for ARMs with particularly desirable features. These include a low current rate, a long period to the next rate adjustment, a low rate adjustment cap, a low maximum rate, and a small margin.

FRM Features: The rate on the new FRM will usually be higher than the ARM rate, but much depends on how much higher it is. Further, account must be taken of refinance costs, including points, other lender fees, and other settlement costs, all of which reduce the benefit of a refinance.

Prepayment Penalty: A prepayment penalty on the ARM acts just like an additional fee on the FRM since you only pay it if you refinance.

Mortgage Insurance: If the borrower is paying for mortgage insurance on the ARM but the house has since appreciated, the FRM might not require the insurance. This would be a partial offset to the costs of the FRM. On the other hand, the ARM could have been taken without mortgage insurance, and subsequent price depreciation might require mortgage insurance on the FRM. That situation killed many potential refinances after the financial crisis.

Assumptions About Future Interest Rates: A critical factor affecting the results is the assumption you make about future interest rates. Calculator 3e allows you to assume many different future rate patterns, including "stable index" and "worst case." Another approach allows you to specify a rate increase each year, beginning in a specified year and continuing for a specified number of years.

A Refinancing Decision Strategy Using the Calculator: One decision strategy is to try rising-rate scenarios of increasing severity until you find the one in which the costs of the ARM and FRM in your case are about the same. This tells you how big a rise in rates is required to make refinance into an FRM profitable for you. If I did this, for example, and found that any increase in rates greater than 0.5% per year for 3 years made the refinance profitable, I would refinance. If I found that it took a 2% rise each year for 5 years for the refinance to be profitable, I would stay with my ARM. If the results fell between these two, I would consult my astrologer.

Refinance to Reduce Monthly Payments: Since a refinance that lowers finance costs reduces the interest rate, it will also reduce the mortgage payment unless the borrower selects a shorter term. A borrower who needs a lower payment will not select a shorter term.

But some borrowers are in the uncomfortable position that they must reduce the payment, even though there is no way they can refinance into a lower rate. If the alternative is default, they must lengthen the maturity or switch to interest only, both of which result in a higher financing cost. Before the financial crisis, borrowers in this situation sometimes took out an option ARM, on which the payment in the early years was less than the interest. After the crisis, because of their horrendous default rates, option ARMs were no longer available.

Refinancing to Raise Cash: Borrowers who want to raise cash should compare the cost of a cash-out refinance against the cost of a second mortgage. This will depend on the interest rates, points, and terms of both loans; the amount of cash required relative to the loan balance; the borrower's tax rate; and other factors.

A cash-out refi with an interest rate below the existing rate is likely to be less costly than a second mortgage. If the cash-out refi rate is higher than the existing rate, the second mortgage is likely to be cheaper, even though the second mortgage rate may be well above the cash-out refi rate. The reason is that the second mortgage allows the borrower to retain the lower rate on the existing mortgage.

For example, assume the existing loan has a balance of $200,000 at 5%, the borrower needs $40,000 in cash, the rate on a $240,000 refi is 5.5%, and the rate on a $40,000 second mortgage is 6.5%. The second mortgage is the better deal. While the borrower is paying 1% more on $40,000, he avoids paying 0.5% more on $200,000.

Other factors are involved, however, including mortgage insurance, settlement costs, and taxes. Calculator 3d on my Web site pulls all of them together to determine the less costly option. If you want to use the cash to consolidate existing debt, use calculator 1b or 1c.

Warning: Because the APR on a cash-out refi ignores the loss of the existing first mortgage, comparing it with the APR on a second mortgage is meaningless. *See* **Annual Percentage Rate (APR)**.

Refinancing with the Current Lender: Borrowers interested in refinancing face the problem of whether they approach their current lender, go to another loan provider, or both. Here are the pros and cons.

The Pros: Perhaps the major reason people approach their current lender is that it is convenient. They are spared having to decide whom and where to shop. If their payment record has been good, furthermore, their existing lender has immediate access to their record, where other lenders would have to investigate. There is comfort in "being known" and a belief that this should earn them special treatment.

There is some validity to this belief. The current lender—defined as the firm to which you now remit your payments—may be in a position to offer lower settlement costs than a new lender. How much lower, however, can vary from case to case.

The greatest potential for lower settlement costs arises where the current lender was the originating lender and still owns the loan, a common situation with loans made by banks and savings and loan associations. If the payment record has been good, the current lender may forgo a credit report, property appraisal, title search, and other risk control procedures that are otherwise mandatory on new loans. This is strictly up to the lender.

If the current lender was the original lender but later sold the loan and is now servicing it for the owner, the potential for lower settlement costs is less. A lender servicing for others must follow the guidelines set down by the owner. If the owner is one of the federal secondary market agencies, Fannie Mae or Freddie Mac, the guidelines are theirs. While both agencies have provisions for "streamlined refinancing documentation," the discretion granted the lender, and therefore the potential cost savings, is quite limited.

Refinance

The potential for lower settlement costs is least when the current lender is neither the originating lender nor the current owner. This is a fairly common situation that arises when the contract to service the loan is sold. In this case, the lender may not be in a position to use all the streamlined refinancing procedures because its files do not contain some of the information those procedures require, such as the original appraisal report.

The Cons: The major argument against refinancing with your current lender is that the lender may not give you the market price. It will try to minimize its loss by taking advantage of your preference for staying put and your reluctance to shop the market. Any settlement cost benefits that your current lender can offer that other lenders cannot may serve to draw attention away from the fact that the rate and points offered are not competitive.

Above-market offers are especially likely if the lender takes the initiative in soliciting its own customers. Lenders that do that are likely to base their offer on the borrower's existing rate. For example, in a 5% market, the borrower with a 7% mortgage might be offered 6% while a borrower with a 6% mortgage (but who is otherwise identical) might be offered 5.5%. The objective is to provide a saving over the existing loan that is attractive enough to discourage the borrower from looking elsewhere. This way, the lender gives up as little as possible.

An even greater hazard is that the borrower dealing with the existing lender will get the runaround because that lender has no interest in completing the deal. Why rush to convert a 7% loan into a 5.5% loan? I saw one situation where the lender charged an unsuspecting borrower a lock fee and then let him dangle indefinitely.

In addition, borrowers who refinance with a new lender have a **Right of Rescission**, whereas if they refinance with their existing lender, they don't.

A Suggested Strategy: In general, a good strategy is to first inquire about the settlement cost savings the existing lender can offer, then find the market price by shopping elsewhere, and then return to the existing lender.

Title Insurance on a Refinance: Borrowers who refinance do not need a new owner's title policy. They must purchase a new policy for the lender, however, because the lender's policy terminates with the repayment of the old mortgage. Such policies are customarily available at a discount, which is usually larger the shorter the period from the previous policy.

Rescinding a Refinance: On a refinance with any lender other than the one holding the existing loan, the borrower has three days after closing to rescind the loan. *See* **Right of Rescission**.

The Tangible Net Benefit Rule: In December 2009, I counted nine states in which legislation aimed at predatory lending had been enacted that prohibited lenders from refinancing a mortgage unless there was a "tangible net benefit" to the borrower. In my view, the tangible net benefit rule would make lenders responsible for something over which they have little or no control. *See* **Tangible Net Benefit Rule**.

Required Cash *The total cash required of the homebuyer or borrower to close the purchase plus loan transaction or the loan transaction on a refinance.*

Required cash includes the down payment, points and fixed-dollar charges paid to the lender, any portion of the mortgage insurance premium that is paid up front, and other settlement charges associated with the transaction such as title insurance and per diem interest. It is shown on the **Settlement Statement (HUD-1)** that every borrower receives at closing.

RESPA *The Real Estate Settlement Procedures Act, a federal consumer protection statute first enacted in 1974.*

RESPA was designed to protect home purchasers and owners shopping for settlement services by mandating certain disclosures and prohibiting referral fees and kickbacks.

Disclosure Requirements: Different disclosure rules under RESPA kick in at different stages of the homebuying or borrowing process. The disclosures listed below are in addition to those mandated by **Truth in Lending (TIL)**.

At Time of Loan Application: Within three business days of receipt of a loan application, the lender must provide the applicant with a Special Information Booklet that describes the various real estate settlement services; a Good Faith Estimate (GFE) of settlement costs, which lists the estimated charges the borrower may have to pay at closing (*see* **Settlement Costs**); and a Mortgage Servicing Disclosure Statement, which discloses whether the lender intends to service the loan or transfer it elsewhere.

RESPA

Before Closing: If settlement service provider A has an ownership or other beneficial interest in service provider B, before referring a client to B, A must provide the client with a disclosure of the Affiliated Business Arrangement (AfBA). In addition, an applicant may request the HUD-1 Settlement Statement, which shows all charges imposed on buyers, borrowers, and sellers, one day before settlement.

At Settlement: The borrower receives the final HUD-1 Settlement Statement at settlement and an Initial Escrow Statement that itemizes the estimated taxes and insurance premiums to be paid from the escrow account and the amounts to be paid into the account.

After Settlement: Borrowers must be provided with an Annual Escrow Statement that shows all inflows and outflows to and from the escrow account and gives the balances during the year. If the firm servicing the loan transfers the servicing to another firm, the borrower must be notified at least 15 days before the effective date of the transfer. There is no requirement that borrowers receive monthly statements showing interest, principal, escrows, and end-of-period loan balance, but there should be.

Prohibited Practices: RESPA prohibits the following practices:

Kickbacks, Referrals, and Unearned Markups: A real estate settlement service provider cannot give or receive anything of value for the referral of business in connection with a mortgage and cannot charge fees or markups when no additional service has been provided.

Seller-Required Title Insurance: A home seller is prohibited from requiring a borrower to use a particular title insurance company.

Escrow Accounts Larger Than Necessary: A lender may not require a borrower to pay into an escrow account more than 1/12 of the total payments out of the account during the year, plus any shortages, plus a safety cushion for unexpected disbursements. The cushion cannot exceed 1/6 of the disbursements for the year.

Loan Servicing Complaints: RESPA provides a complaint procedure for borrowers who believe they are being taken advantage of by the firm servicing their loan. *See* **Servicing/*Predatory Servicing***.

Proposals for RESPA Reform: The existing HUD rules have not prevented a number of market abuses and have not been effective in driving down settlement costs. In response, in July 2002, HUD announced a wide-ranging set of proposals "to simplify and improve the process of obtaining home mortgages and reduce settlement costs for consumers." Because of strong industry resistance, these were never enacted. However, a new and much improved GFE was enacted effective January 1, 2010. *See* **Settlement Costs/*Good Faith Estimate***.

Retail Lender *A lender that offers mortgage loans directly to the public.*

See **Mortgage Lender/*Retail, Wholesale, and Correspondent Lenders***.

Reverse Mortgage *A mortgage loan that is made to an elderly homeowner on which the borrower's debt rises over time, but that need not be repaid until the borrower dies, sells the house, or moves out permanently.*

The "forward" mortgages that are used to purchase homes *build equity*— the value of the home less the mortgage balance. Borrowers pay down the balance over time, and by age 62, when they become eligible for a reverse mortgage, loan balances are either paid off or much reduced.

Reverse mortgages, in contrast, *consume equity* because loan balances rise over time. If there is a balance remaining on a forward mortgage at the time a reverse mortgage is taken out, it is paid off with an advance under the reverse mortgage.

Need: Most of the elderly are homeowners. For many, especially those with low incomes, homeowner equity constitutes a major part of their net worth. Most of them built that equity during their working lives, in part by paying down their mortgages.

As their incomes decline in their later years, many would like to consume their equity rather than leave it to heirs who don't need it. Without reverse mortgages, however, the only way to do that is to sell the house and live elsewhere. Reverse mortgages allow elderly homeowners to consume some or all of the equity in their homes without having to move—ever.

Reverse mortgages are not for everyone. Some seniors do better living in a retirement community, with family, or in a rental unit. Reverse mortgages are for those who want to stay in their own home.

Suspicion: In the 1970s and early 1980s, when I was actively involved in trying to develop reverse mortgage programs and bring them to the market, the need was as great as it is today. However, they were a very tough sell. I was involved in two projects that offered excellent products, but neither project survived.

Reverse Mortgage

The major problem was that elderly homeowners were extremely cautious and suspicious. Even when they seemed convinced, they often backed out at the last moment. Unfortunately, some programs being offered around that time did not guarantee lifetime occupancy—borrowers could be forced out of their homes if they lived too long. The complexity of reverse mortgage programs was also a deterrent.

This situation began to change in 1988 with the development of a federal program under the FHA. This was the Home Equity Conversion Mortgage (HECM) program. The borrower protections built into this program, along with the imprimatur of the federal government, paved the way toward increasing acceptance by elderly homeowners. Other reverse mortgage programs were introduced, including one by Fannie Mae and a number of private firms (*see **Other Reverse Mortgage Programs** below*). By 2009, however, all had disappeared except the HECM program. *See **Impact of the Financial Crisis***.

FHA's Home Equity Conversion Mortgage (HECM): The HECM program began slowly, with only 157 loans written in 1990. Ten years later, the number had grown to 6,600, and by 2009, to about 130,000. This suggests that the program had come of age, but the most recent numbers constituted a small portion of the total potential market.

The great strengths of the program are the security provided by the federal guarantee and the payment options available to the borrower. These options are available at the outset and also throughout the life of a transaction in that borrowers can shift from one to another.

The weakness of HECM is that it is complicated, which is why Congress made it mandatory that borrowers undergo a counseling session before they sign on.

In 1999, a sample of homeowners who had taken FHA reverse mortgages was surveyed regarding their experience under the program. The survey found that about 80% were either "very satisfied" or "satisfied" and only about 15% were "very dissatisfied" or "dissatisfied." In a 2007 survey, "83 percent reported that their loans had completely or mostly met their financial needs, and 93 percent reported that their reverse mortgages had had a positive effect on their lives."

Safeguards: Under the HECM program (as well as the private programs that followed but later became casualties of the financial crisis), borrowers have the right to live in their house until they sell it, die, or move out permanently, regardless of how much their mortgage debt grows.

Reverse Mortgage

If the debt comes to exceed the value of the property, the lender takes the loss, except that on the HECM program, FHA reimburses the lender for any loss out of insurance premiums paid by borrowers. FHA also assures the borrower that any payments due from the lender will be made, even if the lender fails.

In addition, loans under these programs are without recourse. This means that lenders cannot attach other assets of borrowers or their heirs in the event that the reverse mortgage debt comes to exceed the property value.

Borrowers do have reasonable obligations. They must pay their property taxes and homeowners insurance and maintain the property. Further, they cannot change the names on the title, take out a second mortgage, take in boarders, or use the home as a business. The lender can demand repayment of the loan if the borrower transgresses in any of these ways.

Eligibility: To be eligible for a HECM, all owners must be 62 or older and must occupy the home as their permanent residence. There are no income or credit requirements since borrowers don't assume any payment obligation, but borrowers must certify that they have been counseled by a HUD-approved counselor.

Eligible properties include one-family houses, two- to four-family houses if the borrower occupies one of them, HUD-approved condominiums, and manufactured homes that meet FHA requirements. Mobile homes and co-ops are not eligible.

The house may have an existing mortgage, but it must be repaid out of the reverse mortgage proceeds. If the balance is high relative to the value of the property, the amount the borrower can withdraw may be too small to make the HECM attractive. However, even if paying off the existing mortgage exhausts the borrowing power of the HECM, the borrower is relieved of the payment burden on the existing mortgage.

Options for Drawing Funds: Borrowers can choose from five payment plans.

- **Line of Credit:** Borrowers may make withdrawals at times and in amounts selected by them, within a specified maximum draw. This includes drawing the maximum amount as a lump sum at the outset.

- **Tenure:** Borrowers receive a fixed monthly payment for as long as they remain in the house.

- **Term:** Borrowers receive a fixed monthly payment for a period specified by them.

- **Modified Tenure:** A combination of tenure and line of credit.

- **Modified Term:** A combination of term and line of credit.

These options are designed to meet diverse needs. Borrowers who want to repay what is left on their existing mortgage can do it with a line of credit. A borrower who plans to sell in 5 years but needs more income in the meantime can elect a term loan for 5 years. And so on. *See* **Lifetime Annuities and Credit Lines**.

The Net Principal Limit: The different options can be visualized as different ways of removing money from a pot with a fixed amount in it. The starting point for all the options is the amount in the pot at the outset.

Assume a hypothetical owner Smith, aged 70 with a house worth $400,000 and no existing mortgage, selecting a monthly adjustable-rate HECM. Based on the shopping I did for Mr. Smith on December 1, 2009, the "principal limit" (PL) on his house was $216,800. The PL is the present value of Smith's house to an investor, who has to wait until Smith dies or moves out permanently before she can take possession.

The PL is determined by three factors: the borrower's age, which determines how long the investor is likely to have to wait to be repaid; the expected interest rate, which measures the cost of having to wait; and the lower of the property value and the FHA loan limit, which affects the risk that the debt won't be fully paid when it comes due because it will exceed the property value.

But Smith can't actually draw the PL without paying all the upfront expenses connected to a HECM: origination fees, mortgage insurance, third-party closing costs, and a servicing-fee set-aside. These expenses are deducted from the PL to yield a "Net Principal Limit" (NPL), which is $193,340. NPL is the money in the pot that Smith could withdraw as a lump sum immediately or use to support the other withdrawal options. It is a critically important number on which borrowers can base their shopping. *See* **Shopping for a HECM**.

Property Value Versus FHA Loan Limits: The greater the value of the borrower's property, the larger should be the credit advances and monthly payments available under the program. But this is true only so long as the property value does not exceed the FHA loan limit. Borrowers receive no credit for value in excess of the loan limit. For example, if the FHA loan limit is $200,000, a borrower with a home worth $400,000 receives the same credit line and tenure or term payments as a borrower with a house worth $200,000. HUD terms the lower of property value and loan limit the "Maximum Claim Amount."

This is not a major problem for borrowers who view a HECM as a stopgap measure and want to retain as much equity as possible. A borrower who takes a term payment for 5 years, for example, intending to sell at the end of that period, will retain the equity that FHA did not use in calculating the payments.

But borrowers who want to live in their house until they die, who are usually viewed as the major intended beneficiaries of reverse mortgage programs, are disadvantaged. The borrower with the $400,000 house must pay the same insurance premium as the borrower with the $200,000 house, but there is a substantial difference in risk of loss to FHA.

Until the financial crisis, such borrowers could resort to a private program that had much higher loan limits. Their rates were higher than those on the HECM, but the draw amounts were larger because they were calculated on the full value of the house. But the private programs disappeared with the financial crisis. *See **Impact of the Financial Crisis/Private Reverse Mortgages Disappear***.

In 2008, as part of its broader efforts to support the housing market, Congress replaced the system of setting maximum loan amounts on HECMs for each county with a uniform national limit of $417,000. Early in 2009, the limit was raised temporarily (through 2010) to $625,500. This helped fill the void left by the loss of the private programs.

Types of Mortgage: Before the financial crisis, mortgage selection involved choosing between two ARMs, one that adjusted monthly and one that adjusted annually. The monthly adjustable is indexed to 1-month LIBOR and has no rate caps. The ARM that adjusts annually has rate caps, and although it was available in 2009, it was priced so poorly that none were being written. In the meanwhile, a fixed-rate HECM was authorized in 2008. The choice thereafter was between the monthly LIBOR ARM and the new FRM.

When I checked in December 2009, the FRM version had a lower effective interest rate than the ARM, generating a higher NPL. The downside of the FRM is that the entire NPL must be drawn immediately. No unused credit line and no term or tenure annuities are permitted. Borrowers who want to use only part of their credit line immediately will select the ARM.

Because of its higher NPL, the FRM does meet the needs of some borrowers. These include seniors who want to sell their existing house and buy one that better meets their current needs. They may want to exchange a large house for a smaller one, for example, or move to a condominium in a retirement community.

Under a "HECM for Purchase" program authorized by Congress in 2008, seniors can buy a house and take out a reverse mortgage on that house at the same time. In most cases, the senior would want the reverse mortgage to be as large as possible so as to minimize the use of other assets. Absent this program, the senior would have to purchase the new house with a forward mortgage, then take out a HECM to retire the forward mortgage, incurring two sets of settlement costs in the process.

Seniors who draw on their HECM to purchase a lifetime annuity from an insurance company will also prefer the FRM because it allows them to buy a larger annuity. *See* **Lifetime Annuities**.

Interest Rates: Among the complexities of the HECM program is that it uses three interest rates for three different purposes. The note rate is the rate the borrower pays on the loan balance, which determines how fast the balance grows over time. Note rates are the rates on the monthly LIROR-based ARM and the FRM referred to above.

The second rate, called the "expected rate," is used in calculating the NPL, which determines the size of the credit line and payments borrowers can draw. On the ARM, the expected rate is the 10-year Treasury constant maturity rate plus the margin on the ARM note rate. On the FRM, the expected rate is also the note rate.

The third rate, which doesn't seem to have a name, is used to calculate the growth of unused credit lines. It is equal to the note rate plus the mortgage insurance premium of 0.5%.

Total Annual Loan Costs (TALC): Federal law requires lenders to report a single interest cost figure for all reverse mortgages. The TALC is designed to allow borrowers to compare one lender's offerings (or one type of reverse mortgage) with another and also to illustrate how the cost of a reverse mortgage declines as the transaction ages.

The TALC is somewhat analogous to the APR required on forward mortgages, except that the TALC covers all costs and the APR does not. In addition, the TALC is calculated over 2 years, half of life expectancy, life expectancy, and 1.4 times life expectancy, whereas APR is calculated over the term of the loan. In principle, therefore, TALC is a much better tool than APR. Ironically, however, lenders are required to display the APR wherever they display an interest rate, but there is no such requirement for the TALC. Borrowers usually don't receive it early enough to help with shopping alternative lenders. That's why I don't mention it below in **Shopping for a HECM**.

Because origination and closing costs are incurred up front, the TALC is always lower over longer periods. In December 2009 when I shopped for a HECM for an 86-year-old, I found the TALC on a tenure annuity (one that lasts as long as the borrower stays in the house) would be 27.7 % if he terminated after 2 years, 14.8% over 3 years, 6.4% over 6 years, and 5.0% over 8 years. Reverse mortgages are costly for borrowers who expect to be out of their homes within a few years.

Costs: HECMs involve upfront costs, which are almost always financed, which means they are deducted from the NPL. FHA allows lenders to charge an origination fee of 2% of the first $200,000 of house value, plus 1% of the amount above $200,000, with a maximum fee of $6,000. FHA charges an insurance premium of 2% of value at closing, while a monthly premium of 1/2% per year is added to the interest rate. Other closing costs vary by area and also by lender. I found a range of $2,100 to $7,800 on a HECM I shopped in Pennsylvania.

In addition, a servicing fee is added to the loan balance each month. The fee is set by the lender and can be $25, $30, or $35. To ensure that there is enough money available to pay for servicing over the life of the loan, the present value of these payments is deducted from the NPL as a servicing fee "set-aside." This is a needlessly confusing feature of the HECM program. However, a borrower shopping for the lowest NPL will automatically take the servicing fee, as well as the upfront costs, into account. *See* **Shopping for a HECM**.

Lifetime Annuities: Seniors who want the security of a lifetime annuity can fund it with a HECM in two ways: by taking a "tenure" annuity from the HECM or by withdrawing the maximum amount and using it to purchase an immediate annuity from a life insurance company. I shopped both options in December 2009 for a male of 86 with a house worth $400,000.

The net principal limit for this borrower was $288,019, which purchased a tenure annuity of $2,444. The same borrower could draw the

$288,019, maxing out the HECM, and purchase an annuity of $3,778 from a life insurance company. (I found this quote on www.immediateannuity .com.) The difference in the two annuities is substantial, but they are not completely comparable.

First, the HECM tenure annuity is guaranteed by the federal government. The life company annuity is only as good as the promise of the insurance company, loosely backed by state guarantee programs. I would not purchase an annuity from a company that did not have a AA rating.

Further, the borrower who takes a HECM annuity retains ownership of the reserve account underlying the annuity. This allows him to change his mind after a few years and switch to a credit line for the reserve amount still available. And if he dies after a few years, the reserve will go to his estate. On a life company annuity, early death terminates all payments unless the policy has a guaranteed payout, which would reduce the annuity amount.

To be sure, if the borrower gets sick and has to go to a nursing home, the HECM annuity will terminate after a year of nonoccupancy, while the life company annuity will continue until death. But the HECM annuitant who is required to go to a nursing home and has little prospect of returning home can switch to a credit line and withdraw the remaining reserve within the year. The HECM annuity is thus more valuable, though whether the additional value is worth the difference in annuity amount is not clear.

The borrower who seeks the largest possible monthly payment, and has little regard for how much equity passes to heirs, will purchase a life company annuity. I hesitate to say this because some of the worst abuses connected to reverse mortgages have involved purchased annuities. However, seniors can easily avoid the hazards by following one simple rule: keep the two transactions separated and do not be solicited.

The abuses invariably involve package deals that are sold to seniors who have been solicited by fast-talking scamsters. Refuse to be solicited, shop for a HECM following the suggestions below in **Shopping for a HECM**, and use a similar approach to shop for an annuity.

You want a fixed annuity, one that pays the same guaranteed amount every month, beginning immediately. If you don't yet need the payments, you can take the credit line and sit on it—it will grow over time. Alternatively, you can wait until you need the income before taking out the credit line (*see* **Credit Lines** *below*).

Reverse Mortgage

Credit Lines: Most borrowers who take a HECM elect credit lines rather than term or tenure payments because of the greater flexibility. Borrowers can draw on the line as they wish; meanwhile the unused portion increases every year at the same rate as the borrower pays on accumulated debt—the note rate plus the insurance premium.

An important question faced by many seniors with no immediate need for funds is whether their HECM credit lines will be larger in, say, 5 years if they take it immediately or if they wait for 5 years. If they take it immediately, the line grows at the note rate plus the insurance premium. If they wait, the line they can get in 5 years will be larger because the borrower will be older, and because the house may be worth more. If there is no appreciation, the line will grow faster if it is taken out immediately, but appreciation can flip the result in the other direction.

In December 2009, a 75-year-old senior with a house worth $400,000 could obtain a line from a competitive lender for $207,000. If unused, the line would grow to about $253, 000 at 4.06%, which was the initial rate on the ARM. If the senior waited for 5 years and the house did not appreciate, the line would be only $230, 000. If the house appreciated by 3% a year, the line would be $328,000. The breakeven rate of appreciation where the line in 5 years was the same, whether it was taken immediately or in 5 years, was about 1.8%.

In general, therefore, if you don't need the money now and you expect your house to appreciate by 1.8% a year or more, it is better to wait until you need the money before taking out the HECM. Even if the house does not appreciate, if it is currently valued well above the FHA loan limit, future increases in the limit may make it worthwhile to wait.

In 2009–2010, however, the loan limit of $625,500 was temporary and scheduled to be *reduced* at the end of 2010, though it was far from clear when this was written what the lower limits would be or even if any reduction would occur. If the limit is reduced to $417,000, which is what it was before the last increase, seniors with houses worth more than $417,000 will find their lines reduced unless they take out their HECMs before the new limits become effective.

Warning: Do not use a lump sum drawn under a reverse mortgage credit line, whether a HECM line or any other, to invest. There are no safe investments available that pay a return higher than the cost of the reverse mortgage to you. Borrowing at 4% to invest at 2% is dumb.

Refinancing: In some cases, borrowers who have taken out HECMs in the past and still live in their house could increase the amount they draw by refinancing. Because they are older and their house may have appreciated, a recalculation of the net principal limit will provide an increased line. Even if the house has not appreciated, if its value exceeded the FHA loan limit at the outset, increases in the limit have the same effect as appreciation.

When this edition was written in 2009, house values had been in decline for about 3 years, which was not favorable for refinancing. Increases in the FHA loan limit, however, opened the door for seniors with house values higher than the FHA loan limit at the time the HECM was originally taken out.

Refinancing does require a new set of settlement costs, including a new upfront insurance premium. That premium, however, is levied only on the increase in the "maximum claim amount"—the lower of property value and FHA loan limit.

Borrowers must compare the increase in their potential draw by refinancing with the cost of refinancing. HUD will waive the counseling requirement on a refinance if the increase in the draw is five times or more larger than the refinance cost.

Shopping for a HECM: Shopping for a HECM can be very difficult or very easy. If you shop in the conventional way of compiling all the price components for each lender, the process is tedious and prone to error. Interest rates, origination fees, servicing fees, and third-party charges are all costs to the borrower that can vary from deal to deal.

But there is a shopping shortcut that is close to foolproof. You shop for the largest amount of cash you can draw at the outset, which is the NPL. The NPL is the bottom line because it is reduced by higher interest rates, origination fees, third-party charges, and servicing fees.

Just make sure that when you shop NPLs among different lenders, you give them all the same property value, age, and existing debt, because these also affect the NPL. If you tell lender A that you are 72, for example, and only remember that you have a spouse of 68 when you get to lender B, you will be comparing apples and oranges.

To select a lender, I recommend going to www.reversemortgage.org, which lists reverse mortgage lenders by state and has links to all their Web sites. Narrow your choice to lenders who provide calculators that you can use anonymously to find their NPLs. These calculators do not show the TALC, which you typically won't get until you have applied with a lender.

As a test case, I did this for Pennsylvania, where I live. Of the 22 lenders listed in the state, 6 had anonymous calculators on their Web sites. That's enough. The 6 included 3 national lenders that would come up in all other states. Two other lenders in Pennsylvania had calculators on their sites, but to use them you have to provide contact information. There is no need to expose yourself to solicitations.

To avoid being solicited, your name must not appear on lists of reverse mortgage leads. Compiling leads and selling them to lenders is a thriving business. You keep from becoming a lead by not responding to teaser ads, such as "Great New Government Program, See How Much You Qualify to Receive."

If a lender talks to you about the possibility of drawing funds from a HECM to purchase an annuity, run like a thief. He is looking to make two commissions from you, and they both are likely to be extortionate.

It is very hard to get into trouble if you initiate the HECM. When someone else initiates it and you go along with the solicitation, the likelihood of a bad deal for you escalates dramatically. If the soliciting party ties the HECM to an annuity or house purchase, you are almost certainly going to be scammed.

Other Reverse Mortgage Programs: Before the financial crisis, the HECM program had some competition from other reverse mortgage programs. One such program was Fannie Mae's Home Keeper Mortgage. It carried a higher interest rate than the HECM, and the credit lines it offered did not grow if not used; but its loan limit was higher than those on the HECM, which made it a better choice in some circumstances. When the HECM loan limits were raised in 2008, however, Fannie Mae decided that Home Keeper was no longer needed and shut it down.

The HECM program also encouraged the development of a number of private programs, of which the earliest and largest was Financial Freedom's Cash Account. This program offered only a line of credit, no term or tenure payments, and had no loan limit. The interest rate and costs were higher than on HECMs, but seniors with houses worth substantially more than the FHA loan limits could draw larger credit lines on Cash Account. It also had an equity participation feature where the interest rate was reduced by 1% in exchange for the payment of 5% of property value at termination. Cash Account, along with a number of other private programs, was a victim of the financial crisis; *see **Impact of the Financial Crisis***.

Reverse Mortgage

Equity-Based Products: On HECMs and other reverse mortgage programs, the investor acquires a debt instrument that pays a rate of interest. It is also possible to fashion instruments for the same purpose that are wholly or partly equity based—meaning that the investor acquires an ownership interest in the property.

Indeed, the oldest known instrument for "home equity conversion" was of this type. At least as far back as the nineteenth century, notaries in France arranged deals between homeowners and individual investors where the investor paid the owner an annuity for life. Such deals were very simple. The annuity was determined by dividing the current value of the property by the owner's life expectancy. The investor took possession of the house upon the owner's death, whether that happened after a month or after 40 years.

However, these deals were extremely risky to both parties. Occasionally the owner would outlive the investor. And occasionally the owner would die before the ink was dry on the contract. While investors can diversify their risk by writing many contracts, owners cannot because each owner has only one house with which to transact.

Combined debt-equity arrangements are also possible, and several of these have appeared in the United States. In these deals, the investor makes a loan and also receives either a share of the appreciation in the home's value or a share of the value at termination. The equity participation feature permits the investor to pay the owner more than in a straight debt transaction.

None of the programs of this type have been successful, however. The American Homestead program during the 1980s failed because the expected rate of appreciation did not materialize and investors did not earn an adequate return. In 2000, Fannie Mae terminated an equity option in connection with its Home Keeper reverse mortgage (see above) for essentially the opposite reason.

In exchange for paying up to 10% of the value of their home at the termination of the contract, owners received larger payments under Home Keeper than if they took a straight loan. With this equity option, owners who terminated early paid a lot more than those who terminated late. When a syndicated columnist wrote up the news that early terminators were paying a high cost, as if it were a scandal, Fannie Mae was embarrassed; and in 2000 it terminated the equity option.

Reverse Mortgage

Single-Purpose Programs: Much the simplest types of reverse mortgages are those offered by some states and cities, which are either for property improvement or for the payment of property taxes. These loans require no repayment so long as the borrower lives in the house. Loans for property improvement are one-time advances, while those for payment of property taxes are annual advances.

Single-purpose programs are invariably good deals, but they usually have eligibility criteria that limit their availability. The criteria may apply to income, house value, age, area, or borrower health. There is no one comprehensive source of information on these programs, but a good place to start looking is the directory of "homes and communities organized by state" on www.hud.gov.

Impact of the Financial Crisis: The reverse mortgage market was *not* impacted by the crisis-induced tightening of credit standards that plagued the market for forward mortgages. There are no credit requirements for reverse mortgages. Similarly, the requirement that all forward mortgage borrowers must fully document their incomes did not affect reverse mortgage borrowers, who are not subject to income requirements.

Private Reverse Mortgages Disappear: For a time, the HECM program served as a "demonstration," stimulating the development of private programs. Just before the crisis, I counted seven such programs. By the end of 2009, they were all gone.

The cause was a loss of funding. Private reverse mortgages were all securitized, and when the private mortgage securities market collapsed, the relatively small part of it directed to reverse mortgages collapsed with it. The originators of private reverse mortgages had no place to sell them.

The major focus of the private programs had been the high end of the market that the HECM program did not serve well because of FHA loan limits. The private programs had allowed owners of higher-value houses to borrow larger amounts than were possible with a HECM. Their loss left a hole in the market which was only partially filled by increases in the loan limits on HECMs.

Declines in Home Values Reduce Borrowing Power: Seniors with properties of modest value who, prior to the crisis, were not constrained by FHA loan limits, found their HECM borrowing power reduced. If a senior's house declines in value by 30%, the amount that can be borrowed against it also declines by 30%.

Declines in Home Values Create Losses for FHA: Losses to FHA from insuring HECMs arise when loan balances come to exceed property values. If home prices are rising, as they were until 2006, most HECMs will terminate before this loss point is reached, and FHA's insurance premiums generate net profits for the government. The sharp decline in house values after 2006, however, converted those profits into losses. In response, HUD in 2009 reduced the payment factors on HECMs—the percentage of property value that a senior of given age can borrow—by 10%. A second decline was being considered when this book went to press.

Funding of HECMs Under Pressure: Fannie Mae had been the major source of HECM funding since the program began, but the financial crisis raised doubts about whether this would continue. In September 2008, the heavy losses suffered by Fannie Mae and Freddie Mac forced the government to place the agencies in conservatorship. They became wards of the government with a very uncertain future. *See* **Secondary Mortgage Markets/***Fannie Mae and Freddie Mac***/Role in the Housing Bubble**.

To deemphasize its role and hopefully attract other investors, Fannie Mae in 2009 increased its rate margins on adjustable-rate HECMs. This shocked many seniors because higher-rate margins reduce the amounts they can borrow, and it traumatized many lenders who had to explain the bad news to seniors who had HECMs in process.

No private investors came forward. But Ginnie Mae, a federal agency that insures securities issued against FHA and VA forward mortgages, initiated a program of insuring HECM securities in 2007 and began gradually expanding into the space being vacated by Fannie Mae.

Right of Rescission *The right of refinancing borrowers to cancel the transaction within 3 days of closing.*

Under the federal Truth in Lending Act, borrowers who refinance a loan on their primary residence with a lender, other than their current lender, can cancel the deal at no cost to themselves within 3 days of closing. This "right of rescission" is designed to give borrowers who may have been sweet-talked into a transaction an opportunity to think it over and, if they decide the deal is not really in their interest, to back out and retrieve any monies they have paid out.

Right of Rescission

You Have Three Years to Rescind If the Lender Didn't Provide Proper Disclosures: If you were not given the disclosures to which you were entitled, including a written statement of your right to rescind, you have three years to rescind instead of 3 days. The disclosures to which you are entitled include most of the items on the Truth in Lending statement. This is a possible avenue of redress for those who require more than 3 days to realize they have been abused.

Recovering Outlays: Truth in Lending says that "Within 20 calendar days after receipt of a notice of rescission, the CREDITOR shall return any money . . . that has been given to anyone in connection with the transaction . . ." This suggests that payments to a broker must be refunded by the lender. I have never heard of this happening, but as noted below, there have been very few rescissions.

The Mechanics of Rescission: In a very useful article on rescission, Holden Lewis explains how to go about it.

> To exercise your right of rescission, you must inform the lender in writing—a phone call won't do. The letter doesn't have to be postmarked by the deadline—you merely have to drop it in a mailbox by the deadline. That means that if your right of rescission ends at midnight Saturday night, and you mail the letter just before the deadline, and Monday is a federal holiday so the letter isn't postmarked until Tuesday, you still have rescinded the loan. (See http://www.bankrate.com/brm/news/loan/20040212a1 .asp.)

There is one important qualification to his last sentence. Under the conditions he spells out, the loan is *rescinded if the lender acknowledges that the letter has been received.* If the lender just drops the letter in the shredder, the refinance will proceed. This happened to a reader who told me about it. MORAL: SEND YOUR LETTER OF RESCISSION REGISTERED MAIL WITH RETURN RECEIPT REQUESTED.

Some Types of Refinance Have Greater Potential for Regret Than Others: A third party can never say conclusively that a particular deal is not in a borrower's interest. Only the borrower can make that decision. But it is possible to rate the different kinds of refinance transactions by the likelihood that the borrowers will regret what they did. The following list scales refinances from the lowest to the highest regret potential.

Refinancing from an adjustable-rate to a fixed-rate mortgage to lower the risk (*Lowest*)

Refinancing into the same type of mortgage to lower the interest rate

Refinancing two mortgages to lower the rates

Refinancing from one mortgage to two to get rid of mortgage insurance

Refinancing from a fixed-rate to an adjustable-rate mortgage (ARM) to lower the mortgage payment

Refinancing to get "cash out"

Refinancing to get "cash out" when there are two existing mortgages

Refinancing into an option ARM or interest only to reduce the payment (*Highest*)

Very Few Refinancing Borrowers Rescind: The right of rescission is only valuable to borrowers if they use the 3-day period to reflect on all the costs and benefits of the transaction, preferably having it scrutinized by an objective third party. My own experience suggests that this rarely happens. I receive very few letters from refinancing borrowers soliciting my help within the 3-day period. I receive many letters from borrowers, long after their rescission period ended, asking what recourse they have against the loan provider who abused them!

Congress gave borrowers the right of rescission so that borrowers who had been hustled and deceived into deals that were not in their interest could escape. In principle, it should be a very powerful weapon against abuse. Borrowers who have had a deal changed on them, from what they understood was promised earlier, can use the threat of rescission to obtain redress at the closing table.

Yet very few borrowers use it. To those who thought it would level the playing field, it has been a major disappointment. Why is this?

Cognitive Dissonance: Borrowers who have taken the time and trouble to go through the refinance process have an emotional investment in their decision. They want it to be right, and most of them tend to ignore or explain away information that comes their way suggesting that the decision might have been wrong. Psychologists have coined a term for this widespread phenomena. They call it "cognitive dissonance."

The reluctance of refinancing borrowers to admit they are wrong is strengthened by a reluctance to confront their loan provider with such a message. The broker or loan officer may be extremely personable (the most effective ones usually are), they have invested a lot of time in the deal, and most borrowers are reluctant to send them off with nothing to show for their efforts.

For most borrowers, 3 days just isn't long enough for them to work their way past these barriers. I hear from many borrowers who have come to realize that their refinance was a mistake, but almost always the letters come in months after the fact. Since it is not possible to extend the rescission period enough to make a difference, a question arises about whether there is some way to induce borrowers to confront the issue within 3 days. I'm thinking about it.

Scenario Analysis of ARMs *Determining how the interest rate and payment on an ARM will change in response to specified future changes in market interest rates, called "scenarios."*

Whether an adjustable-rate mortgage (ARM) or fixed-rate mortgage (FRM) turns out better usually depends on what happens to interest rates in the future, which no one knows. Shoppers faced with this decision should ask themselves, "Is this a risk worth taking?" and "Can I afford to take it?" The best way I know to deal with these questions is by determining what will happen to the rate and payment on the ARM if market interest rates change in ways that you specify. This is what "scenario analysis" is all about.

What Scenario Analysis Does: Scenario analysis provides a measure of the risk if rates on the ARM increase and the benefit if they don't. It also allows you to determine the extent to which you can reduce the risk on the ARM by making the larger payment that you would have made had you selected the FRM.

Scenario Analysis of ARMs

A side benefit is that you can't do scenario analysis without knowing all the features of the ARM that affect future rates and payments. The information you are forced to compile for this purpose you should have anyway. Otherwise, you don't know whether you have found the best deal on your ARM.

Example of a Scenario Analysis: An example sent by a reader involved comparing an FRM at 5.875% with a 3/1 ARM at an initial rate of 4.625%. After 3 years, the rate adjusts every year to equal the 1-year Treasury index, which had a recent value of 1.28%, plus a margin of 2.75%, subject to an adjustment cap of 2% (no rate change can exceed 2%) and a maximum rate of 10.625%. The numbers cited below all assume loan amounts of $100,000 and came from calculator 7b on my Web site.

Stable-Rate Scenario: A stable-rate scenario provides the best measure of the potential benefit of the ARM. The payment would be $514.14 for the first 36 months and $481.76 thereafter, as compared with $591.54 on the FRM. If you made the $591.54 payment on the ARM, you would pay it off in 257 months.

Rising-Rate Scenarios: I used four rising-rate scenarios of gradually increasing severity: (1) Small rate increase: after 2 years, the index increases by 0.5 % a year for 3 years. (2) Moderate rate increase: after 1 year, the rate index increases by 0.75% a year for 4 years. (3) Large rate increase: starting immediately, the index increases by 1% a year for 5 years. (4) Worst case: the index rises to 100% in month 2.

With the small-rate-increase scenario, the payment remains lower on the ARM than on the FRM over the entire 30 years. If the borrower makes the FRM payment, he will pay off in 304 months. The borrower thus benefits if rates are stable or decline or have a delayed rise of 1.5% over 3 years.

With the large-rate-increase scenarios, the benefits of the ARM over the first 3 or 4 years are followed by losses. Skipping to the worst case, the payment would rise from $514.14 to $630.64 in month 37, to $754.44 in month 49, and to $883.74 in month 61, where it would remain until payoff. It is useful to know whether you could deal with these increases, even though the likelihood of their occurring is very low.

These payment increases could be reduced by making the larger FRM payment in the first 3 years. If you paid $591.54 rather than $514.14 for 36 months, you would reduce the worst-case payment in months 61–360 from $883.74 to $856.01. The complete results for all the scenarios are shown below.

Scenario analysis doesn't provide definitive answers to the questions posed earlier. However, it does allow you to make an informed judgment based on all available information. In the face of an uncertain future, that's the best anyone can do.

	No Change		Small Increase		Moderate Increase		Large Increase		Worst Case	
Interest Rates and Monthly Payments Under Five Interest Rate Scenarios										
SCENARIO										
Mons.	Rate %	Pmt $	Rate %	Pmt $	Rate %	Pmt $	Rate %	Pmt $	Rate %	Pmt $
1–36	4.625	514.14	4.625	514.14	4.625	514.14	4.625	514.14	4.625	514.14
37–48	4.03	481.76	4.53	508.90	5.53	565.46	6.625	630.64	6.625	630.64
49–60	4.03	481.76	5.03	536.01	6.28	608.58	8.03	716.66	8.625	754.44
61–360	4.03	481.76	5.53	563.01	7.03	651.97	9.03	779.13	10.625	883.74
Borrower Makes the FRM Payment If It Is Larger Than the ARM Payment										
1–36	4.625	591.54	4.625	591.54	4.625	591.54	4.625	591.54	4.625	591.54
37–48	4.03	591.54	4.53	591.54	5.53	591.54	6.625	610.85	6.625	610.85
49–60	4.03	591.54	5.03	591.54	6.28	591.54	8.03	694.17	8.625	730.76
61–360	4.03	591.54*	5.53	591.54†	7.03	627.26	9.03	754.67	10.625	856.01

*Pays off in 257 months.
†Pays off in 304 months.

Scheduled Mortgage Payment *The amount the borrower is obliged to pay each period under the terms of the mortgage contract, including interest, principal, and where applicable, mortgage insurance and escrows.*

Paying less than the scheduled amount results in delinquency.

On FRMs and ARMs that do not allow negative amortization, the scheduled payment is the fully amortizing payment, unless the loan has an interest-only option for some period at the beginning, such as 5 or 10 years. In that case, the scheduled payment is the interest-only payment until the end of the interest-only period, when it becomes the fully amortizing payment.

On ARMs that allow negative amortization, the scheduled payment may be determined by the lender in a number of ways, which can change over the life of the instrument. Some of these ARMs also allow the borrower to select from alternative payment plans during the early years of the loan. Whatever form the scheduled payment takes in the early years, however, at some point it becomes the fully amortizing payment.

Second Mortgage *A loan with a second-priority claim against a property in the event that the borrower defaults.*

Fixed-Dollar Amounts Versus Home Equity Lines: A second mortgage is any loan that involves a second lien on the property. Some second mortgages are for a fixed-dollar amount paid out at one time, in the same way as a first mortgage. As with firsts, such seconds may be fixed rate or adjustable rate.

A home equity line of credit (HELOC) is usually a second mortgage also, but instead of being paid out at one time, it is structured as a line of credit. (It is frequently referred to as a "home equity line.") A HELOC allows the borrower to draw an amount at any time up to some maximum. HELOCs are always adjustable rate. *See* **HELOC**.

A line of credit is most convenient when cash needs are stretched out over time. A common example is a series of home improvements, one followed by another. Fixed-dollar seconds are best when all the money is needed at one time. Home purchasers may take out such seconds to avoid mortgage insurance on the first mortgage or the higher interest rate on a jumbo loan.

When taking a fixed-dollar second, borrowers can select between fixed and adjustable rates, as they prefer. When taking a HELOC, they take an adjustable; and if they want a fixed, they can refinance into a fixed-dollar second after they have drawn as much as they intend to borrow on the line.

Seconds Priced Higher Than Firsts: Second mortgages are riskier to lenders than first mortgages. In the event of default, the second mortgage lender gets repaid only if there is something left after the first mortgage lender is fully repaid. Hence, the rate will be higher on the second, provided everything else (mortgage and property type, borrower credit, etc.) is the same. If the second mortgage is a line of credit, however, the initial adjustable rate may well be below the fixed rate on a first mortgage.

Refinancing a First with a Second: As a general rule, it is not a good idea to take out a second to pay off a first, because seconds are priced higher. If you take out a second mortgage to repay the first, the second becomes the first, which is a gift to the lender: you are paying a second mortgage price on a first mortgage.

But there is at least one exception to this rule. Borrowers with a high-rate first mortgage with a small balance may find it more advantageous to pay off the first with a second rather than refinance the first. It is very difficult to find first mortgages of less than $50,000.

Some borrowers lower their rate by refinancing a first with a HELOC. In the process, however, they are exposing themselves to the risk of future rate increases. HELOCs are much more exposed than standard ARMs.

Using a Second to Avoid Mortgage Insurance: Borrowers who put down less than 20% on a first mortgage usually must purchase mortgage insurance. However, before the financial crisis, a borrower could take an 80% first mortgage combined with a 5, 10, or 15% second mortgage and avoid mortgage insurance. Such combination loans were referred to as 80/5/15s, 80/10/10s, and 80/15/5s. An 80/15/5 was an 80% first, 15% second, and 5% down.

Second mortgages designed to avoid mortgage insurance are called "piggybacks," and they became very popular during the bubble years 2004–2006. Piggyback lenders suffered horrendous losses during the subsequent financial crisis years, however; and by 2009, the few still around were likely to be 75/5/20.

In the post-crisis market, following substantial declines in house values, second mortgages atop 80% first mortgages were viewed by lenders as excessively risky. Borrowers looking to refinance, who had loan balances in excess of 80% of depreciated value, could not fund the excess with second mortgages. But those with financial assets to spare could earn a high rate of return by paying down their loan balances to 80% of value. *See* **Partial Prepayments/*Repayment Opportunities During Financial Crisis*.**

Using a Second to Avoid Jumbos: Jumbo loans are larger than the maximum-size loan that Fannie Mae and Freddie Mac can purchase. *See* **Conforming Mortgage**.

Borrowers seeking loans modestly larger than the conforming limit of $417,000 in 2009, or the conforming jumbo limit of $729,750, can use a second mortgage to fund the difference, provided the first mortgage is no larger than 75 or 80% of value. My calculator 13a can be used to determine whether the conforming loan plus a second will be less costly than the jumbo.

Second Mortgage

Second Mortgage Versus Cash-Out Refinance:

See **Refinance/Refinancing to Raise Cash**.

Second Mortgage Versus 401(k) Loan: Many borrowers have the choice of borrowing on a second mortgage or borrowing against their 401(k) plan. Several factors bear on this decision.

Relative Interest Cost: The general rule is that you select the one offering the lowest after-tax cost. On a second mortgage, the after-tax cost is the interest rate less the tax savings. You can calculate this by multiplying the interest rate by 1 minus your tax rate. For example, if the rate on a home equity loan is 8.5% and you are in the 28% tax bracket, the after-tax cost is $8.5 \times (1 - 0.28)$, or 6.12%.

The cost of borrowing from your 401(k) is not the rate you charge yourself because that goes from one pocket to another. The cost is what your loan would have earned had you kept the money in the 401(k). This is sometimes called an "opportunity cost." Since your 401(k) accumulates tax free, the total return on the fund is a close approximation of the after-tax cost.

Of course, taxes must eventually be paid on the earnings on your 401(k). But this doesn't happen until you retire, and even then the tax payments will be stretched out over time unless you elect to withdraw a lump sum.

Consequences of Unemployment: The two fund sources have different consequences should you be laid off. Unless the 401(k) loan is repaid within a month or two of losing your job, it is considered by the IRS as a taxable distribution on which income taxes, and perhaps a 10% early withdrawal penalty, are due. A second mortgage loan need not be repaid if you are laid off. On the other hand, you must continue making the payments on the second mortgage or risk losing your home.

Possible Negative Consequences of Second Mortgages: Second mortgages can cause trouble down the road in ways that borrowers seldom anticipate.

Loss of Flexibility from Negative Equity: A second mortgage reduces the equity in your house, in some cases converting positive equity to negative equity. Borrowers with negative equity lose flexibility. It becomes difficult or impossible to refinance should a favorable opportunity to do so arise, and it may also be impossible to sell. Second mortgages cannot be transferred to a new house. The sale requires that all liens be paid off, so if the liens add up to more than the house is worth, the seller must come up with the needed cash.

Second Mortgage

Refinance of First Requires Subordination of Second: A borrower with a second mortgage can't refinance the first mortgage unless either the second is refinanced as well or the second mortgage lender agrees to allow it by signing a subordination agreement. Without such an agreement, paying off the first mortgage automatically converts the second mortgage into a first mortgage, and any new mortgage would become a second.

The problem is that second mortgage lenders have varying policies toward subordination. Some will do it for a modest fee. Some will do it subject to conditions, such as that any new first mortgage not be cash-out, which would weaken the second mortgage. And some won't do it at all! Lenders' policies toward subordination are not a required disclosure, and very few borrowers find out what their lender's policy is until they try to refinance their first mortgage.

If you do take a second mortgage, ask the lender about its subordination policy immediately after asking about the interest rate. *If the lender doesn't allow subordination, march out the door.* There's another second mortgage lender down the street. If the lender does allow it, ask about any conditions and fees, and ask how long it will take. If the answers are satisfactory, get them in writing and make sure they are incorporated in the loan documents, so that if the loan is sold, the new lender will be bound by them.

A Second Can Derail a Loan Modification: Borrowers who have difficulty making their mortgage payments can sometimes negotiate a contract modification with their lender that will reduce the payment to an amount that is affordable. When default rates skyrocketed in 2008 and 2009, modifications came to be viewed as a major defense against foreclosures, and the federal government introduced the Making Home Affordable Program (MHA) that provided financial incentives to both borrowers and servicing agents to modify loans. *See* **Mortgage Modification/*The Government's Making Home Affordable Program*.**

Where there is a second mortgage, however, the first mortgage lender is usually unwilling to make concessions on terms unless the second mortgage lender does the same. Since a large proportion of the borrowers in trouble had second mortgages, this became a major roadblock. Eventually, the MHA program was forced to add incentives, both positive and negative, for second mortgage lenders to participate. How well these work was not clear at the time of this writing.

Silent Seconds: The term "silent second" is used most frequently to describe self-serving or perhaps fraudulent schemes where house sellers accept second mortgages as part of a sale transaction, without the full knowledge of the first mortgage lender. The "silence" refers to the absence of full disclosure to the first mortgage lender.

Silent Second Instead of Down Payment: The smaller of the deceptions arises when the second mortgage replaces part or all of a down payment. For example, the buyer and seller agree on a price of $200,000, the buyer has a commitment for a first mortgage loan of $180,000, but the buyer doesn't have the $20,000 required for the down payment. To make the deal work, the seller agrees to accept a silent second mortgage for $15,000. As far as the first mortgage lender knows, the down payment is $20,000, but in fact, it is only $5,000.

The silent second increases risk to the first mortgage lender because it takes only a 2.5% decline in home value to eliminate the borrower's equity—rather than the 10% decline that the lender counted on.

This silent second is also risky to the seller, because it can't be recorded at the time of the sale—that would give the game away. This means that the seller has an unsecured loan until the transaction is completed and the lien can be recorded. How long the seller must wait before recording the lien is negotiated between the parties. The longer the seller waits, the greater the risk that other liens will be placed on the property, which will endanger the silent second.

Silent Second Inflating the Sale Price: An even more serious deception of the first mortgage lender arises when the silent second is used to inflate the sale price beyond the true value of the house in order to increase the size of the first mortgage. Assume the same house as before with buyer and seller agreeing on a true price of $200,000, but in this case the buyer has no down payment. They collude to set a fictitious price of $222,200, on the basis of which the first mortgage lender agrees to lend $200,000. This is 90% of $222,200 but 100% of the true value of $200,000. The seller agrees to a second mortgage for $22,200.

In this case, the first mortgage lender knows about the second mortgage. What the lender doesn't know—where the silence comes in—is that after the transaction is completed, the seller will forgive the second mortgage. In this way, the lender is deceived into making a 100% loan, believing that it is a 90% loan.

This scheme won't work unless the higher price is ratified by an appraisal. Lenders base loan amounts on the lower of price and appraised value, so if the appraisal comes in at $200,000, which is the true price, the deal can't be done. Unfortunately, many appraisers have great difficulty in setting a value below the price agreed to by a buyer and a seller.

Silent Seconds as a Form of Subsidy: The term "silent second" is also used to describe a benign type of transaction in which a government, labor union, or nonprofit agency assists low-income homebuyers to purchase more costly houses than they could otherwise afford. The "silence" in this case refers to the absence of a payment burden imposed by the second mortgage. Some municipalities in California have such programs.

These second mortgages may carry a zero or low interest rate, or interest may be deferred for some years. Usually, the principal is not repayable until the house is sold. In some cases, the lender may recover part or all of the subsidy on the second mortgage by receiving a share in the house appreciation at sale.

For example, a labor union may offer members who are first-time home-buyers a silent second to finance closing costs or the down payment. The second might bear no interest and might not be repayable until the first mortgage is repaid or the property is sold.

It is a bit incongruous that the term "silent second" is used both to describe deceptions perpetrated on lenders by homebuyers and sellers, and to characterize subsidy programs that assist lower-income buyers. But English is a very flexible language.

Secondary Mortgage Markets *Markets in which mortgages or mortgage-backed securities are bought and sold.*

"Whole Loan" Markets Versus Securities Markets: Secondary mortgage markets are of two general types. "Whole loan" markets involve the sale of mortgages themselves, sometimes on a loan-by-loan basis but more often in blocks. Such markets, which arose in the United States soon after World War II, primarily involve the one-time sale of newly originated mortgages to traditional mortgage lenders.

In the 1970s, markets also developed in mortgage-backed securities, henceforth MBSs, issued against pools of mortgages. Instead of selling, e.g., $50 million of whole loans, the loans are segregated in a pool, and $50 million of securities is issued against the pool. These securities are actively traded after the initial issuance, and they may be attractive to investors that would not ordinarily hold mortgages, such as pension funds or mutual funds.

Secondary Mortgage Markets

Types of MBSs: MBSs in the United States are of two general types: those that are supported by the federal government and those that aren't. The first category includes securities issued by private firms but guaranteed by Ginny Mae, a federal agency, against FHA and VA mortgages. Ginny Mae guarantees the timely payment of principal and interest on these securities. It also includes securities issued by two "government-sponsored enterprises," Fanny Mae and Freddie Mac, against conventional mortgages. On these MBSs, timely payment is guaranteed by the agencies.

MBSs without a federal guarantee are usually described as being "private." Their payment guarantees are supported by "credit enhancements" of various types, which include special reserve accounts and pool insurance from private mortgage insurers. Each security stands on its own, and in a crunch has access only to the credit enhancements of that security.

In that respect, private MBSs differ from mortgage bonds, which are liabilities of the issuing firm. A given bond is supported not only by mortgage collateral but by the capital and income of the issuing firm. Mortgage bonds have never been very important in the United States, but they are central to the Danish system. *See* **Danish Mortgage System**.

Impact on Interest Rates: Secondary markets reduce mortgage interest rates in several ways. First, they increase competition by encouraging the development of a new industry of loan originators. Called different names in different countries (in the United States they are called "mortgage companies" or "mortgage banks"), they all have in common that they require little capital and tend to be aggressive competitors. Absent secondary markets, the only institutions originating mortgage loans are those with the capacity to hold them permanently, termed "portfolio lenders."

In small communities especially, borrowers may be at the mercy of one or a few local banks or savings and loan associations. The entry of mortgage companies that can sell into the secondary market breaks up these local fiefdoms, much to the benefit of borrowers. The development of whole loan markets in the United States is largely responsible for the growth of this industry.

Secondary markets also increase efficiency by encouraging a specialization of lending functions that reduces costs. Portfolio lenders typically do everything connected to originating and servicing loans, even though they may do some things quite inefficiently. Secondary markets, in contrast, create pressures to break functions apart and price them separately, and this imposes a discipline on mortgage companies to concentrate on what they do best. Many mortgage companies have ceased servicing loans, for example, because they can do better selling the servicing to companies that specialize in that function.

In addition, conversion of mortgages into mortgage-backed securities permits a better distribution of the risk of holding fixed-rate mortgages (FRMs). As one example, depository institutions don't want to take the risk of funding long-term assets with short-term liabilities. But they can originate FRMs, convert them to securities, and sell the securities to pension funds, which have long-term liabilities.

Under normal market conditions, mortgage-backed securities also are "liquid," while mortgages themselves are not. This means that in most cases mortgage-backed securities can be sold for full value within the day, whereas selling the same amount of mortgages could take weeks. Because most investors value liquidity and are willing to accept a lower yield to get it, converting illiquid mortgages to liquid securities puts downward pressure on the rates charged to borrowers.

The liquidity of MBSs, however, prevails only so long as investors have confidence in them. Once they lose confidence, as happened when the financial crisis erupted in 2007, private MBSs become extremely difficult to sell—perhaps even more difficult than selling a group of whole loans identical to those in the collateral pool.

Widening the Market: Secondary markets have also expanded the size of the borrower pool. Portfolio lenders generally restrict their loans to "A-quality" borrowers, in large part because of regulatory concerns about their safety and soundness. Secondary markets, in contrast, can access investors who are prepared to hold risky loans if the price is right. The result has been the emergence of risk-based pricing, which places loans in the hands of borrowers who otherwise would have recourse only to family, friends, and loan sharks.

Increased Vulnerability: A housing finance system in which originators depend on their ability to sell the mortgages they originate is vulnerable to shocks that shut down the secondary market. If investors stop buying, originators are forced to stop lending. The danger applies to private securities in which investor confidence is critical.

Private securities are vulnerable in three ways. First, because there is money to be made by widening the market at higher prices, the individual mortgages behind private securities can be relatively weak with low down payments, weak documentation, and low credit scores. Weak mortgages are more vulnerable to unexpected developments, especially to a cessation of property value appreciation.

Second, because default risk is transferred from originators to investment banks to investors, enforcement of underwriting rules tends to become as loose as the purchaser permits. During the euphoria characteristic of a bubble, almost anything goes. This further reduces the quality of mortgages in security pools.

Third, each private security stands on its own bottom, which means that none of the reserves on good securities that are not needed are available to meet losses on one bad security. Yet it takes only one bad security on which investors incur losses to destroy confidence in all of them. *See* **Subprime Market**.

Shopping Complexities: Another downside of secondary markets from a borrower's perspective is that shopping for a mortgage becomes more complex. The secondary market is largely responsible both for market nichification, which makes it difficult for a borrower to determine whether a price quote applies to her particular deal, and for price volatility, which makes it risky to compare a price quote on Monday with one from another loan provider on Tuesday. Nichification and volatility underlie several common scams perpetrated on borrowers by loan providers. *See* **Mortgage Scams and Tricks/*Other Scams by Loan Providers***.

Ginny Mae: The mortgage-backed security market was begun in 1970 by Ginny Mae, a wholly owned agency of the federal government. The agency guaranteed the payments on securities issued by lenders against pools of FHA and VA mortgages. This program makes money for the Treasury and has been relatively free of controversy.

Fannie Mae and Freddie Mac: These firms are "government-sponsored enterprises" (GSEs), which means that they are privately owned, but receive support from the federal government and assume some public responsibilities. The two GSEs are among the largest corporations in the world and are highly controversial. They played a major role in weakening underwriting standards during the housing bubble, and they suffered horrendous losses in the ensuing crisis. In 2008, they were placed in government-administered conservatorships, and (along with Ginny Mae) became the only secondary market game in town, as the private market shut down.

Mortgages Eligible for Purchase: The GSEs purchase conforming mortgages from eligible lenders. Conforming mortgages are those that meet the underwriting requirements of the agencies and are no larger than the largest loan the GSEs are allowed by law to purchase. In 2009 the maximum for a single dwelling unit was $417,000, but in high-priced counties it ranged up to $729,750, with larger amounts for two- to four-family dwellings. *See* **Conforming Mortgage**.

The agencies hold some of the loans they buy in their portfolios, funding them by the issuance of debt. The remainder are "securitized"—sold in the form of MBSs that the GSEs guarantee.

Government Support: The major support the GSEs receive from the federal government is a special claim for government assistance in the event they ever get into financial trouble. This claim is grounded on their right to borrow from the U.S. Treasury and also derives from their history—both were public institutions before they became privately owned. As a result, investors consider the notes they issue and the mortgage securities they guarantee almost as good as securities issued by the federal government itself. Markets have always assumed that in a pinch their guarantees would be supported by the federal government. That assumption was proved correct in 2008; *see* **Role in the Housing Bubble** *below*.

Absence of Competitors: The GSEs have no competitors in the conforming loan market. Because of their government backing, the GSEs can sell notes and securities at a lower yield than any strictly private secondary market firm. This gives them a monopoly—or rather a duopoly since there are two of them—in the market in which they operate.

The GSEs did have emulators, however, in the nonconforming market. While the cast of players changed, before the financial crisis erupted in 2007, there were usually 15 or more strictly private firms that purchased nonconforming loans and securitized them in much the same way as the GSEs. In 2009, there were none because of the horrendous losses suffered by investors, especially those who had purchased securities issued against subprime mortgages. The private MBS market had ceased to function.

Role in the Housing Bubble: Fannie Mae and Freddie Mac played an important role in the excessive liberalization of mortgage terms that occurred during the housing bubble. As stockholder-owned firms that received enormously valuable subsidies from government, they could not resist pressures coming from a powerful political-social movement aimed at increasing the homeownership rate among the disadvantaged.

In 1992, Congress authorized HUD to set annual quotas for agency purchases of "affordable loans," expressed as a percentage of their total purchases. Initially 30%, these quotas rose over time, through both Democratic and Republican administrations, reaching 55% in 2007.

Meeting this objective required the agencies to liberalize their lending terms. Among other things, they reduced down payments to 3% in 1997 and to zero in 2001. The liberalized terms designed to help disadvantaged groups had to be extended to prime borrowers as well. This encouraged them to purchase more costly houses, make smaller down payments, purchase for investment in anticipation of further price increases, and cash out equity by refinancing

Acquisitions of nonprime mortgages by the agencies increased rapidly beginning in 2004 and peaked in 2007 when the crisis erupted. Their holdings of such mortgages were estimated at $1.5 trillion in 2008. This total included private securities issued against subprime mortgages, which HUD allowed the agencies to count toward their quotas of affordable loans. The horrendous default rates and losses on these loans sealed the fate of the agencies, which in 2008 were placed in a government-administered conservatorship.

What Next? Historically, most economists were skeptical or hostile to the Fannie Mae–Freddie Mac model of stockholder-owned firms with public responsibilities. In most cases, the reason was that only about half of the taxpayer-funded subsidy provided to the agencies was realized as a benefit by borrowers. We now see that that was the least of it. The more compelling argument against the mixed private-public model is that it corrupted the political process and destabilized the system.

In the first edition of this book, written in 2003, I sketched out a relatively simple way to phase out the public support and public responsibilities of the agencies. It would have converted them into strictly private firms without hurting investors who had relied on government support. In 2009 when this second edition was written, that plan was no longer feasible.

In conservatorship, the agencies had enormous capital deficits and could not be given away without substantial outlays by government. Furthermore, with the private MBS market no longer functioning, the system was more dependent than ever on the agencies. Some 60–70% of all new mortgages were being sold to them; about 20–30% were FHA and VA, and only about 10% were untouched by a federal agency. How to get the agencies out of the government without crashing the system was a major challenge.

Self-Employed Borrower *A borrower who must use tax returns to document income rather than information provided by an employer.*

This complicates the process and sometimes derails it. *See* **Qualification/ Qualifying Self-Employed Borrowers**.

Seller Contribution *A contribution to a borrower's down payment or settlement costs made by a home seller, as an alternative to a price reduction.*

See **Down Payment/*Home Seller Contributions*.**

Seller Financing *Providing a second mortgage to a buyer in order to facilitate the sale.*

Most sellers who take back second mortgages from buyers view them as a way to facilitate the sale and, hopefully, get a better price. In the process, they become investors in a risky asset that they often are not in a position to manage effectively.

The Second Mortgage Might Result in a Higher Sale Price: One useful way to think about the question of whether or not to provide a second is to estimate the ratio of the increase in price relative to the risk of loss, which is measured by the size of the second mortgage. For example, if a seller can raise the price to $410,000 from $400,000 by providing a 15-year 10% second mortgage for $20,000, and the appraisal comes in at least at $410,000, the ratio is 50%.

This is a great investment if the buyer repays the mortgage as scheduled. If not, the seller stands to lose up to $10,000 (the $20,000 loss less the $10,000 increase in price). Sellers have to consider how much risk is involved and whether they can manage it.

The Risk on a Single Deal by an Unsophisticated Seller: I don't view a second mortgage as an appropriate investment for a seller who is doing it strictly to get a better price and is not qualified to assess and manage the risk.

Second mortgages must be serviced, which few sellers are equipped to do effectively. Keeping records on the back of an envelope is a recipe for trouble. A moderately intelligent seller can learn to keep track of payments and balances using a spreadsheet because this only requires following a few simple rules. The fun begins when the borrower becomes delinquent, and the seller realizes he hasn't a clue how to adjust the books.

Borrowers who get into payment trouble sometimes stop paying on the second while continuing to pay on the first mortgage, gambling that the second mortgage lender won't do anything about it. If the second mortgage lender is a novice at the game, the gamble will probably pay off.

In addition, the one-shot investor is not diversified. Even if he does a great job of risk assessment, reducing the probability of default to one in a hundred, he might be unlucky enough that the one borrower who defaults turns out to be his.

Selling the Second Mortgage to an Investor: A way out for the unsophisticated and undiversified home seller is to sell the second mortgage to an investor who is in the business. The investor has a servicing system in place, and because she buys from many different home sellers, her risk is diversified. Furthermore, she knows how to manage the risk, including the ins and outs of the foreclosure process if a borrower gets into serious trouble.

Preparing to Sell the Second Mortgage: The seller who needs to offer a second mortgage to get the price he wants, but is not equipped to be an investor in second mortgages, should prepare to sell the mortgage before writing it. The way to do that is to find the investor beforehand, obtain a contract form that the investor finds acceptable, and negotiate the terms of the deal, including the rate and the price.

For example, the investor might offer to purchase the $20,000 second mortgage referred to earlier at a discount of 10%, provided the seller uses the investor's contract, the mortgage has an interest rate of 12%, and the buyer retains 5% equity. This means that if the buyer can be induced to pay 12% rather than 10%, the cost of the second to the seller is only $2,000 as against the estimated $10,000 increment to the price.

Servicing *Administering loans between the time of disbursement and the time the loan is fully paid off.*

Servicing includes collecting payments from the borrower, maintaining payment records, providing borrowers and investors with account statements, imposing late charges when the payment is late, and pursuing delinquent borrowers. In many cases, servicing agents also pay property taxes and insurance with money placed in escrow by the borrower.

Servicing

The Poor Quality of Servicing Overall: From a borrower perspective, the quality of servicing is generally low. The Department of Housing and Urban Development (HUD) reports that two of every five complaints it receives from borrowers involve servicing issues. J. D. Powers and Associates, which measures consumer satisfaction with business services of many kinds, reports that only 10% of borrowers are happy with their servicing agent.

The financial incentives to provide good service, which work in other sectors of our economy, don't work for loan servicing. The borrower selects a lender or mortgage broker, not a servicing agent. The major focus is the price of the loan. Rarely if ever does the expected quality of servicing come into the picture.

Information on the quality of servicing is not generally available, and even if it were, the borrower has no way to know that the lender making the loan will also be servicing it. Most loans are sold shortly after origination, and while servicing sometimes is retained by the seller, often it isn't. In addition, servicing contracts are bought and sold in an active market, much like bonds. This means that any borrower at any time can find her loan suddenly being serviced by a different firm.

The fact that borrowers have no say in who services their loan would not be so bad if they could fire their servicing agent for poor performance, but they can't. The only way to rid yourself of a servicing agent is to refinance, but then you are gambling that the new one will be better, which is a bad bet.

Since borrowers can neither choose nor fire their servicing agents, quality of service has no impact on an agent's bottom line. For most, there is no business reason to provide quality service to borrowers.

Quality Servicing by a Few: A few enlightened firms have adopted the view that the borrowers they are servicing are potential customers for new services. A business strategy of "targeted cross-selling" requires attention to service quality. A borrower who is miffed because her taxes weren't paid on time is a poor candidate for cross-selling. Unfortunately, this approach has not made major inroads in the industry.

Predatory Servicing: At the opposite pole are the servicing predators, whose business strategy is to extract as much additional revenue from the borrowers they service as the law allows. Here is an outrageous example:

A borrower made his monthly payment on the 16th of the month—one day after the grace period. Without notice, the lender imposed a late charge on that payment and then proceeded to collect that charge by deducting it from the following month's payment. That payment was made on time but recorded as late because of the deduction of the late charge from the previous month, which generated still another late charge. Seven consecutive payments were made on time but recorded as late because of the deduction of late charges on the prior payments.

Predatory servicing agents who purchase servicing will examine each note to determine whether they are entitled to shorten the grace period or raise the late fee. If there is some excuse for considering the property to be underinsured, the agent will purchase overpriced insurance and add the cost to the loan balance. Extra payments to principal will not be credited in a timely fashion, and the borrower will not know because monthly statements are not provided or are incomplete.

Recourse: Since borrowers can't fire their servicing agents, what can they do to protect themselves? If you have been mistreated, you should file a written complaint with the lender addressed to customer service. Do not include it with your mortgage payment, which you should continue to make separately. State:

Your loan number.

Names on loan documents.

Property and/or mailing address.

This is a "qualified written request" under Section 6 of the Real Estate Settlement Procedures Act (RESPA).

I am writing because:

[Describe the problem and the action you believe the lender should take.]

[Describe any previous attempts to resolve the issue, including conversations with customer service.]

[If it is relevant to the dispute, request a copy of your payment history.]

[List a daytime telephone number.]

I understand that under Section 6 of RESPA you are required to acknowledge my request within 20 business days and must try to resolve the issue within 60 business days.

If this doesn't do the trick, you can file a complaint with HUD. You can also sue. According to HUD, "A borrower may bring a private law suit, or a group of borrowers may bring a class action suit, within three years, against a servicer who fails to comply with the provisions of Section 6."

Servicing

You can also file a complaint with the government agency that regulates the servicing agent. Here are Web sites you can use to contact these agencies:

- For national banks, www.occ.treas.gov/customer.htm
- For federally chartered savings and loan associations, www.ots.treas.gov/contact.html
- For state-chartered banks and savings and loans, www.lendingprofessional.com/licensing.html
- For mortgage banking firms, www.aarmr.org/lists/members-IE.html

If you don't know the proper agency, you can send the complaint to the Consumer Protection Division of the state attorney general. It will be forwarded to the relevant state or federal agency.

Preventative Measures: Borrowers should periodically check their transaction history to make certain that (a) payments are always applied to the balance at the end of the preceding month, (b) tax and insurance payments from escrow are correct and there have been no double payments, (c) rate adjustments on ARMs are in accordance with the method stipulated in the note, and (d) there isn't anything in the history that looks "funny."

Any borrower who does not receive a complete transaction statement at least annually should periodically submit a "qualified written request" for one using the form described above.

Servicing for Borrowers: Under existing arrangements, servicing systems are designed to meet the needs of lenders, and they won't meet the needs of borrowers until they are redesigned for that purpose. This is possible and may be in the cards. Borrowers must be willing to pay for the service.

A servicing system for borrowers (SSB) would not replace existing servicing systems. The firms providing the services described below could be called "second-tier servicers." Borrowers would make their payments to second-tier servicers, which would then make payments to the primary servicers.

With the payments going through its hands, the second-tier servicer has command of information on the borrower's payment history. In contrast to the primary servicer, however, the second-tier servicer will use the information to provide useful services to the borrower. The services, for which the borrower will pay a modest monthly fee, will be provided over the Internet.

Servicing

Access to Payment History: The major purpose is to provide peace of mind that the lender is properly crediting mortgage payments. The SSB would allow borrowers to monitor their accounts continually, and the "what-if" capacity would allow them to experiment with different future payment patterns.

Access to Details of ARM Rate Adjustments: The major purpose is to provide peace of mind that the new rate has been properly calculated. The SSB would show the details of the ARM rate adjustment, rather than just the resulting new rate, which is all borrowers get now. Borrowers will also be able to forecast what the new rate will be months in advance so they can prepare for a possible refinancing.

Cost-Reduction Refinance Opportunities: The purpose is to flag profitable refinance opportunities. The SSB would continually monitor the relationship between the borrower's interest rate, current market rates, and the borrower's credit as affected by her mortgage payment record.

Cash-Raising Opportunities: The purpose is to provide borrowers who request it with a tool for assessing alternative ways to raise cash. The system would already know many of the required data inputs, including the borrower's existing mortgage balance and terms, as well as current market terms. Other data inputs, such as the amount of cash needed, would be entered by the borrower.

PMI Termination: The purpose is to give the borrower a "heads-up" that it may be possible to terminate mortgage insurance. Automatic termination under the federal legislation passed in 1999 does not take account of extra payments to principal or house price appreciation. Earlier termination that does take account of these factors requires that the borrower take the initiative.

Alternative Payment Options: The purpose is to allow borrowers to pay biweekly, bimonthly, or weekly. Borrowers may prefer one of these options because they find the schedule more convenient or because they want to build an early payoff plan around shorter payment periods.

Servicing and Loan Modifications: The financial crisis imposed a new and heavy challenge to servicers for which they were completely unprepared. The challenge was to ramp up the number of loan modifications needed to reduce foreclosures to manageable levels. *See* **Mortgage Modification/ Servicer Inefficiency**.

Servicing Agent *The party who services a loan, who may or may not be the lender who originated it.*

See **Servicing**.

Servicing Fee *A monthly fee retained by a servicing agent as compensation for servicing a loan owned by another firm.*

Servicing fees are expressed as a percentage of the loan balance and are deducted by the servicer from the interest paid by the borrower. If the interest rate is 6%, for example, and the servicing fee is 0.25%, the servicer remits 5.75% to the investor.

Servicing Release Premium *A payment made by the purchaser of a mortgage to the seller for the release of the servicing on the mortgage.*

A newly originated mortgage can be sold with the seller retaining the right to service the mortgage and collect a servicing fee. Alternatively, the servicing rights can be sold along with the mortgage. The difference in price between the two transactions is the servicing release premium.

Servicing Rights *The present value of a future stream of income from servicing fees, shown on the balance sheet of the firm that owns the income stream.*

Since the standard servicing fee of 0.25% is usually substantially larger than the cost of servicing a mortgage, the contract to service has value, the more so the larger the loan balance and the longer the servicer expects to have the mortgage. A decline in market interest rates reduces the value of servicing rights by increasing the volume of refinances, shortening the life of servicing contracts.

Servicing Transfer *When one servicing agent is replaced by another.*

Servicing transfers may occur when the ownership of a mortgage changes hands and the new owner uses a different servicing agent, and they also occur when servicing contracts are sold. Servicing transfers involve a risk to the borrower because of their potential for fraud. The perpetrators pretend to be the new servicing agent and try and induce borrowers to send their payments to them. You can prevent this from happening to you by confirming the legitimacy of the new firm before sending any money.

Under federal law, a firm that is relinquishing the servicing of a mortgage to another firm must notify the borrower of the name of the successor firm along with a physical address, a toll-free telephone number, and a specific date when the changeover is effective. The notice you receive from the new firm should conform to the information you received from the old firm.

If there is any discrepancy between the information provided by the alleged new servicing agent and the information provided by the old one, and if you can't clarify it to your satisfaction over the telephone, don't send the new firm any money. Instead, open a new bank account and deposit your payment in that account. This will assure that you won't get ripped off while evidencing your good faith effort to meet your obligation.

Settlement Costs *Total costs charged to the borrower that must be paid at closing by the borrower, though the home seller or the lender may sometimes contribute.*

In dealing directly with a lender, settlement costs can be divided into the following categories:

1. Fees paid to lender

2. Fees paid to third parties for services required by the lender

3. Other settlement costs

Fees Paid to Lender: Lender fees fall into two categories: those expressed as a percentage of the loan and those expressed in dollars.

Fees Expressed as Percentage of Loan: These consist of points and origination fees. Origination fees are points in disguise. Reporting services that publish information on mortgage rates and points do not show origination fees, so lenders that charge an origination fee may appear to have lower fees. This is pure gamesmanship. The borrower's concern is the total of all charges expressed as a percentage of the loan amount, whatever they are called.

Lender Fees Expressed in Dollars: Some of the common lender fees expressed in dollars cover processing, tax service, flood certification, underwriting, wire transfer, document preparation, courier, and lender inspection. Until 2010, lenders itemized dollar fees, a deplorable practice that goes back to the days when interest rates were regulated and lenders had to justify their fees in terms of reimbursement for costs.

From the borrower's perspective, what fees are called doesn't matter, and whether they are cost justified doesn't matter. All that matters is their sum total, which borrowers should use in shopping. This principle is recognized in the Good Faith Estimate that became effective January 1, 2010, which has no itemization.

While lenders always report points alongside the interest rate, dollar fees and origination fees are not reported in the media and generally are not volunteered by lenders. For this reason, shoppers often fail to consider them in selecting a lender. Trying to negotiate them afterward is usually fruitless.

Fees Paid to Third Parties for Services Required by the Lender: These include title insurance and other title-related services, homeowners insurance, credit report, appraisal, settlement services, and (when needed) flood insurance and pest inspections. Some of these services are ordered by the lender (appraisal and credit report), others are usually purchased directly by the borrower (homeowners insurance), and some can go either way (title insurance).

Third-party services are often overpriced because of referral relationships between lenders and third-party service providers. The latter compete for referrals, which raises their costs, which are passed on to borrowers. At various times, individual lenders have guaranteed some or all third-party charges, but the practice has never caught on.

Some lenders consistently underestimate third-party charges as a way of making their proposals appear more attractive. The Good Faith Estimate form used for 34 years allowed this, but the new one effective January 1, 2010, does not. *See **Good Faith Estimate** below.*

Other Settlement Costs: These are a miscellany of charges, which require little or no vigilance by the borrower.

- Government charges, such as transaction taxes, are what they are.

- Per diem interest is interest for the period between the closing date and the first day of the following month. At worst, the lender might try to tack on an extra day or two.

- Escrow reserve is your money placed on deposit with the lender so the lender can pay your taxes and insurance. The amount is based on a HUD formula.

Good Faith Estimate (GFE): The Real Estate Settlement Procedures Act of 1974 (RESPA) required lenders to provide borrowers with a Good Faith Estimate of settlement costs. Unfortunately, the form developed by HUD for this purpose, which was used for the next 34 years, was a confusing document of little use to borrowers.

The GFE encouraged itemized pricing by providing space for any expense category a lender wished to use. Total lender charges were not shown anywhere, and the individual lender charges were intermixed with charges of third parties for insurance, taxes, and the like. The GFE thus provided borrowers with all the detail for which they had no use, but no total of lender fees, which is a critical number they needed.

Furthermore, because some third-party charges are not known with certainty until late in the process, all costs on the GFE were viewed as "estimates," including the lenders' own charges, which *are* known with certainty. Viewing lender charges as estimates encouraged the practice of some less scrupulous loan officers of "overlooking" certain charges at the outset, only to discover them later when it was too late for the borrower to back out. Charges of other service providers were also vulnerable to upward adjustments late in the process. *See* **Mortgage Scams and Tricks/ Strictly Lender Scams/Pad the GFE**.

While fees paid to brokers by borrowers were shown on the GFE, fees paid to brokers by lenders in exchange for a higher interest rate were not shown in a way that typical borrowers could understand. *See* **Yield-Spread Premium**.

The GFE that became effective January 1, 2010, makes a clear distinction between lender charges and third-party charges, and lender charges are no longer itemized. Lender charges consist of just two items: the first is points that are paid to reduce the interest rate, and the second is the total of all other charges, referred to as the Origination Charge. The Origination Charge cannot change at closing from the amount shown on the GFE. The sum of the points and Origination Charge is the Adjusted Origination Charge.

Charges of third parties who have been referred to the borrower by the lender, or selected by the lender, cannot be more than 10% higher at settlement than the amounts shown on the GFE. The lender would be responsible for any excess. There are no limits on price increases covering services in which the lender has not been involved in referring to or selecting the service provider.

On brokered loans, the Origination Charge includes any fee paid the broker by the lender, called the "yield-spread premium," or YSP. The YSP is shown as an upfront credit to the borrower (negative points) granted in exchange for a higher rate. (It is the second line under item 2.) This allows the borrower to see how much of the Origination Charge is being paid indirectly through a higher rate.

This is useful information to any borrower who has retained a mortgage broker and is not shopping alternatives. But it can be misleading if the borrower is comparing one GFE offered by a broker with another GFE offered by a lender, because the lender is not obliged to show its YSP equivalent. Borrowers in this situation should ignore any YSP and focus on the rate and the Adjusted Origination Charge, which provide an unbiased price comparison between direct and brokered loans

Using the New GFE in Shopping: Where the old GFE provided no help at all to borrowers shopping for a mortgage, the new one can be useful to knowledgeable borrowers. The freeze on total fixed-dollar lender charges (shown as the Origination Charge), along with the 10% cap on any increase in third-party charges, means that borrowers can meaningfully compare these figures across different loan providers. This includes brokers, whose fee to the borrower is included in the Origination Charge. If there is a payment to the broker by the lender, the interest cost of the payment to the borrower is shown immediately below the Origination Charge.

However, total fixed-dollar lender fees and third-party charges are only a part of the price. The dynamic part, which changes every day and sometimes within the day, is the interest rate and points. Unless the GFE is returned to the borrower the same day the prices are set, the prices will have lapsed when the borrower receives them.

To use the new GFE to compare prices from loan provider 1 and loan provider 2, the borrower must receive GFEs from both and must arrange with both to have the rate and points updated daily by e-mail or fax. (Don't use the telephone—you want a written record.) After the borrower has compared quotes on a few days, she can make a decision and request that the selected loan provider lock the price.

Settlement Statement (HUD-1) *A statement received by every borrower at closing that details all payments and receipts connected to the purchase transaction, all settlement costs connected to the loan, and reserves deposited with the lender.*

The revised version effective January 1, 2010, provides a comparison of items on the HUD-1 with those shown earlier on the **Good Faith Estimate (GFE)**.

Shared Appreciation Mortgage (SAM) *A mortgage on which the borrower gives up a share in future price appreciation in exchange for a lower interest rate and/or interest deferral.*

SAMs in the private market had a brief flurry in the early 1980s but died out quickly, and an attempt to revive them in 2000 was unsuccessful. Some cities on the West Coast offer second mortgage SAMs to residents with incomes below some maximum. Reverse mortgage SAMs have also appeared in small numbers.

Shopping Site *A multilender Web site that offered borrowers the capacity to shop among multiple competing lenders.*

At one point, there were five such sites, including one sponsored by Microsoft and one by Intuit. By 2003, they were all gone. A new one, **Home-Account**, was in development at this writing.

Short Sale *An agreement between a mortgage borrower in distress and the lender which allows the borrower to sell the house and remit the proceeds to the lender as repayment of the debt.*

A short sale is an alternative to foreclosure or a deed in lieu of foreclosure. The lender may or may not retain the right to pursue a deficiency judgment against the borrower for claims in excess of the proceeds of the short sale. *See* **Payment Problems/*Position of the Lender*/Permanent Problem**.

Silent Second *A second mortgage that is used to deceive the first mortgage lender; also a second mortgage offered to borrowers at preferential terms.*

See **Second Mortgage/*Silent Seconds*.**

Simple Interest *A transaction in which interest is not paid on interest—there is no compounding.*

For example, if you deposit $1,000 in an account that pays 5% a year simple interest, you would receive $50 interest in year one and another $50 in year two. If interest were compounded annually, you would receive $52.50 in year two.

All deposit accounts compound interest, however, because if they didn't, depositors would shuffle accounts between banks. In my example, you could withdraw the $1,050 at the end of year one, put it into another bank, and earn $52.50 in year two.

Simple Interest Biweekly Mortgage *A biweekly mortgage on which biweekly payments are applied to the balance every two weeks, rather than monthly, as on a conventional biweekly.*

See **Biweekly Mortgage/*Simple Interest Biweeklies*.**

Simple Interest Mortgage *A mortgage on which interest is calculated daily based on the balance on the day of payment, rather than monthly, as on the standard mortgage.*

See **Amortization/*Amortization on a Simple Interest Mortgage*.**

Single File Mortgage Insurance *Lender-pay mortgage insurance offered by MGIC.*

See **Lender-Pay Mortgage Insurance.**

Single-Lender Web Site *A Web site of an individual lender offering loans to consumers.*

They are easy to identify because the name of the lender usually will be prominently displayed on the screen. They are not easy to shop, however, because only a small percentage of the thousands of sites provide prices that are customized to the individual transaction. Among those that do, many require the user to input personal information before they will provide transaction-based prices.

Most Internet shoppers want a list of lenders in whom they can have confidence, who will provide them with the information they need to make an informed decision *before* applying for a mortgage, and who also guarantee them fair treatment during the period *after* they apply through to closing. To meet this need, I developed the Upfront Mortgage Lender (UML) program. *See* **Upfront Mortgage Lender**.

Stated Assets *A documentation rule where the borrower discloses assets and their source but the lender does not verify the amount.*

> *See* **Documentation Requirements/*Stated Assets or No Asset Verification*.**

Stated Income *A documentation rule where the borrower discloses income and its source but the lender does not verify the amount.*

> *See* **Documentation Requirements/*Stated Income–Verified Assets*.**

Streamlined Refinancing *A refinance that omits some of the standard risk control measures and is therefore quicker and less costly.*

The rationale for streamlined refinancing is that while it is an entirely new loan, the information from the previous loan available to the lender retains validity. In addition, valuable information may be available on the borrower's payment history.

The extent to which a lender can offer streamlining depends on how much information and how much discretion the lender has. A new lender that was the original lender and still owns the loan has the greatest leeway. A new lender that was the original lender but is now servicing the loan for someone else has the same information but less discretion. A new lender that was not the original lender and is not servicing the old loan doesn't have the information needed to justify streamlined refinancing.

> *See* **Refinance/*Refinancing with the Current Lender*.**

Subordinate Financing *A second mortgage on a property that is not paid off when the first mortgage is refinanced.*

The second mortgage lender must allow subordination of the second to the new first mortgage. *See* **Second Mortgage/*Possible Negative Consequences of Second Mortgages*/Refinance of First Requires Subordination of Second.**

Subordination Policy *The policy of a second mortgage lender toward allowing a borrower to refinance the first mortgage while leaving the second in place.*

See **Second Mortgage/*Possible Negative Consequences of Second Mortgages*/Refinance of First Requires Subordination of Second.**

Subprime Borrower *A borrower who, at the time her mortgage was originated, did not meet the underwriting requirements of mainstream lenders.*

The subprime market evolved slowly beginning in the late 1990s, expanded rapidly during the bubble that peaked in 2006, and then gradually disappeared. *See* **Subprime Market.**

The description of subprime borrowers below applies to the period when the market was thriving. By 2009, consumers who would have been accepted as subprime borrowers during the earlier period either became FHA borrowers or were shut out of the market altogether.

Qualifying Subprime Borrowers: Subprime borrowers did not qualify for prime financing primarily because of their poor credit. A very low credit score would disqualify. A middling score might or might not, depending mainly on the down payment, the ratio of total expense (including debt payments) to income, and the ability to document income and assets.

Some other factors could also enter the equation, including purpose of loan and property type. For example, a borrower who was weak on some but not all of the factors indicated in the paragraph above might squeak by if purchasing a one-family home as a primary residence. But the same borrower purchasing a four-family home as an investment might not make it.

Subprime Borrower

Characteristics of Subprime Borrowers: The development of the subprime market made mortgages (and homeownership) available to a segment of the population that otherwise would have been shut out of the market. And some of them succeeded. They took a 2/28 ARM, rebuilt their credit score during the two-year window that they had, and refinanced into a fixed-rate mortgage at prime terms. *See* **Subprime Lender/***The 2/28 ARM*.

But a large segment of them didn't make it. They were unsuccessful in rebuilding their credit and probably should not have been homeowners in the first place. Others might have made it but were torpedoed by a stiff prepayment penalty that they didn't realize they had. And many who hit the two-year mark after the financial crisis erupted in 2007, who might have made it earlier, found that nobody wanted to refinance them. The experience of those who were sweet-talked into cash-out refinances was probably even worse than that of homebuyers.

The Problem of Prime Borrowers Getting Subprime Loans: Some borrowers who were eligible for loans from mainstream lenders ended up in the subprime market. They were prime borrowers, but they paid subprime prices.

This happened partly because of the difficulties some borrowers had in determining whether or not they qualified in the mainstream market. Underwriting requirements can differ from one mainstream lender to another, so it is quite possible that a borrower with problems may not have been eligible at one lender but would have been eligible at another.

However, the main reason some prime borrowers ended up paying subprime prices is that they were solicited by subprime lenders and went along with the deal pitched to them without ever contacting a mainstream lender. This is sometimes referred to as "steering."

Very few subprime loan officers would give up a commission by referring a qualified applicant to a mainstream lender. The deal went down at subprime prices, regardless of how qualified the borrower might be.

Subprime lenders marketed aggressively to homeowners who already had mortgages. A major pitch was the cash that borrowers could take out of their properties through a cash-out refinance. Another common pitch was the low initial payment on 2/28 ARMs.

These lenders targeted groups and areas that promised to have many subprime borrowers. Many occupants of such neighborhoods were subprime, but those who weren't and who went along with the soliciting firm paid subprime prices.

Subprime Lender *A lender who specialized in lending to subprime borrowers.*

Most subprime lenders began as independents, but over time many became affiliates of mainstream lenders operating under different names. They began to scale down operations in 2007 as the secondary market shut down, and many of them failed. By 2009, they were all gone.

Subprime lenders seldom if ever identified themselves as such. The only clear giveaway was their prices, which were uniformly higher than those quoted by mainstream lenders.

Subprime Pricing: Subprime lenders based their rates and fees on the same factors as prime lenders, but more so. For example, a mainstream lender might vary the price with credit score, where a subprime lender would use the score plus three or four other items from the credit report. The price sheet of a mainstream lender might cover a price range of 2%, where for a subprime lender it could be 8%.

The same loan on both price sheets would be priced higher on the subprime. Lending costs were higher because more applications were rejected, marketing costs were higher, lenders expected to earn a larger markup, and loan officers and mortgage brokers expected to earn a larger commission.

Subprime Underwriting: Where underwriting prudence clashed with marketability, prudence lost out. Escrow of taxes and insurance, which is usually required in the prime market unless the borrower pays for a waiver, was seldom required in the subprime market despite the shaky finances of many subprime borrowers. Down payments were low, but mortgage insurance was often not required. Prepayment penalties were almost always required because, in contrast to escrows and mortgage insurance, they imposed no immediate financial burden on the borrower.

The 2/28 ARM: A very common mortgage in the subprime market, which I had never seen outside of that market, is the 2/28 ARM. This is an adjustable-rate mortgage on which the rate is fixed for two years and then reset to equal the value of a rate index at that time, plus a margin. Because the margins are large, the rate on most 2/28s would often rise sharply at the two-year mark, even if market rates did not change during the period.

For example, if the rate was 6% for two years, the initial index value was 4% at time of origination, and the margin was 6%, assuming the index remains at 4% after two years, the loan rate would jump to 10%.

This created a hurdle at the two-year mark that many borrowers could not jump. *See* **Subprime Borrower/*Characteristics of Subprime Borrowers*.**

Subprime Market *The network of investment banks, credit reporting agencies, investors, subprime lenders, warehouse lenders, and mortgage brokers and loan officers, who made possible the delivery of loans to subprime borrowers.*

Players in the Market: A large number of cooperating entities were required to create the subprime market.

Investment Banks: All subprime mortgages were intended to be placed in asset-backed securities that would be sold to investors. Without a market for such securities, there would have been no subprime mortgages.

The critical role of the investment banks was to buy the mortgages from originators, pool them into securities designed to meet the requirements of credit reporting agencies, and sell the securities to investors. The securities were divided into separate tranches carrying varying degrees of risk, but most of the securities received AAA ratings. They all included "credit enhancements," consisting of reserves of various kinds embedded in the securities that were required by the credit rating agencies to obtain the desired AAA ratings.

Credit Rating Agencies (CRAs): Their critical role was to dictate the amount of credit enhancement that was required to earn a AAA rating on most of the securities issued against a pool of subprime mortgages. The CRAs based these judgments on estimates of potential losses under adverse conditions, using the data available on subprime defaults, which went back to the year 2000. Since house prices had risen over the entire period 2000–2006, this experience vastly understated the potential losses in an environment of house price declines, which emerged in late 2006.

Investors: The subprime securities had to be sold to investors, who in many cases were the least informed of all the players in the process. Many investors were foreigners with dollars to invest who were attracted to the high returns being offered on AAA-rated securities. Fannie Mae and Freddie Mac also purchased these securities as a way of meeting their obligation to provide more credit to disadvantaged borrowers.

Retail and Wholesale Lenders: The first operated through loan officer employees, the second through mortgage brokers, but both sold their loans in the secondary market. Many smaller originators were lightly capitalized and could operate only with large warehouse lines of credit secured by originated loans that had not yet been sold.

Subprime Market

Warehouse Lenders: These were commercial banks, investment banks, and wholesale lenders that made secured loans to loan originators. Typically, these loans were for a high percentage of the mortgage value, which allowed originators with little capital to generate a large volume of subprime loans. Warehousing lenders were usually the first ones to "pull the plug" on subprime lenders having difficulty selling their loans. *See Rise and Decline/Subprime Lender Failures*.

Mortgage Brokers and Loan Officers: These were the frontline soldiers who found the clients and sold the deals. They were highly motivated because their incomes were 100% dependent on the volume of loans they closed. Part of their skill set was being able to sooth anxieties about future payment increases. Their favorite gambit was the promise to refinance before anything bad happened. Of course, when the crisis emerged, these promises could not be honored.

Federal Reserve and Bank Regulators: Nonplayers who largely kept their hands off the subprime market until the housing bubble had run its course and had morphed into a financial crisis.

Rise and Decline: The subprime market flourished, and then it crashed, bringing the remainder of the housing finance system down with it, all within less than a decade.

Profitability During the Housing Bubble of 2000–2006: Profits arising out of subprime activities were high for every participant group so long as house prices were rising. Rates, fees, markups, and commissions were high, and default rates were low. Borrowers who couldn't meet an increased payment after 2 years could refinance, or they could sell the house at a profit. When foreclosures did occur, the loss was small because recovery from the property covered most of the loss. *See* **Housing Bubble**.

Disaster Myopia: Why was the mortgage lending industry willing to make loans that were workable for a large percentage of borrowers only if their properties appreciated? In 1986, with my colleague from Wharton, Richard Herring, I published an academic paper called "Disaster Myopia in International Banking." The paper set out to explain the international banking crisis of the early 1980s, but on rereading it recently, I realized that it also goes a long way toward explaining the crisis in the subprime market.

The disaster myopia thesis is that if potential shocks that can cause major losses to lenders occur very infrequently, they will not be fully reflected in loan prices and conditions. If the market is competitive and some lenders are willing to discount the likelihood of a shock altogether, other lenders who might be inclined to be more cautious are forced to go along or lose market share.

In the mortgage market, disaster myopia meant basing mortgage prices and underwriting rules on the assumption that because house prices had risen for a very long period, they would continue to rise. The cessation of price increases was thus a shock for which lenders were no better prepared than borrowers.

Disaster myopia was especially prevalent among aggressive subprime lenders, who could make a lot of money in a very short time so long as house prices kept rising. Other subprime lenders who might not have been disaster myopic were forced to operate as if they were in order to remain competitive.

Underwriting requirements in the subprime market are set by the investment banks that buy the loans and securitize them. While the investment banks may or may not have been disaster myopic, those that were willing to accommodate the more aggressive lenders did more business (so long as house prices were rising) than those that insisted on being more cautious.

Party Started to Unwind During Late 2006: House prices peaked at midyear and began a steep and prolonged decline. Many subprime borrowers having payment trouble were not able to refinance or sell at a profit, and foreclosure losses began to mount. Some subprime securities defaulted, leading to panic selling by investors. The CRAs began to downgrade some issues, and markets shut even for securities still rated AAA. The market for new subprime issues became increasingly selective and then disappeared altogether.

Subprime Lender Failures: As their access to secondary markets began to fail, subprime lenders were forced to write down the value of the unsold loans in their pipelines. In many cases this caused their warehousing loans to become undermargined and gave the warehouse lender the right to call the loans. Unless the subprime lenders were prepared to invest more capital, which under the circumstances they were not, loan calls forced the lenders to cease operations. With delinquencies rising, some lenders were also faced with heavy buy-back obligations imposed by the firms to which delinquent loans were sold. By the end of 2007, many if not most subprime lenders had ceased operations.

The Crisis Spreads to the Broader U.S. Mortgage Market: The financial crisis that began in the subprime market of the United States spread to the entire U.S. home mortgage market—and then to the world financial system.

Increase in Risk Premiums, Tougher Underwriting: The table below draws from a new series on wholesale mortgage interest rates I began to compile on May 4, 2007. The table shows the zero-point rate on a 30-year FRM for a prime and for a risky loan, at various credit scores. The risky loan was a cash-out refinance with stated income documentation.

On the earliest date, the riskier mortgage carried only modest rate premiums over the prime mortgage. On May 2, 2008, however, the risk premiums were substantially larger, and risky loans with credit scores below 680 were no longer being offered. On May 1, 2009, the rate on the prime loan was substantially lower, a result of the easing measures taken by the Federal Reserve. But the risky mortgage was no longer being offered at any credit score.

This combination of very low rates for prime borrowers, large rate premiums on risk features, and extremely rigid underwriting rules—rules that made many potential borrowers ineligible at any price—was unchanged when this was checked in early 2010.

		Wholesale Interest Rates at Zero Points on 30-Year FRM					
		Risky Loan					
Date	Prime Loan FICO Score 720 & Over	FICO Score 740 & Over	FICO Score 700–739	FICO Score 680–699	FICO Score 660–679	FICO Score 620–659	FICO Score Below 620
4/5/07	5.78%	6.15%	6.19%	6.24%	6.30%	6.45%	NA
2/5/08	5.73%	6.47%	6.54%	6.58%	NA	NA	NA
1/5/09	4.65%	NA	NA	NA	NA	NA	NA

Transaction Characteristics of Prime Loan: Loan amount $400,000, property value $500,000, single-family home purchased as permanent residence with full documentation, borrower escrows taxes and insurance, lock period 60 days.

Transaction Characteristics of Risky Loan: Same except that loan is a cash-out refinance and has stated income documentation.

Penalty Rates on Jumbo Mortgages: The collapse of the subprime mortgage security market led to the collapse of all private securitization, including those involving jumbo loans of high quality. The result was a large increase in the rate difference between jumbos and conforming loans eligible for purchase by Fannie Mae and Freddie Mac. To ameliorate this situation, the conforming loan limit was increased in selected areas from $417,000 to a maximum of $729,500, with conforming loans above the lower limit referred to as "conforming jumbos." However, the agencies charged higher prices on conforming jumbos than on nonjumbos.

On May 4, 2007, the wholesale rate was 5.78% on a prime conforming loan for $417,000, 6.05% on a prime nonconforming loan for $418,000, and 6.10% on a prime nonconforming loan for $2 million. These were the tight spreads one associates with a well-functioning system.

On August 21, 2009, the rate was 4.85% on a prime conforming loan for $417,000, 5.47% on a prime conforming jumbo for $418,000, and 11.84% on a prime jumbo of $2 million. For technical reasons, the last figure is not reliable; the correct figure could be as low as 8%. Even with the lower figure, the spread over the nonjumbo conforming rate was eight times larger than it was in early 2007.

Disappearance of Piggybacks: The emerging crisis also saw the gradual disappearance of piggyback second mortgages as a substitute for mortgage insurance.

In early 2007, piggybacks were still widely available as a substitute for mortgage insurance in cases where borrowers made down payments of less than 20%. These deals were known as 80/20/0, 80/15/5, 80/10/10, and 80/5/15, where the first number is the percent of the property value provided by the first mortgage, the second number is the percent provided by the second mortgage, and the third number is the percent down payment. The riskiest of these to the second mortgage lender was the 80/20/0, with the risk declining as the borrower's down payment increased.

Deals for 80/20/0 were available until September 28, 2007, for 80/15/5s until December 28, 2007, for 80/10/10s until February 8, 2008, and for 80/5/15s until March 28, 2008. That was the end of the piggybacks. Borrowers who put less than 20% down thereafter had to purchase mortgage insurance at premiums well above those charged before the crisis.

Exporting the Crisis: Foreign investors were among those who purchased subprime mortgage-backed securities. When the market collapsed, the value of these securities plummeted, and their liquidity disappeared. Some foreign firms actually owned subprime lenders.

In addition, foreign investors held collateralized debt obligations (CDOs), which were issued by banks and investment banks in the United States against pools of other securities as a second level of securitization. Some CDO collateral pools included low-rated tranches of subprime securities. Similarly, foreign investors held asset-based commercial paper (ABCP) issued by structured investment vehicles created by banks, which were secured by asset pools that might include subprime securities or CDOs. Even a relatively small amount of subprime mortgages in a collateral pool could severely depress the market value of a CDO or ABCP.

Mortgage Crisis Evolves into Worldwide Financial Crisis: The mortgage crisis became a worldwide financial crisis essentially because the world financial system was overleveraged. The system did not have enough capital to absorb the losses in the home mortgage sector and the other sectors that weakened afterward as economies went into recession. Investment banks in the United States were particularly exposed, but capital shortages were worldwide.

In addition, there was an enormous erosion of confidence in the solvency of major institutions associated with the lack of reliable information on the extent of value declines of securities that were no longer actively traded. Information was also lacking on net exposures under credit default swaps, which had grown to enormous proportions and were largely unregulated and undocumented.

Swing Loan

Same as bridge loan, see **Bridge Financing**.

Tangible Net Benefit Rule *A rule aimed at predatory lending that would prohibit lenders from refinancing a mortgage unless there is a "tangible net benefit" to the borrower.*

At least eight states have tangible net benefit rules, including New York and Illinois, and the rule has been proposed many times at the federal level.

All or virtually all refinanced mortgages provide tangible benefits; otherwise borrowers wouldn't do them. Even predatory lenders, who are the focus of the tangible net benefit legislation, provide a benefit to the refinancing borrower.

Tangible Net Benefit Rule

The problem is that in exchange for the benefit, the predator extracts a pound of flesh. That's why the proposed legislation requires a "net" benefit, meaning that the benefit outweighs the cost. Unfortunately, there is no way that a lender can determine this. Whether or not the benefit outweighs the cost in any particular case depends heavily on what is in the borrower's head.

This will become clear from looking at the four main reasons that borrowers refinance: to reduce costs, reduce interest rate risk, reduce monthly payments, and raise cash.

The Net Tangible Benefit in a Cost-Reduction Refinance: A cost-reduction refinance is one in which the new interest rate or mortgage insurance premium is lower than the existing one. In most cases, however, the borrower incurs costs up front. If there is to be a "net benefit," therefore, the future savings must outweigh the upfront costs.

But future savings depend heavily on how long the borrower expects to have the mortgage. This critical piece of information, if it is anywhere, is in the borrower's head.

The Net Tangible Benefit in a Risk-Reduction Refinance: When interest rates are expected to rise, many holders of ARMs consider converting them to FRMs. The borrowers making the switch are willing to pay a higher rate now in exchange for future rate certainty. Among other factors, their judgment is based on expectations of future interest rates and on their capacity to absorb higher payments from ARM rate increases. On these questions, lenders are in no position to substitute their judgment for the borrower's.

The Net Tangible Benefit in a Payment-Reduction Refinance: Some borrowers are willing to pay a stiff price, in the form of wealth reduction in the future, in order to reduce their monthly payments now. Frequently this involves converting a fixed-rate loan into an adjustable carrying a lower rate, often with an interest-only option, for a limited period. Costs are usually tacked on to the balance.

Whether there is a net benefit depends on how critical it is to the borrower to lower the payment. Perhaps the alternative to a payment reduction is default. Only the borrower knows.

The Net Tangible Benefit in a Cash-Out Refinance: Some of the worst market abuses arise on "cash-out" refinances, where the motive is to raise cash. Suppose that in raising $5,000 this way, Doe has to accept a 7% loan as a replacement for his current 6% loan, and $5,000 in refinance costs is tacked on to his loan balance. The tangible benefit of $5,000 in cash is clear, but is it a net benefit?

There is no objective way for the lender to answer the question. The price seems high, but maybe the borrower needs the $5,000 to pay for life-saving medicine for his children. Again, the answer is in the head of the borrower.

It could be argued that whether or not there is a net benefit also should depend on the borrower's options. If the borrower could raise the $5,000 elsewhere at a much lower cost, the finding should be that there is no net benefit. It is neither feasible nor fair, however, to make lenders responsible for assessing their customers' options.

In sum, regardless of why borrowers refinance, the question of whether they receive a net benefit from it is for borrowers alone to answer. Lenders do not have the information needed to second-guess them.

On the other hand, borrowers often make their decisions on the basis of incomplete and sometimes misleading information. Instead of requiring lenders to assume responsibility for borrowers' decisions, let's make them responsible for providing borrowers with the information they need to make their own decisions.

The formulation of disclosure rules has long been viewed as a proper responsibility of government, since this is the only way to assure uniformity of disclosures across the market. But the federal government has proved it is not up to this task. The existing mandatory disclosure rules are obsolete and shamefully inadequate. Every attempt to fix them gets bogged down in political in-fighting. It is time to try an approach that makes lenders responsible for providing the information borrowers need.

Tax Deductibility (of Interest and Points) *The provision of the U.S. tax code that allows homeowners to deduct mortgage interest payments from income before computing taxes.*

Points and origination fees are also deductible, but not lender fees expressed in dollars or any other settlement costs. Interest deductibility is politically untouchable in the United States, although it is often criticized by economists and is found in few other countries.

Interest deductibility enters a number of decisions made by home-owners or purchasers, sometimes when it shouldn't.

Borrow for the Deduction? It never makes sense to borrow for the sole purpose of obtaining a tax deduction, even if you are in the highest tax bracket. If you are in the 40% bracket, for example, and you borrow $100,000 at 5%, you pay $500 of interest in month one and save $200 in taxes. Your net loss is $300.

If you invest the $100,000, the interest earnings reduce the loss. However, borrowing at 5% to invest does not become a profitable strategy unless you can earn *more than* 5% on the investment. Since this is not possible without incurring default risk, the required return on the investment must be above 5% plus an increment sufficient to compensate for this risk.

Assuming that the interest on investment is taxable, comparisons of mortgage rate with investment return can be made either before tax or after tax. For example, if the borrower in the 40% tax bracket would pay 5% on the mortgage and earn 4% on investment, the investment is a loser before tax (5% less 4%) or after tax (3% less 2.4%). If the investment is tax exempt, however, its return should be compared with the after-tax cost of the mortgage.

Note that the very same principles hold when the issue is whether to invest in mortgage loan repayment as opposed to acquiring some other type of investment. *See* **Partial Prepayments (or Paying Off Early)/***Making Extra Payments as an Investment.*

Should Mortgage Insurance Also Be Deductible? The IRS is inconsistent in not allowing mortgage insurance premiums to be deducted in the same way as interest. *See* **Private Mortgage Insurance (PMI)/***Deductibility of PMI Premiums?*

Teaser Rate *The initial interest rate on an ARM when it is below the fully indexed rate.*

See **Adjustable-Rate Mortgage (ARM)/***The Fully Indexed Rate.*

Temporary Buy-Down *A reduction in the mortgage payment made by a home-buyer in the early years of the loan in exchange for an upfront cash deposit provided by the buyer, the seller, or both.*

How Temporary Buy-Downs Work: Temporary buy-downs are a tool for borrowers purchasing a home who don't have enough income, relative to their monthly mortgage payment and other expenses, to meet lender requirements. To use a temporary buy-down, the borrower must have access to extra cash. The cash can be the borrower's, or it can be contributed by a home seller anxious to complete a sale. The cash funds an escrow account from which the payments that supplement the borrower's payments are drawn.

While the borrower's payments are reduced in the early years, the payments received by the lender are the same as they would have been without the buy-down. The shortfalls from the borrower are offset by withdrawals from the escrow account.

Temporary buy-downs are not a type of mortgage. They are an option that can be attached to any type. Most temporary buy-downs, however, are attached to fixed-rate mortgages.

Temporary Versus Permanent Buy-Downs: Another way in which borrowers with excess cash can reduce their mortgage payment is by paying additional points in order to reduce the interest rate. This is sometimes called a "permanent buy-down" because the reduced payment holds for the life of the loan. For the same number of dollars invested, however, temporary buy-downs reduce the monthly payment in the first year, which is the payment used to qualify the borrower, by a larger amount than a permanent buy-down. This reflects the concentration of the payment reduction in the early years of the loan.

The table below illustrates the three most common temporary buy-downs. On a 3-2-1 buy-down, the mortgage payment in years one, two, and three is calculated at rates 3%, 2%, and 1%, respectively, below the rate on the loan. On a 2-1 buy-down, the payment in years one and two is calculated at rates 2% and 1% below the loan rate. And on a 1-0 buy-down, the payment in year one is calculated at 1% below the loan rate.

	Payment Received by Lender	3-2-1 Buy-Down		2-1 Buy-Down		1-0 Buy-Down	
Payments by Borrowers and Payments from Escrow Accounts on a $100,000 30-Year 7% Fixed-Rate Mortgage with 3-2-1, 2-1, and 1-0 Temporary Buy-Downs							
Year	Payment Received by Lender	Payment by Borrower	Payment from Escrow	Payment by Borrower	Payment from Escrow	Payment by Borrower	Payment from Escrow
1	$665.31	$477.42	$187.89	$536.83	$128.48	$599.56	$65.75
2	$665.31	536.83	128.48	599.56	65.75	665.31	0
3	$665.31	599.56	65.75	665.31	0	0	0
4–30	$665.31	665.31	0	0	0	0	0
Needed escrow		$4,586		$2,331		$789	

The 3-2-1 buy-down involves the largest reduction in the borrower's payment in the first year, but it also requires the largest amount placed in escrow, as shown on the bottom row.

The required escrow shown in the table assumes that no interest is paid on the account. If the borrower were credited with 4% interest on the 3-2-1 illustrated above, the required deposit to the buy-down account would fall from $4,586 to $4,369. Only a few lenders credit interest, however.

Some lenders not only do not pay interest on the buy-down account, but dispense with the account altogether, replacing it with additional points equal to the sum of the buy-down digits. That is, they charge an additional six points for a 3-2-1, three points for a 2-1, and one point for a 1-0. This is a ripoff.

Calculator 7d on my Web site will allow you to experiment with a variety of temporary buy-down options that are available in the marketplace. In general, you want the smallest buy-down you need to qualify. The calculator will also show you the proper deposit to escrow for any buy-down.

Temporary Lender   *A lender that sells the loans it originates, as opposed to a portfolio lender that holds them.*

Same as **Mortgage Company**.

Term *The period used to calculate the monthly mortgage payment.*

The term is usually but not always the same as the maturity, which is the period over which the loan balance must be paid in full. On a 7-year balloon loan, for example, the maturity is 7 years, but the term in most cases is 30 years.

Selecting the Term

Impact on Monthly Payment: The longer the term, the lower the mortgage payment, but the slower the growth of equity. Borrowers who want to make their payments as small as possible select the longest term available. The reduction in payment from lengthening the term, however, becomes less and less effective as the term gets longer. This is illustrated in the following table, which shows the mortgage payment on a $100,000 loan at various interest rates and terms.

Mortgage Payment per $100,000 of Loan Amount							
	4%	**5%**	**6%**	**8%**	**10%**	**11%**	**12%**
5 years	$1,842	$1,887	$1,933	$2,028	$2,125	$2,174	$2,224
10 years	1,012	1,061	1,110	1,213	1,322	1,378	1,435
15 years	740	791	844	956	1,075	1,137	1,200
20 years	606	660	716	836	965	1,032	1,101
25 years	528	585	644	773	909	980	1,053
30 years	477	537	600	734	878	952	1,029
40 years	418	482	550	695	849	928	1,008
Interest only	333	417	500	667	833	917	1,000

Let's take the example of 4%. Extending the term from 10 years to 20 years reduces the payment by $596, but extending it to 30 years and 40 years reduces the payment by only $129 and $59, respectively. The furthest you can possibly go in extending the term is to infinity, which is an interest-only loan—you never repay any part of the loan. On a 4% loan, the monthly interest is $333, only $85 less than the payment at 40 years.

Extending the term to reduce the payment also becomes less effective at higher interest rates. For example, at 4%, extending the term from 20 to 30 years reduces the payment by $139, but at 12% the reduction is only $72.

Term

Impact on Equity Growth: Borrowers who want to build equity in their home as quickly as possible select the shortest term they can afford. As illustrated in the table below, the shorter the term, the more rapid the increase in equity. For example, after 10 years the borrower with a 15-year term at 7% has repaid 54.6% of the original balance, whereas the borrower with a 30-year term at the same rate has repaid only 14.2% of the balance. Since 15-year loans usually carry a lower rate than 30-year loans, this understates the difference in the rate of equity buildup.

Percent of Loan Balance Repaid After Specified Periods at 7%							
Term	After 5 Years	After 10 Years	After 15 Years	After 20 Years	After 25 Years	After 30 Years	After 40 Years
5 years	100%	100%	100%	100%	100%	100%	100%
10 years	41.4%	100%	100%	100%	100%	100%	100%
15 years	22.6%	54.6%	100%	100%	100%	100%	100%
20 years	13.7%	33.2%	60.8%	100%	100%	100%	100%
25 years	8.8%	21.4%	39.1%	64.3%	100%	100%	100%
30 years	5.9%	14.2%	26.0%	42.7%	66.4%	100%	100%
40 years	2.7%	6.6%	12.1%	19.8%	30.9%	46.5%	100%

Interest Rate Differences: In general, the longer the term, the higher the interest rate. Longer terms are priced higher primarily because the default risk is greater, which is why the financial crisis widened the spreads. Before the crisis, the rate spread between the 15 and 30, the two most popular options, ranged from 0.25 to 0.50%; after the crisis, it was 0.375 to 0.625%. This rate difference strengthens the case for the 15 by reducing the payment advantage of the 30 and increasing the advantage of the 15 in the rate at which equity grows.

Shorter Term Versus Extra Payments: A borrower can always shorten the realized term of a mortgage by making extra payments. For example, a borrower who selects a 15-year loan but wants to pay it off in 10 years can make an extra payment every month to bring the payment to what it would be on a 10. Assuming the interest rate is the same, the outcome is the same.

For example, the monthly payment on a $100,000 loan at 6% for 15 years is $843.86. On a 10-year loan at the same rate, it is $1,110.21. If you take the 15-year loan and make an extra payment every month equal to the $266.35 difference, you will pay it off in 10 years.

This is hardly surprising since the sum of $843.86 and $266.35 is $1,110.21, which is the payment on the 10-year loan. The extra payment in effect converts the 15-year loan into a 10-year loan.

There is one difference, however, between the 10-year loan and the 15-year loan with the extra payment. With the 10-year loan, $1,110.21 is the **Scheduled Payment**, the amount you are obliged to pay every month. With the 15-year loan, the scheduled payment is only $843.86; the extra payment of $266.35 is optional. Which is better for you depends on whether you attach greater value to discipline or to flexibility.

The 10-year loan may also have a lower rate than a 15. This was seldom true before the crisis, but afterward a 0.125% spread was common.

Investing Excess Cash Flow on the 30: Most borrowers electing a 30-year term do it because they can't afford the monthly payment on a shorter term. Some elect the 30-year term, however, because they plan to invest the difference in payment. There is nothing wrong with this, provided they understand how much they must earn on other investments to make it a paying strategy. The yield on other investments must exceed the yield on investment in the shorter term, which is generally high.

An investment in a shorter-term mortgage is a little different from most other investments. Typically, an investment consists of a lump sum paid out at the beginning, and the return is a series of payments received over time. This is the way it is, for example, with an investment in a deposit or bond.

By contrast, when you invest in a shorter-term mortgage, your investment is a series of payments equal to the difference between the monthly payment at the shorter term and the payment at a longer term. And the return is a lump sum, equal to the larger proceeds you receive at time of sale because of the smaller loan balance that must be repaid at the end of the period.

Let's say you are borrowing $100,000 and choosing between a 30-year fixed-rate mortgage (FRM) at 7.5% and a 15-year FRM at 7.125%. Monthly payments of principal and interest are $699.22 for the 30-year loan and $905.84 for the 15-year loan. The difference is $206.62 each month. That's your investment.

You expect to stay in your home 7 years. At that point, the balance of the 30-year loan will be $91,833, and the balance of the 15-year loan will be $66,137, for a difference of $25,696. That's your return. On an annual basis, it amounts to 10.72%. That is the yield you would have to earn to break even if you invested the cash flow savings on a 30, rather than taking a 15. If the difference in interest rate had been greater than 0.375%, the return on investment would be higher, and vice versa.

The calculation above assumes the interest rate is the only difference between the two loans. But if the down payment you expect to make is less than 20%, you will have to pay for mortgage insurance, and the premiums are higher on the 30-year loan. This increases the return on the 15-year loan considerably. If you anticipate paying 5% down, for example, the higher premium on the 30-year FRM will raise the 7-year return on the 15 from 10.72% to 15.74%.

Calculator 15a on my Web site lets you calculate the return on your own deal. You enter two terms, their interest rates, your anticipated down payment, and your expected period in the house. The calculator determines your rate of return.

Staying on Schedule When Refinancing: Some borrowers want to refinance while staying on the same amortization schedule. For example, they took out a mortgage 7 years ago that has 23 years to run, and they want to stay on that schedule, rather than start with a new 30-year schedule.

Lenders won't ordinarily make a 23-year loan. The best option, therefore, is to refinance for 30 years, but increase the payment by the exact amount required to amortize over 23—or any other period you wish. Use calculator 2c on my Web site. You tell the calculator when you want the loan to pay off, and it will tell you the extra payment required to do it.

3/2 Down Payment *Programs offered by some lenders under which borrowers who are able to secure a grant or gift equal to 2% of the down payment will only have to provide a 3% down payment from their own funds.*

Time Horizon Cost (THC) *The total cost of a mortgage measured in future value dollars as of the end of the period the borrower expects to be in the house.*

Comparison to APR: THC is an alternative to the APR, but better. It is comprehensive in its coverage, which the APR is not. It makes more intuitive sense to borrowers than the APR and is easier to understand. It can be broken into its components for a deeper comprehension, which the APR cannot. And it takes account of differences between borrowers in time horizon, tax rates, and opportunity costs, which the APR does not.

Comparison to IC: The advantage of THC relative to interest cost (IC) is that it can take account of opportunity cost and that it can be broken into components, as follows:

The THC is the sum of:

Total monthly payments of principal, interest, and mortgage insurance

Lost interest on monthly payments

Points paid up front

Lost interest on points

Other settlement costs paid up front

Lost interest on other settlement costs

Less cost offsets:

Tax savings on interest, points, and mortgage insurance

Reduction in loan balance

Many of the calculators on my Web site are programmed to generate THCs.

Title Insurance *Insurance against loss arising from problems connected to the title to property.*

A home may go through several ownership changes and the land on which it stands through many more. There may be a weak link at any point in that chain that could emerge to cause trouble. For example, someone along the way may have forged a signature in transferring title. Or there may be unpaid real estate taxes or other liens. Title insurance covers the insured party for claims and legal fees that arise out of such problems.

Lender Versus Owner Policies: All mortgage lenders require title insurance to protect their lien against the property. A lender policy is for an amount equal to the loan and lasts until the loan is repaid. As with mortgage insurance, the borrower pays the premium, which is a single payment made up front.

To protect her equity in the property, the owner needs an owner's title policy for the full value of the home. In many areas, sellers pay for owner policies as part of their obligation to deliver good title to the buyer. In

Title Insurance

other areas, borrowers must buy it as an add-on to the lender policy. It is advisable to do this because the additional cost above the cost of the lender policy is relatively small.

Coverage Period: With the exception noted below, title insurance only protects against losses arising from events that occurred prior to the date of the policy. Coverage ends on the day the policy is issued and extends backward in time for an indefinite period. This is in marked contrast to property or life insurance, which protects against losses resulting from events that occur after the policy is issued, for a specified period into the future.

On a title policy, the owner's protection lasts as long as the owner or any heirs have an interest in or any obligation with regard to the property. When they sell, however, the lender will require the purchaser to obtain a new policy. That protects the lender against any liens or other claims against the property that may have arisen since the date of the previous policy.

Extended Coverage: The standard title insurance policy provides no protection against false claims that arise after the property is purchased. Yet such events occur. Identity theft can result in a new mortgage the owner knows nothing about. Or a neighbor could build on the land without the owner's knowledge and, after a period without challenge, could acquire ownership rights.

A new policy is available in most states that protects against such contingencies. It is usually referred to as the ALTA Homeowner's Policy. It may cost a bit more than the standard policy.

Title Insurance on a Refinancing: A borrower who refinances does not need a new owner's policy, but the lender will require a new lender policy. Even if the borrower refinances with the same lender, the lender's policy terminates when the old mortgage is paid off. Furthermore, the lender is concerned about title issues that may have arisen since the purchase. However, insurers generally offer discounts on policies taken out within short periods after the preceding policy. In some cases, discounts are available as far out as six years from the date of the previous policy. But the borrower may have to ask for the discount to get it.

Cost Structure of Title Insurance: Because title insurance protects against what may have happened in the past, most of the expense incurred by title companies or their agents is in loss reduction. They look to reduce losses by finding and fixing defects before the policy is issued, in much the same way as firms providing elevator or boiler insurance. These types of insurance are very different from life, property, or mortgage insurance, which protect against losses from future events over which the insurers have no control.

A consequence of this is that the amounts paid out by title companies in claims is a small part of the insurance premiums collected. This is sometimes cited, erroneously, as evidence that title insurance is overpriced. I believe that title insurance is overpriced, but not because of low claim rates.

Cross-Subsidization: The cost of providing title insurance is not much different for a small policy than for a large one. The reason is that most title insurance costs arise in preventing loss rather than paying claims, and prevention costs are not related to the size of a policy. Despite this, premiums are scaled to the amount of coverage, which is the amount of the mortgage or the value of the property, suggesting that smaller policies may be underpriced and larger policies overpriced.

Geographic Variations in the Cost of Title Insurance: The cost of title insurance varies widely from one area to another. One major reason is that the services covered by the title insurance premium vary in different parts of the country. In some areas, the premium covers not only protection against loss but also the costs of search and examination, as well as closing services. In other areas, the premium covers protection only, and borrowers pay for the other related services separately.

To complicate it further, in some states the charges for title-related services are paid to title insurance companies, which perform the functions but charge separately for them. In other states, borrowers may pay attorneys or independent companies called abstractors or escrow companies.

Of course, what matters to the borrower is the sum total of all title-related charges. These also differ from one area to another in response to a variety of factors. The 50 states have 50 different regulatory regimes, which affect charges. So do local costs, competition in local markets, and other factors. To my knowledge, there has never been a comprehensive study of geographical variability in premiums and in the causes of variability.

Shopping for Title Insurance: Most borrowers leave it to one of the professionals with whom they deal—real estate agent, lender, or attorney—to select the title insurance carrier. The result is that competition among title insurers is largely directed toward these professionals rather than toward borrowers. This "perverse competition" drives up costs and is the major reason for believing that title insurance is overpriced.

Borrowers may be able to save money by shopping for title insurance themselves, although it is difficult to generalize because market conditions vary state by state and sometimes within states. I would certainly shop in states that do not regulate title insurance rates: Alabama, District of Columbia (OK, technically not a state, but it counts anyway), Georgia, Hawaii, Illinois, Indiana, Massachusetts, Oklahoma, and West Virginia.

There is no point shopping in Texas because the state sets the prices for all carriers. New Mexico did the same until 2009, when it switched from setting premiums to setting maximum premiums. Florida sets title insurance premiums but not other title-related charges, which can vary.

In the remaining states, the situation is murky, and it may or may not pay to shop. Insurance premiums are the same for all carriers in "rating bureau states": Pennsylvania, New York, New Jersey, Ohio, and Delaware. These states authorize title insurers to file for approval of a single rate schedule for all carriers through a cooperative entity. Yet in some there may be flexibility in title-related charges. More promising are "file and use" states—all those not mentioned above—which permit premiums to vary among insurers.

Even where all the insurers in a state set the same premiums, local title agencies that broker title insurance may discount the price to the borrower. While it varies from state to state, the agency receives as much as 75% of the total premium, which leaves room for haggling.

It is a good idea to ask an informed but disinterested local whether it pays to shop in the area where the property is located. Just keep in mind that those likely to be the best informed are also likely to have an interest in directing your business in the direction that is most advantageous to them.

Borrowers would do well to see what is available on the Internet. In 2008, EnTitle Insurance Company began offering title insurance directly to borrowers through its Web site www.entitledirect.com. The premiums it charges undercut the posted prices of existing insurers by about 35%.

Total Annual Loan Cost (TALC) *A measure of loan cost on a reverse mortgage similar to the APR, except that the TALC covers all costs and is calculated over four different periods.*

See **Reverse Mortgage/***FHA's Home Equity Conversion Mortgage (HECM)/*
Total Annual Loan Cost.

Total Expense *The sum of housing expense and nonhousing debt payments.*

Total Expense Ratio *The ratio of total expense to borrower income.*

This ratio is used (along with other factors) in qualifying borrowers. *See*
Qualification/*Meeting Income Requirements/***Expense Ratios**.

Total Interest Payments *The sum of all interest payments to date or over the
life of the loan.*

This is an incomplete measure of the cost of credit to the borrower
because it does not include upfront cash payments, and it is not adjusted
for the time value of money. *See* **Interest Cost**.

Truth in Lending (TIL) *The federal law, administered by the Federal Reserve
Board, that specifies information that must be provided to borrowers on different
types of loans and that stipulates how and when disclosures must occur.*

Truth in Lending (TIL) is a great idea, in principle. The idea is to require
lenders to provide one uniform set of price disclosures that are consistent
from loan to loan and from lender to lender. Then consumers can make
apples-to-apples price comparisons across loan types and across lenders.

The idea has worked concerning the methodology used to calculate the
interest rate. Borrowers no longer have to contend with noncomparable
ways to calculate interest: discount rates, add-on rates, and internal rates
of return. The last has become the standard; *see* **Mortgage Equations**.

Unfortunately, in all other respects, TIL as it has been applied to
mortgages has been a disaster.

APR: The internal rate of return used to measure interest cost on a mortgage is called the annual percentage rate, or APR. The APR on a mortgage
is misleading because upfront fees are a major cost, and yet only some of
them are included in the APR. In addition, the APR assumes all loans run

to term, when in fact most mortgages are paid in full well before term. *See* **Annual Percentage Rate**.

Useless Information: The TIL also includes useless information that distracts borrowers and causes confusion.

Total Payments: This is the monthly payment multiplied by the term.

Amount Financed: This is the loan amount less *"prepaid finance charges,"* which are the selected upfront charges that are included in the calculation of the APR. If the loan is $100,000 and fees are $3,000, the amount financed is $97,000.

Finance Charge: This is the sum of all interest payments over the term of the loan plus the prepaid finance charges.

All these numbers are totally useless for comparing loans of different type or for shopping different loan providers.

Notice of Prepayment Penalty: This is hopelessly confusing, worse than no disclosure at all. *See* **Prepayment Penalty/*Surreptitious Penalties***.

What Isn't Disclosed That Should Be: In addition to making the prepayment disclosure comprehensible to borrowers, the TIL should replace the useless information listed above with information that is critically important to borrowers.

Total Lender Fees: In addition to points, which are an upfront charge expressed as a percentage of the loan, lenders also charge a variety of fees that are expressed in dollars that do not change with the size of the loan. These fees are disclosed on the TIL only indirectly. Subtracting the "amount financed" from the loan amount will yield the fees. If 1 borrower in 100 knows enough to do this, I would be surprised.

In the first edition of this book, I recommended that the TIL show total lender fees and commit the lender to those fees. This was not done, but HUD did both in its revision of the Good Faith Estimate effective January 1, 2010. *See* **Settlement Costs/*Good Faith Estimate***.

Margin on ARMs: The margin on an ARM is the lender's markup—the amount the lender adds to the interest rate index on a rate adjustment date to obtain the new interest rate. It can be 1.5%; it can also be 6.5%.

Lenders always quote the initial rate on an ARM, but they seldom quote the margin, and it is not a required disclosure. On some ARMs, the initial rate holds only for one to three months. (This includes all flexible-payment or option ARMs and all home equity lines.) On these loans, the borrower knows the interest rate for the first few months, but often doesn't know the lender's markup over the remaining 29-plus years. It should be a required disclosure.

Is the Loan Simple Interest? On simple interest loans, interest accrues daily instead of monthly, imposing a stiff penalty on borrowers who pay past the due date. *See* **Amortization/*Amortization on a Simple Interest Mortgage*.** Most borrowers who write me about their problems with simple interest loans never knew they had one until the problems emerged. TIL should require lenders to disclose it.

Subordination Policy on Second Mortgages: Very few borrowers who take out a second mortgage are aware that the second mortgage lender can prevent them from refinancing their first mortgage. When the existing first mortgage is repaid, the existing second mortgage automatically becomes the first mortgage *unless* the second mortgage lender is willing to subordinate his claim to that of the lender providing the new mortgage into which the borrower is refinancing. *See* **Second Mortgage/*Possible Negative Consequences of Second Mortgages*/Refinance of First Requires Subordination of Second.**

Policies of second mortgage lenders regarding subordination vary all over the lot, from a small fee and no conditions to absolute prohibition. Borrowers taking a second mortgage should see the lender's subordination policy on the TIL.

Early Disclosures: At the time this was written, the Federal Reserve was in the process of formulating revised regulations that might address some or all (or none) of the issues noted above. In addition, the Fed introduced an intriguing proposal to require new disclosures at the point of application, as opposed to three days after application, which is when the TIL disclosures are now due. The purpose is to help borrowers select a loan provider before they apply, which is a great idea.

The Proposed Disclosures at Point of Application: Unfortunately, the disclosures proposed by the Fed would be of no use to borrowers in selecting a loan provider because they would be answered in the same way by every lender. The questions are all about the features of the mortgages the lender offers, such as "Can my interest rate increase?" All lenders will respond with some version of "The rate can increase if you select an adjustable-rate mortgage (ARM), but we also offer fixed-rate mortgages on which the rate cannot increase." This response is useless to borrowers trying to select among different lenders.

Truth in Lending (TIL)

My Suggested Disclosures: To help borrowers select from among different lenders, the questions must apply to lenders' operating policies, not to their mortgages. There are important differences in operating policies that borrowers currently have no way of knowing. Here is the list I proposed to the Fed—if they are not incorporated into TIL, there is nothing to prevent borrowers from using them on their own.

Q: Do you allow your loan officers (LOs) to charge "overages"?

Comment: An overage is a price higher than the price the lender shows on its price sheets, which show the prices the lender will accept. Overages are usually shared with LOs, encouraging them to charge what the traffic will bear. I would not want to deal with an LO who has a financial incentive to overcharge me. Some lenders do not allow overages, and this disclosure at the point of application would give them the edge they deserve.

Q: Do you have a financial interest in or a financial arrangement with any of the third parties providing services to your borrowers?

Comment: Overcharges on third-party services are chronic, and lender deals with service providers are a major reason. I would not want to deal with a firm that referred me to title agents or other service providers in which they had a financial interest. The RESPA restrictions on payment of referral fees has had no impact, but a disclosure requirement would. This is also a good question for house purchasers to ask their Realtor.

Q: Are any of your mortgages (other than HELOCs) simple interest or convertible into simple interest?

Comment: I would not knowingly take a simple interest mortgage because it accrues interest daily, eliminating the benefit of having a payment grace period. It has never been a required disclosure, and some borrowers have been surprised to find themselves with one. In some cases, borrowers have been converted to simple interest after their loan was sold because their note could be interpreted as permitting it.

Q: What must a borrower do before you will lock the price of her loan, and will you provide a written lock confirmation?

Comment: I would not deal with a lender that did not have well-defined rules regarding exactly when I was able to lock the price, with confirmation of the lock in writing. Ambiguity that in effect allows the lender to lock when it wants to lock can seriously disadvantage borrowers who have no place else to go.

Q: What fees must a borrower pay to lock, and under what circumstances are they refundable?

Comment: This is another essential part of a lender's lock policy.

---

12 MTA *The average of the most recent 12 monthly values of the one-year Treasury constant maturity series.*

The 12 MTA is used as the rate index on some ARMs. *See* **Adjustable-Rate Mortgage (ARM)/ARM Rate Indexes**.

Underage *A mortgage price paid by a borrower that is lower than the posted price.*

An underage is the opposite of an **Overage**. *Also see* **Posted Prices**.

Underwriting *The process of making a final determination on approval or rejection of a loan application.*

Underwriting involves verifying the information that has been obtained from the borrower and that served as the basis for qualification, as well as assessing information on the applicant's creditworthiness.

Underwriting Requirements *The standards imposed by lenders in determining whether a borrower can be approved for a loan.*

These standards are more comprehensive than qualification requirements in that they include an evaluation of the borrower's creditworthiness.

Upfront Mortgage Broker (UMB) *A mortgage broker who sets a fee for services, in writing, at the outset of the transaction, and acts as the borrower's agent in shopping for the best deal.*

Customers of UMBs pay the broker's fee plus wholesale loan prices, which are disclosed at the customer's request. In contrast, other mortgage brokers (MBs) add a markup to the wholesale prices and quote only the resulting "retail prices" to customers. Most MBs reveal their markup only in required disclosures after an application has been submitted.

UMBs credit customers with any rebates they receive from lenders or home sellers that would otherwise increase the broker's fee beyond what was agreed upon. Such rebates are often an added source of revenue to MBs.

Once the UMB's fee has been established, the UMB's interests are largely aligned with those of customers. In contrast, MBs are in a conflict situation with customers.

A list of UMBs, showing their Web site addresses and the states in which they operate, is available on www.upfrontmortgagebrokers.org.

Many brokers who are not listed as UMBs are willing to operate in the same manner with borrowers who understand the value of broker services and who won't faint when they hear the fee. Here is a form you can use.

Broker Compensation

The total compensation to [Name of broker], including any rebates from the lender, will be: _____

A separate processing fee will be: _____

I developed the UMB program in 2001. In 2003 when I wrote the first edition of this book, 53 UMBs were listed on my Web site. In 2006, I transferred administration of the program to the Upfront Mortgage Brokers Association. In November 2009, there were 87 dues-paying members of that organization.

Upfront Mortgage Lender (UML) *A lender offering loans on the Internet who provides mortgage shoppers with the information they need to make an informed decision before applying for a mortgage and guarantees them fair treatment during the period after they apply through to closing.*

The specific requirements, and how they meet the needs of shoppers, are as follows:

Requirement 1: *A UML provides quick access to the market niches it prices online.* Shoppers need a quick way to determine whether a particular lender prices the niche in which that shopper falls. If not, the shopper can go elsewhere without wasting time.

If the shopper's niche *is* priced online:

Upfront Mortgage Lender (UML)

- The shopper can make valid comparisons of one UML's prices against those of another, prior to paying any fees and prior to filling out an application.

- After selecting the lender and applying for the desired loan, the applicant is not exposed to a future price change based on information that the lender claims not to have had at the time of the original quote.

- The applicant who elects to move to a different niche, perhaps to reduce the term from 30 years to 15, or to pay more points to reduce the rate, can check online to ensure that the new niche has been correctly priced.

- The applicant who elects to float rather than lock can monitor the price as it is reset daily with the market and, therefore, will not be overcharged on the lock day.

UMLs comply with this requirement by filling out a table on their Web site called "Market Niches Priced On-Line." The table format is the same at every UML, making it easy for a shopper to tell at a glance whether the lender is pricing the shopper's niche.

Requirement 2: *A UML discloses all lender fees, including points, origination fees, and any fixed-dollar fees, and guarantees them to closing.* This assures borrowers that new fees won't be added or existing ones increased after they have committed themselves to working with the selected lender.

Requirement 3: *A UML provides a clear explanation of its lock requirements and discloses them prominently.* Because locking was more problematic after the financial crisis, reflecting the increased difficulty in getting loans approved and the increased time required to get properties appraised, I asked UMLs to be as responsive as possible to the following questions:

- What must be done before we will lock your loan?

- What happens if the market price rises before we can approve your application and lock your loan?

- What happens if the market price drops before we can approve your application and lock your loan?

- How long are locks good for?

- How and when can a borrower request a lock?

- What is covered by a lock?

Upfront Mortgage Lender (UML)

- What fees must the borrower pay to lock?
- Under what circumstances are fees refunded?
- What happens if the market price increases after the loan is locked?
- What happens if the market price drops after the loan is locked?
- What happens if critical information in the application, such as the borrower's employment, changes after the lock?
- What happens if the borrower wants to change the type of mortgage (or the rate-point combination) after the price is locked?
- What happens if the loan cannot be closed within the lock period?

Requirement 4: A UML discloses to shoppers all the information they need about its ARMs to make intelligent decisions. It is very difficult today to obtain the information about ARMs that is needed to make an informed decision. Loan officers selling ARMs stress one or another feature, usually the index, and leave the remainder of the ARMs' features in the dark. Shoppers need information on potential ARM performance—what will happen to the interest rate and mortgage payment under assumptions about future interest rates that make sense to the shopper.

UMLs can comply with this rule in two ways. One way is to offer schedules of monthly payment and interest rate under no-change and worst-case scenarios. The first assumes that the most recent value of the index remains unchanged through the life of the loan, while the second assumes that the ARM rate increases by the maximum amount allowed in the contract.

The alternative is to provide the information needed for the shopper to calculate these (and perhaps other) scenarios using calculators on my Web site or other sites. The required information is shown on a form that is identical for all UMLs.

Requirement 5: A UML informs borrowers if its loan officers are compensated in a way that gives them a financial incentive to overcharge the borrower. Off the Internet, many lenders credit loan officers with overages. An overage is a price higher than the price delivered to the loan officer by the lender's pricing department. If the loan officer gets a piece of it, there is a conflict situation that the customer ought to know about.

When I was writing the first edition of this book in 2003, there was one UML. The program had just been launched. In February 2010, there were six: AHC Lending, Aimloan, Amerisave, Century Point Mortgage, Integrity First, and National Mortgage Alliance.

USDA Mortgage *A mortgage insured by the U.S. Department of Agriculture for which eligibility is limited to properties in rural areas and to borrowers with incomes below maximums set for each area.*

The USDA program is very similar to the VA home mortgage program in that both allow loans with little or no down payment and limit eligibility to those targeted by the program. In addition, both programs charge borrowers an upfront fee designed to cover losses, which is typically included in the loan balance. Both programs are usually less costly to the borrower than a comparable FHA, but with 20% down, they are more costly than a comparable conventional mortgage.

Additional information can be found at http://eligibility.sc.egov.usda .gov/eligibility/welcomeAction.do?home.

VA Mortgage *A mortgage available only to ex-military personnel (including National Guard reserves), on which the lender is insured against loss by the Veterans Administration.*

The critical question for those eligible for VA loans is whether, given their qualifications and financial status, the terms available on a VA will be better than those available on a conventional, FHA, or USDA loan. The question is best answered in terms of the down payment the veteran is capable of making. The comparisons below are based on total costs over six years for a borrower with excellent credit.

At zero down on a house purchase, the only loans available are VAs and USDAs. A borrower eligible for both will do better with the USDA. However, USDA loans are not available for a refinance or for houses not located in a rural county.

At 5 and 10% down, the VA is the lowest-priced option, though only marginally better than USDA.

At 20% down, the conventional loan is the best, with VA and USDA tied for second.

Provisos: There are two important provisos to these generalizations. One is that the comparisons, done December 15, 2009, are heavily impacted by mortgage insurance charges on the federal programs, which can change. The second is that the comparisons are based on wholesale prices, which may or may not be reflected in the retail prices borrowers actually pay. Some loan providers view veterans who need no-down-payment loans, and who trust the loan provider to give them the market rate, as sheep to be fleeced.

To protect themselves, veterans should consult a Web site that prices all four types of loans. The only site I know that does this is www.Amerisave .com. *Note:* I have a relationship with this lender that is explained on my Web site.

The VA Web site, www.homeloans.va.gov, will tell you who is eligible, how you go about obtaining a Certificate of Eligibility, and whether eligibility can be used more than once. The site will also specify the types of properties that can be purchased with a VA loan, the range of insurance premiums for different categories of veterans and different loan purposes, the conditions under which VA loans can be assumed by a buyer, the types of VA home loans, and more.

Waiver of Escrows *Authorization by the lender for the borrower to pay taxes and insurance directly.*

This is in contrast to the standard procedure, where the lender adds a charge to the monthly mortgage payment that is deposited in an escrow account, from which the lender pays the borrower's taxes and insurance when they come due. On some loans lenders will not waive escrows; and on loans where the waiver is permitted, lenders are likely either to charge for it in the form of a small increase in points or to restrict it to borrowers making a large down payment. *See* **Escrow Account**.

Warehouse Lender *A bank, investment bank, or large mortgage lender that lends to temporary lenders against the collateral of closed mortgage loans prior to the sale of the loans in the secondary market.*

Warehouse lenders require that loans be repaid as the mortgages collateralizing them are sold, and they can call loans if the mortgage collateral declines in value.

See **Subprime Market/*Players in the Market*/Warehouse Lenders**.

Warrantable Condo *A condominium project with features that lenders view as favorable in terms of their risk exposure on loans secured by individual condo units.*

The requirements of warrantability include such features as the following: the project (including all common areas) is fully completed and the common areas are insured, the homeowners association has been controlled by unit owners (as opposed to the developer) for some period, most units are owner occupied, and no one person owns more than 10% of the units. Loans on units in warrantable condos receive better terms than loans on units in nonwarrantable condos.

Weekly Payment Mortgage *A mortgage on which the payment is due weekly rather than monthly, biweekly, or bimonthly.*

The weekly payment is calculated by multiplying the monthly payment by 12 and dividing by 52. Weekly payments increase servicing costs to lenders, which may charge borrowers a processing fee.

The only benefit to borrowers is that those who are paid weekly may value the convenience and budgetary discipline imposed by having to pay their mortgage weekly. Borrowers won't pay down the balance any sooner because weekly payments are credited monthly, not weekly, and no extra payments are involved.

Wholesale Lender *A lender that provides loans through mortgage brokers or correspondents.*

See **Mortgage Lender/*Retail, Wholesale, and Correspondent Lenders***.

Wholesale Mortgage Prices *The interest rates and points quoted by wholesale lenders to mortgage brokers and correspondent lenders.*

Wholesale mortgage price data are a superior way to measure day-to-day changes in the market as a whole and to gauge how prices vary with loan features at any one time. Retail price data have much more "noise" because of the varying markups and fees charged by retail lenders and because retail data are not broken down by credit score, down payment, and other variables that affect the price.

Consumers shopping for a loan cannot borrow at wholesale prices, but they can use the wholesale data to protect themselves against one of the most pervasive frauds in this market: price escalation between the day they are quoted a price and the day the price is locked. If the market price goes down, the borrower's price will stay the same, and if the market price goes up, the borrower's price may go up even more. Loan providers explain a price increase as stemming from "changes in the market," but the market price on the lock day is what they say it is. Borrowers with access to wholesale prices have a good way to check it. I show wholesale prices daily on my Web site.

While the wholesale data are an excellent measure of what has happened, they have no predictive power, so don't waste time trying to spot "trends." Even if the price rises 10 days in a row, view the probability that it will rise in day 11 as 50%.

Another purpose I had in developing the data was to provide accurate measures of how, at any one time, mortgage prices vary with different features of the loan transaction. These features include loan size, FICO score of borrower, down payment, type of documentation provided, and loan purpose. Data designed for this purpose are shown weekly on my site.

You can't borrow from a wholesale lender, though some borrowers try. Mortgage brokers often conceal the identity of the wholesale lender whose product has been selected for a potential borrower because they fear the borrower will go directly to the wholesale lender. The borrower may, indeed, find a lender with the same name, but it will be the retail arm of the same firm, and the borrower will be charged retail prices. Large lenders usually have both retail and wholesale divisions, but the wholesale division does not have the infrastructure required to originate loans, so forget about the possibility of "getting it wholesale." That occasionally works in men's suits, but never in mortgages.

Workout Assumption *The assumption of a mortgage, with permission of the lender, from a borrower unable to continue making the payments.*

See **Payment Problems/*Position of the Lender*/Permanent Problem**.

Worst-Case Scenario *On an ARM, the assumption that the interest rate rises to the maximum extent permitted by the loan contract.*

See **Scenario Analysis of ARMs/*Example of a Scenario Analysis*/Rising Rate Scenarios**.

Wraparound Mortgage *A mortgage loan transaction in which the lender assumes responsibility for an existing mortgage.*

Usually, but not always, the lender is the home seller. For example, S, who has a $70,000 mortgage on his home, sells his home to B for $100,000. B pays $5,000 down and borrows $95,000 from S on a new mortgage. This mortgage "wraps around" the existing $70,000 mortgage because S will continue to make the payments on the old mortgage.

A wraparound can be attractive to home sellers because they may be able to sell their home for a higher price. In addition, if the current market interest rate is above the rate on the existing mortgage, the seller can earn an attractive return on the cash foregone from the sale. For instance, if the $70,000 mortgage in the example has a rate of 6% and the new mortgage for $95,000 has a rate of 8%, S earns 8% on his $25,000 investment plus the difference between 8% and 6% on $70,000. The total return is about 13.5%. I have a spreadsheet on my Web site that calculates the yield on a wraparound.

But the high return carries a high risk. The new mortgage owned by S is a riskier asset than the house he previously owned. The new owner has only $5,000 of equity in the property. If a small decline in market values erases that equity, the owner has no financial incentive to maintain the property. If the buyer defaults on his mortgage, S will be obliged to foreclose and sell the property in order to pay off the old mortgage.

Only assumable loans are legally able to be wrapped. Assumable loans are those on which existing borrowers can transfer their obligations to qualified house purchasers. Today, only FHA and VA loans are assumable without the permission of the lender. Other fixed-rate loans carry "due-on-sale" clauses, which require that the mortgage be repaid in full if the property is sold.

Sometimes wraparounds arise on loans with due-on-sale clauses without the knowledge of the lender. This is looking for big trouble. *See* **Assumable Mortgage/Illegal Assumptions—Wraparounds**.

Yield Curve *A graph that shows, at any given time, how the yield varies with the period to maturity.*

Usually, a yield curve slopes upward, but occasionally it slopes down or is flat. A flat yield curve means that yields on long-term bonds are no higher than those on short-term notes. In a flat-yield-curve market, the initial rate on an ARM may not be much lower than the rate on an FRM, while the risk of a sizable rate increase at the end of the initial rate period on the ARM will be sizable.

Yield-Spread Premium *A payment made by a wholesale lender to a mortgage broker or correspondent lender for delivering an above-par loan.*

A par loan is one on which the lender charges zero points. Lenders charge points on loans carrying interest rates below that on the par loan and pay points or rebates on loans carrying rates above that on the par loan. *See* **Points/Points and Rebates as Borrower Options**.

On loans involving mortgage brokers, the rebate on above-par loans is credited to the broker, and it is referred to euphemistically as the "yield-spread premium" (YSP). YSPs are a major part of broker income. Because borrowers pay YSPs indirectly in the interest rate, they resist them less than they would broker fees paid directly out of their pockets. YSPs are an abuse only when borrowers don't realize they are paying the broker in the interest rate.

Since correspondent lenders deliver loans to wholesale lenders against firm price commitments, YSPs arise on their loans as well as on brokered loans, and the potential for borrower deception is the same. *See* **Mortgage Scams and Tricks/Other Scams by Loan Providers/Pocket the Borrower's Rebate**.

In the new Good Faith Estimate that became effective January 1, 2010, the YSP and the rate increase associated with it are clearly disclosed on brokered loans but not on loans by correspondent lenders. *See* **Settlement Costs/Good Faith Estimate**.

Zero Balance *The amount the borrower owes at maturity.*

Zillow Mortgage *A mortgage Web site that complements the Zillow real estate site and has some interesting features.*

Zillow allows prospective borrowers to shop anonymously, posting their financial information but not their identity among participating loan

Zillow Mortgage

originators who are free to quote prices. Originators are individual loan officers and mortgage brokers. Borrowers take the initiative in contacting originators based mainly on their price quotes, but they are vulnerable to lowballing.

About the Author

Jack M. Guttentag is now Professor of Finance Emeritus and was formerly the Jacob Safra Professor of International Banking at the Wharton School of the University of Pennsylvania. Earlier he was Chief of the Domestic Research Division of the Federal Reserve Bank of New York, was on the senior staff of the National Bureau of Economic Research, and served as managing editor of both the *Journal of Finance* (1974–1977) and the *Housing Finance Review* (1983–1989).

Professor Guttentag has been a student of the home loan market for many years, and his bibliography of scholarly articles, books, and monographs is large and diverse. He has also been an active practitioner, serving as a consultant to many government agencies and private financial institutions. In addition, he has been a director of Teachers Insurance and Annuity Association, Federal Home Loan Bank of Pittsburgh, Guild Mortgage Investments, and First Federal Savings and Loan Association of Rochester.

Throughout his career, Professor Guttentag has been concerned with the difficulties faced by consumers in the home loan market. In 1985 he and a colleague at Wharton founded GHR Systems, Inc., which developed a nationwide electronic network that lenders use to deliver complex mortgage information quickly to loan-officer employees, to mortgage brokers, and to consumers using the Internet. GHR was sold in 2005.

In 1997 Professor Guttentag began to phase out his teaching at Wharton to focus his efforts more fully toward helping consumers navigate the home loan market effectively. He began a weekly nationally syndicated column on mortgages and established www.mtgprofessor.com. The major purpose of both is to help consumers make better decisions. Most of the materials in this book were extracted from his Web site.